Cases in International Relations

Sixth Edition

DONALD M. SNOW

Professor Emeritus

University of Alabama

Boston   Columbus   Indianapolis   New York   San Francisco   Upper Saddle River
Amsterdam   Cape Town   Dubai   London   Madrid   Milan   Munich   Paris   Montréal   Toronto
Delhi   Mexico City   São Paulo   Sydney   Hong Kong   Seoul   Singapore   Taipei   Tokyo

Publisher: Charlyce Jones Owen
Project Manager: Rob DeGeorge
Program Manager: LeeAnn Doherty
Editorial Assistant: Maureen Diana
Senior Marketing Manager: Wendy Gordon
Marketing Coordinator: Theresa Rotondo
Marketing Assistant: Rebecca Schoenfeld
Operations Specialist: Mary Ann Gloriande

Cover Designer: Suzanne Behnke
Text Permissions Project Manager: Barbara Ryan
Image Lead: Beth Brenzel
Full-Service Project Management: S4Carlisle
  Publishing Services
Printer/Binder: Courier Companies, Westford
Cover Printer: Courier Companies, Westford
Text Font: 10/12 Sabon LT Std

Credits and acknowledgments borrowed from other sources and reproduced, with permission, in this textbook appear on page 331.

Library of Congress Cataloging-in-Publication Data
Snow, Donald M., 1943-
  Cases in international relations / Donald M. Snow, Professor Emeritus,
University of Alabama.—Sixth edition.
     pages cm.
  Includes index.
  ISBN-13: 978-0-205-98353-7
  ISBN-10:   0-205-98353-7
  1. International relations.   I. Title.
  JZ1242.S658 2014
  327—dc23
                                        2013044636

10 9 8 7 6 5 4 3 2 1

PEARSON

ISBN 10:   0-205-98353-7
ISBN 13: 978-0-205-98353-7

BRIEF CONTENTS

DETAILED CONTENTS

PREFACE

The issues that dominate international relations constantly change, as new dynamics appear on the stage and enduring trends and factors change and are changed by events. Since the last edition of this book appeared in 2011, the most seismic new dynamic has been the so-called Arab Spring, a series of uprisings that began to erupt in 2011 and that continue to roil the Middle East region and to radiate more broadly in international politics. At a slightly less visible level, the emergence of shale oil and gas as a major fuel source promises to have enormous impacts on future geopolitics and matters like global warming.

New trends have been augmented and changed by the evolution of existing dynamics, often in frustrating ways. The contemporary world, for instance, has not produced progress on the problem of global warming, in movement toward an enduring peace between the Israelis and the Palestinians, nor in resolving the contentious relations between the United States and North Korea or Iran. The economic malaise has indeed spread about the globe, infecting particularly the European Union (the Greek crisis of 2010 as prime example), but the global economy is also clearly in a process of readjustment, most notably in the continuing rise of China and India as world economic powers and in institutional recognition of that status through the replacement of the Group of Seven (G-7) by the Group of Twenty (G-20) as the prime international economic consultative mechanism.

The fifth edition assessed many of these dynamics, all of which have changed to some extent since then. Part of the burden of this volume, which has sought through its various editions to spotlight changing global trends, is to update and modify the discussion of situations with regard to a variety of evolving matters, from the international humanitarian disaster in Syria to the breakdown of the global warming summit in Copenhagen in December 2009 to the ongoing gyrations of the U.S.–North Korean conflict over the proliferation of nuclear weapons.

The intention of this volume is to present material that is readable, understandable, relevant, illustrative, and important to the reader and the instructor assigning this book. By avoiding an excess amount of technical jargon and consciously trying to engage the reader with the material, the hopeful result is an enjoyable and understandable read. The cases were largely chosen because of their relevance to both the world in which we all live and the illustration of the important principles covered in these pages. The intent is a volume that is both valuable and important to understanding contemporary international relations.

NEW TO THIS EDITION

Each edition of *Cases in International Relations* has been different from its predecessor in at least three distinctive ways. First, in order to accommodate dynamics that have appeared or been accentuated since the last edition, the author has added more contemporary cases and concepts. To keep the book manageable in length, each addition has been matched by scrapping or amending a case from the previous edition. Second, each edition has seen updating, modifying, and even replacing of the case applications from the previous edition, and this has been done in this edition as well. Third, there has been some reordering and restructuring of the order of cases within and between sections of the book.

Substantively, two entirely new chapters have been added to this edition. In order to deal with the changing nature of the global economic system, Chapter 8, "Revolutionary Change," has been added. It emphasizes underlying dynamics of political revolutions both historically and in conceptual context, applying its observations to ongoing events in two of the countries where the Arab Spring has most made a mark: Libya and Egypt. Chapter 15, "Secession and Self-Determination," examines the most severe form of national disintegration, with the case application centering on the creation of the Republic of South Sudan in 2011. To accommodate these new subjects, two chapters, "Peace-keeping" and "Failed and Failing States," have been eliminated.

In addition to these entirely new chapters, four others have received extensive modification or refocusing. Chapter 2, "Resource Scarcity," now focuses on the changing nature of energy production, consumption, and thus dependency, with a special emphasis on the growing impact of shale gas and oil production in the United States and elsewhere and possible impact of a movement toward this fuel source. Chapter 3, "Limits on International Cooperation," features a new case emphasis on alleged war crimes in Syria. Chapter 11, "Rising Economic Powers," has added emerging economic giant Brazil to the discussion of countries that have a growing impact on the global economy. Chapter 12, "Globalization and Development," has been refocused to emphasize how international economic change is driven and affected by demands for development in much of the less developed world.

Although it runs the risk of some oversimplification, the most important of the changes in this edition can be summarized as follows:

- An emphasis on change in the international economic order, accentuated by the emergence of the G-20 and the rise of India, China, and Brazil as world economic powers, and the sovereign debt crisis in the European Union;
- A much clearer and more focused examination of asymmetrical warfare and the perils of involvement in these kinds of conflicts;
- An updated and focused examination of the issues that divide Israel and its neighbors and friends and that demonstrate the difficulties of irresolvable conflicts;
- A new emphasis on the evolving nature of the terrorist threat and the emergence of new problems that have arisen since the death of Osama bin Laden;

- An introduction to the potential for shale gas and oil exploitation and its implications for energy patterns and politics;
- An examination of the trajectory of the Arab Spring through the lens of existing understandings and theories of revolutionary change;
- A systematic discussion of the issues surrounding secession as a rising international phenomenon in the successful separation of South Sudan from Sudan; and
- A placement of international atrocities such as those occurring in Syria within a framework of international norms.

The structural rearrangement of the book begun in the last edition has been continued. Chapter titles identify the concept being explored as the primary title in each chapter, with the case application as the subtitle. The table of contents has also been rearranged in two ways. The format of four parts introduced in the last edition has been retained, with each section containing four chapters dealing with the general topic of the part. The order of the parts was changed in the last edition to bring the table of contents more into line with standard core texts in the field, and this feature has been retained as well. The organization by parts is as follows: Conflict and Cooperation, National and International Security, International Political Economy, and Human Security.

Part I, "Conflict and Cooperation," consists of chapters dealing with sovereignty and intervention and the impact of the American invasion of Iraq on those concepts (Chapter 1); resource scarcity and change as a source of ongoing conflict among states (Chapter 2); the collision of sovereignty and limits of cooperation in the areas of war crimes and international norms in places like Syria (Chapter 3); and conflicts that are extremely difficult to resolve, like the Israeli–Palestinian conflict (Chapter 4).

Part II, "National and International Security," looks at problems affecting the security of states and the international order. Topics include asymmetrical warfare as a dominant feature of the future (Chapter 5), the proliferation of weapons of mass destruction and especially nuclear weapons (Chapter 6), the influence of important, pivotal regional powers like Iran (Chapter 7), and revolutionary change (Chapter 8).

Part III, "International Political Economy," shifts the focus of the cases to the economic realm. Topics include the concept and evolution of free trade (Chapter 9); the evolution of the most economically integrated region of the world, particularly in light of the sovereign debt crisis: the European Union (Chapter 10); rising economic powers like China, India, and Brazil (Chapter 11); and the changing dynamics of an expanded and extended globalized world to the developing world (Chapter 12).

Part IV was renamed "Human Security" in the fourth edition to reflect its emphasis on problems that are international in scope and that have a direct impact on people and their well-being and safety, and this designation has been retained. Topics include efforts to address global warming following the lapse of the Kyoto accords (Chapter 13), international migration (Chapter 14), the dynamics of national disintegration through secession (Chapter 15), and the changing nature of post–bin Laden terrorism (Chapter 16).

FEATURES

What distinguishes this effort from other supplementary texts in the field? One answer is that all the essays included in the volume are original papers written by the author specifically for this volume. The reason for doing so was to allow for more timely coverage of ongoing situations than is possible with the publication lag time of scholarly journals and their availability to readers and other compendia. It also allows casting the cases in a common format that makes it easier to compare and contrast the contents of the various cases. In addition, journal articles are written for academic peers rather than more-or-less lay students, meaning they are generally rendered in language and theoretical trappings that are less than accessible to student readers. Finally, writing original articles facilitates updating and modifying materials as events and dynamics change, which hopefully adds to the freshness, accuracy, and timeliness of the materials contained in these pages. Presenting the most contemporary set of portraits possible has certainly been a major purpose of this and earlier editions.

A word about what this book is—and is not—is appropriate at this point. It is a case book, presenting a series of individual instances of dynamics and trends within the international arena. The effort is neither inclusive nor encyclopedic; it covers selected concepts and events, not the universe of international concerns. A series of 16 important, underlying concepts and principles of the international system have been chosen and discussed, and the discussion of these principles has been applied to contemporary, important, and interesting real-life examples. The result is not a systematic overview of the international system or its history, which is the province of core textbooks in the field. Likewise, it does not offer a unifying theoretical explanatory framework of international politics, a task that more specialized books purporting grand "theories" of international relations propound. Rather, the intent is to introduce and apply some basic concepts about international relations and how they apply in real situations.

The book's pedagogy reflects this approach. Each of the cases begins by identifying a particular problem or dynamic of the international system (indicated as the main chapter title). After describing the concept, it applies that concept to an actual case. Thus, for instance, Chapter 8 begins with the concept and dynamics of revolutionary change and how it has evolved in the contemporary system and applies it to two major Arab Spring examples in Libya and Egypt. Each case concludes with a series of questions for study or discussion, a bibliography of contemporary articles and books useful to the intended readers of the book, and some suggested websites for additional reference.

MYSEARCHLAB WITH ETEXT

A passcode-protected websites that provides engaging experiences that personalize learning, MySearchLab contains an eText that is just like the printed text. Students can highlight and add notes to the eText online or download it to an iPad. MySearchLab also provides a wide range of writing, grammar, and research tools plus access to a variety of academic journals, census data, Associated Press news feeds, and discipline-specific readings to help hone writing and research skills.

ACKNOWLEDGMENTS

The result of this endeavor is a new stack of portraits of the future that the reader hopefully will find both broad and enriching. This edition of the book, like the original, is dedicated to my good friend and colleague, the late D. Eugene Brown. Gene and I met in 1989 at the U.S. Army War College, where we both served as visiting professors and shared an office for two years before he returned to his permanent home at Lebanon Valley College in Annville, Pennsylvania, and I returned to the University of Alabama in Tuscaloosa. In the ensuing decade, we were collaborators on several book projects; *Cases in International Relations*, which was mostly Gene's idea, was to be a continuation, even culmination, of those efforts. Unfortunately, Gene left us before the original project was complete. His shadow remains, I hope with a smile on his face.

DONALD M. SNOW
PROFESSOR EMERITUS
UNIVERSITY OF ALABAMA

Conflict and Cooperation

Although the dynamics of the international system are in a more or less constant state of flux, some issues, problems, and themes recur across time. A major theme of international relations has been the existence of a state of conflict among the countries of the world and the dynamic tensions between conflict and cooperation as the principal approaches by which countries attempt to manage or settle their differences. The four studies in Part I address various aspects of that dynamic tension.

Chapter 1, "Sovereignty," addresses the concept of sovereignty, the bedrock principle of international relations for at least the last 300 years. Sovereignty means exclusive political authority over territory and people, and maintaining and protecting national sovereignty is a core value of the members of the international system. Intervention into the affairs of states, most extremely employing military force, directly challenges the sovereignty against those who are the objects of that force. The case application deals with the ramifications for the concept of sovereignty of the American invasion and occupation of Iraq, an event that clearly violated Iraqi sovereignty.

Chapter 2, "Resource Scarcity," examines a major source of conflict in international relations, the competition for scarce resources. The examination represents an extension and application of principles raised in Chapter 1, as the pursuit of scarce resources is one of the reasons why states cling to sovereignty and demonstrate a willingness to engage in sometimes extreme actions in the quest for scarce resources deemed vital to the state. The case concentrates on the problem of access to petroleum energy, a vital resource in increasingly short supply and over which states vigorously compete for access and control. It looks particularly at changes in patterns of production associated with the emergence of shale gas and oil and the possible geopolitical impact such exploitation could create.

Chapter 3, "Limits on International Cooperation," deals with why it is often difficult to induce cooperation between states, even in an area, such as war crimes, where such cooperation would seem mutually advantageous to all states and the international order. The chief barrier in this case, as in other instances, is sovereignty, and the case examines how this bedrock principle impedes cooperation about what kinds of actions are permissible and impermissible during or leading up to war. A modern judicial body, the International Criminal Court (ICC), has been created to try alleged violations of war crimes, and one of the areas of war crimes currently under scrutiny is the use of torture, which is a war crime when committed during war and is thus within the purview of the ICC. Despite condemnation of war crimes, major countries, including the United States, resist the application of these cooperation-based efforts on the grounds of intrusions on national sovereignty.

Chapter 4, "Irresolvable Conflicts," looks at the problem caused by disagreements between states and entities that are so fundamental that there appears to be no way to create solutions acceptable to the parties—to engage in cooperative resolution of conflicts. Although there are relatively few of these irresolvable conflicts in the international arena, those that exist are particularly vexing and upsetting to international peace and stability. The most famous contemporary case is the confrontation between the Israelis and the Palestinians over the disposition of the territory they both claim in the Holy Land.

Sovereignty: The Violation and Restoration of Iraqi Authority

PRÉCIS

The principle of sovereignty, or supreme authority, has been the bedrock principle of operation of the international system since the end of the Thirty Years' War in 1648, a process known as the Peace of Westphalia. Over time, sovereignty has come to reside in the governments of states, where it is generally conceded to exist today. One of the most controversial areas involving sovereignty is its relationship to war and the effects on sovereignty that acts of war create under different circumstances. War is a primary result of the international system that has evolved around the principle of sovereignty, as a way to resolve differences between sovereign states. The outcomes of war often affect the sovereignty of the parties. The sovereignty of losers is most often affected.

The issue of sovereignty came under particularly close scrutiny as one consequence of the U.S. invasion of Iraq in March 2003. The invasion clearly involved the violation of Iraqi sovereignty by intruding on Iraqi territory, and thus contributed to legal and moral questions about whether the invasion was justified. This case will examine the invasion of Iraq, its impact on sovereignty, and the process by which that sovereignty was restored in 2011.

There is no more basic principle in the relations between the world's countries (states) than that of sovereignty, the supreme authority of the state over its territory. Sovereignty is the conceptual linchpin from which the formal pattern of dealings derives, and it represents a value held particularly dearly by the arguably two strongest and most consequential countries, the United States and the People's Republic of China. As a result, state actions that appear to violate, challenge, or dilute state supremacy are particularly important and potentially traumatic to the world order.

The American invasion and occupation of Iraq that ended in December 2011 has been controversial on many grounds, including its legality and its impact on the practices of states in the international system. Both of these areas of contention revolve around the question of whether the U.S. action represented a fundamental challenge to the sovereignty of Iraq, which was interrupted by the eight-and-a-half-year American military occupation of the country. Although that occupation has been made politically moot by the American withdrawal, the fact of American violation of Iraqi authority retains precedential importance.

For more than 350 years, the bedrock principle of international relations has been the evolving concept of sovereignty, and more specifically, the idea of state sovereignty. Although its philosophical roots extend back farther, this concept was first introduced formally in a book written in the sixteenth century by the Frenchman Jean Bodin as the philosophical underpinning for the consolidation of power by Europe's monarchs, and in particular, the authority of the king of France. With the settlement of the extraordinarily brutal, religiously based Thirty Years' War in 1648, the triumphant secular monarchs of northern Europe adopted the concept as part of asserting their independence from papal authority.

State sovereignty, the idea that state governments have supreme authority in the international system and that there can be no authority superior to the state, has been a first principle by which international relations is organized ever since. The primacy of sovereignty has never lacked its critics, either in terms of the concept's validity or its philosophical and practical implications. Nevertheless, the principle has endured, and all governments cling tenaciously to their possession of sovereignty.

Sovereignty has always done more than provide the philosophical underpinning of international relations. The idea—even the necessity—of possessing and protecting sovereignty has formed the basis of much state action, and particularly the geopolitical task of protecting the state from its enemies. The idea of a "national security state" that became popular during the Cold War was based in the need to protect American supreme authority over its territory from predators that threatened that authority.

The sacrosanct status of unfettered sovereignty is being increasingly questioned. Part of the assault has come from the traditional critics of sovereignty; opponents of war, for instance, argue that armed conflict is an integral, inevitable, and regrettable consequence of a world in which sovereignty reigns. From this view, dismantling sovereignty is the necessary prerequisite for world peace. At the same time, the rise of other concerns such as human rights collides with state sovereignty. Why? Because a major historical justification for mistreatment of individuals and groups within states is that sovereign states possess absolute authority over their citizens, and thus how states act within their sovereign jurisdiction is strictly their own business. This is roughly the position that the Russian government has taken with regard to its treatment of Chechnya during the attempted Chechen secession during the 1990s and into the 2000s, and that the Assad government in Syria took during its civil disturbances more recently. More indirectly, but no less fundamentally, the Bush Doctrine's assertion of an American "right" to attack foes preemptively, as in Iraq, represented a de facto denial of the absolute sovereignty it seeks to preserve.

Indifference toward humanity in the guise of sovereignty may seem incredible in contemporary terms, but it is an idea that was virtually unchallenged as recently as the end of World War II. Consider a real example. When the war crimes trials at Nuremberg were being organized in 1945, there were questions about what crimes the Nazi defendants could be charged with committing. The leading U.S. jurist at the trials, a member of the U.S. Supreme Court, offered the official view that the Nazis could be charged with killing non-German citizens on German soil, but not with exterminating German Jews, because, as German citizens, they could treat them any way the Germans saw fit. The position was not particularly challenged at the time, partly because, as a practical matter, there were plenty of war crimes with which to charge the defendants.

The bloody internal conflicts in places like the Balkans and parts of Africa have challenged the idea that state sovereignty provides an unfettered license for governments to do as they please to their citizens or, where governments are incapable or nonexistent, not to protect portions of their populations from ravage. Using the United Nations as a vehicle to justify actions, the international system has, on numerous occasions that will almost certainly continue into the future, intruded itself into these situations in order to prevent further abuse and to protect citizens.

The collision of traditional conceptualizations of sovereignty with the evolution of the contemporary world generally is thus a major question in international relations, a question of whether the world and its values are changing so much that the principle of sovereignty must be modified or abandoned to adjust to a new reality. One aspect of that reality is the collision between sovereignty and the assertion of an international right or need to intervene in civil wars within states or, more recently, to pursue international terrorists. The outcome of the ensuing debate will help answer the broader question of the role of sovereignty in the twenty-first century and is thus the focus of this case study.

What role does sovereignty play in defining what acts by states are permissible or impermissible in the international environment? Do the sovereign rights that states possess allow them to act as they wish and remain immune from international repercussions? Or, are there overriding considerations that permit states to violate the sovereignty of others in ways such as the physical invasion of one state by another? Examining these questions requires looking first at the content and evolution of sovereignty and some major criticisms of sovereignty in theory and action. That discussion will form the context for examining the U.S. invasion and long occupation of Iraq, in terms of both its legality and the precedent it may serve for future interpretations of sovereignty.

THE CONCEPT OF SOVEREIGNTY

The basic concept of sovereignty has three distinct elements that collectively define what it means to possess sovereignty. The first element is legitimate authority. Authority is simply the ability to enforce an order; the qualifier "legitimate" means that authority is invested with some legal, consensual basis. Put another way, sovereignty is more than the exercise of pure force.

The second element of sovereignty is that it is supreme. What this means is that there is no superior authority to the possessor of sovereignty; the sovereign is the highest possible authority wherever the sovereign holds sway. The third and related element is that of territory; sovereignty is supreme authority within a defined physical territory. Since the Peace of Westphalia, the political state came to embody the territorial definition of sovereignty. Thus, states (or countries) have supreme authority over what occurs within their territorial boundaries, and no other source of authority can claim superior jurisdiction to the sovereign within those territories.

Before turning to why sovereignty has developed the way it has as a concept, it is worthwhile briefly to look at the consequences of these characteristics politically. In the *internal* workings of states, sovereignty is the basis of the political authority of state governments; the idea of supreme authority provides the state with the legitimacy to order its own affairs and for the government to create and enforce that order. When the concept of sovereignty was first developed, this internal application was the emphasis. *Externally,* in the relations between states, this same sovereignty creates disorder, because there can be no superior authority to the sovereign within the defined territory of states. The result is *anarchy,* or the absence of government (political authority) in the relations among states. Thus, sovereignty has the schizophrenic effect of creating order and disorder, depending on the venue in which it is applied.

Early Origins and Evolution

The anarchical consequence was not so clear when Bodin formally enunciated the concept of sovereignty in his 1576 book *De Republica.* Bodin decried the inability of the French monarchy to establish its authority throughout the country, because lower feudal lords instead claimed what amounted to sovereignty over those realms—especially through charging taxes (tolls) to cross their territories. Bodin countered with the idea of sovereignty, which he defined as "supreme authority over citizens and subjects, *unrestrained by law.*" (Emphasis added.) The added and italicized element, Bodin felt, was necessary to avoid the unifying monarch being hamstrung by parochial laws in his quest to establish the power of the French monarchy. This part of the definition has fallen from common conceptions of sovereignty, but its implications remain and are part of the ongoing controversy central to this case: If the sovereign is above the law, then nothing he or she does can possibly be illegal, at least when committed within the sovereign jurisdiction over which the sovereign reigns.

When Bodin enunciated the principle of sovereignty, he was unconcerned about it as a maxim for international relations. This is not surprising in that the period of its gestation was a time when monarchs were consolidating their holds on what became the modern states of Europe and thus creating the modern state system. Given that all these states were absolute monarchies, it is further not terribly surprising the presumption quickly evolved (aided by philosophical publicists like Thomas Hobbes) that sovereignty resided with the monarch (which, among other things, helps explain why monarchs are sometimes referred to as sovereigns).

The concept of sovereignty was extended to international relations as the state system evolved and the structure of the modern state emerged and solidified. Hugo Grotius, the Dutch scholar generally acknowledged as the father of international law, first proclaimed state sovereignty as a fundamental principle of international relations in his 1625 book *On the Law of War and Peace*. By the eighteenth century, the principle was well on its way to being in place, and by the nineteenth it was an accepted part of international relations.

By the nineteenth century, the content of sovereignty had evolved from its original context. Because virtually all countries were still ruled by more or less absolute monarchies (the fledgling, and not very important, United States, revolutionary France, and slightly democratizing Great Britain being the exceptions), the idea of absolute state sovereignty was the rule, and this principle governed both domestic and international relations. From the view of the international system, a prevailing way to describe international politics was in terms of something called the *billiard ball* theory. The idea, never to be taken entirely literally, was that state authority resembled an impermeable billiard ball, and that international relations consisted of these impermeable objects bouncing against one another, causing them to change course in their international behavior from time to time. Important to the theory, however, was that the balls were impermeable, which meant that nothing in international interactions could affect what went on within the balls, for instance, how states treated their citizens. Under this principle, it was simply impermissible for states to interfere in the internal affairs of other states, no matter how distasteful or disgusting domestic practices might be.

Even during its heyday, this conceptualization was not universally accepted. In fact, conceptual challenges tended to be grouped around two related questions that continue to be important. How much authority does the sovereign have in the territorial realm over which it is exercised? Within whom, or what body, does sovereignty reside? Different answers have decidedly different implications for what sovereignty means in the relations among states.

As sovereignty was originally formulated and implemented, the answer to the first question was that sovereignty is absolute, that the possessor has total authority over his or her realm. This interpretation flows from, among other sources, the idea that the sovereign is "unrestrained by law," to repeat Bodin's term. The contrary view emerged during the eighteenth and nineteenth centuries and reflected the growing notion of political rights asserted in the American and French Revolutions, each of which claimed the sovereign's powers were limited and could be abridged. Among the primary publicists of this view were the English political philosopher John Locke and his French counterpart, Jean-Jacques Rousseau.

The assertion that there are limits on sovereignty reflects the second question: Where does sovereignty reside? It is a question about the basis on which that authority is legitimately claimed by those who seek to wield power within their political jurisdictions. The traditional view was that sovereignty resides in the state. In the sixteenth and seventeenth centuries when sovereignty was taking hold as an organizational principle, this meant the king or queen had sovereignty, because the monarch was the unchallenged head of government. It was what is now called a "top-down" concept; the government exercised sovereignty over the population, whose duty it was to submit to that authority.

Beyond the philosophical positions taken by Locke and Rousseau, the contrary argument had its base in, among other places, the American Revolution. A major theme of the American complaint against the British monarch was his denial that the colonists had *rights* in addition to obligations. From that assertion, it was a reasonably short intellectual odyssey to the assertion that the *people*, not the state (or monarch) were the possessors of sovereignty. Under the notion of what became known as *popular sovereignty*, the idea was that the people, as possessors of sovereignty, ceded some of that authority to the state in order to provide the basic legitimacy for the social and political order. Ultimately, however, sovereignty resides with individual citizens, who can grant, withhold, or even, in some interpretations, rescind the bestowing of authority to the state.

These distinctions are more than abstract, academic constructs. Their practical meanings and implications become particularly clear if one combines the two ideas in matrix form.

Sources and Extent of Sovereignty			
		Extent of Sovereignty	
		Absolute	Limited
Source	State	(Cell 1)	(Cell 3)
	Individuals	(Cell 2)	(Cell 4)

The idea that sovereignty is absolute can be associated with authoritarian governance of one sort or the other. Traditional authoritarian regimes derive their claim to authority on the combination of absolute sovereignty and the state locus of authority (Cell 1). The populist/fascist regimes in Italy and Germany that arose between the world wars combined absolutism with some popular, individual base, Cell 2 (both regimes originally came to power popularly). On the other side of the ledger, the idea that sovereignty is limited is associated with democratic regimes. The idea of state sovereignty derived from the people is the backbone of traditional western democracy (Cell 3). When the conferral of sovereignty to the state is denied and maintained by subnational individuals or groups, the result can be the kinds of instability one associates with many of the unstable regimes in the developing world (Cell 4). The controversial "right" to secede from existing state, the topic of Chapter 15, is an extreme example of this combination. Much of the debate about intervention in the internal affairs of states also derives from the situation depicted in Cell 4. If one accepts the notion that sovereignty resides with individuals, then the possibility of legitimate interference on behalf of those sovereign individuals can be argued to override the sovereignty of the state.

Objections to Sovereignty

The idea and consequences of sovereignty came under increasing assault as the twentieth century evolved into the twenty-first century. Two broad categories of criticism, however, relate directly to the question of international intervention in the affairs of states and thus have direct relevance to the task of examining the impact of intervention on sovereignty. Both are attacks on the operationalization of the concept.

The first critique is aimed at absolutist conceptions of sovereignty. Critics of this argument maintain that sovereignty in application has never been as absolute as sovereignty in theory. The myth of the impenetrability of states by outside forces, including other states, is no more than a fiction to buttress the principle. States have always interfered in the internal affairs of other states in one way or another. The billiard ball theory is not, in the scientific sense, a theory at all, but instead a false hypothesis.

According to this argument, not only has sovereignty never been as absolute as its champions would assert, but it is becoming increasingly less so. A major reason for this dilution derives from the scientific revolution in telecommunications, which is making national borders entirely more penetrable from the outside, a trend anticipated nearly 60 years ago by then-Prime Minister Sir Anthony Eden in a speech before the British House of Commons on November 22, 1954: "Every succeeding scientific discovery makes greater nonsense of old-time conceptions of sovereignty."

Those "old-time" conceptualizations refer, of course, to state-centered, absolutist interpretations of sovereignty. Forces such as the spread of the Internet, economic globalization, the emergence of a homogenized commercial and popular culture around the world, and the desire to embrace the globalized world economic system all make the factual content of total sovereign control by governments over territory increasingly suspect. One must ask, however, whether this factual dilution of sovereign control extends to the "right" of the international system to infringe on the sovereign ability of the state to treat its citizens in ways that the international community disapproves. Is the spread of popular global culture, for instance, any kind of precedent to assert the rightfulness of forceful interposition by foreign troops into civil strife or to effect domestic change?

The other objection to absolute sovereignty has to do directly with the consequences of a system based in state sovereignty. Once again, a number of assertions are made about the pernicious effects of this form of organization on the operation of the international system. Two of them will be explored here.

The first, and most commonly asserted, objection to state sovereignty is its legitimization and, in some constructs, even glorification of war as a means to settle disputes between states. In a system of sovereign states, after all, there is no authority to enforce international norms on states or to adjudicate or enforce judgments resolving the disputes that arise between them. The exceptions are when states voluntarily agree to be bound by international norms or, ironically, when they can be forced to accept international judgments. If states cannot agree amicably on how to settle their differences, then they must rely on their own ability to solve favorably the disagreements they have.

The principle involved is known as *self-help*, the ability to bring about favorable outcomes to differences, often at the expense of the other state. This resolution becomes an exercise in *power* (the ability to get someone to do what he or she would not otherwise do), and one form of power available to states is military force. In situations that states deem to be of sufficient importance to settle with armed force, war may be the conflict resolution means of choice. In a system of self-help, there is thus no alternative to possessing, and in some instances using, armed force to protect one's self.

Despite the fact that all member states of the United Nations have renounced the waging of war as a means to resolve conflict (they are not called *wars* anymore), the resort to force is understood and accepted in international practice (with some reservations). A fairly large number of analysts, including many scholars and practitioners of international relations, however, decry this situation, because they abhor war and would like to see it end. Because sovereignty and the legitimate recourse to war are closely related, therefore, they welcome its dilution and replacement as an international principle.

The other, more contemporary, objection to the consequences of sovereignty is the power it gives governments over their people. In an international sense, governments still are, after all, legally "unrestrained" by international norms in dealing with their own populations, except, once again, to the extent that states have voluntarily limited their rights by signing international agreements. Historically, the notion that governments could do horrible things to their citizens was abhorred by many in the international community, but the right to such behavior was unchallenged on the basis of sovereignty. The phrase "Patriotism is the last refuge of a scoundrel," first uttered by the English author Samuel Johnson in 1775, could easily be paraphrased as "sovereignty is the last refuge of a scoundrel." Arguments defending practices like torture are de facto extensions of this "right" to use all available means to protect sovereign territory.

Whether this is good or bad is debatable. Governments strongly support sovereignty because it preserves the ability to conduct affairs without undue interference from outside. Unfortunately, the greater the protection of internal actions, the greater is the potential for abuse. In those cases in which abuse results in atrocity and human suffering, calls for outside intervention arise as a challenge to that sovereign authority. The case of Syria, explored in Chapter 13, is an example.

The sanctity of this concept of sovereignty began to erode with the global reaction to the reality of the Holocaust that surfaced after World War II. The active revival of this objection came at the end of the Cold War. Scoundrel-like behavior did not, of course, go into hibernation during the Cold War (Pol Pot and the Khmer Rouge in Cambodia guaranteed that), but condemnation—and especially proposing action to combat it—tended to get entangled in Cold War politics. Could, for instance, the United Nations have proposed a peacekeeping mission to Cambodia in 1975 (when the Khmer Rouge seized power and began their slaughter), when the fighting and killing involved two communist factions, each aligned with a different communist superpower (China and the Soviet Union), each of which had a veto in the Security Council? Of course not!

The Assault on Sovereignty Through the United Nations

Since the end of the Cold War, traditional concepts of sovereignty have become increasingly questionable, both intellectually and practically through a series of actions organized by the United Nations (UN). To borrow a term from military tactics, these attacks on sovereignty emanating from actions have not constituted a "frontal assault." None of the actions authorized by the UN Security Council has directly challenged the concept of state sovereignty or aligned itself explicitly with a particular interpretation of the concept. Rather, they have been justified under Chapter VII of the UN Charter, which gives the council the authority to determine threats to or breaches of the peace and to authorize responses, including the use of military force.

The assault on sovereignty has thus been conducted indirectly and inductively. It began when the Security Council authorized a peacekeeping force (UNOSM I) to go to Somalia on December 3, 1992. The official reason for the mission was to alleviate human suffering (the threat of massive starvation) due to a five-year-long drought and a civil war, one consequence of which was that international relief efforts to get food to the afflicted were being interrupted by the combating factions. The motivation for the mission was hence humanitarian, to alleviate suffering in what would subsequently be referred to as a major humanitarian disaster.

The UN action was a major precedent in at least two ways, influenced by the unique circumstances in Somalia at the time. First and possibly most important, it was a mission authorized and implemented without any consultation with the government of the country to which it was dispatched. The idea that the United Nations would in effect invade a member state presumably for its own good was a major change of policy for the international community working through the world body.

Circumstances on the ground in Somalia made this an easy course to take. The government of Somalia was not consulted before the intervention because *there was no legal government to consult.* Since the overthrow of Siad Barre the previous year, Somalia had been in a state of anarchy. The United Nations in effect skirted the sovereignty issue by invoking Chapter VII of its Charter and using its provisions to determine a breach of the peace had occurred and to take appropriate action to restore the peace. One could argue, although no one did publicly at the time, that the absence of a government meant there was no sovereign territory involved; the sovereignty issue was officially ignored.

The second precedent was that Somalia was the first occasion when the Security Council interpreted its jurisdiction to include purely humanitarian crises. Without going into the legislative history of the Charter, it is clear that the framers meant for Chapter VII to be invoked primarily in the case of cross-border invasions by states (interstate wars). The Persian Gulf War effort of 1990–1991 was the prototype the framers had in mind. Although the United Nations had (rather unhappily) intervened in a civil war in the former Belgian Congo (later Zaire, now the Democratic Republic of Congo) in 1960, the decision to engage in humanitarian intervention in a civil war in a country for which the term *failed state* was later coined represented a major change of direction. To reiterate, sovereignty in theory and in practice have not always been the same thing.

THE ASSAULT ON SOVEREIGNTY OUTSIDE THE UNITED NATIONS: THE IRAQ PRECEDENT

On June 30, 2009, citizens of Iraq celebrated "National Sovereignty Day." The occasion was the formal withdrawal of American combat troops from the Iraqi cities they had occupied since the American conquest and occupation of the country in 2003, an event that had "interrupted" Iraqi sovereignty (the term is provided by Wikipedia). This event was hardly noted in the United States, which of course had provided the interruption of Iraqi sovereignty but did not like to describe the occupation in those terms. Jeremy Scahill, an opponent of the war, termed the occasion a "fake holiday." Yet, the declaration and celebration highlighted both that the American attack violated Iraqi sovereignty and that the Iraqis were anxious to reassert that status, a process completed when the last American forces exited the country before Christmas 2011.

The American invasion has been controversial on a number of grounds largely concerned with whether it was necessary or whether it accomplished its purposes. Lurking behind these questions, however, is a more fundamental systemic concern: Did the invasion represent an illegal, precedent-setting assault on the very principle of sovereignty of which the United States has been among the most ardent defenders?

The Bush administration argued the invasion was not illegal on two debatable grounds. One was the principle of preemption, which says that a state can legally attack another whenever it faces an imminent threat that can be thwarted by preemptive action. The other is the authorization to use force under Article VII of the UN Charter. Alleged Iraqi possession and intention to use weapons of mass destruction in support of terrorism formed the justification for preemption. UN Security Council Resolution 1441, which demanded Iraqi compliance with weapons inspections and warned of unspecified consequences (that did not specifically include force) were used to justify Chapter VII. A large portion of the international community denied both claims.

The assault on sovereignty and challenges to international law represented by the American invasion must be placed in their international context. Two factors stand out. The first is the fluidity and change ushered in by the post–Cold War world. Although the Cold War was a very dangerous environment because it contained the possibility of general nuclear war, it was also a reasonably orderly system wherein the major powers knew where and when they could and could not intervene in the affairs of third-party states based on Cold War impacts such as the prospects for escalation of any contemplated action. This calculation provided a barrier to intervention except within the acknowledged spheres of influence of the superpowers. The end of the Cold War removed that barrier and made more states "eligible" for potential actions against them, including actions breaching national sovereignty. Iraq fell into the category of newly "eligible" states.

Second, the terrorist attacks of 9/11 created an urgency and intensity that tended to sweep aside the theoretical and legal barriers to action. The "war on terror" was cast as a life-or-death struggle against an opponent that honored no rules of civilized conduct, and the lawlessness and atrocity of the enemy made restrictions based in legal restraints seem irrelevant to some people. The mentality of the time suggested that if the alternatives were counter-terror measures or less effective measures bounded by international legal conventions, it was the boundaries that would suffer. Extraordinary circumstances justified extraordinary actions.

These factors help to frame the environment in which a decision to invade Iraq that most experts consider a direct violation of sovereignty could occur. To understand these dynamics, the discussion moves to attitude toward the intervention response that was so common in the years leading up to the invasion of Iraq, then to the decision itself and its legality and impact on international relations, and to the restoration of Iraqi sovereign control of its territory.

The Intervention Atmosphere

The pattern of international response to intervention questions beginning in the 1990s was not uniform. The international community has been willing to act forcefully in places like the Balkans, but not in Africa (Darfur is a particularly poignant example), for instance. In this atmosphere of change, the principle of absolute sovereignty had lost some of its sacrosanct position, although the strongest states could (and did) maintain and enforce its application *to them*. For other states, the status was evolving.

One common mechanism for authorizing an international response that violates territorial sovereignty has been to take it to the Security Council of the United Nations for a United Nations Security Council Resolution (UNSCR) under Chapter VII. The precedent for this route was Somalia, which in turn was the outgrowth of the successful use of UNSCRs in the Persian Gulf War of 1990–1991. The effect, on an ad hoc basis, was to legitimize violations of states' sovereignty. But how?

First, because most of the world's countries are members of the world body, passing a resolution serves as a kind of statement of world opinion, a legitimating action indicating the support of the international community. The second, and more controversial, purpose of the use of UNSCRs is to create a kind of legal basis for intervention in civil wars. Intervention in civil wars violates traditional international law and, especially when done without invitation, is clearly a violation of the sovereignty of the country where the intervention occurs.

The UN Charter, however, does authorize the United Nations to act in the name of peace. Articles 39 and 42 (both part of Chapter VII) create the authority. Article 39 states, "The Security Council shall determine the existence of any threat to the peace, breach of the peace, or act of aggression and shall make recommendations or decide what measures shall be taken. . . to maintain or restore international peace or security." Article 42 makes the military option explicit: "[T]he Security Council . . . may take such action by air, sea or land forces as may be necessary to maintain or restore international peace and security." These provisions appear to refer to *international* rather than internal disputes. Earlier in the Charter, Article 2 (7) makes an ambivalent statement to that effect: "Nothing contained in the present Charter shall authorize the United Nations to intervene in matters which are essentially within the domestic jurisdiction of any state or shall require the members to submit such matters to settlement under the present Charter; but this principle shall not prejudice the application of enforcement measures under Chapter VII." One can use this language to justify intervening in a country's civil strife under two apparent circumstances: if there is a question about whether there is a domestic institution with jurisdiction (Somalia); or if one determines that whatever is happening within a given country constitutes a threat to or breach of "international peace and security. The latter standard was applied to Iraq.

Why would the members of the United Nations go to all this trouble to justify interfering in internal matters? At least part of the answer has to be that it is a way to avoid the direct assault on national sovereignty that such actions involve. The UN Charter is quite explicit in its defense of the "territorial integrity or political independence of any state" (Article 2 [4]), or, in other words, its sovereignty. The organization cannot directly admit that it is violating sovereignty without violating its own constitution. And yet violating sovereignty is exactly what the members do when they pass UNSCRs authorizing intervention in the internal affairs of countries and then dispatch their troops to foreign shores to enforce those decrees. Manipulating the Charter effectively finesses the underlying issue of the violation of sovereignty by making intervention appear to be an expression of international will.

The Legality of Invading Iraq

The legitimacy of outside intervention in the affairs of countries has come into question in the United States most dramatically over Iraq. The primary reasons for questioning have been political and practical. The issue has two facets.

In the 2000 presidential election campaign, Republican George W. Bush came out strongly against the use of American forces in peacekeeping operations. The reason was practical: These deployments had arguably placed a strain on declining manpower and financial resources that could be devoted to more traditional military priorities. The implication was clear: Such interventions should be strictly limited or avoided in the future. Yet, the new president had been in office for less than nine months before the terrorist attacks of September 11, 2001, opened the window for new interventions—possibly protracted—in Afghanistan and later in Iraq.

Questions of Iraqi sovereignty were not raised in the deliberations over that intervention, although the administration later made a point of "restoring" Iraqi sovereignty in June 2004. Does this mean there is a reluctance to open a Pandora's box of problems if the relationship is addressed directly? Is there a fear of raising a question that might produce a negative answer? Or is the question simply unimportant?

In some ways, the invasion of Iraq was simply the culmination of trends inherited from the 1970s. The breakdown of the Cold War had left the United States as the remaining superpower more-or-less unilaterally seeking to create a new world order for an increasingly unruly, contentious array of states. The attacks of 9/11 enraged the United States and most of the rest of the world and reminded everyone the world was still a dangerous place, parts of which required subduing. In that atmosphere, the United States deputized itself to restore order where it deemed it necessary to do so. Then President Bush made this policy official in his 2004 State of the Union address, declaring that the protection of U.S. interests overrode all other concerns; indeed, the United States would no longer ask for "permission slips" before it acted.

The invasion of Iraq was the emotional apex of this process. At the time (and to a large degree since), questions of international legality and sovereignty precedent were hardly raised in a very muted debate about the *policy* wisdom of the action. In retrospect, however, it is possible and prudent to raise questions about the broader implications of the action. Was the invasion legal under international law? What effect does it have on the principle of sovereignty?

The requirements to legalize a military action are specified in the UN Charter, to which all signatory states (including the United States) are obliged to conform. The most basic statement is found in Article 2 (4): "All members shall refrain in their international relations from the threat or use of force against the territorial integrity or political independence of any state." As J. L. Brierly and other legal scholars point out, the exceptions are narrow and specific. The Charter specifies two circumstances in which the use of force is justified, both under Chapter VII: Actions with Respect to Threats to the Peace, Breaches of the Peace, and Acts of Aggression. The first is as part of enforcing a UNSCR authorizing the use of force against a state "to maintain or restore international peace and security." This use of force is included in Article 42 of the Charter. The other use, specified in Article 51, entails "the inherent right of individual and collective self-defense if an attack occurs."

On their face, neither of these requirements was met before the U.S. invasion. The United States did not have an Article 42 mandate to use armed force on behalf of the United Nations, and it had clearly not been the victim of an armed aggression by Iraq prior to the invasion.

The U.S. government did attempt a legal defense of its actions under both articles. It invoked UNSCR 1441 on November 8, 2002, which threatened "serious consequences" if Iraq failed "full compliance" with a list of demands centering on UN inspections of Iraqi weapons facilities (looking for weapons of mass destruction, or WMD). Resolution 1441 did not, however, specifically authorize the use of force specified in Article 42, and American and British efforts to obtain such permission failed.

The Bush administration also claimed authority under Article 51. Their device was the so-called Bush Doctrine of *preventive war*, which justifies the use of force when a preemptive attack is planned by an enemy. This is an extension of the legal justification of so-called preemption. Most interpretations argue that preemption is justified only when an attack is imminent; an enemy massing its troops on one's border is an obvious case in point. Jeffrey Record makes this point explicitly: "preemptive attack is justified if it meets Secretary of State Daniel Webster's strict criteria, enunciated in 1837 and still the legal standard, that the threat be 'instant, overwhelming, leaving no choice of means and no moment of deliberation. Preemptive war has legal sanction. . . . Preventive war has none. . . . This makes preventive war indistinguishable from outright aggression.'"

Most foreign and domestic analysts outside the Bush administration have concluded the U.S. legal position was questionable at best. UNSCR 1441 does not clearly authorize an Article 42 action (most argue it clearly does not), and the doctrine of preventive war is a statement of U.S. policy, not law. One leading U.S. neoconservative, Richard Perle, admitted the legal deficiency in a backhanded fashion: "I think in this case international law stood in the way of doing the right thing."

Unless one is willing to argue that international law is unjust in a general sense regarding the resort to violence, Perle's comment is enigmatic. Does it mean that whenever law gets in the way of state policy it is permissible to ignore that law? Such a position would be difficult to justify for a country that professes an abiding commitment to the rule of law. In legal fact, the United States committed an illegal act of aggression against Iraq. Given the tenor and circumstances of the time, one can argue "so what?" as many defenders of the decision in effect have done.

What can be made of the precedential impact of the invasion? At heart, the U.S. invasion represented a violation of Iraqi sovereignty, and the UN Charter provisions on the legality of intervention are based in the defense of sovereignty, largely at the insistence of one of sovereignty's fiercest defenders, the United States. What does it mean when the world's most ardent supporter of the concept of sovereignty ignores or contravenes that principle?

Whether admitted openly or not, international intrusion into the domestic politics of states, no matter how objectionable or horrific the behavior of states may be, reflects a far different conceptualization of sovereignty than the one that reigned for the first 300 years of the modern state system. Had one asked in 1946 whether it was permissible to mount Operation Restore Hope in Somalia without the permission of the Somali government, the answer would have been overwhelmingly negative. The explanation would have been that such a mission would have been a direct violation of Somalia's sovereignty.

The unintended (or ignored) effect of recent interventions like that in Iraq has been to move the rationale for outside interference into alignment with the conceptualization of sovereignty based in the individual and the limited grant of individual sovereignty to the state. In terms of the meaning of sovereignty, there can be no other rationale for violating state sovereignty other than saying that state sovereignty *is no longer an inviolable principle of international relations*. To make that assertion, in turn, it is necessary to locate sovereignty somewhere else, such as in individuals and groups whose rights are being violated and to whose rescue international efforts are directed to support higher international values like the eradication of terror. The alternative, ironically, is to admit that violations of sovereignty such as the invasion of Iraq are illegal. In that case, the United States was a law breaker, but the principle of sovereignty of which it is a staunch defender is left relatively intact.

The Restoration of Iraqi Sovereignty

The last American military combat—effectively, occupation—forces left Iraq at the end of 2011. The only American military presence in the country since then has been some military guards protecting the American Embassy in the so-called Green Zone, and their jurisdiction is limited to the embassy grounds (the normal status of embassy security guards everywhere). With no foreign troops on Iraqi soil, the country's sovereignty has been effectively restored.

The government of Iraq was most insistent on this outcome in negotiations leading to the final withdrawal of all American troops. The great symbol of this determination was the Iraqi refusal to accept a continuing American presence in talks on the Status of Forces Agreement (SOFA) signed by the two countries in 2008, but the subject of controversy and unsuccessful attempts to modify afterward. The United States had argued for a limited continuing American "footprint" after almost all American forces withdrew, including the crucial provision that those forces would fall under U.S. rather than Iraqi jurisdiction in the event of accusations of law-breaking by those forces or individual American soldiers. The Iraqis obdurately refused to cooperate and accept those provisions in SOFA negotiations.

The Iraqi objections were based in the ongoing violation of Iraqi sovereignty the proposed American conditions would perpetuate. On one hand, foreign troops on their soil were an affront to their sovereignty on the face of it: Would Americans have accepted an Iraqi military presence on U.S. soil? More particularly, Americans exempt from Iraqi laws magnified the indignity by placing those forces beyond Iraqi sovereign control. The result was an impasse. The Iraqis would not agree to a continuing American military presence unless they had legal jurisdiction over the remaining troops, and the United States would not stay without that provision. Americans would either stay on Iraqi terms or they would have to leave.

Ultimately, the Iraqis won and the Americans signed the SOFA (technically the "Agreement of the United States and the Republic of Iraq on the Withdrawal of American Force from Iraq and the Organization of Their Activities During Their *Temporary* Presence in Iraq") (Emphasis added) acceding to Iraqi demands. At no time did the American government acknowledge the sovereignty issue or admit that it had in any way formally violated Iraqi sovereignty by its invasion and occupation.

The public explanation of the withdrawal was that it was possible because the United States had somehow accomplished its purposes in Iraq and thus could leave, an explanation many observers questioned. Practically, the United States withdrew on Iraqi terms because the American public had turned against the war and because President Obama had promised in 2008 to end the war as part of his election campaign. The Iraqis understood these practical political forces, held firm in their positions, and prevailed.

CONCLUSION

The impact of American actions of violating, effectively abrogating, and then restoring Iraqi sovereignty on the principle itself has assiduously been omitted from official discussions and evaluations. Doing so avoids a debate that the United States would just as soon not open. The United States has long been and continues to be one of the staunchest defenders of national sovereignty and its implications. To admit that its 2003 actions against Iraq violated the very principle it so strongly defends is undesirable on two grounds.

First, it runs the risk of being seen as hypocritical by implying that some countries' sovereignty is more inviolable than that of other countries. Although such a factual inconsistency may exist in a world of power politics (one of the bases of which *is* sovereignty), it is not anything any state would publicly admit. Second, admitting a breach would also be a precedent-setting action. Does the American violation of Iraqi sovereignty mean sovereignty as a universal principle is no longer so important? If one admits that sovereignty is not sacrosanct, how can the American insistence on the sanctity of its own sovereignty be justified in principle?

No powerful country, least of all the United States, will admit that the universality of sovereignty has been compromised by the American invasion and occupation of Iraq, but such an erosion is clearly arguable. The consequences of this breach have not been systematically investigated and debated, but it is probably just a matter of time until they are.

SUGGESTED ACTIVITIES AND QUESTIONS

1. What is sovereignty? How is the question of the American war against Iraq a sovereignty question? Explain.
2. With which conception of sovereignty do you agree? Are, in other words, the rights of states more important than the rights of individuals and groups within states? How would the international system be different without the supremacy of state sovereignty?
3. Does American participation in military operations in countries torn by civil war or allegedly involved in terrorism violate American principles, such as our position on sovereignty? Or should the question of our participation be made on pragmatic grounds rather than on principles? If you were in a position to do so, how would you advise President Obama when the next intervention is proposed at the United Nations or elsewhere?
4. Under the UN Charter, when is it permissible to interfere in the sovereign affairs of states? Did the United States seek to invoke these conditions to justify the invasion of Iraq? If so, how, and did the arguments succeed?
5. Did the United States violate Iraqi sovereignty by invading and occupying that country? Was the invasion legal, or is the question moot, as U.S. interests overrode questions of legality?
6. What was the SOFA? What role did it play in the restoration of Iraqi sovereignty? How did it symbolize the entire issue of whether the U.S. action represented a breach of sovereignty?
7. Assess the U.S. position on the sovereignty principle. Is it reasonable or hypocritical? Should the United States modify its position on sovereignty or its practice of violating the sovereignty of other countries? Is there any way to resolve this apparent inconsistency?

SUGGESTED READINGS AND RESOURCES

Bodin, Jean. *Six Books on the Commonwealth*. Oxford, UK: Basil Blackwell, 1955.

Brierly, J. L. *The Law of Nations,* 6th ed. New York: Oxford University Press, 1963.

Burkeman, Oliver and Julian Borger. "War Critics Astonished as US War Hawk Admits Invasion Was Illegal." *The Guardian* (online), November 20, 2003. (http://www.guardian.co.uk/uk/2003/nov/20/usa.iraq/print)

Cusimano, Mary Ann, ed. *Beyond Sovereignty*. Bedford, MA: Bedford St. Martin's, 1999.

Grotius, Hugo. *The Rights of War and Peace: Including the Law of Nature and Nations.* New York: M. W. Dunne, 1981.

Hashami, Sohail H., ed. *State Sovereignty and Persistence in International Relations.* University Park, PA: Pennsylvania State University Press, 1997.

Hobbes, Thomas. *Leviathan*. Oxford, UK: Clarendon, 1989.

International Institute for Strategic Studies. "Reconciling Iraqi Sovereignty." *Strategic Comments* (online) 15, 10, December 2009.

Kantor, Arnold and Linton F. Brooks, eds. *U.S. Intervention Policy for the Post–Cold War World.* New York: The American Assembly, 1994.

Lewis, Charles and Mark Reading-Smith. *False Pretenses: Iraq: The War Card.* Washington, DC: Center for Public Integrity, 2008.

Locke, John. *Two Treatises on Government*. New York: Cambridge University Press, 1988.

Lyons, Gene M. and Michael Mastanduno, eds. *Beyond Westphalia: State Sovereignty and International Relations.* Baltimore, MD: Johns Hopkins University Press, 1995.

Mason, R. Chuck. *U.S.—Iraq Withdrawal/Status of Forces Agreement: Issues from Congressional Oversight.* Washington, DC: Congressional Research Service, July 13, 2009.

Parker, Sam. "Is Iraq Back?" *Current History* 108, 722 (December 2009), 429–431.

Record, Jeffrey. *Dark Victory: America's Second War Against Iraq.* Annapolis, MD: Naval Institute Press, 2004.

Rousseau, Jean-Jacques. *The Collected Works of Jean-Jacque Rousseau.* Hanover, NH: University Press of New England, 1990.

Scahill, Jeremy. "Iraq's 'National Sovereignty Day' Is U.S.—Style Trademark Hype." *Huffington Post* (online), June 30, 2009.

Snow, Donald M. *What After Iraq?* New York: Longman, 2009.

———. *When America Fights: The Uses of U.S. Military Force.* Washington, DC: CQ Press, 2000.

——— and Eugene Brown. *International Relations: The Changing Contours of Power.* New York: Longman, 2000.

Steinberg, James B. "Real Leaders Do Soft Power: Learning the Lessons of Iraq." *Washington Quarterly* 31, 2 (Spring 2008), 155–164.

Yaphe, Judith S. "Iraq: Are We There Yet?" *Current History* 107, 713 (December 2008), 403–409.

Resource Scarcity: The Changing Dynamics and Implications of Global Energy

PRÉCIS

The desire, even necessity, to control scarce resources, and conflict over those resources, are as old as human history and have acted as a major source of friction in the international order through time. Major wars have been fought over access to precious metals, water, food, and exotic spices, to name a few examples. In the contemporary world, the most publicized resource conflict has been over access to petroleum reserves, principally those of the Middle East region. The conflict over petroleum is a continuing major source of conflict and disorder. There are signs, however, that it is also changing.

This case examines the changing general parameters of the problem of energy security. The major change agents are shifts in emphases on different sources of energy and changes in who demands greater parts of global energy, trends that are only emerging but promise to become more important. The center of the global energy problem, with economic and geopolitical implications for the world's largest and most powerful countries, has been on petroleum, which will remain a scarce and valuable resource. Global energy patterns are, however, changing, with major geopolitical ramifications for all countries.

Conflict and war over the ability to control, monopolize, or deny access to valued resources is as old as human history. Men have fought and died, armies have swept across countless expanses, and empires and states have risen and fallen in the name of precious resources. Whether it was control of the silk routes across Asia, the exotic foodstuffs of the Spice Islands, the diamonds and gold of southern and central Africa, El Dorado in the New World, or the petroleum wealth of the Middle East, the struggle for scarce and valuable natural resources has been a recurrent theme of human history and relations.

How will this historical theme be acted out in the early twenty-first century? What is striking is that the resources over which there is the most competition are also the most basic resources for the human condition. At the top of the list is potable water. With 70 percent of the earth's surface covered by water, water per se is hardly a scarce resource, but water that is usable for human purposes like drinking, bathing, and agriculture is in selective shortage across the globe. As world population grows, existing shortages will be multiplied. The other scarce resource, and the one to which this chapter is devoted, is energy. The heart of the global energy debate has centered on petroleum, making security of access to oil a prime concern for all states. The balance between oil and other sources of energy is, however, changing, and the needs of different states for different energy sources and forms are changing as well.

As has always been the case, resource scarcities are politically important, because domestic and international political decisions help define scarcities and responses to them. Where resources are in short supply, the political, including geopolitical, competition between those who have adequate or surplus supplies and those who do not has acrimonious consequences for the relations between the haves and the have-nots. The worldwide demand for energy, of which petroleum has been the spotlight, is growing and will likely continue to swell despite the emergence of alternate sources. As long as demand is increasing and those in control of supplies can exercise some level of power over how much of the resource is available to whom, there will be continued friction and conflict between the possessors and those who do not have but need energy resources.

Scarcity exists whenever all claimants to a resource cannot simultaneously have all of that resource they need or want. When scarcity exists between sovereign states, there are four possible ways to allocate the resource. First, if some method can be found to increase supply so that all claimants can have all the resource they desire, scarcity disappears and so does the basis for conflict. The problem with this solution is that increased supply usually results in lower prices, an outcome unattractive to producers. If their narrow (normally nationally driven) interests prevail, they will prefer scarcity, as it keeps the prices up.

If existing suppliers are reluctant to make more of the resource available, what can make supplies more plentiful? Finding new sources of petroleum, for instance, is the most obvious way to increase supplies, but it face two barriers. One is that cheaply exploitable supplies are increasingly difficult to find and extract, and this trend will only magnify as time passes and current sources are depleted. The traditional approach to petroleum supply has been more exploration and exploitation of traditional repositories, such as the Middle East. New sources of petroleum and other carbon-based energy such as shale oil and natural gas are beginning to alter these calculations, especially in the United States.

The second approach is to decrease demand for the resource by using less and thereby lowering demand closer to available supply. In the case of traditional energy sources like oil, this approach is bedeviled by the fact that global demand is actually increasing, mostly because of new claimants to the resource. As will be discussed later in the chapter, countries like China and India are rapidly expanding their demands for petroleum and other forms of energy, and their demands are growing at a faster pace than conservation in places like the United States. Thus, efforts to increase gasoline mileage standards for vehicles in the United States may reduce *American* demands for petroleum and improve the American energy prolife in the world, but increased Asian demands more than counteract those gains on a global scale.

The third option is substitution, an alternative with growing appeal. The most important current uses of petroleum energy are for power generation and transportation, and the question is whether alternatives can be found to substitute for burning petroleum. An additional criterion for alternatives is whether they produce lower (or no) carbon dioxide emissions that are a byproduct of petroleum burning and that have harmful ecological effects. In the area of energy production, substitution includes coal and natural gas (both carbon emitters), nuclear power, and renewable sources like wind and solar, which do not have a carbon dioxide residue. Each of the alternatives has its own advantages and disadvantages, as discussed later in the chapter.

If the other three options fail, then a power struggle remains, pitting the suppliers against the consumers over how much energy will be available at what prices. Up until now, the geopolitical struggle has largely been over petroleum. The emergence of new technologies such as shale oil and natural gas exploration could alter the geopolitical map. The exact nature, direction, and outcome of those alterations remain uncertain.

The structure of the contemporary energy problem is changing. Although changes in the overall energy equation may lessen the stranglehold of petroleum, the dynamics of petroleum remain important central illustrations of the energy security problem. They also show how the pattern of global demand is changing as well.

According to 2006 figures, oil production was at about 85 million barrels a day. Global consumption was at about 83 million barrels a day, meaning a "surplus" of only about 2 million barrels each day. Although numbers are slightly different today, this balance between supply and demand has not changed much. This means the oil market is extremely "tight," in the sense that a fairly marginal increase in demand or decrease in supply can throw the equation out of balance and create a situation of scarcity where demand exceeds supply. This is one reason the oil market always seems nervous about geopolitical events. There are, for instance, 14 countries in the world that produce over 2 million barrels a day, and one of them suddenly withholding their oil could upset the balance. The balance is further made precarious by who is placing demands on global energy sources, notably petroleum.

One way demand is traditionally measured is the balance between the countries of the Organization for Economic Cooperation and Development (OECD) and non-members. OECD members encompass the traditional developed, industrialized world: North America, Western Europe, Japan, and Australia and New Zealand, and the non-OECD group, which contains everyone else, historically defines the less developed or less industrialized world. Because energy consumption is one of the best indicators of economic activity, this means that most of the world's energy demands have come from the OECD members, whereas the non-OECD members have made more modest demands.

Led by the burgeoning development of non-OECD members like China and India (with other countries like Brazil not far behind), that balance is changing. Using data from the *CIA World Factbook 2012*, American import figures, which a decade ago were just short of 20 million barrels a day (bbd), have shrunk to 10.27 million bbd, and that number is expected to continue to grow smaller. The major drivers of this decrease are increased domestic production (largely from shale oil) and decreased demand due to conservation. The same is not true for China and India, countries that between them now import about 1.25 million bbd per day more than the world's largest single national importer, the United States. Chinese imports have risen from about 3 million bbd in 2004 to 2011 levels of over 9 million, and Indian imports have almost doubled since the middle 2000s. The dual effects of this change are to further tighten markets by increasing the overall demand for oil and to create a larger pool of purchasing countries, thereby increasing the ability of oil exporters to determine to whom they will and will not sell. The result is to increase the leverage of the sellers by making pursuit of any country's production an increasingly important part of importer's energy security calculations. This factor is particularly evident in the Middle East, an area that gains almost all of its international importance because of its oil leverage.

The energy crisis has been driven almost exclusively by petroleum supply and demand since the early decades of the twentieth century, and "black gold" continues to be the largest single driver in this equation. The calculus is, however, changing, impelled by two major dynamics, the technology-driven changes and diversification of energy sources, especially since 2008, and changes in the sources of demand away from OECD toward non-OECD countries. Individually and collectively, these two dynamics are altering visibly the international geopolitical energy security landscape. Examining these two dynamics and their resultant impact on the global geopolitics of energy forms the heart of the rest of the chapter.

THE PROBLEM OF ENERGY SUPPLY AND SCARCITY

Petroleum has been the primary energy source in the developed world for nearly a century, during which vast sources of oil have been discovered and exploited in a number of places around the globe, but especially in the Middle East, where the largest and most accessible sources have been found and mined. World dependence has become so great that two basic trends have emerged that will be of great importance in the twenty-first century. One of these is that increasing demand and exploitation have begun to reveal limits on the eventual supply of this non-renewable resource (non-renewable because it does not naturally replenish itself when used). The result has been to look for alternative sources of energy for the future, including petroleum from non-traditional sources recovered in new ways.

The other trend has been to create a changed aspect of the world power map, where countries and regions that would not otherwise have great geo-political significance gain such status because they are significant petroleum repositories. Once again, the Middle East is the most obvious example. As traditionally exploited sources of oil lose some salience, the geopolitical map is likely to change again, away from traditional oil suppliers to possessors of other energy sources.

The current importance of petroleum thus derives from the centrality of its usage to modern society, including the worldwide trend toward globaliza-tion (see Chapter 9). The great demand for petroleum makes it a particularly valuable resource, and its concentration within various regions and control by different governments makes it scarce or potentially scarce and thus a source of leverage for its possessors against those non-possessors dependent upon it. The United States, for instance, has not had access to the petroleum of two of the world's largest possessors, Iran and Iraq, since the late 1970s, when regimes hostile to the United States came to power in those countries.

Some scarcities, of course, are more important than others. A shortage or withholding of cinnamon from world markets, for instance, would be dis-tressing to many people who regularly use it as a spice, but a sharp rise in price or reduction of supply would not be catastrophic. People would simply decrease their consumption without life-threatening consequences. Energy is different; without adequate energy, many people could not survive, and many more could not prosper.

Historically, prime human reliance on different energy sources has fea-tured the dominance of one source until its eclipse by an alternate source. For most of human history, the dominant source of energy was from burning wood. As long as the human population was relatively small and the demands on fuel by individuals were modest (mostly cooking and heating), wood was essentially a renewable resource, as more trees grew than were harvested and burned for energy, among other uses for trees.

Both the adequacy of wood as an energy source and the equipoise be-tween its exploitation and natural replenishment began to break down in the eighteenth and nineteenth centuries. Lower death rates (people living longer) caused human populations to begin to grow rapidly, and industrialization caused per capita demand for energy to explode, as energy was applied to more uses than simple survival. As a result, wood gradually became both less adequate as an energy source and increasingly non-renewable. There are a few relatively isolated places in the world where wood remains a prime energy source, but depletion of trees is a problem in virtually all of them. The growing spread of the Sahara Desert southward into greater parts of Africa is largely the result of this dynamic. Wood became an inadequate source of energy for human usage.

Oil provided the alternative. Since petroleum overtook wood as the primary worldwide means of energy generation early in the twentieth century, world dependence on it has gradually increased to the almost total dependence on oil for such basic human needs as energy provision and transportation. All analysts agree that the period of petroleum dominance of the energy cycle will be considerably shorter than that of wood because of burgeoning global population and increasing per capita demands for energy as more and more of the world develops economically. At the same time, the world supply of petroleum is finite and depleting, because oil is non-renewable. Until very recently, it was fashionable to talk about the concept of "peak oil," roughly the point at which half the world's reserves are depleted and after which supply can be expected to shrink. Some of the projections have been quite dire and ominous, raising the prospect that the mid-point has already been or will shortly be passed, with potentially serious consequences. Very recent discoveries, especially of shale oil deposits in many parts of the world, are rendering many of the more apocalyptical predictions questionable and are suggesting that much greater supplies are available than those from tradition means of extraction, thereby stretching the length of the cycle for petroleum dominance. That dominance will not, however, last indefinitely.

The resource struggle for petroleum is, from this vantage point, largely a struggle over managing the transition from petroleum as the world's primary energy source to alternate sources that will assume the role oil plays in contemporary societies. Predictions about the pace and content of that transition are debatable, and for the foreseeable future, there is no clear successor to petroleum as the world's primary source of energy. Most extrapolations suggest that there will be multiple "contestants" in this transition, and that the next cycle may be one where several sources contribute to energy supply. Fusion energy is seen by some as the long-term solution, but whether or when it will emerge is a point of contention among scientists. In addition, the current transition is influenced by factors not present in past periods of change, notably the question of environmental impact (the subject of Chapter 13).

There are five sources of energy production for the future, all of which are currently in use at various levels and with different prospects. The three largest of these sources in terms of current usage involve the burning of fossil fuels, with the inevitable byproduct of carbon dioxide emission into the atmosphere. These three sources are petroleum, natural gas, and coal. They differ in quantity available, geographic distribution, and contribution to environmental degradation. The other two source categories are nuclear power generation and renewable energy sources, a cover designation for a variety of specific energy-generating technologies. These sources share the characteristic of being non-carbon burning and thus producing no carbon dioxide emission. Nuclear power, of course, presents its own special environmental problems in terms of the disposal of nuclear residue and the danger of power plant accidents, and the various renewable sources present supply adequacy problems that have not yet been overcome. Most observers do not believe that these latter sources will ever become dominant in the overall energy supply equation.

Each of these sources also creates specific concerns that go beyond the physics of energy production. One of these concerns is the question of supply adequacy: How much of the resource is available, and is that amount enough for current and projected needs? A related matter is the cost of this supply. Can adequate supplies at acceptable and predictable prices be guaranteed or at least reasonably assured? As well, there is the question of energy security: Can necessary supplies at acceptable supplies be guaranteed, or are they potentially subject to uncontrollable fluctuations in amount of resource availability and cost? All of these concerns have been prominent parts of the debate over petroleum dependency. The other major concern has been environmental impact: Do some energy sources create such environmental degradation that their use should be restricted or precluded on the damage such production will do to the global ecosystem? Each of these concerns will be addressed in a brief review of each source as part of the global energy problem. Because of its prominence, that survey begins with and features the traditional use of petroleum.

Petroleum

Worldwide dependency on petroleum-based energy is not accidental. At the end of World War II, the international community was faced with the replacement of energy sources and generation facilities destroyed or crippled in the war. The problem was especially acute in Europe and parts of Asia (notably Japan), where much of the wartime destruction occurred. The conscious solution to the problem was to rebuild the energy system based on petroleum as the primary energy source. The premises of this decision, heavily influenced by the United States, included the abundant availability of petroleum for a long time at a low, controllable cost, as most oil production was controlled by Western oil companies (the so-called "seven sisters"), and much of the source was in the Persian Gulf region, where the seven sisters held sway and assured that compliant local governments would grant concessions perpetuating the low costs. These projections of abundant, cheap, and secure oil led to the conversion of most European and Asian energy systems to a petroleum base (France being a notable exception). In 1945, these assumptions seemed realistic and sustainable. They no longer are.

Both assumptions have proven questionable or entirely false. Petroleum that can be extracted in great quantities at minimal costs is rapidly disappearing (the relatively unexploited Iraqi oil fields are an exception, which helps explain their great attraction to many countries). Thus, the physical costs of extraction have increased. At the same time, those supplies are no longer controlled by the oil companies, allowing them to manipulate access costs. Instead, a major consequence of forming the Organization of Petroleum Exporting Countries (OPEC) in 1960 has been the nationalization of oil assets.

Although oil has been used primarily as an energy source for economic activity (its conversion to electricity) and transportation, its uses go well beyond the production of energy, and some of those usages are more important than its use as an energy source. Petroleum is, after all, the basic commodity used in the petrochemical industry, which is the basis, among other things, for most of the plastics industry. Because there are no ready alternative materials to substitute for petroleum in making plastics, there is a case to be made that using oil to produce energy is a waste of a resource that is indispensable for other, more important purposes—a claim that does not attach to other energy sources that lack this range of utilities. The late Shah Reza Pahlavi of Iran (as quoted by Fleischman) captured this dilemma before his fall from power in 1979. "There is a limited amount of petroleum in the earth. Oil is used for making plastics and other products," he said. "Oil is too valuable to burn. When we run out, what will we do? Fight each other for the last drop?"

Arguments over whether producing energy is the best use of petroleum were considered esoteric when petroleum availability seemed virtually (if not literally) endless. Before the implications of the exploitation of shale oil exponentially increased likely reserves, concerns surrounded peak oil and the prospect of dwindling availability in the future. These calculations have been plagued by two uncertainties. One is the amount of petroleum left to be discovered. Estimates made in 2008 top out at around 1.3 trillion barrels of untapped discovered oil, with uncertain amounts that are undiscovered. These calculations are rough and probably underestimate reserves for three reasons suggested by Hirsch: proprietary interests of oil companies keeping secret the amount of oil they control or seek, state secrets in the petroleum-exporting countries, and politically biased calculations. The result is fairly wide disagreement among estimations, and this uncertainty is magnified by the attempt to calculate exploitable oil shale formations that are widely spread around the globe and the potential of which is only now being explored. The second uncertainty is the rate at which oil still in the ground will be depleted. While demands are increasing due to greater demand from non-OECD states, rates of petroleum usage are decreasing in much of the traditionally developed world due to a combination of conservation, conversion to other fuel sources, and a slowing of economic growth rates. Where these trends will go in the future is not clearly nor consensually understood. Although it is no longer certain *when* peak oil will be reached and decline will occur, both *will* occur eventually.

The joker in supply calculations has, of course, been the emergence of shale-formation oil and natural gas as an energy source. Since 2008, the United States—and to a lesser extent Canada—have moved progressively and aggressively to the extraction of oil and natural gas from shale formations common throughout much of the world and specifically in North America. The prototype of this activity has been the so-called Bakken formation, named after the North Dakota farmer on whose property near Tioga, North Dakota, the initial formation (part of the Williston Basin covering parts of North Dakota, Montana, and Saskatchewan) was exploited. This type of formation is amenable to exploitation through a process known as "fracking" that yields natural gas and petroleum. These discoveries are the major source of change in the economic geography of energy, but are controversial, as discussed in the next section on natural gas. Among the possible impacts are a reduction of American (and other countries') dependence on imported petroleum, notably from the Middle East.

Supply costs also affect the petroleum equation. The cost of petroleum worldwide has leveled off at around $100 a barrel in recent years, and despite periodic fluctuations, these costs are likely to be enduring. Although such costs have negative consequences like the high price of gasoline at the pump, they also create opportunities for greater supply availability, particularly in the United States and for Americans. The dynamics of the calculation are straightforward. There is a good bit of petroleum in the United States, but it is relatively expensive to extract. In essence, all the cheap, easily accessible oil has been extracted, leaving petroleum that can only be recovered if its price is high. At $25 to 50 a barrel for imported oil, for instance, it is not economically feasible to go after American residues, but at $100 a barrel, extraction can be done profitably. Among other things, these costs have made shale and other difficult petroleum sources economically feasible to extract. The current American push toward something like net energy self-sufficiency thus depends upon high prices for a barrel of oil. A decline in cost would mean, however, noticeable consumer benefits in the prices of gasoline or fuel oil but could only occur at a loss of energy sufficiency.

Energy sufficiency is, of course, a goal of all energy-importing states, as sufficiency is a major component of energy security. As noted, energy security is the product of availability and cost, in the sense that the goal is secure access to adequate supply at acceptable cost. Were petroleum (or other) energy sources distributed worldwide according to consumption (i.e., energy produced where it is used), this would not be a problem. Table 2.1, for instance, depicts crude oil reserves by region in 2010 according to figures supplied by the Energy Information Administration (EIA) of the U.S. Department of Energy. These figures reveal that oil reserves are not found in the parts of the world that historically have used the most oil (the OECD countries of Europe and North America) or in non-OECD countries like India and China (both part of Asia and Oceania) where demand is growing fastest.

TABLE 2.1

World Oil Reserves, 2010

Region	Reserves (in Billions of Barrels)
North America	210
Central and South America	239
Europe	12
Middle East	800
Eurasia	99
Africa	124
Asia and Oceania	45

Source: International Energy Statistics Database. Washington, DC: Energy Information Administration, U.S. Department of Energy, 2012 (cited in *World Almanac and Book of Facts*. New York: World Almanac Books, 2013).

As these figures unsurprisingly reveal, oil reserves and oil consumption are not coterminous: Slightly less than half of petroleum energy is used in the OECD countries, whose reserves make up about 15 percent of the global total (mostly in Canada). The vast bulk of supply (more than 50 percent) comes from the volatile Middle East, giving that part of the world an importance and leverage in world politics it would not otherwise have. Because a number of the states with the largest reserves and thus the potential for the largest amount of supply are Middle Eastern, the region further has multiple candidates that could withhold the 2 million barrels a day that would throw the tight balance between supply and demand out of kilter and precipitate a crisis in the oil market.

In addition, the politics of petroleum control and exploitation can corrode the domestic politics of countries, including otherwise unstable Middle Eastern states, as well. Iraq is a prime example. The long struggle between the Shiite Arab, Sunni Arab, and Kurdish populations of that country has religious and ethnic bases, but in the wake of the American occupation and withdrawal, it also has a deep oil-based economic cleavage as well. The current major division among the groups is over who will receive the vast revenues from exploitation of Iraqi oil fields. The principal fields are in the Kurdish north (and especially around the contested city of Kirkuk) and in the Shiite south, whereas there are no known, exploitable oil deposits under lands dominated by the traditionally politically dominant Sunnis (although there are reports of potentially great reserves in the so-called Sunni Triangle). Any attempt to reconcile ethno-religious differences are currently stymied by disagreements over which groups should receive how much of the revenues from leasing drilling rights to different countries and companies. Until this dispute, which has dominated the Iraqi landscape since the American withdrawal, is resolved, Kurdish separatism and Sunni insurgency remain major concerns.

In a previous edition of this book, petroleum was described as the "lubricant that corrodes," a reference primarily to its effects on world politics. This corrosiveness is the result of a great demand for a resource necessary to energize the world economy by producers seeking to maximize their individual benefits from that resource, often at the apparent expense of the consumers. The United States was the poster child for this corrosion, as the United States at its nadir had an extreme dependence on fickle foreign oil sources for nearly half its consumption. Thanks to the emergence of other fuel sources, the distribution of the "rust" of that corrosion is changing somewhat, but increased demand by some consumers is making the friction no less real. One of the ways in which countries like the United States may be able to relieve some of the resulting stress is through conversion of its energy demands to alternate sources. Bakken oil and natural gas provide one such major avenue for this kind of transformation.

Natural Gas

The major change agent in the energy equation is the expansion of availability and usage of natural gas as an energy source. Natural gas has been part of the energy equation since the transition to petroleum as the world's most favored and used fuel, because natural gas is found essentially everywhere there is oil. Natural gas has, however, generally been seen as a less valuable than oil, particularly in the United States. Anyone with a long memory who has ever driven across the Oklahoma or Texas panhandles at night will remember parts of the horizon lit up by the fires used by oilmen to burn off and get rid of extra, superfluous gas they were uninterested in exploiting.

Despite its devaluation, natural gas has always been part of the energy equation. In the United States, for instance, natural gas from traditional sources coterminous with oil reserves has always accounted for nearly as much of total U.S. energy production as its major rivals, fellow carbon-based petroleum and coal. In 1980, for instance, EIA figures show each had roughly 20 percent of overall production, and although there has been a gradual decline in oil production using traditional methods, gas has been a steady part of the production equation.

In 2011, gas production passed the production of coal as the single greatest source of American energy production at around 22 percent, and the gap is projected to widen by the year 2040, when natural gas production will account for just 35 percent of production, with coal and petroleum occupying second and third places, according to EIA figures. In addition, the EIA's *Annual Energy Outlook 2013* extrapolates that total American energy production, largely driven by increased production of natural gas, will exceed consumption through 2040, making the United States a net energy exporter.

The major reason for this change, of course, has been the emergence of shale oil and gas production, which has gradually been growing since about 2008 and has reached a point where it is becoming a transformational factor in the global energy picture. The United States has been the leader of this development and likely will continue to be at the forefront of this technology in the near future, and thus it is worthwhile to examine some of the factors for the rising prominence of shale oil in the United States, as they may provide some framework for considering future developments of Bakken formations— which have been widely identified worldwide—in other parts of the world.

For Americans, shale gas production is cheaper than the production of other natural gas and fossil fuel alternatives. It is particularly cheaper than petroleum as an energy source, and because there is a great deal of it in reserve, it is tempting as a substitute to oil on this ground alone. It is apparently also cheaper than traditional mining of other natural gas forms.

The distribution of Bakken formations globally is also a long-term advantage to the United States and China, which have the world's largest known availability of these formations but not such large reserves of traditional natural gas. International Energy Agency (IEA) figures for 2009, for instance, show that the two countries with the greatest proven shale gas reserves are China (1,275 trillion cubic feet) and the United States (862 trillion cubic feet). Of the remaining 11 countries listed in descending rank order of possession, Russia, which has the world's largest known reserves of traditional natural gas, does not even appear on the list. On the list of traditional gas reserve holders, Iraq, Qatar, and Saudi Arabia also have larger natural gas reserves than the

United States (and China). None of these countries even appears on the shale gas table; in fact, the only Middle Eastern state that does is Algeria, whose technically recoverable shale gas reserves are a little over one-fourth of American reserves.

The other great attraction for the United States is geopolitical, specifically as a prospect for lessening dependence on foreign petroleum importation and thus contributing to greater energy security, even overall sufficiency. As noted, the movement toward the United States ceasing to be a net energy importer to being a net exporter is under way, and shale oil and gas are major contributors to this shift. The change is also charged by an increasing movement of the United States away from alternate, including foreign, sources of oil. On the domestic level, the American power grid is seeing a shift from coal to natural gas burning as the energy source. The major reason is that natural gas emits less than half the carbon dioxide levels of coal burning (a ratio the coal industry, of course, denies). One spinoff has been the ability of the United States to adopt air pollution projections committing the country to carbon-dioxide-emission reductions in international follow-on negotiations since the collapse of the Kyoto Protocol (see Chapter 13). As more shale oil and greater conversions of energy source occur, American reliance on imported, and especially Middle Eastern, petroleum is decreasing as shale oil and gas supplant petroleum as a component in the American energy equation. In fact, as a larger percentage of the American energy sector converts to this source, it is accompanied primarily by a decline in the use of energy derived from petroleum. No one is predicting that the United States will become oil self-sufficient, but the size of imports will decrease, and the United States, largely by increasing shale gas exports, will become a net energy exporter.

Shale gas exploitation also has political advantages within the United States, two of which stand out. Unlike petroleum, shale formations are found in exploitable amounts in over 30 American states (as opposed to about five petroleum-producing states), meaning that political support for exploitation is likely to be more broad-based than for alternatives. At the same time, unlike traditional petroleum and associated natural gas reserves, most of the shale formations are found on privately owned land, meaning federal permission to exploit is not so much a problem as with using federal land.

The other country that can benefit greatly from the shale oil and gas "revolution" is China. China's need for energy is growing rapidly, as economic development and higher standards of living in the People's Republic of China (PRC) occur in energy-intensive ways, such as burgeoning sales of automobiles in the country. China and India, the world's two most populous countries, are leading the surge in demand for increased energy that is shifting the balance of demand away from the OECD countries. To meet its increasing needs, China is attempting to increase its access to all energy sources. It must, however, import most of its petroleum, as its reserves of traditional oil sources are about the same as those of the United States unless its claims to South China Sea oil are included, a prospect discussed later in the chapter. Its increasing reliance on coal is creating enormous environmental difficulties for the country (especially urban atmospheric pollution) and demands for decreased carbon dioxide emissions from international environmentalists.

Shale oil and gas may provide a useful alternative for both the Chinese energy need and pollution problem. According to EIA figures cited earlier, China has the world's largest reserves, and it has begun to test fracking techniques to explore the prospects of mining its vast shale oil formations. On the negative side, most of its reserves are in remote locations difficult to access, and China lacks the technology and infrastructure (gas pipelines, for instance) to exploit its reserves in the near- to mid-term. As a result, shale gas will not solve all of China's energy and pollution problems, but it could certainly reduce its dependence, particularly on coal, following an apparent American lead to replace coal-generating power plants with facilities that burn shale-derived gas instead. It is too early to see how much of an impact such a conversion would have in China, as the shale oil industry is in its earliest infancy, but it is likely to be of some value.

It should be added that India faces a similar set of problems—increasing energy demands and growing pressure to reduce pollution from coal burning, but with the significant difference that India lacks shale oil potential on a major scale. At 63 trillion cubic feet of technically recoverable shale gas, its reserves are twelfth on the global list and less than 5 percent of Chinese totals, meaning its conversion away from energy sources like coal is more problematic.

Coal

Coal is the third major carbon-dioxide-emitting fossil fuel. Coal preceded petroleum in helping to power the Industrial Revolution in eighteenth- and nineteenth-century Europe and North America, and it remains a significant source of energy production and consumption in many countries. Coal currently produces about 22 percent of American energy through the operation of coal-powered electrical energy plants, and this market share is predicted to remain fairly steady through 2040. What is most notable about coal usage is that it is such an important part of the gradual shift in energy patterns toward the developing world. As noted earlier, the vast majority of the growing disparity in OECD versus non-OECD energy consumption is occurring in China and India, and will continue as both these population giants progress through the economic development process.

The situation is particularly sharp and, to some observers, worrisome in China. Using an EIA-supplied graph, China now uses nearly 47 percent the coal consumed in the world. In 2011, for instance, China consumed 3.8 billion tons of coal, whereas the rest of the world combined to use 4.3 billion tons. China has coal reserves in abundance (it ranks third in the world in known reserves, behind the United States and Russia), and coal mining is a large industry in the country. Moreover, coal mining is relatively cheap, and the Chinese power industry does not have to worry about dependency on foreign sources for the coal it needs. In economic and security terms, a growing reliance on coal for power generation makes sense, and the Chinese reliance on coal is increasing.

China already has about 620 coal-burning power plants in operation, and is planning for or already building over 350 more (the Indians, starting from a smaller base, are being even more aggressive in their construction efforts). In 2013, a *Time* magazine report titled ominously "The Scariest Environmental Fact in the World" publicized this growing dependency. China, for instance, got 69 percent of its power from coal plants in 2006, and up to 80 percent of Chinese power is now estimated to come from this source.

There is, however, a major downside to this growing situation. Coal, for all its availability and cost-effectiveness benefits, is also the worst carbon-dioxide-emitting form of carbon-based fuel, and it also contributes significant amounts of other pollutants such as mercury and chemicals that produce acid rain to the atmosphere in significant amounts. This impact was shown particularly dramatically in Beijing in January 2013, when particulates achieved levels well above toxic and virtually blackened the skies. The chief culprit was, of course, pollution caused by the emissions from coal-powered electricity plants, including a huge Beijing plant that provides most of the electricity to the Chinese capital.

Demands for environmental cleanups are certain to put additional pressure on all countries that use coal as a primary energy source to slow the growth of that reliance and probably to try to reduce or curtail that usage. Given coal's economic and security allures, that pressure will be resisted, and in places like the United States with a very active coal lobby, there will be political pressures as well to maintain or even increase the reliance on coal as an energy source. Given the growing pressures associated with environmental concerns like climate change, it is hard to imagine coal as a "growth industry" for very long, and the pressure to find alternatives will grow.

Nuclear Energy

Power generation using nuclear rather than carbon-based fuel is one of those alternatives. Like the fossil-based energy sources, nuclear power has both advantages and disadvantages. Its primary advantage is that nuclear power generation does not, like generation from fossil fuels, contribute to carbon dioxide overload in the atmosphere and is thus an environmentally friendly source of energy. Its primary disadvantages, on the other hand, are the problem of disposal of spent nuclear fuel after it has been expended to produce energy, dogged questions of plant safety, and the expense of building nuclear power plants. These disadvantages have combined to make nuclear power a relatively small contributor to worldwide energy, and its contribution is unlikely to grow markedly worldwide. A few countries, such as China, are building nuclear power plants and expanding their nuclear power capacities, but they are very much the exception.

The United States is the world leader in overall power generation from nuclear sources, with over 100 nuclear power plants in operation, according to 2011 European Nuclear Society data. These produce a little less than 10 percent of American power needs, and that proportion is forecast to remain flat or slightly decline as the American power grid gradually converts to shale gas as its primary fuel. No new nuclear plants have been built in the United States since the 1970s, and despite periodic calls for new construction, environmental and nuclear safety concerns continue to frustrate such efforts.

France is the second largest nuclear power user in terms of plants and output. It currently has 58 plants in operation that produce about 77 percent of French electricity. This dependence reflects the post–World War II decision of the French government not to join in the general trend of rebuilding its power grid based on petroleum. Japan, with 50 operating plants, is third in nuclear power generation, followed by the Republic of Korea (South Korea), India, Canada, and China. Of these, China has the most aggressive program of nuclear power expansion as it attempts to reduce its environment-choking reliance on coal. Nearly half of the nuclear plants under construction worldwide (31 of 68) are in China; India, the other world power whose demand for power is growing rapidly, currently has 20 nuclear plants, with 9 more under construction.

The disadvantages of nuclear power continue to depress its expansion as an energy source. The costs of nuclear plant construction are much higher than those of other forms of power generation (notably coal and natural gas) because of the requirements to protect against radioactive leakage at nuclear sites. This problem is obviously most burdensome for non-OECD developing countries, but it is also a concern for more developed countries as well.

Two problems create particular public resistance to nuclear power. One of these is the problem of waste disposal. The used (or "spent") fuel from a nuclear reactor is highly toxically radioactive, and the half-life of its toxicity (the point at which it is no longer dangerously environmentally threatening) is measured in hundreds of years. The only way to deal with this problem is to bury nuclear fuel so deeply in the ground that it cannot possibly leak into the environment or to store it in secure waste sites until it loses its radioactive peril. The problem, highlighted by the long battle in the United States about nuclear waste sites, is that nobody wants these sites located anywhere near them for fear of a contaminating accident.

The other, and more spectacular, fear arises from the danger of nuclear power plant accidents that foul the environment. Although these are relatively few in number globally, they are often spectacular and memorable. The most recent major disaster occurred in 2011 at the Fukushima nuclear plant in Japan, whose containment safeguards were breached as a result of the so-called Sendai tsunami. The most famous and devastating occurrence was the meltdown of a nuclear reactor at Chernobyl in the Ukraine (then part of the Soviet Union) in 1986, an accident that still leaves large parts of the surrounding countryside uninhabitable. For American nuclear opponents, memories of the 1979 Three Mile Island calamity near the Pennsylvania capital of Harrisburg remain a powerful evocation of what can go wrong at nuclear power sites.

There are other concerns with nuclear power that arise from geopolitics as much as from a pure energy perspective. One is the danger that nuclear power plants will become the target for terrorists. This fear emerged in the

United States after the 9/11 terrorist attacks and resulted in extensive, costly measures to reduce the likelihood that terrorists might be able to penetrate security and breach a reactor core, sending deadly particulates into the atmosphere. Due to the nature of the 9/11 attacks, the crashing of an airplane into a power reactor provided a popular horror scenario. This problem could become worse if nuclear power generation facilities are built in many non-OECD countries that lack strong security mechanisms. The other danger is the conversion of nuclear power facilities to producing weapons-grade materials that can be converted into nuclear weapons. International agreements prohibit such activity, which is monitored by the International Atomic Energy Agency of the UN, but it has arisen specifically regarding nuclear programs in both the Democratic People's Republic of Korea (DPRK) and Iran. This aspect of the problem is discussed in Chapters 6 and 7.

Under optimal conditions, the contribution of nuclear power to the world energy situation would be marginal, and residual fear of nuclear accidents and the spread of radioactivity continue to provide an important barrier to expansion of this source. Like fossil-based energy sources, the forms of uranium that are used in nuclear power generation are also finite and non-renewable. One result has been a movement, particularly among environmentally conscious groups and individuals, for alternative sources that are both non-polluting and renewable.

Renewables

Concerns with arresting and reversing air pollution and over the depletion of non-renewable energy sources have contributed to a global concern with so-called renewable forms of energy generation. Generically, the term *renewable energy sources* refers the use of natural phenomena like wind and the sun that are not degraded or depleted by their conversion to generate usable energy, generally in the form of electricity. The movement toward renewable energy sources is most advanced in the United States, where it has become an integral part of so-called "green energy" solution to the country's energy problem. The difficulty is whether there is enough potential in any or all of these sources to make any real dent on global energy dilemmas.

There are a number of different natural phenomena and technologies that are lumped together as renewable by alternateenergysource.org. One of these, hydropower (electricity generated by damming rivers and gathering energy from the water flowing over or through the dams) has been in existence for some time. In the United States, for instance, building dams to capture and claim the energy of western rivers has been in practice since the early twentieth century. These efforts, however, generate only about 2 percent of the country's needs, and that proportion is unlikely to increase. A few countries with the appropriate terrains and conditions like China and Turkey have invested in hydropower, but the process of damming and building power facilities is very expensive and largely unavailable in countries that do not have significant mountainous terrains through which rivers flow.

There are various other newer technologies. Several involve the use of the sun as a power source, the most prominent being photovoltaic (the use of large solar panels to capture the sun's heat and convert it to energy) and thermal. In addition, renewable sources include wind power (the use of large windmills), geothermal, and various natural oceanic phenomena like tides and waves to generate power and thus energy.

The renewable sources face two major limitations. First, they are all dependent on the abundance of whatever natural phenomena they seek to exploit: Solar power requires generous amounts of sunlight and spacious deserted terrain not available everywhere, wind power requires steady and predictable winds, and the exploitation of oceanic sources requires contiguity to one of the world's major bodies of water. Second, it is not at all clear that the renewable can make a large contribution to the overall problem. By the year 2040, for instance, the contribution of renewable sources will be only a little over 10 percent of American needs, and even if traditional hydropower is added, the proportion only comes to about one-eighth.

Changing Demand Patterns

This shift in the composition and importance of various energy sources comes within the context of a changing pattern of demand for greater and lesser changes of global energy production. As noted, the basic trend is a movement away from larger proportional demands by the OECD developed countries to the non-OECD developing world. Given the centrality of energy usage to economic development, this change is a natural and, for most purposes, laudable phenomenon that contributes to an improved condition for increasing proportions of humankind. At the same time, the developing world both needs additional energy and has multiple demands on the scarce resources it possesses to pursue additional supplies. As a result, there will be a natural tendency for countries whose demands are greatest to look for more economical sources that are often associated with increased environmental degradation, thus creating a dynamic tension between global priorities for development and environmental protection.

The countries that will make the greatest demands for increased energy are China and India. EIA projections estimate that these two countries alone will account for half of the growth in global energy between now and 2035. As the International Energy Agency's *World Energy Outlook, 2012*, points out, much of this demand will come for petroleum, at the same time that major OECD countries like the United States are reducing their needs for foreign oil. Whereas India and China will need more Persian Gulf oil, for instance, the United States will require less, both as the country converts away from traditional petroleum (thanks largely to shale oil and gas production) and as dynamics such as conservation lower the demand for petroleum products like gasoline. The EIA projects that by 2035, nearly five-eighths of world energy demands will come from non-OECD countries—488 of a total of 770 quadrillion British thermal units (BTUs)—compared to a 2008 figure of 260 quadrillion

BTUs for the non-OECD world (52 percent). Projected world growth between 2008 and 2035 is thus estimated at 166 quadrillion BTUs, of which China and India will account for about a half, or something above 80 quadrillion BTUs. Much of that will come from petroleum demands, and whereas China has the world's largest shale oil reserves, India is not so well endowed.

This differential trend is also illustrated by changes in the American pattern. The United States will remain a major global energy consumer, but the exploitation of shale oil and gas will change its energy profile considerably. The IEA projection, for instance, suggests that "by around 2020," the United States will surpass Saudi Arabia as the world's largest petroleum producer, and that the United States will be a net oil exporter by 2030. The progressive transformation of American energy (notably electricity) production away from coal and other fuels will also result in reduced energy costs for American industries, helping to support a competitive renaissance for American industries in world markets. Once again, shale gas and oil provide the major driver in these changes.

IEA projections also provide some forewarnings about energy changes and their possible consequences that are warnings for dealing with the geopolitical impact of energy change. For the near and medium term, there will be an increased global demand for petroleum, and the largest contributor to guaranteeing that supply and demand does not go out of balance is projected to be increases in Iraqi oil production. Iraq's centrality as a future oil producer arises from the fact that it has the world's third largest known reserves of petroleum and that these reserves are also relatively unexploited. At the same time, political turmoil that continues in Iraq after the American departure raises serious questions about whether, or how much of, that petroleum will find its way out of Iraqi soil and into the international petroleum lifeline.

At the same time, changing emphases will also alter the contribution of energy source distributions to world power maps. As the IEA outlook points out, three countries with large exploitable Bakken formations will likely dominate supplies of oil and gas from these sources: the United States, China, and Australia. Those who will likely suffer the most are the major oil-producing countries—and especially the oil-rich countries of the Middle East—which do not have noticeable known reservoirs of shale oil and gas formations. The traditional oil producers do have impressive supplies of more traditional natural gas supplies, and these will be helpful in their energy dealings with the rest of the world, but their total dominance of the world geopolitical energy map will inevitably lessen.

All of these trends, especially the farther into the future they project, are decreasingly precise and subject to other, only partially foreseeable or unforeseeable events and discoveries. Between now and 2035, the target dates of both EIA and IEA projections, things could change. The most transformational change might well be scientific and engineering breakthroughs in fusion energy, a potentially inexhaustible form of energy (it is based on the fusion of deuterium and tritium molecules, each of which is abundant in sea water) on which concerted research is ongoing. While predictions about whether or when feasible fusion generation of energy will be attained, the possibility exists and cannot be entirely discounted.

Uncertainty is thus a part of predicting energy futures, just as it is part of most projections into the future. What is not uncertain is that change is occurring, and some of that change has potentially major international political implications that are quite different than trends might look in the absence of changes in energy futures.

Geopolitical Implications

Energy security has been one of the most important goals, and its pursuit among the highest priorities, of the state system since at least the early twentieth century, when petroleum became the dominant source of world energy and changed important dynamics of how the world operates. Petroleum-based energy unlocked the door to vastly increased energy availability around the world, and provided both the lubricant and fuel empowering the resolution in transportation. At the same time, the derivative petrochemical industry that is often the forgotten component in the petroleum equation has produced enormous change in the way the world produces an enormous number and variety of the materials that underpin modern life. Imagine, for instance, a world without plastics or synthetic fibers, both of which the petroleum revolution makes possible and widely available.

This change in energy source transformed the geopolitical map of the last century. Most notably, parts of the world, such as the Middle East, became important for the first time in many years of history. Before the petroleum phenomenon, after all, most of the oil-rich countries that are such important international forces today were regarded as little more than hot, dusty global backwaters. As the world became dependent on the "black gold" beneath their soil (or, in some cases, off their shores), they became influential, even deciding, players on the world stage. For a country or region now to claim security, its relations with and access to the vital petroleum of the Middle East, and to a lesser degree other parts of the developing world, has been crucial.

Although it is probably premature to try to predict with any precision, the power map associated with traditionally derived petroleum energy may be changing. Petroleum geologists and associated scientists and engineers have known for years about the potentially enormous amount of energy locked in the shale gas and oil reservoirs commonly called Bakken formations in the United States. The application of techniques like fracking, which is not in a new technique but rather the adaptation of a decades-old method for exploiting these reserves, however, has only emerged in a commercially viable way in the past few years. As this exploitation emerges, it could have transformational effects on how the world treats and thinks about energy resources, especially in a world of continuing growth in demand and change in those who demand this and other forms of energy.

Consider the mouth of the Persian Gulf as a prominent example. The Persian Gulf has been the point of egress of major components of the world's petroleum, and thus energy, supplies since the period surrounding World War II: Almost all the oil flowing from the major OPEC states—Saudi Arabia, Kuwait, Iran, and Iraq, for instance—flows on oil tankers out of the Gulf and around the world to feed the needs of an energy-addicted world. Making that lifeline secure and safe has been a major security concern of all states with a dependence on that source.

Traditionally, most of the ships leaving the Persian Gulf have made a right turn into the Indian Ocean, heading west for destinations in Europe and North America, and the result is that protecting the oceanic highways out of the Gulf has been a major priority of Western OECD states, notably the United States. Thanks to changes, notably the increasing use of shale oil and gas not found in the Persian Gulf, Western reliance of Persian Gulf oil will gradually decrease, and this is especially true for the United States. For Americans, there will be a need to import some traditional petroleum, but the quantities will be much smaller than at the peak of dependence when Middle Eastern oil was absolutely necessary to meet American needs. Instead, it is possible that much of the continuing need can be fulfilled from alternate locations, thereby reducing the need for Persian Gulf sources to a comparative trickle. To a lesser degree, the same is likely true for other OECD countries, including those in Europe.

At the same time, non-OECD countries, and especially countries in eastern Asia, are almost certain to increase their need for petroleum, and Persian Gulf oil is closer and more convenient for them than oil from other sources. Despite massive amounts of shale oil and gas potential, the Chinese are the largest growing market for energy, and that thirst is likely to increase: Oil as both a fuel and lubricant will increase as more and more Chinese become automobile drivers, and China will be under both domestic and international pressure to reduce the percentage of coal it burns for power consumption for environmental reasons. Although shale reserves offer a long-term solution to much of this need, in the interim traditionally produced petroleum is the obvious solution, and much of that will most readily come from the Persian Gulf. The same is even more pronounced for India, which does not have China's shale potential.

The result could be to alter the "traffic pattern" for tankers exiting the Persian Gulf. Rather than making their traditional westward, right turn into the Arabian Sea, instead the tankers will be turning left toward destinations in eastern Asia. Such a change could have major geopolitical implications for countries like the United States.

The major implication is strategic. It has been a cornerstone of American security policy since at least 1979 (when the shah of Iran fell and with him protection of American energy supplies by the Iranian armed forces ended). Particularly for the U.S. Navy, the protection of the shipping lanes through the Persian Gulf and the critical Straits of Hormuz (ironically, from the same Iran that used to protect them) has been a major priority that has necessitated committing an American carrier-based battle group in the narrow, shallow Persian Gulf full-time to protect international, including American, oil tankers exiting the Gulf.

The shift from a right- to a left-hand turn out of the Gulf changes that calculation. If it is principally Chinese or Indian oil that is heading through the Gulf and heading eastward, should it be the U.S. Navy that provides the primary protection of the shipping lanes from hostile interdiction? Or should others like the Chinese or the Indians provide that guarantee of transit? The idea of the Chinese Navy operating in the Persian Gulf would clearly give pause to many observers (see Chapter 11), but the case for a large and expensive American presence would seem less compelling.

China and its increasingly bellicose stance toward the South China Sea provide another example. China has recently announced its intention to "close" this sea contiguous to the Chinese mainland to international commerce, despite the objections of others whose territories are also washed by the sea, such as the Philippines and Vietnam. Beyond its assertion over national prestige and standing and thus its desire to treat the South China Sea as a Chinese "pond" (analogous to American attitudes toward the Caribbean Sea), the real issue that makes the area important is the vast reserves of traditional petroleum in the sea, which are claimed by multiple parties. The declaration of supremacy is not only a matter of prestige but also a matter of strengthening China's claim to South China Sea oil. A movement toward exploitation of shale deposits in China could lessen some of that imperative and appeal and thus decrease the basis for Chinese belligerence over this body of water.

These are isolated examples of possible geopolitical impacts that could derive from the shift toward shale oil and gas as an energy source. There are undoubtedly others that will emerge, as well as some unexpected sources of international political concern and possibility. Exactly where these may be and where they may lead is, at this point, a matter of conjecture, but that the change in energy patterns will have geopolitical impacts is difficult to deny.

CONCLUSION

The problem of resource scarcity of one kind or another has been a ubiquitous feature of human history. Humankind has always wanted or needed resources that all of the claimants could not possess simultaneously in the amount they desired (the definition of scarcity). The content of the resource in question has changed at different points in time, but the basic problem has always been with us and likely always will be.

In the current epoch, scarcity tends to be centered on two resources necessary to maintain the human condition: water and energy. At this point in time, potable, usable water is only a selectively scarce commodity, but it is likely to become a more pervasive scarcity in the future as the human population continues to grow and changes in climate alter the availability of fresh water globally and in individual locales. The quest to find a way to convert the waters of the 70 percent of the globe covered by salt water will remain a major global scientific imperative, just as harnessing the ocean's deuterium and tritium for the production of fusion energy may be the ultimate means for solving energy security.

Energy scarcity is currently the most salient global resource problem. The pressures of a growing global population, increasing portions of which demand a greater and more reliable supply of energy, and finite, dwindling reserves of traditional sources of energy combine to create this problem. Because energy consumption is tied so closely to economic productivity, the demand is both a matter of survival and an increasingly prosperous physical condition for people. Like the solution of the problem of adequate potable water, supplying the world with a steady, even growing supply of energy is a changing problem, not all the answers to which are clearly apparent. Like all scarcities, as long as supply and demand remains out of balance, one result will be political disagreement and conflict.

Although it is clear that the world energy map is in the beginnings of a process of considerable change driven largely by advances in the exploitation of shale oil and gas deposits found widely worldwide, much of this change remains uncertain and speculative. One is reminded of the small boom of enthusiasm for fusion energy in the early 2000s, where projections of inexhaustible supplies of energy from the world's oceans seemed to promise a major revolution in the world's energy future, both in terms of global availability and even the structure of national power grids (fusion plants would naturally be built along coastlines with ready access to the deuterium and tritium in the oceans, with power grids radiating out from the coasts). That technology has proven premature, and although it may offer a long-term solution, the enthusiasm for the shorter term has disappeared. The beneficial prospects and degree of change predicted then proved to be an illusion. That realization should temper current projections as well.

There is, of course, a difference between the impact of fusion and shale-formation energy: Fusion remains a scientific possibility that has not yet been actualized, whereas shale reserves are being exploited today with existing technology. The effects are currently most dramatic in North America, where exploitation has made North Dakota the United States' second largest producer of oil among American states, where conversion of electricity-producing power plants to shale gas is reducing carbon dioxide emission, and where dependencies on imported petroleum are definitely on the decline. The Obama administration, largely on the basis of these changes, has been willing to commit the United States to a goal of absolute carbon-dioxide-emission reduction as it enters negotiations on atmospheric pollution.

The impact will be slower elsewhere in the world where shale repositories are smaller and the technology is less well developed. Because the United States remains the second largest energy consumer in the world, there will undoubtedly be a ripple effect. The most obvious place for such effects to take place is in China, which is simultaneously the world's largest energy user, its greatest atmospheric polluter, and the possessor of the world's largest shale-formation reservoirs. The stars could hardly be in more perfect alignment than for a Chinese move toward the development of shale technology.

One should, of course, take all of this with a grain of salt. There are critics, especially vocal within the United States, warning that the exploitation of the new shale reserves could have ecological effects that could negate much of the allure of this source and that there are other problems that have either been identified or that may pop up. It is not clear to everyone, for instance, if the injection of pressurized water, sand, and chemicals (the basic process of fracking) into shale seams to liberate oil and gas deposits might not leave fissures in the earth's sub-stratum, with resulting great long-term liabilities. Some activists also complain about water and air quality issues arising from the injection of foreign substances into the seams to free the oil and gas. Proponents of shale energy, citing past experience with the technique on a smaller scale, dismiss such concerns; others wonder. At the same time, shale formations are rapidly depleted of their oil: Some estimates are that over half the available products are mined in the first couple years of exploitation, leaving declining assets after that. One cannot help but wonder what this could mean for the "boom towns" spreading across places like North Dakota. Other problems will almost certainly surface as the movement toward more shale usage expands.

It is always a perilous task to predict the future with too much certainty, because there are always uncertainties that arise and can bedevil even the best-laid-out plans and projections. What can be said with some certainty is that the pattern of energy usage and production is changing and that the effects will be important. But they will also be to some extent unpredicted and unpredictable. If one doubts that assertion, go back and look at projections made a decade ago and see how much of a future contribution they predicted for shale energy.

SUGGESTED ACTIVITIES AND QUESTIONS

1. What is resource scarcity? Why has it always been a problem in international relations? Define *scarcity*. What are the possible solutions to a condition of scarcity?
2. What have been the major dynamics of energy scarcity? How has this problem evolved across time? When did petroleum become the leading component of the problem?
3. The possession of a scarce resource may give particular leverage and power to its possessor. Using petroleum as an example, show how this leverage has worked.
4. What are the leading sources of scarcity in the contemporary world? Why has petroleum been such an important component of the global scarcity problem?
5. What are the leading alternative sources of energy in the world today? What are the advantages and disadvantages of each, both globally and within different regions of the world?
6. How is the energy "equation" changing? What kinds of geopolitical implications do these changes suggest?
7. How specifically is the energy supply problem changing? What is shale oil and gas? What is the current and potential promise of this energy source?
8. In terms of OECD versus non-OECD demands on energy, how is the global pattern of demand changing? What are some of the implications of these changes?
9. What are some of the economic and geopolitical implications of changing energy supply and demand patterns? In particular, how do these changes affect the United States?

SUGGESTED READINGS AND RESOURCES

Alternate Energy Source. *Global Energy Supplies: Pros and Cons,* 2012. (http://www
.alternativeenergysource.org/pros_cons.htm)

Central Intelligence Agency. *CIA World Factbook 2012.* Washington, DC: U.S. Central
Intelligence Agency, 2012.

European Nuclear Society. (http://www.euronuclear.org/)

Fleischman, Stephen E. "Too Valuable to Burn." *Common Dreams Newsletter* (online),
November 29, 2005.

Friedman, Thomas L. "The First Law of Petropolitics." *Foreign Policy,* May/June
2006, 36–44.

Hirsch, Robert L. *Peaking of World Oil Production: Recent Forecasts.* Washington,
DC: National Energy Technology Laboratory, February 5, 2007. (http://www.netl
.doe.gov)

Holt, Jim. "It's the Oil." *London Review of Books* (online edition), October 18, 2006.

Homer-Dixon, Thomas. "Environmental Scarcities and Violent Conflict: Evidence from
Cases." In Sean Lynn-Jones and Stephen Miller (eds.), *Global Dangers: Changing
Dimensions of International Security.* Cambridge, MA: MIT Press, 1995, 144–179.

International Energy Agency. *World Energy Outlook, 2012.* Paris: International Energy
Agency, November 2012. (http://www.iea.org/publications)

Kumins, Lawrence. "Iraqi Oil: Reserves, Production, and Potential Resources." *CRS
Report to Congress.* Washington, DC: Congressional Research Service, April 13,
2005.

Kurlantzik, Joshua. "Put a Tyrant in Your Tank." *Mother Jones* 33, 3 (May/June 2008),
38–42.

Maugeri, Leonardo. "Two Cheers for Expensive Oil." *Foreign Affairs* 85, 2 (March/
April 2006), 149–160.

Pope, Carl and Bjorn Lomborg. "The State of Nature: The *Foreign Policy* Report."
Foreign Policy, July/August 2005, 66–74.

Roberts, Paul. "The Seven Myths of Energy Independence." *Mother Jones* 33, 3 (May/
June 2008), 31–37.

Rohter, Larry. "Shipping Costs to Crimp Globalization." *New York Times* (online),
August 3, 2008.

Snow, Donald M. *National Security for a New Era,* 3rd ed. New York: Pearson, 2014.

U.S. United States Energy Information Administration (Department of Energy). *Annual
Energy Outlook 2013,* April 15–May 2, 2013. http://www.eia.gov/forecasts/aeo/
index.cfm

Walsh, Bryan. "The Scariest Environmental Fact in the World." *Time* (online), January
29, 2013.

"World Fossil Fuel Reserves." *The World Almanac and Book of Facts, 2013.* New
York: World Almanac Books, 2013 (source International Energy Statistics Database, Energy Information Administration, U.S. Department of Energy).

World Nuclear Organization. *Nuclear Power in the World Today* (online), April 2012.
(http://www.world-nuclear.org/info/inf01.html).

Yergin, Daniel. "Ensuring Energy Security." *Foreign Affairs* 85, 2 (March/April 2006),
69–82.

———. *The Prize: The Epic Quest for Oil, Money, and Power.* New York: Simon and
Schuster, 1991.

Zweig, David and Bi Jianhai. "China's Global Hunt for Energy." *Foreign Affairs* 84, 5
(September/October 2005), 18–24.

Limits on International Cooperation: War Crimes, the International Criminal Court, and Syria

PRÉCIS

Although events in the 1990s in places like Bosnia and Rwanda and more recently Syria have made the idea of war crimes and their prosecution a widely recognized part of international relations, the notion is a relatively recent concept. There have always been more or less well-accepted and enforced rules for conducting war, the violation of which was deemed criminal, but the ideas of crimes against peace and, especially, crimes against humanity are largely the result of the prosecution of German and Japanese officials after World War II. The 1990s revived this interest, which had receded during the Cold War.

Although there is near-universal condemnation of war crimes as a general rule, efforts at international cooperation in regulating and prosecuting violations of war crimes norms have been less successful. The case examines why such limits on cooperation exist. It begins by looking at the content and evolution of the war crimes concept as background, then moves to its central thrust, which is an examination of the primary efforts to regulate war crimes, and why international cooperation and progress have been limited in this important international area, using Syria as an example.

Τ he idea that war crimes are reprehensible, that their commission should be outlawed, and that those who commit war crimes should be punished seem noncontroversial on their face. War is horrible enough, involving the violent taking of human life (if within certain boundaries or rules for its conduct), and criminal behavior is universally condemnable and generally unacceptable. When crime is committed in the violent context of war, the result can be particularly horrific, and one would assume that the area of war crimes would offer fertile grounds for international cooperation aimed at eliminating their occurrence. And yet, international cooperation in the area of war crimes has lagged behind international solutions in other, often less compelling, areas.

Efforts to address the subject of war crimes have been attempted. The most obvious case was the war crimes trials against German and Japanese defendants at the end of World War II, which are discussed later in the chapter. The subject lay largely fallow between the end of those efforts and the early 1990s, when outrageous instances of war crimes occurred in places like Bosnia and Rwanda and reinvigorated interest in the war crimes issue. The major result of that emphasis was the negotiation of the International Criminal Court (ICC) through the Rome Treaty of 1998; although the jurisdiction of the ICC is accepted by many states today, exceptions remain.

The evolution of these efforts demonstrates, in important ways and for reasons worth noting, the limits of international cooperation in the war crimes/ torture area. As of February 1, 2012, only 120 of the 190 or so countries of the world had ratified the ICC statute and become parties to the treaty. Of those countries that have not joined are five of the six most populous states in the world (China, India, the United States, Indonesia, and Pakistan), which between them have a population of 3.21 billion of a world population estimated at 6.83 billion, according to 2009 United Nations (UN) estimates. Of the six largest states, only Brazil has ratified the ICC treaty. When other nonsignatories' populations are added to the total, over half the people living in the world are not covered by the international regime forbidding war crimes. Within the volatile Middle East where violence and atrocity are widespread, the only signatories of the ICC are Afghanistan and Jordan. Syria, accused in a February 2013 report of the commission of the United Nations Human Rights Council of extensive war crimes by both sides in its civil war, is also a nonmember.

The purpose of this case is to study the problem of war crimes and why finding concrete ways to eliminate their occurrence demonstrates the limits, rather than the positive possibilities, of international cooperation. At a commonsensical level, the idea that war crimes should be condemned and perpetrators punished seems obvious—a "no-brainer." Yet, within the more byzantine workings of international relations, other concerns, such as the protection of state sovereignty introduced as a bedrock principle in Chapter 1, may come into conflict with apparently consensual concerns that would seem to militate toward cooperation between states. War crimes are not the only place where this anomaly appears, but they are one of the most dramatic.

The phenomenon of war crimes reentered the international dialogue during the 1990s. The immediate precipitant had been a rash of so-called humanitarian disasters, in which intolerable acts against groups within states, often grouped under the name "ethnic cleansing," occurred during the decade. The worst of these occurred in Bosnia during the early 1990s and in Rwanda in 1994. A somewhat more limited case occurred in Kosovo in 1998–1999.

The result, according to one source, was a paradox: "Humanitarian law and international human rights has never been more developed, yet never before have human rights been violated more frequently. This state of affairs will not improve absent a mechanism to enforce those laws and the norms they embody." The ongoing and historical tragedy in South Sudan, discussed in detail in Chapter 15, accentuates these concerns.

This quote suggests that the contemporary concern with war crimes stems from two parallel developments. One is the assertion that there are universal human rights to which people and groups are entitled and that, when they are violated, are subject to penalty. The second is an interest in some form of *international* mechanism for dealing with violators of these norms.

Although the ideas of defining criminal behavior and enforcement of laws in international, universal terms may not seem extraordinary, both are in fact of recent origin in international affairs. The idea of universal human rights transcending state boundaries is really a post–World War II phenomenon; the primary crime that has been identified in war crimes, genocide, was not identified until the word was coined by Richard Lemkin in 1944, and the United Nations Convention on Genocide, which bans the commission of genocide, was not passed until 1948. The term *war crimes,* which now refers to a broad range of activities associated with war, was basically linked with violations of the so-called laws of war (actions permissible and impermissible during wartime) until war crimes trials were convened in Nuremberg and Tokyo to prosecute accused Nazi and Japanese violators after World War II.

The subject of war crimes is unlikely to disappear from international discourse, for at least five reasons. First, acts now defined as war crimes continue to be committed in many places. Exclusionary nationalism (when national groups persecute nonmembers) in some developing-world states may actually increase the number of savage acts that are now considered war crimes. Second, the war crimes trials involving Bosnia and Rwanda that were empanelled in the early 1990s are still ongoing, and the international legal community fully recognizes that the outcomes of those trials will influence the subject in the future. Third, definitions are rapidly evolving. Rape, for instance, has only recently been added to the list of punishable crimes against humanity. Terrorist mass murders almost certainly qualify as well. The trial of Saddam Hussein gave wide publicity to these phenomena. Fourth, one outcome of the concern for war crimes has been the establishment of a controversial permanent International Criminal Court with mandatory jurisdiction over war crimes. Fifth, accusations of war crimes in places like Syria assure that the subject does not disappear from public awareness. The commission of atrocities seems to occur most frequently in internal violence within states, and such conflicts are the most common form of violence and instability in the contemporary world.

This statement of the problem suggests the direction this case study will take. It begins with a brief historical overview of war crimes, emphasizing the major point that whereas the idea of crimes of war has long been part of international concerns, war crimes as they are now defined are of recent vintage. The case will then look at the various categories of war crimes that arose from the experience of the war crimes trials at the end of World War II, and how the existence of well-documented atrocities in places like Bosnia and Rwanda rekindled interest in the subject. With the principles surrounding war crimes and enforcement of prohibitions established, the case will be applied to controversies surrounding the ICC and to the contemporary case of war crime allegations in Syria to illustrate the core concern with war crimes as a prime example of the limits of international cooperation.

THE PROBLEM OF WAR CRIMES

The idea of war crimes is both very old and very new. Throughout most of history, the term has been associated with conformity to the so-called laws of war. This usage can be traced back as far as 200 B.C., when a code of the permissible behavior in war was formulated in the Hindu Code of Manu. Enumerated codes of warfare were part of Roman law and were later practiced throughout Europe. These rules began to be codified into international law following the Thirty Years' War (1618–1648), when most of Europe was swept up in very brutal religiously based warfare. The first definitive international law text, Hugo Grotius's *Concerning the Law of War and Peace,* was published in 1625 and included the admonition that "war ought not to be undertaken except for the enforcement of rights; when once undertaken, it should be carried on only within the bounds of law and good faith." Definitions of the laws of war, and hence violations of those laws, developed gradually during the eighteenth and nineteenth centuries, culminating in the Geneva and Hague Conventions of 1899 and 1907.

The concerns expressed in the laws of war continue to be an important part of international law, but the idea of war crimes has been expanded to cover other areas of conduct in war in the twentieth century. The precipitant for this expansion was World War II and wartime atrocities committed by the Axis powers (notably Germany and Japan). Some of the crimes fit traditional definitions of war crimes—the mistreatment of American and other prisoners of war (POWs) by the Japanese during the infamous Bataan death march, for instance. Many actions, however, went well beyond the conduct of war per se, as in the systematic extermination of Jews, Gypsies, and other groups in the Holocaust by Germany and the so-called Rape of Nanking, in which Japanese soldiers went on a rampage and reportedly slaughtered nearly 300,000 citizens of that Chinese city (some Japanese sources dispute the numbers) on the pretext that some of them were soldiers hiding among the civilians.

Contemporary Evolution of War Crimes

World War II thus provided the impetus for change. It was a truly global and brutal war, and one of its major "innovations" was to extend to civilian population what the American general William Tecumseh Sherman called the "hard hand of war" during the Civil War. The Allies discussed the problem throughout the war. The first formal statement on the subject was the Moscow declaration of 1943, which stated that Nazi officials guilty of "atrocities, massacres, and executions" would be sent to the countries in which they committed their crimes for trial and appropriate punishment after the war ended.

The London Agreement. The document that defined modern war crimes precedent was the London Agreement of August 8, 1945. It did two major things. First, it established the International Military Tribunal as the court that would try alleged war crimes and thereby set the precedent for a formal, permanent body later on. At the time, it specifically set the groundwork for the Nuremberg and Tokyo tribunals. Second, the agreement established the boundaries of its jurisdiction, which have become the standard means for defining war crimes.

The London Agreement defined three kinds of war crimes. The first is *crimes against peace,* "namely, planning, preparation, initiation, or waging of a war of aggression, or a war in violation of international treaties, agreements or assurances, or participation in a common plan or conspiracy for the accomplishment of any of the foregoing." This admonition was reinforced by the United Nations Charter that same year, in which the signatories relinquished the "right" to initiate war. Under this definition, the North Korean invasion of South Korea in 1950 or the invasion and conquest of Kuwait by Saddam Hussein's Iraq in 1990 both qualify as crimes against peace. What should be clearly noted is that this definition applies most obviously and directly to wars between independent states because of its emphasis on territorial aggression. The U.S. invasion of Iraq arguably also qualifies as a crime against peace.

The second category reiterates the traditional usage of the concept. *War crimes* are defined as "violations of the laws or customs of war. Such violations shall include, but not be limited to, murder, ill-treatment or deportation to slave labor or for any other purpose of civilian population of or in occupied territory, murder or ill-treatment of prisoners of war or persons on the seas, killing of hostages, plunder of public or private property, wanton destruction of cities, towns or villages, or devastation not justified by military necessity." This enumeration, of course, was a virtual laundry list of accusations against the Germans and the Japanese (although the Allies arguably committed some of the same acts). Although acts against civilians are mentioned in the listing, the crimes enumerated are limited to mistreatment of general civilian populations rather than their systematic extension to individuals and segments of the population.

The third category was the most innovative and controversial. It is also the type of war crimes with which the concept is now most closely associated. *Crimes against humanity* are defined as "murder, extermination, enslavement, deportation, and other inhumane acts committed against any civilian population, before or during the war; or persecutions on political, racial or religious grounds in execution of or in connection with any crime . . . whether or not in violation of the domestic law where perpetrated." The statute goes further, establishing the basis of responsibility and thus vulnerability to prosecution. "Leaders, organizers, instigators, or accomplices participating in the formulation or execution of a common plan or conspiracy to commit any of the foregoing crimes are responsible for all acts performed by any persons in execution of such plan." This latter enumeration of responsibility justified the indictment of former Yugoslav president Slobodan Milosevic, who was never accused of personally carrying out acts qualifying as war crimes, and also against Saddam Hussein. It would also undoubtedly be included in an indictment against Syrian President Bashar al-Assad and possibly against some leaders of the opposition against him.

To someone whose experience is limited to the latter part of the twentieth century, this notion of crimes against humanity may not seem radical, or possibly even unusual. At the time, however, the concept clearly was, for several reasons. First, wars against humanity criminalized actions by states (or groups within states) that, although not exactly common in human history, were certainly not historically unknown but had previously not been thought of as criminal. Imagine, for instance, Genghis Khan and the leaders of the Golden Horde being placed in the docket for their brutal actions while conquering much of Eurasia in the thirteenth century. The same applies to the Ottoman Turk executors of the genocidal campaign against the Armenians early in the twentieth century. Or, for that matter, the post–Civil War campaigns by the U.S. government against the Western Indian tribes (e.g., Wounded Knee) probably qualifies as well.

The second radical idea contained in the definition is that of jurisdiction. By stating that crimes against humanity are enforceable "whether or not in violation of the domestic law" in the places they occur, the definition adds a universality to its delineation that seems to transcend the sovereign rights of states to order events as they choose within their territory. That assertion remains at the base of controversy about the institutionalization of war crimes, because it entwines war criminal behavior (the reprehensibility of which is agreed upon) with the controversy over sovereignty (about which there is considerable disagreement). Third, the statute seeks to remove the defense that crimes against humanity can be justified on the basis they were committed on orders from a superior. Thus, anyone with any part in crimes against humanity is equally vulnerable under the law, and this provision allows the tribunal to delve as deeply as it wishes into the offenders' hierarchy.

The statute does not address one element about war crimes prosecution that is almost always raised. It is the problem of the so-called victors' law: the charge that war crimes are always defined by the winning side in a war, and those tried are always those from the losing side. The Nuremberg and Tokyo tribunals labored hard and long to make the proceedings as judicially fair as they could; it is nonetheless true that it was Germans and Japanese in the dock, not Americans or Britons. It is possible, but not very likely, that no one on the Allied side ever committed a war crime or a crime against humanity during World War II. It is arguable, however, that the officials who ordered and carried out the firebombing of Tokyo or the leveling of Dresden, in which many innocent civilians were killed, were guilty of crimes against humanity. None of these officials came before the war crimes tribunal. The recognition of the potential charge that any trial applies victors' law has been an ongoing concern in the further development of the concept of war crime and is reflected in the jurisdiction of the International Criminal Court.

This concern carried over into the postwar world. In 1948, the General Assembly of the United Nations passed the International Convention on the Prevention and Punishment of the Crime of Genocide, known more compactly as the Convention on Genocide. Building on the assertion of crimes against humanity, the Convention on Genocide provided clarification and codification of what constituted acts of genocide. According to the convention, any of the following actions, when committed with the intent of eliminating a particular national, ethnic, racial, or religious group, constitute genocide: (1) killing members of the group; (2) causing serious bodily or mental harm to members of the group; (3) deliberately inflicting on the group conditions of life calculated to kill; (4) imposing measures intended to prevent births within a group; and (5) forcibly transferring children out of a group.

In important ways, enunciating the Convention on Genocide (and the parallel UN Declaration on Human Rights) was a form of international atonement for Axis excesses, and especially for the Holocaust. Most countries signed and ratified the Convention, which took force—without, one might quickly add, any real form of enforcement. A few countries, notably the United States, refused to ratify the document for reasons based in infringement of sovereignty discussed later.

Reemergence of the Problem

With the completion of the war crimes tribunals after World War II and the flurry of activity that produced the Convention on Genocide, the subject of war crimes dropped from the public eye, not to reemerge publicly until the 1990s. Well beneath the surface of public scrutiny, attempts were made to create some sort of enforcement mechanism for dealing with these issues, but they never received much public attention, nor did they generate enough political support to gain serious international consideration.

Why was this the case? It is not because crimes against humanity became less unacceptable; those kinds of acts and traditional war crimes certainly continued to occur, at least on a smaller scale than had happened during World War II. Rather, the more likely explanation is that the subject matter became a victim of the Cold War, as did other initiatives such as the aggressive promotion of human rights.

It is almost certainly not a coincidence that the emergence of a broad international interest in war crimes emerged at a time of U.S.–Soviet cooperation right after World War II, that concern and progress ground to an effective halt during the ideological and geopolitical confrontation between them, and that the subject has resurfaced and been revitalized since the cessation of that competition.

Why would the Cold War competition hamstring progress on a subject that would, on the face of it, seem noncontroversial? No one, after all, officially condones war crimes, and yet, in the Cold War context, neither was their clarification or codification aggressively pursued internationally.

The problem was similar to, and had the same roots as, the advocacy of human rights, which also lay fallow on the international agenda through most of the Cold War period. In a sense, war crimes are a flip side of human rights: The crimes against humanity clearly violate the most basic of human rights, and traditional war crimes violate those rights in times of combat.

In the Cold War context, issues like human rights tended to get caught up in the propaganda war between the superpowers. The Soviets would assume that American advocacy of certain principles (for instance, free speech) was championed to embarrass the Soviet Union, where such rights were certainly not inviolate. Had the Soviets decided to push for greater progress on war crimes during the American participation in the Vietnam War between 1965 and 1973, the United States would have assumed the purpose was to embarrass American servicemen and discredit the American military effort. The My Lai incident during the Vietnam War (in which a platoon of U.S. servicemen destroyed a Vietnamese village and slaughtered its residents) illustrates the extension of this dynamic to war crimes. Innocent civilians were slaughtered at My Lai in what was a clear crime against humanity, but dispassionate consideration was drowned out by wartime propaganda duels over Cold War issues. In such circumstances, little if any progress could be expected on issues with a Cold War veneer; by and large, there was little attempt to pursue agreements where one side or the other might impose a formal veto in the United Nations Security Council or an informal veto by convincing its friends and allies not to take part.

There was a second problem with extending the idea of war crimes, and especially the codification of the idea into some enforcement regime, that has been a particular sticking point for the U.S. government: the issue of sovereignty. As noted in Chapter 1, the United States (as well as nondemocratic states like China) has been among the staunchest supporters of the doctrine of state sovereignty. Because the Convention on Genocide is universally applicable to all states that have signed and ratified it and thus have acceded to its provisions, it can be viewed, and was by powerful political elements in the United States, as an infringement of the authority of the U.S. government to regulate its own affairs. This argument may seem strained in the area of genocide: One way of looking at the objection is that it preserves the right of the United States to commit genocide. Nonetheless, the argument against diluting American national sovereignty was sufficient politically to prevent the U.S. Senate from ratifying the convention until 1993, when it was submitted to the Senate by President Clinton and approved by the necessary two-thirds majority.

Two other things had changed between the 1970s and the revived international concern about crimes against humanity in the 1990s, and these help explain earlier international indifference and international activism in the 1990s. The first change was the emergence of much more aggressive global electronic media with the physical capability to expose and publicize apparent violations. During most of the Cold War, there was no such thing as global television; Cable News Network (CNN), for instance, was not launched until 1980 and did not become a prominent force for some time thereafter. Moreover, media tools such as handheld camcorders and satellite uplinks were theoretical ideas, not the everyday equipment of reporters. Telephones with video cameras were a science fiction or a cartoon fantasy (the oldest popular version was a wristwatch camera phone in the cartoon "Dick Tracy"). In this atmosphere, governments could and did obscure some of their most atrocious behavior, a practice that has become much more difficult, as governments from countries like Sudan (see Chapter 15) and Iran (see Chapter 7) have learned in recent years, and countries like Syria are learning today.

The other change has been the growing *de facto* (in practice) if not *de jure* (in law) acceptance of the permissibility of international intervention in the internal affairs of states or factions within states that grossly abuse other people or groups—in other words, commit crimes against humanity and especially genocide. Without an elaborate statement of the principle of *humanitarian intervention,* this is what the United Nations authorized when it sent UN forces into Somalia in 1992. More recently, this "principle" has been called the "responsibility to protect (R2P)." By the early 1990s, the dynamics affecting international politics had changed sufficiently to raise the prospects of dealing with war crimes onto the international agenda. The end of the Cold War meant atrocities were less likely to be hidden or accusations about them suppressed on ideological or propagandistic grounds. A more aggressive and technologically empowered electronic media with global reach was available to report and publicize atrocities wherever they were found. At the same time, the UN operation in Somalia had established something like a precedent about the notion of humanitarian intervention. Two particularly egregious cases during the 1990s, in Bosnia and Rwanda, drew particular focus on the problem and its solution. Libya and Syria in 2011 raised the same kind of concern.

Individually and in combination, Bosnia and Rwanda thrust two unavoidable imperatives before the international community. First, they made the subject and horror of war crimes so public that it could no longer be ignored. Second, it created the need for some mechanism to prosecute those accused of committing war crimes, and the result was the formation of ad hoc war crimes tribunals to deal with each case. A major outgrowth of this process was a growing belief that there should be a permanent international institution both to deter potential future war criminals and to try future undeterred perpetrators.

WAR CRIMES AND COOPERATION APPLIED: THE INTERNATIONAL CRIMINAL COURT

The precedent of the Bosnian and Rwandan special war crimes tribunals inevitably created momentum for a permanent court. There was very little objection in principle to the idea of a war crimes court to deal with these two instances. Moreover, it was increasingly clear from atrocities being committed in other countries that there would be no shortage of situations in which allegations of crimes against humanity would emerge. Internal conflicts in places as widely separated as Sierra Leone in Africa, Kosovo nearby the Bosnian border, and

East Timor on the Indonesian archipelago provided evidence of both geographic diversity and numerous opportunities to enforce sanctions against a new breed of war criminals, who perpetrated gross crimes against their fellow citizens. Beyond the anticipated amount of demand there would be for a permanent structure was the hope that the existence of such a court and the knowledge that it could bring criminals to justice might deter some future crimes against humanity. But how should the international community react?

One aspect of the evolving debate over war crimes stands out in the contemporary international scene, and each is a matter of special interest to the United States. That concern is the desirability of a permanent institution (the ICC) with mandatory jurisdiction both to determine instances of war crimes and their prosecution. The heart of that concern is the *mandatory* nature of jurisdiction and thus authority over accused war criminals. Sovereignty-based concerns have made the United States the world's most vocal and prominent opponent of international institutionalized efforts to foster international cooperation in this area. An examination of the ICC thus illustrates the limits of international cooperation in this area.

Proposals for a Permanent War Crimes Tribunal

The initial advocacy of a permanent court to adjudicate war crimes accompanied the flurry of activity surrounding Nuremberg and Tokyo and the adoption of the Convention on Genocide. In 1948, the UN General Assembly commissioned the International Law Commission (a private body) to study the possibility of establishing an ICC. The commission examined this problem until 1954 and produced a draft statute for the ICC. Unfortunately, it appeared during the darkest days of the Cold War; there were objections from both sides of the Iron Curtain, and the United Nations dropped the proposal.

The idea of an ICC lay dormant until 1989, when the tiny Caribbean island country of Trinidad and Tobago revived the proposal within the United Nations. Trinidad and Tobago's motive, oddly enough, was to provide an instrument in its struggle against drug traffickers from South America. Nonetheless, the events in Bosnia and Rwanda revived broader interest that suggested the wisdom of a permanent body to provide a more effective, timely response to war crimes.

The idea of a permanent war crimes tribunal illustrated dramatically the clash between order and disorder inherent in the world system, the conceptual core of which is the sovereignty of its units. No country, to repeat, endorses the right to commit war crimes, but some states and groups or individuals within states from time to time violate the moral and legal norms that constitute war crimes. In some cases (some terrorist groups, for instance), the validity of these norms may be rejected, but this does not mean the mainstream does not accept the idea that war crimes are punishable acts.

The idea that these include crimes against *humanity* suggests universality in the condemnation of war crimes and enforcement of norms coterminous with that universality. Because virtually every country joins in the condemnation, the international institution of war crimes mechanisms would seem a ripe place for international cooperation. Such impulses, however, collide with other system values and come to a head in concrete instances like the ICC.

The proposal for an ICC has been controversial, especially surrounding the matter of jurisdiction. Champions contend that the court must have mandatory jurisdiction over all accused instances of war crimes and that its jurisdiction must supersede national sovereignty to be effective. Opponents object that this infringement on national sovereignty is unwarranted and could form the basis for future abuses of sovereignty. The ICC statute contains provisions for mandatory jurisdiction.

The Case for the ICC

The idea of an ICC flowed from renewed interest in dealing with war crimes and the perception that a permanent war crimes institution had several advantages over impaneling ad hoc tribunals. First, a permanent body would avoid having to start essentially from scratch each time suspected war crimes are uncovered. A permanent ICC would have, among other things, a permanent staff of investigators and prosecutors, and its staff would have the authority and jurisdiction to ascertain when crimes against humanity have indeed occurred.

Second, and related to the first point, a permanent ICC could be much more responsive to the occurrence—or even perhaps the possibility—of war crimes in the future. Not only would permanent staff members have or develop the expertise for efficient identification of war crimes situations, they could be rapidly mobilized and applied to the problem.

Third, it was hoped that a permanent ICC would act as a deterrent to future potential war criminals. Would, for instance, the Bosnian Serb leaders indicted (mostly in absentia) for authorizing ethnic cleansing in Bosnia have been dissuaded from doing so if they knew there was an international criminal authority to bring them to justice for their deeds? What influence would a permanent ICC have had on the planners and implementers of the slaughter in Rwanda? Although no one can know the answers to these questions, the existence of the ICC might have made a difference.

Fourth, the idea emerged in a time period when international cooperation was being instituted on a broad range of vexing issues, from human and women's rights to free trade (see Chapter 9). The end of the Cold War seemed to usher in an atmosphere where the narrow, conflict-driven paradigm of world politics was being replaced by a more open and cooperative atmosphere. The time for an ICC seemed ripe.

As a result, pressure to negotiate a treaty to create an ICC grew during the 1990s. As early as 1995, the Clinton administration became an activist in the movement in support of the idea. The movement culminated with the Rome Conference of 1998 (technically the United Nations Diplomatic Conference on the Establishment of a Permanent International Criminal Court). The conference produced a draft treaty to establish the ICC as a permanent body for trying individuals accused of committing genocide, war crimes, or crimes against humanity and gave the court jurisdiction over individuals accused of these crimes. When the draft was put to a vote, it passed by a vote of 120 states in favor, 7 opposed, and 21 abstentions. In order for the treaty to come into force, at least 60 states had to ratify the treaty. It reached that level in 2002 and came into official existence on July 1, 2002. As noted, there were 120 members as of February 1, 2012.

In what would prove a harbinger of future difficulties, the U.S. government was one of the seven states to vote against the treaty in Rome and has neither signed nor ratified the document, despite the Clinton administration's involvement in promoting and drafting its statute. In one of his final acts in office, President Clinton signed the statute in December 2000. In February 2001, Secretary of State Colin S. Powell announced that President George W. Bush had no intention of submitting it to the Senate for ratification; the Bush administration subsequently announced it was "unsigning" the treaty, an ambiguous international legal act punctuating its high level of opposition.

Objections to the ICC

That the United States advocated and then opposed the ICC statute may seem anomalous, but it is not entirely unusual. The apparent schizophrenia represents different views of America's place in the world, the American attitude toward the world, and especially the question of sovereignty. The Clinton administration saw the ICC statute as a way both to demonstrate responsible U.S. leadership and to improve the quality of the international environment, and thus became a champion of a war crimes court with "teeth." Other powerful political forces, however, summoned the specter of the loss of sovereignty that joining the treaty might entail. The problem came to focus on the potential loss of control of the U.S. government over its own forces in the field. This objection has been the basis of American refusals to turnover service members accused of war crimes to international authorities or authorities in countries where the alleged acts occurred. The March 2012 American refusal to relinquish control of an American soldier accused of killing 16 Afghan villagers and to try him instead in an American military court is an example.

David Sheffer, head of the American delegation, delivered the heart of the United States' objection at the end of the Rome Conference. He began by pointing out that the ICC would have jurisdiction only in countries that were parties to the treaty, and he noted that a number of countries that were accused of war crimes could and would evade prosecution by simply not joining the treaty. Iraq was an example, and Syria is today. The qualifying point of this objection was that a UN Security Council Resolution (UNSCR) can extend that jurisdiction in a given case. Helena Cobban argues this extension of jurisdiction is itself objectionable, as it extends authority over countries to which the court has only "an indirect line of accountability."

The heart of the objection was that the treaty forces countries to relinquish their sovereign jurisdiction over their forces and leaves those forces vulnerable to international prosecution with no U.S. ability to come to their aid when the United States participates in UN-sponsored peacekeeping operations, such as those in Bosnia and Kosovo or in Iraq or Afghanistan. As Sheffer put it, "Thus, the treaty purports to establish an arrangement whereby U.S. armed forces operating overseas could be conceivably prosecuted by the international court even if the U.S. has not agreed to be bound by the treaty. Not only is this contrary to the most fundamental principles of treaty law, it could inhibit the ability of the U.S. to use its military to meet alliance obligations and participate in multinational operations, including humanitarian interventions to save civilian lives." Jennifer Elsea summarized U.S. objections in a 2006 Congressional Research Service study, the gist of which remains American policy. "The ICC purports to its jurisdiction citizens of non-member nations," she wrote. Moreover, lack of adequate due process "will not offer accused Americans the due process guaranteed them under the U.S. constitution." The sovereign control of American forces potentially accused of war crimes thus stands at the base of the United States' refusal to sign off on the ICC statute.

In order to get around the problem of sovereignty forfeiture, the United States has dredged up a tactic it used after World War II to ensure Senate ratification of the statute of the International Court of Justice (ICJ, or World Court), with which the ICC is affiliated. In the case of the ICJ, the United States insisted that the statute include the provision that the court would only have jurisdiction in individual cases if *both* (or all) parties granted jurisdiction for that action alone. In other words, countries, including the United States, can only be sued and have judgments made against them in situations in which they have given their permission: Sovereign control is only abrogated by explicit consent.

The same argument is incorporated in the American approach to the question of the jurisdiction of the ICC. The American proposed "supplement" to the Rome Treaty read: "The United Nations and the International Criminal Court agree that the Court may seek the surrender or accept custody of a national who acts within the overall direction of a U.N. Member State, and such directing State has so acknowledged *only in the event (a) the directing State is a State Party to the Statute or the Court obtains the consent of the directing State, or (b) measures have been authorized pursuant to Chapter VII of the U.N. Charter against the directing State in relation to the situation or actions giving rise to alleged crime or crimes.*" (Emphasis added.) Parties to the statute have consistently rejected this American position.

Why does the United States object to this cooperation-inducing regime? The U.S. government, and especially the military, argues that the United States, as the remaining superpower, is uniquely vulnerable to international harassment in the absence of this kind of protection. More specifically, there are usually American forces involved in major peacekeeping missions globally, where accusations of war crimes are commonplace. The military fears that unfounded accusations (what the Elsea study refers to as "trumped-up charges") against Americans can become a means of harassment of the United States against which they should guard and that the American amendment seeks to protect.

The U.S. position, which was formulated by the Bush administration but had been neither modified nor renounced by its successor, goes on to add other objections based in the expansion of international authority contained in the ICC statute. Elsea cited two: an "unacceptable prosecutor" who would have "unchecked discretion to initiate cases," and the "usurpation of the role of the UN Security Council" in regulating ICC initiatives. Both find their base in the sovereignty issue: Checks would presumably be exercised by states through the effective veto of prosecution of particular cases, and the Security Council's authority is based in the veto power of the permanent members, including the United States.

These distinctions are more than academic. The question of mandatory jurisdiction forces the United States to join a virtual rogue's gallery of other states that have also not ratified the ICC statute. This list contains both the world's most populous states (of which the United States is one) and its worst human rights abusers (membership in which the United States would deny). The motivation of many (but not all) of these states, which are concentrated in the Middle East and Africa, is to avoid the ICC's reach in cases where they or their top officials might be defendants. One of these states is Syria.

The Specific Case of Syria

The particularly brutal Syrian government reacted to its variant of the Arab Spring revolt against authoritarian rule with a savagery that has created international rage toward the regime of Bashar al-Assad. Most of the reaction has come in the form of condemnations of the bloody repression of anti-government activity, centered around Homs and Aleppo, two of Syria's largest cities. That repression has included a virtual siege of each by Syrian government forces and vicious attacks against civilians in both cities and elsewhere. As of early 2013, the civilian death toll was a reported 70,000 and climbing. As the violence has grown and included considerable amateur video reports of the tragedy, the accusations have included crimes against humanity—war crimes—directed at the regime and more recently at some rebel forces as well.

The U.S. government has been at the forefront of these accusations. On February 28, 2012, American Secretary of State Hillary Clinton argued in a speech (quoted in Spence), "Based in definitions of war crimes and crimes against humanity, there ought to be an argument that he (al-Assad) fits into that category." There were outpourings of agreement from Western capitals, including Great Britain and France (whose governments volunteered to take an indictment of al-Assad to the ICC) and in a few Middle Eastern states, notably neighboring Turkey.

The Milosevic case provided a precedent for indicting a sitting head of state, and a similar action had been taken *in absentia* against Sudanese president Omar al-Bashir for alleged atrocities in Darfur and South Sudan (see Chapter 15). The two precedents differed in that the Serbian government was willing to remand Milosevic to the ICC control for trial, whereas the Sudanese government, where al-Bashir still rules, has not.

Although there are firm bases for dealing with the Syrian case as a war crime within ICC jurisdiction, there are also at least two objections. One of these, raised by Clinton, is that indicting al-Bashar would make efforts to convince him to step down more difficult. As a former leader, he would be much more vulnerable to arrest and deportation to an ICC tribunal (the Milosevic precedent) than if he remains in power (the al-Bashir precedent). Thus, an indictment could simply increase his determination to remain in power.

The other objection arises from the ICC's claimed jurisdiction over accused war criminals from states that are not party to the ICC. Because Syria is not a member, such jurisdiction is necessary to establish for the ICC to have a claim of authority over al-Assad. It is, however, the heart of the American (and Israeli and others') objection to the ICC to deny this extension of authority, as already noted. This obviously puts the United States in a conceptual bind of accusing al-Assad of crimes but denying the authority of the body specifically entrusted with trying him. France, an ICC member, has no such problem. The potential trial of al-Assad thus raises important legal questions regarding the universality of laws against war crimes.

The February 2013 report of the commission of the UN Human Rights Council (a 131-page document) widens the accusation to include war crimes accusations of leaders of the opposition as well. The report, as described in the *New York Times* (see Cummings-Bruce) and elsewhere, argues that alleged violence by both sides is worsening, "aggravated by increasing sectarianism," and made even worse by a growing influx of foreign fighters into the country. Speaking for the commission, Carla del Pante, described as a "UN human rights investigator," summarized what the report views as the necessary international response. "It's incredible the Security Council doesn't take a decision," she says. "Crimes are continuing, and the number of victims is increasing every day." The report recommends sending the case to the ICC, but two of the permanent members of the Security Council with veto power, China and the United States, are also nonmembers of the ICC.

The issue came to a head in mid-2013 with the accusation of chemical weapons use against Syrian civilians by the government. If confirmed, such usage clearly constitutes a crime against humanity and would place the perpetrators in the jurisdiction of the ICC. Doing so would have required a direct accusation against the regime and Assad and created a dilemma for the world community. If the norm has any teeth, it would have to be enforced. Assad, along with supporters such as Russia, would have resisted, and in all probability, the only way to enforce the norms would have been through the application of force, something countries like the United States were reluctant to contemplate given their recent experiences in Iraq and Afghanistan.

The problem was resolved through a UN resolution UN Security Council Resolution—UNSCR—2118) that demanded Syrian disarmament of its chemical weapons under international supervision, but with no mention of or blame assigned to chemical uses against civilians. The international community was thus able to enforce the ban on chemical weapons without forcing itself to enforce ban on crimes against humanity. The result was no entirely satisfying to all, but it did allow the crisis to pass.

CONCLUSION AND DILEMMAS

The question of war crimes is not likely to go away as a concern in international relations. In a gradually democratizing world in which authoritarianism is still practiced but rarely extolled, there is no longer any organized, principled objection to the notion that there are limits on both the conduct of war and how individuals and groups can be treated. Although the development of something like a consensus on this matter is quite recent in historical terms (particularly the idea of crimes against peace and humanity), it nonetheless seems well on its way to being established as an international norm.

The major remaining question is institutionalization of war crimes enforcement. As noted in a quote at the beginning of this study, the emergence of a consensus has coincided with a spate of war crimes, principally in the bloody, brutal internal wars in a number of developing-world states. Syria is the current symbol of man's inhumanity to fellow man, and it also demonstrates the difficulty of adjudicating such inhumanity due the less-than-universal reach of the ICC. The practical implication of this situation is that there are almost certainly going to be places where war crimes tribunals will need to be formed if the permanent court does not have universal jurisdiction.

Is the ICC the answer? Clearly, it would solve some problems and have some advantages. It would certainly be more responsive when problems arise; it would maximize whatever deterrent value a potential violator would experience knowing the court was waiting for him or her; and it would insulate the system from accusations of victor's law in future cases. Moreover, it would contribute at least marginally to the general promotion of lawfulness in the international system and, in specific cases, might help defuse public passions by removing trials from the places in which alleged crimes took place and in which there was universal international support for action, a limit in the Syrian case. To its proponents, these are powerful and compelling justifications for the ICC.

Then there is the American position. The U.S. objection to the ICC is not a defense of war crimes or an explicit defense of international disorder. Rather, it stems from a longstanding American fixation with state sovereignty and the need for the American government to have sole jurisdiction over its citizens. In practice, this policy puts the United States at cross-purposes with most of the international community, including most of its closest allies, and on the same side as some rogue states on this and similar issues. Within the United States, there is division on the position to take: The Clinton administration did, after all, both champion and subsequently back down into opposition about the ICC. The Bush administration redoubled opposition to the ICC. The Obama administration has remained officially mute on the subject. Given the prominence of the United States as the arguable remaining superpower, the American decision on ratifying the ICC statute or an amended version is probably critical.

In the end, the international debate pitting the United States against most of the rest of the world (and especially its principal allies) is not about war crimes or the establishment of a court. No one is *for* war crimes or *against* a tribunal to prosecute offenders. The debate is over the nature of the court's jurisdiction and what the jurisdiction means for Americans. More specifically, it is a question of whether American forces operating worldwide can or should be subject to international rather than American legal standards and whether the United States should avoid situations where the ICC could be used to harass American soldiers and thus impinge on American sovereign control of its nationals.

The result is a clash between advocacies of war crimes prosecution and defenders of sovereignty. Which is more important? At one level, international cooperation against crimes against humanity (including torture) is clearly virtuous and praiseworthy, but what if such cooperation is detrimental to the ability of the state to protect itself from evils being committed against the state, including evil committed using those very acts the cooperation attempts to but cannot prevent? More concretely, can states advocate the imposition of mandatory war crimes jurisdiction against others but not against themselves?

At another level, the dilemma is over the rule of law versus the primal right of self-protection. International cooperation in adjudicating war crimes, after all, about is self-interest. One reason that crimes against humanity are outlawed is based in reciprocity: If I do not commit these acts, you cannot justify using them either, so it is in both our interests to outlaw them.

But there will always be exceptions. Some people will always break the law, and in the case of war crimes, doing so can endanger the people of sovereign states. Syria is the latest dramatic illustration. What should the state do in these circumstances? It is easy to delineate the extremes: The cooperative rule of law should triumph regardless of the human consequences, or states should do whatever they feel they must to defend themselves, regardless of the impact on law and even civilization. But most cases in the real world lie between the extremes, where the choices are neither so stark nor clear cut.

SUGGESTED ACTIVITIES AND QUESTIONS

1. The commission of war crimes, including torture, is universally condemned, and international cooperation to end and punish these acts seems to be the obvious solution, but this has not always been the case. Why?

2. Discuss the evolution of the war crimes concept. What was the impact of the end of the Cold War and the tragedies of Bosnia and Rwanda on that evolution? How is the International Criminal Court the product of that evolution?

3. What are the various categories of war crimes? Discuss them historically and in terms of their current importance.

4. Are the arguments in favor of the International Criminal Court compelling? How much of the American objection to the question of automatic, overriding jurisdiction should be accommodated?

5. Is the participation of the United States necessary for the success of the permanent war crimes tribunal? Assess the American objection. Is it reasonable, arrogant, or possibly both? If you were the representative of another government, how would you feel about the American position?

6. Most situations in which allegations of war crimes are likely to occur are internal wars in the developing world; how does this affect the value of having a permanent court rather than ad hoc tribunals, as have been formed up to now? Is a permanent ICC more effective in deterring violators or investigating and bringing them to justice? Was Bashard al-Assad affected by his potential vulnerability to ICC prosecution?

7. Should some measure of national sovereignty be surrendered to make the ICC effective? Which value is more important: national control over a country's citizens or justice for the victims and perpetrators of war crimes when those two values come into conflict?

8. How do accusations of war crimes (including the employment of chemical weapons) against the government of Syria illustrate the points of contention over war crimes? Explain.

9. The dilemma of war crimes and torture is that they are both universally condemned, but half the world's population lives outside the regime intended to regulate war crimes and a significant part of the world rejects official condemnation of torture. Can this dilemma be resolved?

SUGGESTED READINGS AND RESOURCES

Cobban, Helena. "Think Again: International Courts." *Foreign Policy*, March/April 2006, 22–28.

Cummings-Bruce, Nick. "U.N. Rights Panel on Syria Urges War Crimes Charges." *New York Times* (online), February 18, 2013.

Dempsey, Gary. *Reasonable Doubt: The Case Against the Proposed International Criminal Court.* Cato Policy Analysis No. 311. Washington, DC: Cato Institute, 1998.

Elsea, Jennifer K. *U.S. Policy Regarding the International Criminal Court.* Washington, DC: Congressional Research Service, August 29, 2006.

Greenberg, Karen Joy. *The Torture Debate in America.* Cambridge, MA: MIT Press, 2005.

Grotius, Hugo. *Concerning the Law of War and Peace.* New York: Cambridge University Press, 2012 (originally published 1625).

Gutman, Roy and David Rieff, eds. *Crimes of War.* New York: W.W. Norton, 1999.

Hersh, Seymour. *Chain of Command: The Road from 9/11 to Abu Ghraib.* New York: HarperCollins, 2004.

Kahn, Leo. *Nuremberg Trials.* New York: Ballantine Books, 1972.

Neier, Aryeh. *War Crimes: Brutality, Genocide, Terror, and the Struggle for Justice.* New York: Random House, 1998. *Nuremburg Trial Proceedings, International Military Tribunal: Trial of the Major War Criminals.* New Haven, CT: Yale Law School Avalon Project, 1945.

Schmid, Alex P. and Ronald D. Crelinsten. *The Politics of Pain: Torturers and Their Masters.* Boulder, CO: Westview Press, 1994.

Spence, Richard. "Syria: Bashar al-Assad Could Be Regarded as a War Criminal, Says Hillary Clinton." *The Telegraph* (online), February 28, 2012.

Tusa, Ann and John Tusa. *The Nuremberg Trial.* New York: Atheneum, 1983.

Welsh, Jennifer. "The Responsibility to Protect: Dilemmas of a New Norm." *Current History* 111, 748 (November 2012), 291–298.

WEB SITES

Collaboration of journalists, lawyers, and scholars on laws of war and war crimes
   Crimes of War Project: http://www.crimesofwar.org
Overview of documents and events leading to Rome Statute
   Rome Statute: http://www.un.org/law/icc/index.html
Arguments about the ICC and U.S. security interests
   "A Summary of United Nations Agreements on Human Rights": http://www.hrweb
   .org/legal/undocs.html
   "Sheffer on Why U.S. Opposed International Criminal Court": http://www.usembassy
   .org/uk/
   Human Rights Watch: http://www.hrw.org/english/docs/2003,12/19/ira_6770.htm
   http://hrw.org.europe/083104milo.htm

Irresolvable Conflicts: The Israeli– Palestinian Impasse

PRÉCIS

A difficult problem facing the international system that largely arises from sovereignty is the existence of irresolvable conflicts between states, disputes so difficult that they defy successful attempts at resolution. The most extreme contemporary example of such conflicts is the conflict between the Israelis and the Palestinians, which is the subject of this case study.

The case begins with a description of irresolvable conflicts, including their common characteristics and the basic methods that are available to try to resolve them. With that framework established, the dynamics of irresolvable conflicts will be applied to the conflict between Israelis and the Palestinians arising from the partition of the "holy lands" that began n 1948 and has evolved since. Following a brief description of the issues involved, the discussion looks at the American-brokered peace process that has been ongoing for well over a quarter century, both in terms of its successes and ultimate failures. It then looks at the difficult and intractable differences between the two sides that have come to center on and be symbolized by the growing presence of Israeli settlements on the West Bank, and will conclude with the prospects of moving this conflict to some form of resolution—resolving the irresolvable.

In a world composed of sovereign states, conflict is an unavoidable, ubiquitous aspect of international relations. In most cases, the conflicts are not so basic and fundamental that the states cannot find means to resolve or learn how to live with those differences. Ideally, outcomes can be found that are mutually acceptable and thus satisfactorily resolve the differences in ways with which both sides can live. In some cases, differences cannot so easily be resolved and, at least some of the time, armed force in some guise becomes the way in which attempts are made—not always successfully—to resolve these differences. It is in these circumstances of deep, even irreconcilable, conflict that some of the most difficult problems reside.

IRRESOLVABLE CONFLICTS

Thoroughly vexing conflicts that present irreconcilable, irresolvable differences between the parties represent an important genre of international reality. In these kinds of conflicts, the issues that divide the two (or more) sides are so deep and fundamental that they cannot be resolved peaceably through diplomatic methods, either because the positions are so far apart and deeply held or because the animosities between the parties are so great (or both) that they cannot find a basis on which to reach accord. Moreover, in these situations a military resolution wherein one side imposes its will on the other is either impossible or unacceptable to influence parts of the international community as a whole, so a coerced solution cannot be implemented.

These kinds of situations, fortunately enough, are comparatively infrequent, but they do occur and are particularly intractable and difficult for the system to accommodate. Within the contemporary international system, the ongoing differences between Taiwan and mainland China about the status of the island Republic of China and the Indo-Pakistani conflict over Kashmir stand out, but the most difficult example is the division between Israel and the Palestinian people over the political future of the piece of real estate known as Israel or Palestine, depending on the person to whom one is talking. The Israeli–Palestinian conflict is such a textbook example of irresolvable conflict that it is the subject of this chapter.

Irresolvable conflicts share at least seven common characteristics. The first is that the scarce resource normally involved is territory, the scarceness of which arises from the fact that there are multiples claimants to sovereign control of a piece of territory over which only one side can exercise sovereignty. In the case of China and Taiwan, for instance, both sides agree that Taiwan is rightly a part of China (some native Taiwanese disagree), and the question is over which political groups should exercise that sovereignty. The Kashmir question similarly revolves around whether India, Pakistan, or the Kashmiris should exercise sovereignty over the mountainous formerly princely state of Jammu and Kashmir. The centerpiece of the Israeli–Palestinian feud is over who should rule all or different parts of the pre-partition territory once known as Palestine and has come to be centered on the Israeli-occupied West Bank of the Jordan River.

The second characteristic is that these territorial conflicts tend to be extremely emotional, deep, and fundamental. The emotion and depth arises from the fact that the territory is generally viewed as the rightful homeland of one or both sides, or the claims are rooted in some deep and fundamental division such as religion or ethnicity. Often individual plots of land in the disputed territories are viewed as the rightful home sites of individuals on both sides of the conflict, making their emotional attachment all the deeper than it might be otherwise. Palestine is an example. This emotional element can be—and often is—politically manipulated by those either seeking to avoid resolution of the conflict or wanting to subvert outcomes that do not work to their advantage. The fundamental source of division also makes compromise solutions extremely difficult to discover: It is, for instance, daunting to try to figure out how to divide a single dwelling between two hostile families that claim it.

Third, this emotional, fundamental base creates positions that become mutually exclusive and that consequently require mutually exclusive outcomes. Irresolvable conflicts tend to be viewed by both or all parties as strictly zero-sum exercises in which one side's success is the other side's loss; there is little effort made or point in trying to find an accommodation in which both sides can benefit (a positive-sum exercise) or in which losses are equitably and acceptably apportioned (negative-sum games). In irresolvable conflicts, both sides will only accept outcomes in which they succeed and the other side does not.

Fourth, this intractability resonates throughout the populations affected in such a way as to reinforce the unwillingness and unacceptability of compromise. The position of each side often becomes "righteous" to the antagonists to the point that the simple idea of compromise becomes virtually a sacrilege and those who promote compromise become suspect. Such depth of emotion may be limited to the extremists on both sides of the conflict, but their influence may be disproportionate to their numbers. One way this can occur is by the extremists succeeding in establishing the rhetorical high ground and thus being able to relegate the compromisers to the status of infidels or traitors. Another way is to resort to violence to pump up the emotions of followers against any movement toward resolution by peaceful means. Both these methods have been prominently evident in the Israeli–Palestinian conflict.

A fifth shared characteristic is often the failure of outside mediation to move the dispute toward resolution. When disputes become heated to the point of combustibility, as irresolvable conflicts often do, it is only natural for outsiders with interests on one or both sides of the conflict to want to aid a process that will help defuse the situation, either by resolving it or by at least reducing its intensity so that it loses the ability or likelihood of bubbling over and disturbing international tranquility.

In some sense, the degree to which the particular conflict could endanger the rest of the world affects the degree to which outsiders become interested. Conflicts between the government of Indonesia and East Timorese seeking independence did not attract much notice until reports of large-scale killings focused attention on the island of Timor; the isolation of the region from the global system meant that intervention was effectively regionalized with the lead involvement of Australia (which was mostly motivated by the fear of a stream of East Timorese refugees navigating the 600-mile straits to its shores). Similarly, the conflict over Kashmir attracted less outside interest until both India and Pakistan tested nuclear weapons in 1998. The more volatile Middle East, on the other hand, has ensured a high level of interest by the outside world in making sure its conflicts do not spread to a general conflagration.

The sixth characteristic is the inability of the parties to find acceptable outcomes to the conflict, thereby guaranteeing its continuation. Conflicts over exclusive possession of scarce territorial resources are, of course, inherently difficult to resolve in an amicable manner, meaning that normal methods of conflict resolution have generally failed (that failure is what defines irresolvable conflicts). In this case, the only way to reach a conclusion may be through the imposition of a settlement favoring one side at the expense of the other, which may be impossible for one of two reasons.

One reason may be that neither side has the resources available to force a settlement on the other, at least within acceptable bounds of resource expenditure. The reason Kashmir remains in a state of uncertain de facto sovereignty is that neither India nor Pakistan has the required military might to impose a settlement on the entire territory. The only way either country could conceivably do so would be to escalate the conflict to the point that it might become nuclear, an alternative the international community would find unacceptable (as would the affected populations, presumably). The failure of Israel to eliminate Hezbollah in Lebanon in 2006 suggests the possibility that there is no military solution to the Israeli–Palestinian problem as well.

In other cases, the imposition of force may be physically possible but geopolitically unacceptable. Israel, after all, has maintained authority over a good bit of land jointly claimed by it and the Palestinians since at least 1967, and militarily it is certainly conceivable that Israel could continue to assert its sway over all the contested territories. Doing so, however, keeps the conflict within the region alive, with uncertain outcomes—the worst of which could be catastrophic. As a result, any instincts the Israelis may have toward an imposed solution are effectively stifled by the consequences such an imposition might bring.

A seventh characteristic is that the longer an irresolvable conflict remains unresolved, the more the status quo may harden into a de facto solution that is unattractive to both but that becomes the least unacceptable outcome by default. The situations in Kashmir and Palestine (especially the West Bank) are exemplary. Both conflicts have their roots in 1948 (the partition of the Indian subcontinent and the independence of Israel), and neither has moved toward resolution in the intervening 60-plus years. The issues—Muslim claims on Kashmir and Palestine—remain unresolved, and an unhappy de facto status quo (division of Kashmir along the "Line of Control" and Israeli occupation of the West Bank) has evolved an uneasy permanence. In the Palestinian case, this position has hardened, possibly irredeemably, due to continued and growing Israeli settlement in the disputed territory.

THE ISRAELI–PALESTINIAN CONFLICT

The ongoing conflict between Israel and Palestine meets all the criteria for an irresolvable conflict. It is quintessentially about sovereign control of territory that is coveted with great passion by both sides. The positions that both the Israelis and the Palestinians take toward their claims to the land are fundamental, deep, and emotional, profoundly shrouded in historical tenure and even religious claims and bases. Because "God" has empowered both sides in their own minds, the claims each has are deeply held by their supporting populations and make it essentially impossible for leaders on either side to propose major concessions or compromises, which are viewed as heresy by those at the extremes on both sides. The positions are thus intractable, and outside attempts to mediate (in this case led mostly by the United States) have not succeeded in reducing the issues dividing the sides, despite strong and concerted efforts at trying to act as the midwife of settlement. Moreover, no imposed settlement in which one side is forced to accept great sacrifices is acceptable to that side, and even if it could physically be imposed by one side on the other, such a settlement would be internationally unacceptable and resisted by the side on which it was imposed. The longer the dispute remains at an impasse, the more permanent the current outcome, which is basically unacceptable to both sides, becomes.

In order to understand this conflict as irresolvable, it is necessary to examine it and how it has evolved. This examination begins by looking at the structure of the problem, how it has evolved, and what the basic unresolved obstacles to resolution are. One factor that distinguishes this conflict from other irresolvable conflicts is the extraordinary efforts and prestige a major power—the United States—has ultimately unsuccessfully invested in trying to overcome the conflict, and so the record of attempted solutions, beginning with the efforts of Jimmy Carter at Camp David in 1978 and going forward through George W. Bush's "road map" for peace and efforts by the Obama administration, will be reviewed. This background will form the backdrop for examining the contemporary conflict and its current most vexing manifestations, notably the continuing growth of Israeli settlements on the Palestinian territories (the West Bank). The study will conclude with an assessment of what, if any, prospects exist for resolving the irresolvable.

The Israeli–Palestinian Problem

The heart and soul of the disagreement between Israel and the Palestinians is a real estate dispute over the rightful ownership and sovereign control of the territory known to Muslims as Palestine and now largely controlled by Israel. The contemporary basis of this dispute has its roots in the late 1800s, when the Zionist movement in Europe promoted the migration of increasing numbers of Jews to Palestine to avoid religious persecution and to fulfill what they viewed as a biblical admonition to return to the "Promised Land." The movement gained momentum after World War II and the Holocaust stimulated a surge of Jewish immigration to what they called Israel. It crested and became a problem with the establishment of the state of Israel in 1948.

The piece of territory over which the conflict alternately simmers and rages has been the subject of contention and violence for far longer than is reflected in the current impasse, which is in some ways just the most recent chapter in the saga over the "holy lands." The roots of this disagreement date back to biblical times and have been the subject of innumerable treatises and arguments regarding rightful ownership over centuries and millennia that need not be repeated here, other than to note both that these claims exist and that they form underlying arguments to which both (or all) sides make reference to buttress their claims. For present purposes, suffice it to say that all parties have impressive, if contradictory, historical and scriptural arguments that buttress the cases they wish to make.

The current dispute has its origins in the immediate post–World War II period, although the movement to return much of the largely European Jewish population to the area goes back to the Zionist movement. This movement was essentially peaceful and the Jewish influx was absorbed by the Muslim Palestinians before World War II, when the two peoples, Israeli and Palestinian, essentially lived side by side in peace. Only when the post–World War II flood of Holocaust survivors found its way to Israel did the question of land become critical.

Israeli Independence, War, and Displacement

The movement of a large number of Jews into Palestine (at the time a part of Transjordan) stimulated the desire to create a Jewish state of Israel that had been central to the Zionist appeal and that many Jews believed had been promised them by God. This movement obviously disquieted many of the Muslim Palestinians, who found this possibility inimical to their centuries-long possession of the territory (which had, until the end of World War I, been part of the Ottoman Empire). When the Israelis declared their independence in 1948, after a declaration supported by the United States and the Soviet Union in the United Nations (UN) in favor of Israel's statehood, the result was violence.

There were two basic reactions to Israel's declaration as a sovereign state. One was the exodus of a large part of the Palestinian Muslim population, which feared retribution and repression under the new Israeli government. There had been numerous instances of intercommunal violence on both sides in the months and years leading to the creation of the new state. Most Palestinians fled with little more than the shirts on their backs and a few possessions, so that they became an instant refugee problem in the territories—especially the West Bank of the Jordan River—to which they went. The second reaction was for most of the surrounding Muslim states to declare war on the new Israeli state and to launch attacks designed to destroy Israel. These attacks were ineptly carried out and absolutely uncoordinated, so that military and paramilitary forces within the new Jewish state (which had been part of the resistance to postwar British administration of the area) easily repulsed the attacks. In the process, the original territorial boundaries of the Israeli state were actually enlarged by the outcome.

The 1948 war established the basic conditions that exist today, although the details have changed over time. There were two major effects. The first, most profound, and most relevant was the effect on the Palestinian Muslims. Most of the Palestinian population fled their homes in Israel and became refugees, and collectively the Palestinians constituted a *stateless nation* (a distinct people with no home state that they could claim). Such statelessness had been part of the burden of the Jewish population for nearly a millennium; the status was now transferred to the Palestinians. Because the surrounding territories into which the Palestinians fled were generally poor and incapable of absorbing the new residents, the status of most refugees was wretched, powerless, and, as time went by, increasingly hopeless. This set of circumstances forms the basic rationale for a demand for the creation of an independent Palestinian state. Such a state could be of two natures, which divides the current debate. One possibility is that the Palestinian state could be carved out of part of the original Palestine (leaving both an Israeli and a Palestinian state as the outcome—an arrangement that was part of the original Zionist plan for the area). The other possibility is to return Palestinian domain over the entirety of the area, thereby eliminating Israel. The nature of the resulting Palestinian state remains the most basic division between the two sides, the resolution of which is necessary if the conflict is to be resolved. A particularly vexing part of the territorial puzzle is the final disposition of Jerusalem, the site of religious symbols basic to Islam, Judaism, and Christianity.

The other outcome was to endow the new state of Israel with a kind of special status. On the surface, the Israelis were severely disadvantaged when they were attacked by forces from the surrounding states, including Egypt, Jordan, Syria, Iraq, and Saudi Arabia. Postconflict analysis has shown that the forces arrayed against the Israelis were nowhere near as formidable as a cursory examination would suggest and that the Israelis actually had their attackers significantly outgunned and were better organized militarily than their assailants. Nonetheless, the Israelis emerged from the conflict as the heroes of a David-and-Goliath struggle in which they had prevailed. That aura would gradually fade, but it was a worthwhile adjunct for a period of time.

Two subsequent wars were of greater consequence, if in different ways, one rewriting the map of the region and the other creating the geopolitical incentive to move concertedly toward resolution of the difficulties between Israel and its Muslim opponents. Each is thus important to view at least briefly.

The Six-Day War of 1967

Slightly less than 11 years after the Suez conflict of 1956, war broke out again between Israel and its neighbors. The precipitant of the fighting was the removal of a UN force (the United Nations Emergency Force, or UNEF) from the Egyptian–Israeli border, where it had acted as a peacekeeping tripwire to prevent either country from attacking the other. When UNEF left, Egypt launched an attack on Israel and was joined by the armies of Jordan and Syria. The result was an utter disaster for the Muslim states. The Israelis managed to decimate their opponents in the remarkably short period of six days, changing fundamentally the power balance in the region and setting the groundwork for the current conflict.

When the dust had settled at the end of the war, Israel not only had defeated the armed forces of each of its opponents but had also occupied significant territories belonging to each. From Egypt, the Israelis gained the Sinai Peninsula and the Gaza Strip, a small appendix of Sinai along the Mediterranean coast adjacent to Israel. They also occupied the West Bank of the Jordan River from Jordan and the Golan Heights from Syria.

This territorial exchange greatly enhanced the physical security of Israel, because any future Egyptian attack against Israel would first have to fight its way across Sinai, which the Israelis fortified against such an incursion. At the same time, Egypt was badly embarrassed by having such a large part of its territory taken from it, and the occupation also meant that the east bank of the Suez Canal was now in Israeli hands (although the canal was closed for a time because of ships sunk in its waters during the war). The Israelis seized the West Bank of the Jordan River from Jordan, thereby further increasing its physical security by making it much more difficult for a future enemy to dash across the narrowest parts of Israel and effectively cut the country in two. Jordan, however, lost its most economically productive region. The Israelis completed the occupation by seizing the Golan Heights, a low mountainous region bordering northern Israel that the Syrians had used to launch artillery attacks against Israeli *kibbutzes* before the war.

These outcomes both altered the geopolitical balance in the region and created the physical basis for the peace process that would follow. Egyptian humiliation at the loss of Sinai and Gaza and the consequent desire to regain those lost territories helped form the basis for negotiations with Israel a decade later that would begin the peace process at Camp David. At the same time, Jordan's loss of the West Bank changed greatly the Palestinian situation. Part of the change was that many Palestinian refugees had settled on the West Bank after 1948, and they were again displaced by the events of 1967, as more fled into Jordan and also Lebanon, where they added to political instabilities in those countries. Many Palestinians, however, remained in the occupied West Bank, where they were subjected to Israeli rule over what they considered part of their own historic lands. Some of the fuel for the *intifadas* (uprisings) in the 1990s and 2000s was sown in this change of control. At the same time, the seizure effectively ended the Jordanian claim on the West Bank and allowed negotiators to think of a solution to the Palestinian real estate dispute in terms encompassing both Israel and the occupied West Bank and Gaza. This transformation is especially important in so-called two-state proposals (proposals to create a Palestinian state alongside Israel). Little noticed at the time, the occupation of the West Bank and Gaza created the necessary precondition for Israeli settlements in both areas, a process that began as a trickle and has grown to a possible peace-process-drowning deluge in recent years.

Yom Kippur War of 1973

The Six-Day War created the conditions with which the peace process would have to deal, and the Yom Kippur War created the perceived necessity and impetus to begin that process. The reasons had to do with the conduct and outcome of the war, and more important, what almost—but did not—occur during its conduct.

Two things stand out about the 1973 war. The first is that it was the first time the Israelis suffered significant military defeats against their Muslim rivals. As a result, the Israelis reportedly authorized the arming of their clandestine nuclear arsenal for possible use against neighboring capitals to reverse their fortunes on the battlefield (the Israelis neither confirm nor deny that they either possess such weapons or that they activated them). This prospect greatly increased the likelihood that a Middle East conflict might escalate into a superpower nuclear confrontation, as the United States backed Israel and the Soviet Union backed the Islamic states in the conflict. Second, after the Israelis reversed the tide of military events and routed their opponents, the Soviets threatened to airlift troops to the front to save an Egyptian army from possible extinction, thereby further increasing the possibility of a superpower showdown. Like the nuclear activation by Israel, this possibility was also averted by diplomatic means.

The outcome changed the calculation of Middle East conflict in two ways. The very real prospect that the war could have somehow reluctantly drawn the United States into a confrontation that could have led to World War III convinced both sides, but especially the United States, that such a possibility had to be avoided in the future: The Arab–Israeli conflict was simply not worth a nuclear war that could destroy the United States. This recognition created the determination that finding a peaceful settlement (or at least an accord averting future war) was absolutely necessary. The change made this outcome possible to pursue. The Soviets did not resupply their allies in the war—notably the Egyptians—as fast or as well as they would have liked, and Egypt broke its ties with the Soviet Union. The United States leaped into the power vacuum created by the Soviet departure and quickly established leverage with the Egyptians, in addition to its previous relationship with Israel. The possibility of a peace process was thus added to its perceived necessity.

THE PEACE PROCESS

The process of attempting to end the territorial imbroglio over Palestine was the result of both an outside determination by the United States that such an effort was necessary and an initiative by the parties involved. Some outside pressure was almost certainly necessary, because there had been no formal—or significant informal—relations between Israel and the surrounding Islamic states since the creation of Israel in 1948. Thus, it was necessary for some outsider to create a forum in which to pursue a settlement. Because the United States had supplanted Great Britain as the major outside influence in the area (a position enhanced by the forced withdrawal of the Soviets) and saw the necessity of ending the possibility that the region could ignite a global war, it became a logical candidate for that role.

The process began with the convening of Egypt and Israel for peace negotiations in the United States by U.S. President Jimmy Carter in 1978 at the presidential retreat at Camp David, and President William J. Clinton reprised that process in 2000. Between those events, Israel and Jordan independently negotiated an agreement, leaving only Syria and the Palestinians with unsettled differences with Israel. George W. Bush reactivated outside assistance in the process in 2003 when he presented his "road map" for solving the differences between the two. That initiative did not bear fruit, nor have attempts by the Obama administration broken the impasse.

The result has been minimal progress toward a peace agreement, but a comprehensive settlement of this intractable conflict remains elusive. As is normally the case in complex negotiations, the parties settled what in retrospect appeared to have been the easier differences first, and as they peeled away the onion skin of differences, what remains are the most difficult issues. At the very core is the irresolvable conflict between Israel and Palestine, and notably the issue of territorial control and sovereignty centering on the West Bank.

Camp David I

That there even was a first meeting at Camp David is one of the miracles of twentieth-century diplomacy. Prior to the events that led to the meeting, Israel had never held official meetings of any kind with its neighbors (or the Palestinians), and all the Muslim states in the region were committed, to one degree or another, not only to denying the legitimate existence of Israel but also to destroying the Israeli state and hence to restoring Palestine to Muslim rule.

The process leading to Camp David began with the Yom Kippur War. When Jimmy Carter came to the White House in 1977, a peace in the region was at the top of his list of foreign policy priorities, and one of his first acts was to issue his plan for peace. The governments on both sides rejected the plan Carter proposed, but it became at least a beginning point for future discussions.

Egyptian president Anwar Sadat jump-started the process. In 1977, Sadat flew to Jerusalem, where he pointedly visited the Dome of the Rock and Al Aqsa mosque (the second-holiest sites in Islam, Muslim access to which had been denied since 1967) and met with Israeli Prime Minister Menachem Begin. The move was extremely bold because going to Jerusalem implicitly recognized the existence of Israel and thus broke ranks with his Islamic brethren in the region. Egypt and Sadat were roundly condemned in the region because of this contact, and, after the Camp David accords, were diplomatically and economically isolated. Begin took a chance in the face of considerable Israeli opposition to the potential return of Sinai and Gaza to the Egyptians.

Sadat's visit to Jerusalem proved the stepping-stone for the meeting at Camp David in 1978. At the time, the very idea of accommodation between Israel and its enemies seemed a long shot at best. The meetings succeeded partly because Begin and Sadat showed extraordinary leadership in the face of tremendous opposition to the enterprise, and partly because they both needed something from the other that only the negotiations could provide. At the same time, what they could agree on was less than the entirety of the issues dividing Israel from the other states and from the Palestinians; on those issues that could not be resolved, the result was to defer the matter to future efforts.

There were three basic issues between the two negotiators. The first was Israel's desire to be recognized by its neighbors, including an admission of Israel's right to exist. Movement on this issue was sufficiently important to Begin that he was willing to compromise on other issues to realize it. Egypt represented the second and third interests. Egypt had been enormously humiliated by the forced cessation of Sinai and Gaza and badly wanted both back as a matter of national prestige and pride. At the same time, Egypt hoped that opposition to its discussions with the hated Israelis would be moderated in the Muslim world if it also managed to get the Israelis to move toward a Palestinian state, the third interest.

Two of the three issues could be and were included in a quid-pro-quo agreement, whereas the third was too difficult to settle in detail and was deferred for future consideration. As a result, the Camp David Accord (as it was known) consisted of three agreements:

1. The withdrawal of Israel from the Sinai Peninsula;
2. A peace treaty between Israel and Egypt that included recognition of Israel; and
3. A promise to resolve the Palestinian question in the form of autonomy for the West Bank and Gaza Strip, which were to become the basis for a Palestinian state.

The first two provisions were implemented routinely. The Israelis withdrew from Sinai in two steps in 1979 and 1982, returning control (including control of an oil-producing capability developed by Israel during its occupation) to the Egyptians. The peace treaty between the two countries was signed in 1979, beginning the process leading to normal relations between them. Egypt got back the territory it wanted, and Israel got the recognition it desired.

The agreement foundered on the Palestinian question. The fate of the Palestinian state was much more complex and contentious than the other two issues, and thus it was deferred. The disposition of Jerusalem, a question that was and remains contentious, symbolizes this dispute. The problem is that both sides claimed (and continue to claim) the Old City (East) Jerusalem as their capitals, and there are numerous religious shrines that neither religious group is willing to entrust control over to the other side. The issue was thus intractable and effectively too difficult to resolve, so it was left unresolved for future negotiators. Carter explained the situation in a *New York Times* op-ed piece shortly after the conclusion of the negotiations: "We knew that Israel had declared sovereignty over the entire city but that the international community considered East Jerusalem to be legally part of the occupied West Bank. We realized that no Israeli leader could renounce Israel's position, and that it would be politically suicidal for Sadat or any other Arab leader to surrender any of their peoples' claims regarding the Islamic and Christian holy places." The fate of Jerusalem has remained a major sticking point in the process. At Camp David I, it was deferred for the future.

Camp David II

The peace process evolved between 1978 and the second Camp David summit in 2000. The most prominent example was the peace accord between Israel and Jordan signed in 1994. There was progress on some aspects of the relationship between Israel and its neighbors, but reaching a mutually satisfactory understanding and progress on the question of the Palestinians remained elusive.

The first Camp David Accord had promised a movement toward Palestinian "autonomy," but there was disagreement about exactly what autonomy implied. In the eyes of most of the Muslim world and among Palestinians themselves, autonomy over specific parts of the occupied territory was part of a process leading to full Palestinian control and sovereignty over the West

Bank and Gaza and, eventually, to the establishment of a Palestinian state. To many in Israel, autonomy certainly meant turning over various local governmental functions to the Palestinian Authority (PA), but not necessarily total authority and not necessarily entailing a commitment to a sovereign Palestinian state. Most Muslim states saw this Israeli interpretation of Camp David I as simply further evidence of Israeli duplicity and intransigence.

A major breakthrough appeared to occur in 1993, when representatives of Palestine and Israel met secretly in Oslo, Norway, at the invitation of the Norwegian government. At those meetings, the parties agreed to what became known as the Oslo framework as a way to move talks forward. The Palestinian Liberation Organization (PLO) represented the Palestinians and agreed to end its call for the destruction of Israel and to renounce terrorism. In return, the Israelis agreed to withdraw their authority from Gaza and the West Bank city of Jericho and turn that authority over to the Palestinians. A deadline was also set for a final agreement to all issues by September 12, 2000.

Like Camp David I, progress toward fulfilling the promises of the Oslo accord lagged behind expectations. Violence continued on both sides, in the form of the first *intifada* by Palestinians and in isolated acts such as the assassination of Israeli Prime Minister Yitzhak Rabin by an Israeli extremist in 1995 and an attack against a Jerusalem mosque that left over 25 dead. At the same time, each side accused the other of not living up to its side of the Oslo accords. The Israelis accused the PLO of failing to renounce violence and terrorism and used Palestinian suicide terrorist attacks as evidence. The Palestinians countered that the Israelis were not living up to the agreements they had made for turning over jurisdiction to the PA.

With the September 2000 deadline looming and the end of his second term impending, American president William J. Clinton sought to revive the peace process in July 2000 by inviting Yasser Arafat, head of the PA, and Israeli prime minister Ehud Barak for a reprise of the 1978 meeting at Camp David. His hope was to achieve a comprehensive peace agreement that would simultaneously end the world's most intractable conflict and provide a pinnacle to his own term in office. Because of what proved to be irresolvable differences, the process ultimately failed.

By the time Clinton convened the parties at Camp David II, there were four major outstanding issues facing the conferees. They are presented here from easiest to most difficult to resolve.

The largest and most public issue was the pace and extent of transfer of the West Bank and Gaza from Israel to the PA. Both sides had their own, very different timetables and formulas; as might be guessed, the Palestinians consistently insisted that more territory be transferred more quickly than Israel proposed. Israeli settlements in both Gaza and the West Bank exacerbated and, in the case of the West Bank, continue to exacerbate the problem. These housing areas had been built after the 1967 occupation to accommodate the immigration of more settlers to Israel and were permanent enough in appearance to suggest that Israel would not turn them over to the Palestinians, although they were on land claimed as part of Palestine. Moreover, the Israelis placed the settlements on prime territory (for instance, where there was access to water, a scarce commodity), and the settlers stubbornly insisted that these settlements were permanent. These settlers, who feared being abandoned by Israel to what they assumed would be the not-so-tender care of the PA, became a highly emotional, vocal factor in Israeli politics; to many Israelis, abandoning the settlements and the settlers became equated with capitulating to the Palestinians. For some Israelis, permanent possession of the settlements and thus the West Bank is part of their plan for a "Greater Israel." The settlement problem now occupies center stage in the ongoing process.

The size and location of the settlements adds to the problem. Jeffrey Goldberg, for instance, reports that the settlers numbered about 400,000 in 2008, a little less than 10 percent of Israel's population, and were concentrated in more or less equal numbers on the West Bank and in the eastern suburbs of Jerusalem. Tiebel, for instance, asserts that "today, nearly 200,000 Israelis live in Jewish neighborhoods in East Jerusalem" that are claimed by Palestinians. Their continued existence, Goldberg maintains, is toxic: "These settlements have undermined Israel's international legitimacy and demoralized moderate Palestinians. The settlements exist far outside the Israeli political consensus, and their presence will likely incite a third *intifada*. Yet the country seems unable to confront the settlements."

Harry Siegman, former executive director of the American Jewish Council and of the Synagogue Council of America, agrees about the corrosive effects of the settlements: "No government serious about a two-state solution to the conflict would have pursued, without letup, the theft and fragmentation of Palestinian lands, which even a child understands makes Palestinian statehood impossible." Regarding apparent international indifference to the growth of these settlements, he adds, "What is astounding is that the international community, pretending to believe Israel's claim that it is the victim and its occupied subjects the aggressors, has allowed this devastating dispossession to continue." Kodmani reinforces this view: "Settlements and bypass roads amount to daily aggression, daily confidence-destroying measures, inflicted on Palestinians."

The settlement issue remains a central barrier to progress today. In November 2009, the Netanyahu government announced a freeze on new construction on the West Bank—largely at the insistence of the Obama administration—but in January 2010, Eldar reported that "dozens of settlements are experiencing a building boom" in apparent defiance of the Israeli self-proclaimed moratorium.

The second issue was the timing of the declaration of Palestinian sovereignty and total independence. The issue was, of course, related to land transfer by the question of sovereignty over what territory would become part of Palestine. This issue thus could be divided into two questions, on neither of which was there agreement: (1) *when* the transfer of authority would take place, and (2) *the physical extent* of the territory that would be ceded.

To Arafat, the answer to the first question was the deadline set under the Oslo accords, and he proposed that the declaration of the Palestinian state should occur on September 12, 2000, as set at Oslo, and threatened to do so unilaterally if the conference at Camp David failed to reach an agreement. Barak, reflecting Israeli popular sentiment, believed the date should be deferred to when the PA had clearly put an end to terrorism against Israel by Palestinians (a position supported by Israelis who opposed any Palestinian independence).

The other question was the physical extent of the Palestinian state that would be created. At the time of Camp David II, the PA administered about 40 percent of the West Bank, and the question was regarding how much more territory (in addition to Gaza) would be added. As one would expect, the two sides were also divided on this issue, with Israel proposing less expansion than the Palestinians, who wanted the whole West Bank (the entire occupied territory). Such a division would deprive the Israelis of all the settlements they had built and was thus politically unacceptable in Israel. In the end, the two sides agreed that 95 percent of the West Bank would be ceded to Palestine, leaving the Israelis in control only of a few settlements basically contiguous to Israeli territory. Arafat eventually rejected this concession as part of rejecting the entire peace settlement.

Something like a compromise was possible in principle on the first two issues, but the same was not true of the third and fourth issues. The third was the question of East Jerusalem. As Jimmy Carter had noted over two decades earlier, the problem of who would control Jerusalem (or specific parts of it) had been a deal stopper that had been simply shelved in 1978, and no progress toward accommodation had ensued in the interim. The only difference now was that the eventual status of Jerusalem became an open matter of contention, and without a resolution to its status, an overall peace settlement could not be reached in 2000.

The issue itself had not changed. Both Israel and Palestine claim the city as their own, and Israel claims the entire city as its capital, whereas the Palestinians claim the Old City (East Jerusalem) as their capital. The positions are mutually exclusive, which means an agreement can be reached only if one or both sides agree to compromise.

Compromise, of course, is made all the more difficult because of the religious significance of Jerusalem to adherents both of Judaism and Islam (as well as Christianity). Access to the holiest sites (the Wailing Wall and the Little Wall to Jews and the Temple Mount to Muslims) is a *sine qua non* to both, but the physical contiguity of the sites makes the division of jurisdiction difficult or impossible. Because both Muslims and Jews have been denied access when the area has been controlled by the other, there is an understandable reluctance to cede control in any manner.

In the end, the impasse could not be overcome. The status of Jerusalem was not resolved, because the position of each side is absolute (both sides claim sovereignty) and a history of animosity and treachery does not allow them to reach compromise solutions in which trust must inevitably play a part. This intractability is also built into the fourth and most irresolvable issue, repatriation.

The issue underlying repatriation (or what Palestinians call the "right to return") is conceptually simple, if extremely difficult to resolve. Palestinians who fled their homes in what is now Israel or were otherwise displaced from such home sites have never given up their belief that they are entitled to return and reclaim those pieces of real estate. Thus, they cling tenaciously to their supposed right to return to their homes. Israelis, who have since resettled and developed the land claimed by the Palestinians, equally believe they now hold clear legal title and that the Palestinian "right" to repatriation is not a right at all.

The issue is both geopolitical and political. The number of Palestinian expatriates who claim territory in Israel, when combined with the million or so Palestinian Muslims who reside in Israel (about one-fifth of Israel's population) and consider themselves "Palestinian citizens of Israel, not Israelis," according to Gorenberg, would equal or exceed the Jewish population of the country. Thus, allowing the immigration of the Palestinians back to Israel/Palestine would effectively mean Israel would no longer be a Jewish state. Even though there are many Israelis who oppose the idea of a sectarian Jewish state, very few believe Jews should not be the majority in Israel. In addition, the return of the Palestinians would essentially double the population of the country, and it is not clear how such an influx could be physically accommodated. The same demographics result if a binational state (one state housing Israelis and Palestinians) is the final outcome of the dispute. The problem is discussed in some detail in Snow, *Cases in American Foreign Policy*.

These geopolitical facts frame the political dilemma: The question of repatriation is fundamental, absolute, and nonnegotiable on both sides. No Israeli government could even consider repatriation because of the effects on the Jewish state and on individual Israelis who would suddenly find themselves in legal battles over their homes from former Palestinian owners. Equally, no Palestinian politician can possibly renounce or negotiate away the right of the Palestinian refugees to return to what they view as their homes. The immediate prospects of return may be exceedingly dim, but the long-term goal is so strongly held as to be nonnegotiable.

Beyond Camp David: The Road Map

After the Camp David II talks collapsed without a final resolution, Palestinian violence returned in late 2000 in the form of the second *intifada* that has included Palestinian suicide/martyr bombings and reprisals by the Israeli Defense Forces (IDF). In February 2001, the Israelis elected a government that made Ariel Sharon prime minister, and he quickly visited the Wailing Wall, sparking predictable violence by the Palestinians. In addition, his government renounced the Camp David II proposals, a spokesman declaring "everything in Camp David is null and void unless it was signed, and nothing was signed." The government also took a hard line on remaining issues. Sharon backed away from Barak's offer of a Palestinian state composed of 95 percent of the West Bank, saying such a state would be based on the 42 percent of the territory administered at the time by the PA. In secret negotiating sessions held in 2007–2008, Yaari reports that the prime minister of Israel at the time, Ehud Olmert, reversed Sharon's course and "offered [PA President Mohammad] Abbas more territory than Ehud Barak had offered Arafat in 2000," but the offer was declined. On Jerusalem, Sharon declared the Old City is "the united and indivisible capital of Israel—with the Temple Mount as its center—for all eternity." On repatriation, he announced the renewal of the Zionist goal of Jewish immigration to Israel, which physically precludes the return of the Palestinians. None of these positions, of course, was or is acceptable to the

Palestinians. At a tree-planting ceremony in early 2010, Kershner quotes Netanyahu as reiterating the hardline Israeli position on these issues: "Our message is clear. We are planting here, we will stay here, this place is an inseparable part of the state of Israel for eternity."

The Bush administration made its contribution to the peace process in 2003, when it announced its "road map" for achieving peace, a set of guidelines to measure progress toward settlement. The road map proposed three sequential steps toward peace. In step one (2003), the Palestinians were to put an end to terrorism by Palestinians operating from Palestinian soil, and the Israelis were to suspend the building of new settlements on the West Bank and Gaza. In step two (2004), a provisional Palestinian government was to be established. In step three (2005), all "remaining differences" were to be settled and a Palestinian state was to be established.

THE CURRENT IMPASSE

The road map failed to move the parties on any of the major issues. Between 2000 and 2004 there were no major changes in the conflict, but four sequential factors have coalesced that could influence the future. The first was the erection of a fence dividing Israel from the West Bank, which began in 2004 and continues to the present. Depending on how it is completed, it could seal off the West Bank, both physically and psychologically, from pre-1967 Israel. Second, in 2005, the government of Ariel Sharon agreed to and carried out the end of the occupation of Gaza, thereby moving the territorial possibilities forward. In 2006, the dynamics changed as governments changed on both sides. Most dramatically, in January, the Palestinians elected a majority of members of Hamas to the Palestinian Legislative Council. When Ariel Sharon was forced to resign his position as prime minister after a massive stroke left him incapable of remaining in office, new Israeli elections in April resulted in the election of Olmert as his successor. Olmert was succeeded in 2009 by Netanyahu after alleged scandals essentially drove him from office. Fourth, the outcome of the Israeli invasion of Lebanon in summer 2006 clouds the military balance in the region. Do these changes make a difference?

"The Fence," as it is simply known in the region, is a physical barrier gradually separating all of the West Bank from Israel proper. The Israelis erected a similar fence between its territory and Gaza in 1994. As David Makovsky explains, "since early 2001, not a single Palestinian suicide bomber has infiltrated Israel from Gaza." The Gaza fence thus serves as a precedent for building the similar West Bank structure dividing the West Bank from Israel proper. Moreover, Makovsky argues that the fence serves the Israeli interests "to reduce terrorism and to find a way out of the settlement morass that lets Israel keep a Jewish majority within its borders." In addition, Yaari argues that the fence creates a psychological barrier that allows Israelis to avoid thinking about the personal impact of the occupation on Palestinians.

The fence has been loudly, and occasionally violently, opposed by the Palestinians on grounds as diverse as cutting through Palestinian territory to preventing (or making exceedingly difficult) Palestinian commuting to jobs in Israel. At the same time, an effective fence is bound to assuage Israeli fears of continued terrorism and thus relieve that barrier to creating a Palestinian state. By now, the fact of the fence is well enough established that its existence is not so much the issue as *where* it is placed, as it may form a boundary between Israel and a Palestinian state.

The most fundamental change has occurred in Palestine, where the January 2006 elections swept Arafat's Fatah party from control of the Palestinian Legislative Council, replacing it with a militant government led by Hamas. Hamas has a dual image as being both a scrupulously honest political movement (in contrast to the notoriously corrupt Fatah) as well as a continuing commitment to violence (including terrorism) and the destruction of the Israeli state. Its election resulted in international isolation (especially from outside assistance) for Palestine as a means to try to force Hamas to moderate its stance, especially on terrorism and the future existence of Israel. The ascension of Hamas, however, creates "a momentous experiment—the results of which will have a major impact on the future of Palestine, Israel, and the Middle East at large," according to Michael Hertzog (the son of Israeli military hero Chaim Hertzog). Having Hamas in control of Gaza and Fatah in control of the West Bank does not, however, create an opportunity for Israel to split the two apart in negotiations, because, as Kodmani asserts, "Gaza cannot be dealt with separately from the West Bank, just as a peace agreement cannot be reached with the West Bank alone."

The impact of Israel's failed attempt to destroy Hezbollah in Lebanon is related. It changes the military factor in two ways. First, as Salem argues, it punctures "the aura of invincibility long projected by the Israeli defence forces." Second, it makes the prospect of a forced resolution less plausible. As Djerejian argues, the "confrontation has further proved what should have been painfully clear to all: there is no viable military solution to the Arab-Israeli conflicts."

The Israeli situation has changed as well. Before his second stroke, Sharon was instrumental in the creation of the Kadima Party, which emerged as the major alternative to the current Netanyahu-led coalition that has ruled since the fall of Olmert. Netanyahu remains in control of a razor-thin majority in the Knesset (the Israeli parliament), although his hold on power was lessened in the Israeli elections in 2013, which may force him into coalition with more moderate Israeli parties.

The same issues that divided the two sides in 2000 remain. Under the stewardship of Netanyahu, the central settlement issue has arguably hardened, and the sincerity or likelihood of Israeli abandonment of the settlements seems increasingly suspect to many. The number of settlements and settlers continues to grow to the point where their permanence seems the clear intent of the Israeli government. Moreover, the spread of the settlements is rapidly changing the geography of the West Bank in ways unfavorable to the Palestinians. Friedman describes the conditions in June 2008: "The West Bank today is an ugly quilt of high walls, Israeli checkpoints, 'legal' and 'illegal' Jewish settlements, Arab villages, Jewish roads that only Jewish settlers use, Arab roads and roadblocks."

CONCLUSION

The Middle Eastern dispute has remained irresolvable despite nearly 30 years of negotiations in which the United States has taken an active lead. Some progress has been made along the way, including the narrowing of the dispute to its current status as an Israeli–Palestinian conflict and the narrowing of the unresolved—and to this point unresolvable—issues of the size and shape of Palestine (of which Israeli settlements on the West Bank are the clearest manifestation); Jerusalem; and the right of return. Each of these issues remains a deep and, to this point, irresolvable area of contention.

The central issue about a Palestinian state is what kind of state it will be (or if it will come into existence). There are three possibilities. None of the possibilities is acceptable to all parties, and all parties arguably suffer from whichever of the three ultimately adheres. The failure to solve the underlying source of disagreement, notably the continued population of the West Bank by Israelis, prejudices the process and its outcomes.

The first possible outcome is a continuation of the status quo of Israeli occupation of the West Bank. Many Israelis, and especially Netanyahu and his supporters, at least implicitly, endorse this outcome. From their viewpoint, a continued occupation allows further settlement and thus the pursuit of the Greater Israel goal of bringing a maximum part of Jewry to Israel by providing a place for these immigrants to live (a large portion of the current settlers are immigrants). Further, this policy, especially combined with the fence's forceful separation of the Palestinians from access to Israel, is popular with a not insignificant part of the Israeli electorate—notably the right. The disadvantages, of course, are that this outcome is totally unacceptable to the Palestinians, thereby ensuring their continued militant opposition, and brands Israel as an international "criminal," as settlement of occupied territory is a violation of international law.

The second possible solution is the two-state settlement, wherein an independent state of Palestine is established on the current occupied land on the West Bank (or at least most of it) and in Gaza. This solution has been the historic preference of the outside world, is favored by the Obama administration, and has support of the Israeli left. Hardline Israelis have always opposed a fully sovereign Palestinian state on the grounds it would be a legally protected source of terrorist violence against Israel. There are, in addition, indications that the Palestinians may not really support this outcome either. As Yaari explains, "Many Palestinians now feel that by denying Israel an 'end of conflict, end of claims' deal, they are increasing their chances of gaining a state for which they would not be required to make political concessions." The reasoning is that the two-state solution offers only a partial recovery of Arab lands seized by the Israelis, when the real desire is for a return of *all* Palestinian lands (the issue of right of return).

The third possibility is a single Israeli/Palestinian state encompassing both pre-1967 Israel and the West Bank and Gaza, which might fulfill the Palestinian dream. Demographically, such a state would have a majority of Palestinian Muslims in the near future, meaning it could remain a Jewish state (or Jewish-dominated state) only by becoming what former U.S. President Jimmy Carter referred to as an "apartheid" state wherein the Israeli minority would have full political rights that would be denied to the Palestinian majority. A democratic (one-man one-vote) state would be dominated by the Palestinians, which is the ultimate Israeli nightmare.

The ongoing impasse prejudices these options as realistic alternatives. The most notable example is the continuation (and especially expansion) of the settlements on the West Bank and the two-state solution. Given the sheer volume of Israelis now living in the occupied territories, it may already be impossible to implement a two-state outcome simply because of their presence: No Israeli government is likely to try to remove all of them (where they would put them is a virtually insurmountable problem), and such an action would ignite a domestic firestorm against any Israeli government that attempted it. At the same time, the continued presence of the settlers relieves the Palestinians of any need to push for a West Bank/Gaza state that many apparently privately oppose, because a continued Israeli presence would be intolerable in such an entity. Effectively, this may mean the two-state solution is already effectively off the table, leaving the unpalatable options of the status quo or a unified state.

The settlements issue remains the most prominent face of continued intractability in the peace process. In late 2009, the Israelis instituted a moratorium on new construction in the disputed territories (while allowing continued construction of dwellings already begun) for 10 months, and the result was a flurry of peace negotiations in September 2010, notably a Washington meeting between Palestinian leader Mohammed Abbas and Netanyahu sponsored by President Obama that temporarily rekindled hope for progress. The moratorium expired on October 1, 2010, however, and building resumed on the West Bank, effectively dampening hopes for peace again. As long as this impasse continues, however, the settlements issue will continue to preclude any real progress toward peace.

The settlements issue frustrates any peace process. President Obama, now in his second term, favors a two-state solution and is more free to pursue it then before his reelection, when he had to worry about the possible electoral consequences of defying pro-Netanyahu American Jews. Whether that freedom will matter crucially is anyone's guess. President Abbas managed to get a vote of recognition of the Palestinians and their state aspiration in the UN General Assembly in 2012, but the practical effect of that action (which was opposed by the United States) remains negligible on the peace process.

The Jerusalem and repatriation issues are both either/or propositions with little leeway for compromise, but an outcome on each is necessary for any overall settlement. Both also meet the criteria for irresolvable conflicts: They are territorial; they are based on mutually exclusive perceptions of outcomes; they are deeply held and emotional; the positions held on both sides do not facilitate compromise; outside efforts at mediation have failed to remove the issues; and unilateral solutions are unacceptable internationally.

Of the two issues, Jerusalem is—at least in principle—resolvable. A formula for dividing physical sovereignty over parts of Jerusalem is conceptually possible, if both sides find ways to lower the emotional trappings of devotion to their religious shrines and the question of what parts of the city might be the capital of each state. Some resolution is critical, because as Palestinian negotiator Ahmed Qurei put it in June 2008, "If there is no Jerusalem there is no agreement," as quoted in Kershner.

Repatriation, the right of return, is another matter. Palestinians either have or do not have a right to return to their former homes, and Israelis either do or do not have a legal or moral imperative to accommodate the Palestinians. The only possible forms of compromise are possible to state, but not to implement. One solution is deferment of the problem, which is the de facto current nonsolution. Under this arrangement, neither side must compromise, but the implementation of the outcome is put off to a future time. This solution simply puts off the problem. The other solution is to allow *some,* but not all Palestinians to return. Such a solution eliminates the outcome of a non-Jewish state of Israel, but leaves for future resolution *who* gets to return and *which* Israelis have to forfeit their property. It is hard to imagine how that can be done, but until it is, the Israeli–Palestinian conflict remains a classic example of an irresolvable conflict.

SUGGESTED ACTIVITIES AND QUESTIONS

1. What is an irresolvable conflict? What distinguishes such a conflict from differences that can be resolved?
2. What are the characteristics of an irresolvable conflict? How do they build on and reinforce one another?
3. In terms of the six characteristics of an irresolvable conflict, assess the Israeli–Palestinian conflict.
4. Discuss the basic dynamics of the Israeli–Palestinian conflict. How did it come about? How did it evolve between 1948 and the beginning of the peace process in 1978? Why are the Six-Day and Yom Kippur Wars so important in that evolution?
5. What have been the steps in the peace process between the Israelis and Palestinians? Discuss each step in terms of accomplishments and failures.
6. What basic issues continue to divide the two parties? Rate and discuss each in terms of intractability and thus its contribution to the inability to resolve the conflict.
7. What is the current status of the conflict? What recent events have occurred that might affect the dynamics? What might their effects be?
8. Is there realistic hope for a resolution of the Israeli–Palestinian conflict? What forms could such a resolution take? Assess each.

SUGGESTED READINGS AND RESOURCES

Bronner, Ethan. "Carter Says Hamas and Syria Are Open to Peace." *New York Times* (online), April 22, 2008.

Brown, Nathan J. "The Palestinians' Receding Dream of Statehood." *Current History* 110, 740 (December 2011), 345–351.

Carter, Jimmy. "A Jerusalem Settlement Everyone Can Live With." *New York Times* (online), August 6, 2000.

———. *Palestine: Peace Not Apartheid.* New York: Simon and Schuster, 2006.

———. "Palestine: Peace Not Apartheid. Jimmy Carter in His Own Words." *Democracy Now* (online), November 30, 2006.

Djerejian, Edward P. "From Conflict Management to Conflict Resolution." *Foreign Affairs* 85, 6 (November/December 2006), 41–48.

Eldar, Akiva. "Construction in West Bank Settlements Booming Despite Declared Freeze." *Haaretz.com* (online), January 1, 2010.

Friedman, Thomas L. "U.S. Must Shake Up Peace Process to Have Any Hope of Success." *Island Packet*, June 8, 2008, A16 (reprinted from *New York Times,* June 7, 2008).

Goldberg, Jeffrey. "Unforgiven." *The Atlantic* 208, 4 (May/June 2008), 32–52.

Gorenberg, Gershom. "Think Again: Israel." *Foreign Policy*, May/June 2008, 26–32.

_____. *The Accidental Empire: Israel and the Birth of the Settlements: 1967–1977.* New York: Times Books, 2006.

Haas, Richard N. "The New Middle East." *Foreign Affairs* 85, 6 (November/December 2006), 2–11.

Hertzog, Michael. "Can Hamas Be Tamed?" *Foreign Affairs* 85, 2 (March/April 2006), 83–94.

Kershner, Isabel. "Netanyahu Says Some Settlements to Stay in Israel." *New York Times* (online), January 25, 2010.

Khalidi, Rashid. "Palestine: Liberation Deferred." *The Nation* 286, 20 (March 20, 2008), 16–20.

Kodmani, Bassma. "Clearing the Air in the Middle East." *Current History* 107, 709 (May 2008), 201–206.

Makovsky, David. "How to Build a Fence." *Foreign Affairs* 85, 2 (March/April 2006), 50–64.

Ottaway, Marina S. "Promoting Democracy After Hamas' Victory." Washington, DC: Carnegie Endowment for International Peace, March 2006.

Robinson, Glenn E. "The Fragmentation of Palestine." *Current History* 106, 704 (December 2007), 421–426.

Rubin, Barry. "Israel's New Strategy." *Foreign Affairs* 85, 4 (July/August 2006), 111–125.

Sadat, Anwar. *In Search of an Identity: An Autobiography.* New York: Harper and Row, 1978.

Salem, Paul. "The Future of Lebanon." *Foreign Affairs* 85, 6 (November/December 2006), 13–22.

Sharon, Ariel, quoted in Brownfeld, Allen C. "The Growing Danger of Transforming the Palestinian-Israeli Conflict into a Jewish-Muslim Religious War." *Washington Report on Middle East Affairs,* April 2001, p. 79.

Shlaim, Avi. "A Somber Anniversary." *The Nation* 286, 20 (March 20, 2008), 11–16.

Siegman, Henry. "Tough Love for Israel." *The Nation* 286, 27 (May 5, 2008), 7–8.

Snow, Donald M. *Cases in American Foreign Policy.* New York: Pearson, 2013.

Tiebel, Amy. "Netanyahu Stakes Claim to West Bank Settlement." *My Way* (online), January 24, 2010.

Waxman, Dov. "Between Victory and Defeat: Israel After the War with Hizballah." *Washington Quarterly* 30, 1 (Winter 2006–2007), 27–42.

Weymouth, Lally. "We Are Ready for Change." *Newsweek*, April 17, 2006, 34.

Witte, Griff. "Carter: Hamas Ready to Live Beside Israel." *Washington Post*, April 22, 2008, A10.

Yaari, Ehud. "Armistice Now." *Foreign Affairs* 89, 2 (March/April 2010), 50–62.

WEB SITES

UN documents on Palestine question: http://www.un.org/Depts/dpa/qpal
U.S. policy: http://www.state.gov/p/nea
Israeli positions on conflict: http://www.mfa.gov.il
Palestinian positions on conflict: http://minfo.gov.ps

National and International Security

Arguably the most important function that states provide their citizens is physical security against harm from other states or groups (national security), and the security of the entire world (international security) is at least an implied goal of those promoting national security. Security, like any other element of international politics, is a complex and multifaceted problem, and the chapters in Part II attempt to look at four important aspects of that question: the evolution of warfare to a contemporary emphasis on asymmetrical war; the proliferation of weapons of mass destruction, principally nuclear weapons; the problems created by important regional states whose interests come into conflict with those of the leading powers; and the impact of important international phenomena like political revolutions that challenge the existing order. Each problem is viewed through the lens of a contemporary example.

Chapter 5, "Asymmetrical Warfare," looks explicitly at the direction that physical warfare is taking and will likely take in the future. In a world where conventional military power (symmetrical force) is concentrated in the largest countries (notably the United States) but where the disagreements that lead to violence often pit weaker powers against the strongest, the result has been the increasing recourse to unconventional, asymmetrical measures that allow weaker powers to compete with their stronger adversaries. The current best example of asymmetrical warfare is the ongoing war in Afghanistan, which is the subject of Chapter 5.

Chapter 6, "Proliferation," addresses the highly politically explosive problem of the spread of weapons of mass destruction, notably nuclear weapons, to countries that do not currently possess them. The problem of proliferation has been a major concern for nearly a half-century, and the chapter discusses the dynamics of why states seek to gain weapons others do not want them to have and what those who seek to limit proliferation can do to prevent the spread of those weapons. The case of the Democratic People's Republic of Korea (DPRK, or North Korea) is a particularly vivid example of this problem, with major implications for the future.

Chapter 7, "Pivotal States," looks at the impact of prominent regional powers, what are called pivotal states, on regional and international power balances. Pivotal states are countries that are important within their regions of the world, and their interests often clash with the global interests of the largest powers. The problem for the great power is how to gain support for its interests among pivotal states, and the results are not always positive. The case of a nuclear-ambitious Iran in the Persian Gulf region and potentially beyond is a particularly poignant contemporary instance of the role pivotal states play.

Chapter 8, "Revolutionary Change," deals directly with the phenomenon and aftermath of the so-called Arab Spring, a series of uprisings in a number of Middle Eastern states that began in Tunisia and spread more widely through the region. The stated goal of each movement was the overthrow of tyrannical, authoritarian rule and its replacement with popularly based regimes. As the prominent cases of Egypt and Libya clearly indicate, the progress of these "revolutions" has been very difficult.

Asymmetrical Warfare: The Case of Afghanistan

PRÉCIS

Anticipating the nature of future conflict and preparing for that form of combat has always been a primary responsibility for those charged with national and international security. Doing so is always a difficult process involving extrapolation of the past into the future.

Warfare in the twenty-first century, at least as manifested in its first decade, differs significantly from how and why warfare was conducted in the prior century, and those differences extend to the outcomes and expectations that come from war. The dominant characteristic of contemporary warfare is its asymmetrical, or unconventional, nature, and this description is unlikely to change in the near future. This case examines the nature of modern, asymmetrical warfare, applies those characteristics to the war in Afghanistan, and extrapolates those observations into thinking about war in the future.

War is one of humankind's oldest institutions, involving the attempts by groups of people to impose their will on other groups of people by the use of coercive force. Humans have organized in different ways to conduct wars—as ethnic tribes in biblical times, Greek city-states, the Roman Empire against tribal armies to the enormous clashes between coalitions of states locked in the world wars that made the twentieth century humanity's bloodiest epoch. Regardless of the entities that conduct it, warfare has been one of history's constants.

The early twenty-first century is no apparent exception to this historical continuity. In some ways, warfare has changed in the new millennium, but the preparation for and the conduct of war remains an apparently inexorable part of human existence. As a result, thinking about and planning for war always has been, and continues to be, an important endeavor. Warfare in the new century has taken on different characteristics than those that dominated the past 100 years, but the patterns are not historically unfamiliar. War is still war, and it still must be understood.

Gaining such an understanding is, and always has been, a difficult problem. War planning, by definition, is a projection into a future that does not yet exist and that, by definition, cannot be known entirely in advance. Will the same kinds of weapons be available in the future as there were in the past? If there are new weapons, what will they be like, how will they be used, and what will be their effect? Who will have the new weapons, and who will not? How will weapon balances affect patterns of war? For that matter, who will the enemy be? Where will I have to fight the next adversary? What will the enemy be like? How likely am I to succeed?

The answers to any of these questions cannot be known precisely in advance, so uncertainty has always been a major part of the operational universe of the military planner. Uncertainties produce an environment laced as well by an aura of conservatism and seriousness. It is conservative because reckless innovation and lack of preparedness can lead to devastating vulnerabilities. It is serious because the wrong decisions—the failure to prepare properly or adequately—can literally endanger national existence. Because of these potential consequences, there is a built-in propensity to over-prepare—to anticipate more and different threats than realistically exist. Conservatism and the seriousness of mistakes also predispose planners to emphasize ways of doing things that have worked in the past—to stay "inside the box"—rather than to embrace change and its uncertainties. The result is a tendency to prepare "to fight the last (most recently concluded) war."

The problem of gauging the future of war is especially acute today. Since the end of the Cold War, much of the preparation that states have undertaken in planning for war has been an attempt to adapt military planning and practice from its roots in conventional war between large powers to new realities of which the movement toward asymmetrical warfare is the prime example. Will this effort succeed?

It depends. One of the most important aspects of preparing for future war is anticipating against whom one is likely to have to fight. Although many Americans sought to ignore the warning signs during the 1930s, it was pretty clear that World War II would find the United States on one side and countries like Germany and Japan on the other (at least retrospect suggests that structure of the conflict). During the Cold War, it was absolutely clear that the enemy was the Soviet Union and its communist allies. The structure of the situation dictated the content of the planning process.

Not all planning has such a clear focus. In August 1990, Iraq invaded and quickly conquered Kuwait. This act of aggression would ultimately activate a coalition of over 25 states, none of which had given much if any thought to the possibility of war with Iraq as little as a few months before the invasion occurred. The lesson was that some problems can be easily anticipated; others cannot. The largely unanticipated terrorist attacks of September 11, 2001, redouble the point.

The planning process begins by examining how, or if, war is changing. Most of the past century or more was dominated by a style and philosophy of warfare that was heavily Western and that culminated in the way World War II was fought, what is now called symmetrical warfare (both sides fight in the same manner and basically by the same rules). Since early in the post–Cold War world, that has changed. Arguably, warfare is changing fundamentally from the confrontation and clash of mass armies to a more asymmetrical form in which weaker foes seek to negate Western styles with non-Western variants on war in which the two sides are dissimilar in organization and purpose and do not fight while honoring the same rules and conventions. September 11, 2001, may be remembered as the harbinger of this change in the nature of warfare. The effort of the United States and the North Atlantic Treaty Organization (NATO) in Afghanistan may be the precedent for the future.

The problem of preparing for future war boils down to four basic considerations. The first is the conflict environment, and the main factor in that environment is the nature of the adversaries one may encounter in the future, including why and how one may fight them. In the past, war was between the organized armed forces of states. Contemporary conflicts often pit traditional armed forces against so-called nonstate actors, forces with neither territorial base nor governmental affiliation. The second consideration is the physical structure of warfare, which encompasses the means available for adversaries to fight one another and the degree to which the means available are appropriately adapted to achieve military ends. In the contemporary era, the means are widely disparate for different foes, creating the basis for asymmetrical approaches for the disadvantaged. The third concern is determining against whom one might have to fight in an environment that has not witnessed a major war in over 65 years—and where possible enemies are difficult to anticipate in conventional ways. The fourth, and often incompletely considered, factor is the postwar peace: What conditions will be created in the so-called "postconflict environment"? Failure to consider this aspect adequately can result in the so-called "winning the war and losing the peace."

Planning for the wars of the twenty-first century requires applying these criteria to contemporary conflicts and extrapolating into an uncertain future that is unlike the past experience of the twentieth century in several important ways. For one thing, there are no obvious major, conventional adversaries in the system, due in large measure to the ideological harmony among the major powers in the current international system. The answer to the question, "preparing to fight whom?" is especially fraught with uncertainty regarding whom to prepare to fight and how to prepare to fight them. The long gap between major wars has allowed the accumulation of many militarily relevant technologies that have greatly enhanced the conventional capabilities of those who possess them. Some of the electronically based innovations have been employed in "shooting galleries" like the Persian Gulf War and Operation Iraqi Freedom in 2003, and the primary lesson these victims seemed to have learned is not to fight the West (especially the United States) on its terms. The imbalance in symmetrical capabilities has in effect done two things: It has made the development of asymmetrical, technology-negating methods the primary dynamic of the present, and it has arguably rendered symmetrical warfare archaic because no one will fight that way. Finally, fighting against unconventional opponents complicates the task of planning and executing stable postconflict peace arrangements. This is true in part because these wars rarely have decisive "end games" where one side or the other capitulates. The calculation is further muddied by the fact that the real outcome—whose purposes were and were not served by war—is often unknown for some time, often years, after the fighting stops.

The remaining pages of this chapter are devoted to understanding the challenge of asymmetrical warfare to thinking about war—its purposes, its conduct, and its outcomes. It will proceed in two sequential parts. First, it will examine the evolving, often amorphous nature of asymmetrical warfare, the conceptual core of the chapter. Second, it will apply those observations to the international system's most prominent current instance of asymmetrical warfare, the war in Afghanistan. The observations from the general description and Afghan application will then be extrapolated to the problem of war in the future.

ASYMMETRICAL WARFARE: NEW/OLD WAR

Warfare, particularly as it involves major powers like the United States, has changed enormously since the end of the Cold War, for essentially two obvious reasons. The first is the collapse of militarily based major-power rivalry. Unlike the Cold War confrontation between the world's two most militarily powerful countries, such rivalry has receded to economic competition with very little potential to escalate to armed violence. The large, heavy conventional (symmetrical) armed forces and accompanying purposes for war have been made arguably obsolete in the process. Second, the remaining conflicts in the world are mostly developing-world internal conflicts (DWICs), generally in the form of internal conflicts within countries in which the major powers may have an interest. Internal conflicts in the least stable parts of the developing world are largely the result of the breakup of European colonialism, and they have become the major source of military conflict in the contemporary world.

The result is the rising prominence of asymmetrical warfare in the pantheon of modern warfare. Before beginning to explore this phenomenon, however, two preliminary observations are necessary. On one hand, what some have called the "new" way of war is not new at all. Asymmetrical warfare, in its simplest description, features the adaptations an inferior force makes when it is faced with a more powerful force with which it cannot compete successfully on the terms preferred by the superior force. Because this situation has recurred through history, asymmetrical warfare is as old as war itself. Relatedly, asymmetrical warfare is an approach to warfare, not a form of war or combat. Put another way, it is a methodology, a way to organize the problem, not a method or set of battlefield or theater instructions.

For those reasons, planning processes are different than they used to be. The conflict environment and the physical structure of warfare are no longer based on the European model of conflict featuring the clash of similarly organized and equipped mass armed forces. The compositions of likely enemies to be deterred or, if necessary, fought, are more likely to be that of developing-world countries, or even more likely, some subnational group such as insurgent or even terrorist organizations. The nature of stable postconflict environments is much more fluid, indeterminate, and less distinct.

Conflict Environment

Traditional geopolitics has clearly taken a beating since the end of the Cold War. The traditional base—politico-military alliances of states facing one another—has evaporated. The first victim of the end of the Cold War was the structure of adversarial relationships that provided concrete military problems against which to prepare. In some ways, this is a considerable improvement over the past. It means that for now, as noted, there is virtually no likelihood of major war between the most powerful countries of the world on the scale of the world wars. Certainly the tools for such a war are still available, but it is difficult to conjure the circumstances that would ignite such a conflagration. There are a few places in the world, for instance, the Indian subcontinent, where adversaries might become involved in a war of fairly large proportions, but none of those places would raise the distinct likelihood of drawing in other major actors on opposite sides and thus widening the conflict to anything like the scale of World War III (the major planning case of the Cold War).

The conflict environment is thus different in two distinct ways. First, the imbalance in conventional capability between the United States and the rest of the world means no one is likely to confront the United States in large-scale conventional warfare. Those who oppose the United States must devise new ways to do so. As Bruce Berkowitz puts it, "Our adversaries know they cannot match the United States in tanks, planes, and warships. They know they will most likely lose any war with us if they play according to the traditional rules." This innovation is the second new characteristic of the environment: the adoption and adaptation of asymmetrical ways to negate the advantages of overwhelming military capability and the emergence of new categories of opponents, such as nonstate actors. Asymmetrical approaches are intended, in Berkowitz's terms, "to change the rules to strategies and tactics that avoid our strength head-on and instead hit us where we are weak." This problem is progressive, because the core of asymmetrical warfare is constant adaptation, meaning the problem is never exactly the same from instance to instance. Moreover, traditional warfare is directed at state-based political opponents, and it is less clear how one subdues an opponent who lacks such a base.

Asymmetrical warfare is ancient. As Renee de Nevers points out, asymmetrical wars are "perhaps better understood as reversions to very old wars." The Thirty Years' War, for instance, featured marauding bands that would now be called nonstate actors, and the nineteenth-century resistance to colonialism certainly featured highly mismatched forces. It is different in terms of the problems for which it is conducted; how those who carry it out think and act; and in terms of the motives of the asymmetrical warrior. Asymmetrical warfare is not only militarily unconventional but it is also intellectually unconventional.

The United States' first major encounter with asymmetrical warfare was in Vietnam. (The country had previous limited experience in places like the Philippines at the turn of the twentieth century, but on a much smaller scale.) Vietnam mixed symmetrical and asymmetrical characteristics. In terms of its purposes, it was quite conventional: The North Vietnamese and their Viet Cong allies sought to unify Vietnam as a communist country, and the South Vietnamese and the Americans sought to avoid that outcome. In terms of conduct, however, the war was unconventional. The North Vietnamese concluded early in the American phase of the war that they could not compete with the United States in symmetrical warfare because of visibly superior American firepower. Instead, they reverted to tactics of harassment, ambush, and attrition, the purpose of which was to produce sufficient American casualties to convince the American people that the cost of war was not worth the projected benefits. The North Vietnamese could not have succeeded fighting by the American rules. Their only hope was to change the rules and fight in a way that minimized American advantage and gave them a chance. It worked.

The heart of asymmetrical warfare is not a set of tactics or strategies, but instead is a mindset. The potential asymmetrical warrior always begins from a position of military inferiority, and the problem, as Berkowitz points out, is how to negate that disadvantage. Adaptability is at the heart of asymmetrical approaches to warfare. If one asymmetrical tactic does not work, try another. Vietnam was a primer for those who may want to confront American power, but an organization like Al Qaeda or the Taliban could not succeed simply by adopting Vietnamese methods (for one thing, there are no mountainous jungles into which to retreat after engagements). Instead, the asymmetrical warrior learns from what works and discards what does not. Iraq is a case in point.

In 1990–1991, Iraq attempted to confront the United States conventionally in Kuwait and was crushed for its effort. It learned from this experience that a future conflict with the United States, the prospects of which Iraq faced after September 11, 2001, could not be conducted in the same manner as before without equally devastating results, which included the decimation of Iraqi armed forces.

What to do? The answer, largely unanticipated by the United States, was to offer only enough resistance to American symmetrical force application to make the Americans think they were prevailing, while regrouping to resist an occupation that they were powerless to prevent except in other, asymmetrical ways. Thus, the limited form of irregular warfare (ambushes, car bombings, and suicide terror attacks) became the primary method of resisting the Americans, apparently aimed at the same goal the Vietnamese attained 30 years earlier— convincing the Americans that the costs of occupation were not worth the costs in lives lost and treasure expended.

Whether this was some carefully modulated plan formulated in advance of the invasion by the Iraqis or not is not the point (and it is a point for which adequate evidence is not available anyway). What is hardly arguable is that the United States underestimated the likelihood of such an asymmetrical response in planning the invasion in the first place. In postinvasion analysis, the argument is frequently made that American planning was flawed in, among other ways, its failure to allocate sufficient troops to the effort. The criticism is valid but somewhat misses the point. The troop numbers were clearly adequate for a symmetrical invasion and conquest, which is all that was anticipated. The troop levels were inadequate for a protracted resistance to occupation, which was an asymmetrical response that was not anticipated.

Physical Structure of Warfare

The major certainty about future warfare involving asymmetrical methods is that its face is uncertain. Part of the reason is that a primary characteristic of future conflict is that it is itself changing. Vietnam was a prototype, but the experience in Vietnam became the baseline from which others would adapt, changing the problem each time it was applied. Similarly, the next asymmetrical challenge will incorporate elements of Iraq and Afghanistan, but it will not be identical to either of them. Preparing for the next war has become very perilous. Past experience provides the baseline for new asymmetrical applications, and the side that prevails is likely to be the one that correctly determines the necessary adaptations and prepares either to apply or to counter them.

The problem is finding a conceptual frame for organizing considering the permutation of future asymmetrical situations. Writing in 1995, the then–U.S. Army Chief of Staff Gordon Sullivan and Anthony M. Coroalles analogized the problem to "seeing the elephant," a phrase borrowed from the American Civil War (the idea of describing what combat was like from others' descriptions—like having an elephant described). They wrote, "Our elephant is the complexity, ambiguity, and uncertainty of tomorrow's battlefield. We are trying to see the elephant of the future. But trying to draw that metaphorical elephant is infinitely harder than drawing a real one. We don't know what we don't know; none of us has a clear view of what the elephant will look like this time around."

Modern asymmetrical warfare is today's elephant. As a U.S. Marines officer in Iraq has been quoted as saying: "The enemy has gone asymmetric on us. There's treachery. There are ambushes. It's not straight-up conventional fighting." In other words, it does not conform to the accepted rules of symmetrical warfare for which the U.S. Marines had prepared themselves.

In trying to determine the changing shape of the new elephant of asymmetrical warfare, one can begin by looking at predictable problems that asymmetrical warrior will present in the future. With no pretense of being exhaustive, at least five stand out.

First, political and military aspects of these conflicts will continue to merge, and distinctions between military and civilian targets and assets will continue to dissolve. The asymmetrical warrior will continue to muddy the distinction for two reasons. One is that he is likely to see conflicts as pitting societies against societies, so there is no meaningful distinction between combatants and noncombatants, whereas traditional symmetrical warfare draws sharp distinctions between those who fight and those who do not, including prohibitions against attacking noncombatants. The other reason is that imbedding conflict within the fabric of society removes some of the advantage of the symmetrical warrior. Urban warfare, for instance, can only be waged symmetrically by concentrating firepower intensity on areas where civilians and opponents are intermingled, where traditional rules of war prohibit actions aimed at civilians, thereby inhibiting some actions. The asymmetrical warrior likely rejects these distinctions, leaving him free either to attack or fight among civilians.

Second, the opposition in these kinds of conflicts often consists of nonstate actors acting out of nonstate motivations and without state bases of operation. International terrorist organizations, for instance, often carry out operations that cannot be tied to any state, and are not clearly based in any state. This creates a problem of response for the symmetrical warrior. Whom does he go after? Whom does he attack and punish? If the asymmetrical warrior remains in the shadows (or mountains or desert) and the government plausibly denies affiliation or association, then the lever of using force against the opponent's base is weakened. This is a major problem the United States has faced in dealing with Al Qaeda in Pakistan and elsewhere.

Third, the opposition posed by asymmetrical warriors will almost certainly be protracted, even if the tempo and intensity of opposition varies greatly from situation to situation. The reason for protraction flows from the weakness of the asymmetrical warrior compared to his symmetrical foe. Because direct confrontation is suicidal, the alternative is patient, measured application of force not designed to destroy the enemy, but instead to drag out the conflict, testing the will and patience of the opponent. The United States first saw this dynamic in Vietnam, saw it reprised in Iraq, and most recently encountered it in Afghanistan. The antidote is recognition of the tactic and a considerable degree of patience, generally not the long suit of the United States or other political democracies.

Fourth, these conflicts will often occur in the most fractured, failed states, where conditions are ripe for people to engage in acts of desperation that include actions like suicide bombing. Where high desperation and deprivation exist, the systemic obstacles will be extraordinarily difficult to address and solve. The problem is recognizing the multifaceted nature of the wants and needs of the people. The difficulty in rectifying these situations is having the patience and level of physical (including financial) commitment to remove the festering problems that give rise to violence in the first place. As of 2010, the United States, according to Haass, had invested about 1 trillion dollars in directly accountable costs in Iraq, but hardly any resources to helping build a stable Iraqi state, a goal that remains elusive. Studies in 2013 from Harvard and Brown Universities estimated the total, including long-term, costs of American involvement in Iraq and Afghanistan at 4 to 6 *trillion* dollars.

Fifth, asymmetrical warfare will change in the future. The problem of Iraq was more than overcoming the Iraqi resistance, it was a matter of defeating and discrediting its methods, so it would not form the basis for the opposition of others in the future. From the vantage point of potential asymmetrical warriors, the Iraqi resistance had already succeeded enough that parts of it will be imitated. Can anyone doubt the next asymmetrical warriors will come armed with improvised explosive devices (IEDs) to be detonated against symmetrical opponents?

This aspect of the problem, of course, flows from the observation that symmetrical warfare is more an approach (or methodology) than a game plan or set of actions to be taken (a method). The trick is figuring what else will be learned from the experience to be countered and what new and unique elements will be added.

Determining Opponents

Virtually by definition, asymmetrical warfare will take on a variety of forms and be conducted by a variety of opponents in the future. Some variant will occur whenever a technologically inferior force confronts an opponent so superior that it cannot be confronted directly. Although the precise nature of future asymmetrical opponents is impossible to predict with great confidence, this section will look at two current variants as examples of plausible futures. One is hybrid symmetrical–asymmetrical conflicts, of which Afghanistan is a prime example. The other example is internal wars involving factions within a state that are only partially military—or quasi-military—in nature. Each poses a different planning problem. Hybrids are likely to be confused as symmetrical wars, and quasi-military situations are likely to be overly militarized. Both provide harbingers for the future.

Hybrid Symmetrical–Asymmetrical War. One of the most difficult aspects of dealing with asymmetrical war situations is recognizing them for what they are. The United States faced this recognition problem in Vietnam in the 1960s and concluded, after the first major encounter between American and North Vietnamese regulars in the Ia Drang Valley, that the war was conventional, a symmetrical conflict between two similar foes that could be prosecuted in a conventional manner.

The problem was that the strategy of the Vietnamese contained both symmetrical and asymmetrical elements. After the battle of Ia Drang, the North Vietnamese concluded they could not match American firepower and switched their method to guerrilla-style combat, one of the classic forms of asymmetrical warfare. Their purpose was to harass and drain the Americans sufficiently to cause them to give up the fight as unwinnable at an acceptable cost. After the United States abandoned the war, they returned to conventional, symmetrical warfare against a South Vietnamese opponent that they could defeat conventionally. Afghanistan and Iraq are contemporary hybrid symmetrical–asymmetrical examples.

In 2001, the United States entered an altogether symmetrical civil war between the Taliban government of Afghanistan and a coalition of opposition clans collectively known as the Northern Alliance. Both sides relied heavily on guerrilla warfare tactics, but because both sides used the same rules, the situation was symmetrical. The role of the United States was to aid in the overthrow of the Taliban government that was providing sanctuary to Al Qaeda—an extension of the war on terrorism. The American military role was to provide strategic airpower against the Taliban forces facing the Northern Alliance. The tactic was successful in the short run. Taliban forces were decimated, their government was forced to flee, and victory was proclaimed. The problem was that crushing the extant armed forces of the opposition did not destroy their will to resist; the Taliban returned in 2003, and they became the de facto primary opponent of the United States there.

The effort in Iraq was in some ways similar. In the conquest phase of the war, the American effort was almost entirely symmetrical, with U.S. forces quickly brushing aside those Iraqi conventional forces that offered any resistance. The problem was that doing so only solved part of the problem. The remnants of the disbanded Iraqi armed forces and disgruntled Iraqi tribesmen organized a spider web of asymmetrical forces that bedeviled the American occupiers through much of the occupation phase of the war, as well as engaging in ethnic cleansing that effectively partitioned large parts of the country into essentially Sunni, Shiite, or Kurdish enclaves. The American surge beginning in 2007 coincided with and contributed to a decrease in violence, but the underlying dynamic of a restive population remained. Elections in early 2010 and the withdrawal of all U.S. forces in 2011 has placed the overall success of the effort in the spotlight. The success (or failure) of the effort will ultimately be decided by the Iraqis themselves. Whether a peaceful, stable Iraqi state will eventually evolve, which was a large reason for the American involvement, will ultimately be outside American hands to dictate.

Quasi-Military Situations.   A second set of circumstances in which military force may be employed in the future is in quasi-military unconventional roles and missions. Some of these are outgrowths of the struggles between the haves and the have-nots within developing countries and are manifested in things like terrorist acts either within the society or against outsiders, with the objects normally being the major powers (the African embassy bombings against the United States in 1998, and, most dramatically, the attacks against New York and Washington, D.C., in 2001). Others are extensions of the general decay of some of the failed states and often are exemplified in activities such as criminality. Attempts to deal with the prospects of potential WMD attacks also fit into this category. What these phenomena share is that they are only semimilitary, even quasi-military, in content.

The Western, and specifically American, problem with Osama bin Laden illustrates the phenomenon. For a variety of reasons, bin Laden blamed the United States for a large number of the problems afflicting the Middle East and was consequently devoted to inflicting as much pain and suffering on the

United States and Americans as he could through acts of terror committed by his followers and associates. The campaign to eradicate Al Qaeda since 2001 has in fact decimated much of the ranks and leadership of the original organization, but it also spawned a series of spin-off, copycat, and affiliated organizations that make the terrorist threat much more hydra-headed than it was before. Al Qaeda in Mesopotamia (Iraq), in the Arabian Peninsula (Yemen), and in the Maghreb (Mali) are three often-cited examples. Successful actions have, by and large, been the result of intelligence and law enforcement efforts, as in the June 2006 assassination of Abu Musab al-Zarqawi, the leader of Al Qaeda in Iraq, and the assassinations of bin Laden and Yemeni leader Anwar al-Awlaki in 2011.

Postconflict Peace

Planning for the peace that follows these highly fluid asymmetrical conflicts is generally as difficult as their prosecution and, partly as a result, tends to be underemphasized in the planning process. Nevertheless, no durable peace is likely to ensue unless there are concrete plans to alleviate the conditions that gave rise to the violence in the first place or that were created by the violence.

This means wartime planning must work backward, in Clark's terms. Most asymmetrical conflicts begin with prominent internal bases that must be addressed after the fighting in what Clark calls the "four-step minuet" of planning (development, deployment, decisive [military] operations, and postconflict operations). Describing Afghanistan, former minister of the interior Ali A. Jalali argues the need for "human security, which assumes the sustainability of the peaceful environment. . . . Freedom from fear and freedom from want lead to human security, and they require more than building the state's security forces." He cites good governance, social security, economic development, and protection of human and political rights as additional needs. This realization leads backward to military operations, as Gray points out: "The primary objective in counterinsurgency is protection of the people, not military defeat of the terrorists-insurgents." It is not clear that adequate attention to these kinds of concerns was present in American prewar planning for Afghanistan or Iraq or that these goals can be attained in a sustainable manner by outsiders.

CASE: THE AFGHANISTAN WAR

Unless one counts long occupations such as the U.S. Marines' two decades in Haiti between 1915 and 1934, the American military effort in Afghanistan now represents America's longest war, and it is one where any definitive outcome seems no more imminent than it did at the beginning. Those who committed the first American forces to Afghanistan did not envision such an outcome when the first Americans were dispatched there in October 2001.

Spurred by the 9/11 attacks by an Al Qaeda whose principal sanctuary was in Afghanistan and protected by the Taliban government, the overt purpose was to attack, capture, and destroy the terrorist organization and its leader Osama bin Laden. The American action, however, also enmeshed the United States in a conventional civil war between the Taliban and insurgents under the banner of the Northern Alliance.

The campaign against bin Laden and Al Qaeda, of course, failed, as the terrorist leader and his followers managed to elude their pursuers and to slip across the border into areas of Pakistan not under effective control of the Pakistani government, where they remained and from which the survivors continue to operate. Despite this inability to accomplish the primary—and universally supported—goal of destroying Al Qaeda, the United States remained engaged in Afghanistan. After the 2003 return of the Taliban in their attempt to reassert their lost domain, this meant the United States became part of the Afghan civil war, which was not part of the original overt purpose but which became justified as necessary to prevent an Al Qaeda return. The American effort was subdued and limited because of heavy American commitment in Iraq, but as that mission has wound down, American resources have been increasingly deployed in Afghanistan.

The result has been a classic asymmetrical war. On one side is the Afghan government, aided by a NATO-based coalition and the United States, acting both as a member of the coalition and independently of it. Thanks to outside assistance, this side possesses clearly superior conventional force. On the other side is the insurgent Taliban, whose forces are clearly inferior to those of the United States and its allies (NATO and the Afghan government) in physical terms. As a result, the Taliban had no choice but to adopt the methodology of asymmetrical force.

Conflict Environment

By virtually any measure and for virtually any purpose, Afghanistan is one of the most forbidding, unforgiving, and difficult countries in the world. It is an ancient land with a discernible history that dates back three to four millennia; it has always been a harsh and contentious place whose history is punctuated by occasions in which it has united to repel foreign invaders and then fallen back into fractious disunity and violent rivalry once any particular outsider has been repulsed. Rudyard Kipling's nineteenth-century admonition— "Don't let your sons die on Afghanistan's plain"—has been sound advice for a long time.

Historic interest in Afghanistan has largely geographic bases. Although the country has few natural resources to exploit or physical bases for development, it has a strategic location in the heart of Asia that has made it a junction point, what the U.S. government has called a "land bridge," for travelers and traders throughout history. East–West commerce from the Orient to the Middle East and Europe traversed the country, and the north–south axis from Central Asia to the Asian subcontinent has modern Afghanistan in its path as well.

This strategic location has placed Afghanistan on the transit route or made it the object of some of history's greatest conquerors. Alexander the Great passed through what is now Afghanistan in both directions as he sought to subdue India, and Genghis Khan's Golden Hordes swept through and for a time occupied this rugged land of barren mountains and high mountain valleys. More recently, independent Afghanistan (it originally achieved its independence in 1747) was occupied and partially subdued by Great Britain, which fought three wars there in the nineteenth and early twentieth centuries. In the nineteenth century, indeed, Afghanistan was the object of the "Great Game" between the British and the Russians, as the Russians sought to extend their influence southward toward the British Raj in India and the British wanted to retain influence over Afghanistan and part of what is now Pakistan as a buffer area protecting British domain in the area. Most recently, the Soviet Union invaded Afghanistan in December 1979 in a feckless attempt to shore up a communist regime in Kabul. Like virtually all the conquerors that had come before them, the Soviets retreated ignominiously in 1988, having failed utterly in their quest and having weakened themselves to the point of facilitating the downfall of Soviet communism that began in 1989.

The Afghan experience has been enigmatic. For most of its history, Afghanistan has been a deeply divided society, with loyalty being toward tribal affiliations rather than the state. Afghanistan has never evolved a strong, stable central government, and its attempts to create one have been fleeting and ultimately unsuccessful. What passes for unity and peacefulness normally has occurred when geographically based, ethnic tribal groups have had substantial autonomy and where such central regulation as existed was the result of *loya jirgas*, extensive meetings of tribal elders from around the country. Whenever a central government in Kabul has attempted to assert its authority outside the tribal council system, it has been actively resisted, often violently. The exception has generally been when Afghanistan has been invaded by outsiders, at which time the various Afghan tribes have temporarily set aside their differences long enough to expel the foreigners. Once that goal has been achieved, the traditional practice has been to return to rivalry and suspicion.

The result is an Afghan society that is dominated by its tribal parts and that has a xenophobic dislike and suspicion of outsiders. Within the tribal structure of the country, however, one tribal entity has traditionally been most prominent. The Pashtuns are the largest ethnic group in the country, although they are further divided into competing subunits, the most prominent of which are the Durrani and the Gilzai Pashtuns. Throughout most of Afghan history, they were a majority, and for a time the terms "Afghan" and "Pashtun" were used synonymously. Forced migration—largely to Pakistan—has cost the Pashtuns their majority status, but they retain a plurality (currently estimated as about 42 percent). Traditional Pashtun lands are concentrated in the southern and eastern parts of the country adjacent to and overlapping the Durand Line (the legal boundary between Afghanistan and Pakistan but not accepted as valid by many Pashtuns). The Pashtuns are also the second largest ethnic group in

Pakistan (behind the Punjabis), and the territory dominated by the Pashtuns on both sides of the border is also known as Pashtunistan. A sovereign state by that name remains the goal of some tribal members.

The Pashtuns are important in the current context for two reasons. First is that virtually all Afghan governments have been headed by a Pashtun and have had the active support of the Pashtuns. Hamid Karzai, the president of Afghanistan since 2002, is an urban Durrani Pashtun, but his support among the rural Gilzais who are the core supporters of the Taliban is suspect. Karzai is Western-educated, and he has cooperated with other Afghan tribes distrusted by most Gilzai Pashtuns (notably the Tajiks, who are prominently represented in the current government). The Gilzai support base of the Taliban comes almost exclusively from rural-based Pashtuns, and most of the hotbeds of Taliban activity and control are in traditional Pashtun lands. All Pashtuns are by no means Taliban, but virtually all Taliban are Pashtuns. Second, much of the very strong identity and values of Pashtuns derive from Pashtunwali, a code of morals and proper behavior. Among the central tenets of this code is hospitality and protection of honored guests. Arising from their collaboration in the anti-Soviet resistance, one of the recipients of this protection has been Al Qaeda.

Physical Structure of War

The structure and issues underlying the current war in Afghanistan are the direct result of the Afghan resistance to the Soviet occupation during 1979–1988 and its aftermath. In predictable fashion, the invasion produced a fierce resistance by the various Afghan tribes, aided by, among others, the Americans and the Pakistanis. The mujahidin, as the resisters were collectively known, had two distinct elements: native Afghan tribesmen who, in typical Afghan fashion, formed a loose coalition to repel the Soviets that dissolved when the Soviets departed; and foreign fighters, mostly from other Islamic countries. The native Afghans formed the basis for both sides in the later civil war, the Taliban and the Northern Alliance. The foreign fighters, some of whom had been recruited by a then-obscure Saudi activist named Osama bin Laden, became members of Al Qaeda.

The expulsion of the Soviets ended communist rule in Afghanistan. Between 1988 and 1996, a number of governments came and went in Kabul, but they were equally inept, corrupt, and unpopular. In reaction, a new movement primarily comprising students (talibs) from religious schools (madrassas) largely in Pakistan formed and swept across Afghanistan. In 1996, the Taliban became the government of the country. That same year, Al Qaeda was expelled from Sudan, partly because of pressure from the U.S. government. Looking for a new sanctuary, bin Laden and his followers appealed to their old allies in the new Afghan government, who welcomed them and, under the tenets of Pashtunwali, provided them with protection.

The Taliban government's rule—or misrule—is well documented (e.g., tyrannical fundamentalist excesses, including the draconian suppression of women) and this perhaps inevitably spawned its own opposition, and gradually a coalition of primarily non-Pashtun tribes formed under the banner of the Northern Alliance. By 9/11, the Northern Alliance and the Taliban were locked in a full-scale civil war, the outcome of which was very much in doubt. Meanwhile, Al Qaeda continued to operate training facilities in Afghanistan, planning, among other things, the 9/11 attacks.

While decrying the Taliban's policies and providing some small amount of assistance to the opposition, the United States stayed on the sidelines of this conflict before 9/11. The public face of the American decision to intervene physically in Afghanistan was the "war on terror," with Al Qaeda as its centerpiece. When U.S. forces entered the country, they in effect created a second conflict with its own objectives and conduct separate from and independent of the ongoing civil war. Although bin Laden's flight from the country effectively ended the military effort against Al Qaeda in Afghanistan (since the terrorists were now in Pakistan), that did not end the Western (including NATO and U.S.) military involvement. Rather, outside assistance had helped drive the Taliban out of power and into Pakistani exile, and the result was the formation of the new Karzai government as the representative of the victorious Northern Alliance, with American blessing. When the Taliban left, the outsiders remained to mop up residual Al Qaeda and Taliban resistance and to ensure they did not return.

The Taliban did, of course, begin to infiltrate back into the country and to launch a new phase of the civil war with the pre-9/11 roles reversed: The Karzai-led Northern Alliance formed the core of the government and the Taliban were the insurgents. Now reconfigured as the Afghan national force, the Northern Alliance was no more capable of defeating the Taliban than they had been before. As the returning Taliban gradually reasserted its authority over increasing parts of Afghanistan (especially traditional Gilzai Pashtun territories), opposition to them gradually fell to NATO. The current civil war was thus engaged.

It has become a classic asymmetrical war. The Taliban are arguably more powerful than the government forces on their own, but they are far less powerful than and incapable of defeating the NATO/American forces in symmetrical warfare. The Taliban thus adopted an unconventional, asymmetrical approach to the war, aiming most clearly at overcoming American cost-tolerance by prolonging the conflict sufficiently that American public opinion will turn against the effort and force a withdrawal. This is, of course, a classic insurgent strategic approach against an outside occupier and is consistent with the historical Afghan treatment of outsiders. The American response has been that of counterinsurgency (COIN) as outlined in the Petraeus-inspired FM 3-24, which seeks to liberate Taliban territory and engage in a successful campaign for the "hearts and minds" of the Afghan people to turn their loyalty away from the Taliban and toward the government. At the same time, the strategy calls for expanding the size and quality of Afghan government forces to the point that they eventually can defeat the insurgency on their own.

Determining Opponents

The dual nature of the Afghanistan war has complicated the specification of the opposition. This difficulty is particularly acute for the United States, which became the de facto major opponent of the Taliban in the fight, a role it is gradually relinquishing to Afghan forces as it has moved toward its scheduled 2014 withdrawal. The two possible opponents, of course, are the Taliban and Al Qaeda, and they are by no means the same. The Taliban, for instance, are almost all Afghan Pashtuns, whereas members of Al Qaeda are almost all non-Afghans. Thus, the two opponents are distinct. The problem for the United States is that there is widespread, virtually universal public support for opposing Al Qaeda, but because Al Qaeda is weakened and its remnants are physically in Pakistan, it is not the opponent the Americans are fighting. Rather, the physical foe is the Taliban, who are American enemies only in the sense that they might invite an Al Qaeda return to Afghanistan if they win.

The purposes of these two opponents, and thus how they must be opposed, differ substantially as well. Both problems are difficult. Al Qaeda, of course, is a terrorist organization that has goals that are murky to Americans but that include inflicting as much pain and suffering on Americans and others as they can, presumably in order to extract some political concessions—noninterference in Middle Eastern countries and abandonment of Israel are the goals most often articulated. The Al Qaeda opponent is physically small—probably no more than a few thousand operatives worldwide—but elusive and difficult to destroy, which is the obvious goal against them. The problem, of course, is that they are not present in any numbers in Afghanistan. When their locations can be established, the main way to attack them has been through pilotless Predator air strikes, which the Pakistanis oppose and which often result in civilian casualties that simply create new Al Qaeda recruits. Moreover, it is not clear that effective action will not simply cause Al Qaeda to pack up and relocate in sanctuaries elsewhere, such as in Somalia or Yemen.

Opposing the Taliban insurgency is a different, and in many ways more familiar, problem. The Taliban are conducting an asymmetrical campaign using largely guerrilla tactics and insurgent goals, to which the symmetrical warriors have responded with the American COIN strategy. This effort, however, is plagued by at least three difficulties. One is that the Taliban have proven to be tough, adept, and adaptive fighters defending harsh territory with which they are more familiar and comfortable than their opponents: The going is very difficult. The other problem is that the outsiders—who are, to repeat, currently doing most of the fighting—find themselves aligned with what many Afghans view as an anti-Pashtun coalition, Karzai's ethnicity notwithstanding. Afghan history has been remarkably consistent in the sense that no government that is opposed by the Pashtun plurality has much chance of succeeding. Recasting the war as one where the Pashtuns are not the implicit enemies is a necessary (if not necessarily sufficient) condition for success against the Taliban. Third, the outsiders are exactly that—outsiders—and their presence is resented because they are foreigners and unwelcome guests (or at least guests who have overstayed their welcome). Resistance to foreign military occupation is a universal human instinct, and it is especially strong among the Afghans.

Postconflict Peace

The war in Afghanistan became an asymmetrical war and continues to be one because of the outside intervention of the United States and its NATO allies following 9/11. Prior to that involvement, there had been a fairly conventional civil war going on against the Taliban (a not unusual circumstance) that would likely have continued with some internal resolution. Interfering in that internal affair was not a prominent part of the rationale for intervention. Destroying Al Qaeda was the purpose, and the Taliban were in the way. Operationally, the anti-Al Qaeda mission in Afghanistan ended when Al Qaeda fled. The outside mission remained, it became the shield behind which the anti-Taliban government of Karzai was formed, and by staying, it became the protector and sponsor of the new regime. When the Taliban returned, they came back as asymmetrical warriors, the only way they had a chance of prevailing.

How the Afghanistan War will end is a matter of speculation. Its evolution has been conceptually contorted, but it does provide some potential precedent for the future. The international environment is not favorable to symmetrical applications of conventional, Western-style warfare: The developed countries that could wage such wars against one another have scant reason to do so, and the developing countries cannot compete with the symmetrical warriors on their own terms. Regardless of which Afghan faction eventually wins or retains control of the country (which is what the actual conflict and fighting are about), the more general and enduring lesson will be about whether asymmetrical warfare in developing countries is how the major powers wish to expend their armed might and treasure. The content of that lesson remains to be decided; the one thing that is reasonably certain is that the Afghans themselves will determine who prevails, not the outsiders.

CONCLUSION

Warfare is both an ever-changing and never-changing human endeavor. The opponents change, the purposes for which wars are fought change, and the methods and tools of war change. At the same time, the fact that groups of humans find reasons to fight and kill other groups of humans seems ubiquitous, one of history's true constants.

What is now called asymmetrical warfare is part of this larger march of history. The idea, and even some of the methods, underlying this kind of war is as old as warfare itself and has been a recurring part of the historic pattern. What is arguably different is that differential fighting capabilities among and between countries and groups have widened to the point that asymmetrical warfare has become much more prominent than it was in the past. The ongoing war in Afghanistan is only the latest and most currently obvious example of this form of warfare. How it ends will, in turn, have some effect on the form this warfare will take in a future where asymmetrical opponents are the only likely foes for major powers like the United States.

SUGGESTED ACTIVITIES AND QUESTIONS

1. The military planning problem has changed markedly since the end of the Cold War. What is the nature, and what are the causes, of that change? Discuss.
2. What is asymmetrical warfare? Contrast it with symmetrical warfare. Why has it arisen as the major military problem of the twenty-first century? Is it likely to continue to be the dominant problem?
3. Discuss the problem posed by asymmetrical warfare in terms of the conflict environment, physical structure of war, opposition, and postconflict peace.
4. Discuss the background and evolution of the Afghanistan War, beginning with its roots in the Afghan resistance to the Soviet occupation and leading to the 9/11 attacks. Why does the war have two distinct facets? What are they? Explain.
5. Building on the dual nature of the war, describe the Afghanistan War in terms of conflict environment, physical structure, opposition, and postconflict peace.
6. Should it be a major priority of the most advanced countries to involve themselves in trying to ameliorate internal violence in the developing world? If so, what kind of criteria should be adopted to guide involvements? If not, what should we prepare for?
7. Predict where and in what kind of conflict the United States is most likely to be fighting 10 years from today. Try to devise the basic principles for a counter-asymmetrical warfare strategy to deal with that future.

SUGGESTED READINGS AND RESOURCES

Badkhen, Anna. "Afghanistan: Cold and Violent." *Foreign Policy* (online), March 9, 2011.

Barfield, Thomas. *Afghanistan: A Cultural and Political History.* Princeton, NJ: Princeton University Press, 2010.

Berkowitz, Bruce. *The New Face of War: How War Will Be Fought in the 21st Century.* New York: Free Press, 2003.

Biddle, Stephen, Fotina Christia, and Alexander Thier. "Defining Success in Afghanistan: What Can the United States Accept?" *Foreign Affairs* 89, 4 (July/August 2011), 48–60.

Blackwill, Robert D. "Plan B in Afghanistan: Why a De Facto Partition Is the Least Bad Option." *Foreign Affairs* 90, 1 (January/February 2012), 43–50.

Boot, Max. *Invisible Armies: A History of Guerrilla Warfare from Ancient Times to the Present.* New York: Liveright Publishing, 2013.

Brodie, Bernard and Fawn M. Brodie. *From Crossbow to H-Bomb: The Evolution of Weapons and Tactics in Warfare.* Bloomington, IN: Indiana University Press, 1965.

Clark, Wesley. *Winning Modern Wars: Iraq, Terrorism, and the American Empire.* New York: PublicAffairs, 2003.

Coll, Steve. *Ghost Wars: The Secret History of the CIA, Afghanistan, and bin Laden from the Soviet Invasion to September 10, 2001.* New York: Penguin Books, 2004.

Crews, Robert D. and Amin Tarzi, eds. *The Taliban and the Crisis of Afghanistan.* Cambridge, MA: Harvard University Press, 2008.

Ewans, Martin. *Afghanistan: A Short History of Its People and Politics.* New York: HarperCollins Perennial, 2002.

Galula, David. *Counterinsurgency Warfare: Theory and Practice.* Westport, CT: Praeger Publishers (Praeger Classics of the Counterinsurgency Era), 2006.

Giustozzi, Antonio. *Empires of Mud.* New York: Columbia University Press, 2010.

Goulding, Victor J. Jr. "Back to the Future with Asymmetrical Warfare." *Parameters* XXX, 4 (Winter 2000–2001), 21–30.

Gray, Colin S. "Stability Operations in Strategic Perspective: A Skeptical View." *Parameters* XXXVI, 2 (Summer 2006), 4–14.

Haass, Richard N. *War of Necessity, War of Choice: A Memoir of Two Iraq Wars.* New York: Simon and Schuster, 2009.

Jalali, Ali A. "The Future of Afghanistan." *Parameters* XXXVI, 1 (Spring 2006), 4–19.

Jones, Seth G. *In the Graveyard of Empires: America's War in Afghanistan.* New York: W.W. Norton, 2009.

Kaplan, Robert D. "Man Versus Afghanistan." *The Atlantic* 305, 3 (April 2010), 60–71.

Lind, William S. et al. "The Changing Face of War: Into the Fourth Generation." *Marine Corps Gazette*, October 1989, 22–26.

Lowther, Adam B. *Americans and Asymmetrical Warfare: Lebanon, Somalia, and Afghanistan.* Westport, CT: Praeger Security International, 2007.

Nevile, Leigh. *Special Operations Forces in Afghanistan.* New York: Osprey Publishing, 2008.

O'Hanloon, Michael. "Staying Power: The U.S. Mission in Afghanistan After 2011." *Foreign Affairs* 89, 5 (September/October 2010), 63–79.

Rashid, Ahmed. *Taliban: Militant Islam, Oil, and Fundamentalism in Central Asia.* Second Ed. New Haven, CT: Yale University Press, 2010.

Rubin, Barnett E. "Saving Afghanistan." *Foreign Affairs* 86, 1 (January/February 2007), 57–78.

Scales, Maj. General Robert H. Jr. *Future War: Anthology.* Carlisle Barracks, PA: Strategic Studies Institute, 1999.

Snow, Donald M. *National Security for a New Era*, 5th ed. New York: Pearson, 2014.

_____. *What After Iraq?* New York: Pearson Longman, 2009.

_____. and Dennis M. Drew. *From Lexington to Baghdad and Beyond: War and Politics in the American Experience*, 3rd ed. Armonk, NY: M. E. Sharpe, 2009.

Stoessinger, John. *Why Nations Go to War*, 9th ed. New York: St. Martin's Press, 2003.

Sullivan, General Gordon R. and Anthony M. Coroalles. *Seeing the Elephant: Leading America's Army into the Twenty-First Century.* Boston, MA: Institute for Foreign Policy Analysis, 1995.

U.S. Army and U.S. Marine Corps. *Counterinsurgency Field Manual* (U.S. Army Field Manual No. 3-24, Marine Corps Warfighting Publication No. 3-33.5). Chicago, IL: University of Chicago Press, 2007.

U.S. Marine Corps. *Afghanistan: Operational Culture for Deploying Personnel.* Quantico, VA: Center for Operational Cultural Learning, 2009.

Van Creveld, Martin. *The Transformation of War.* New York: Free Press, 1991.

Proliferation: The Case of North Korea

PRÉCIS

Nuclear proliferation, a subject of concern since the dawn of the nuclear age, returned to the world agenda with a vengeance in late June 2006. Two states, Iran and North Korea, occupied the spotlight because of actions they had taken or were contemplating taking with strong overtones for the world's nuclear balance. The Iranian aspect of this problem is discussed in detail in Chapter 7. North Korea, which potentially has a small number of nuclear arms, has gone so far as to test a ballistic missile delivery system potentially capable of delivering payloads to parts of the continental United States, among other places, and has tested a nuclear bomb. How the 2011 change of regime and the increased militancy of its rhetoric (demonstrated in the spring 2013 confrontation on the peninsula) will affect that country's nuclear status is problematical, but the general problem of proliferation of the Koreas remains a lively international security concern.

The spread of different categories of weapons to states that do not possess them and whose possession concerns other states is not a new phenomenon. In the modern world, trying to place limits on the numbers and types of weapons that states possess goes back to the period between the world wars in modern times; the Washington Conference on naval fleet sizes and the Kellogg–Briand Pact, both of which were negotiated in the 1920s, were early prototypes of the concern that is now called proliferation. Dealing with the spread of nuclear weapons has been a concern since the early 1950s.

The post–World War II concern with the spread of nuclear weapons reached a crescendo with the negotiation of the Nuclear Non-Proliferation Treaty (NPT) of 1968. The NPT prohibited additional states that did not already have nuclear weapons from acquiring (or trying to acquire) them.

It also required current possessors not to aid in the spread of nuclear weapons and made them promise to reduce and eliminate their own arsenals. The NPT has enjoyed a mixed level of success.

Concern about proliferation has ebbed and flowed across time. When the membership in the nuclear "club" (the counties that possessed the weapons) was very small during the 1950s and 1960s, there was great concern about additional countries acquiring the weapons, and the body of nuclear proliferation thought was developed to deal with that contingency. During the 1970s and 1980s, that level of concern became more muted, both because the number of nuclear states did not grow perceptibly despite the dire warnings of proliferation theorists whose entreaties increasingly had a kind of "cry wolf" quality, and because of concern with other matters, including the demise of the Cold War and the need to adapt to that change in the international environment.

Interest in proliferation has returned since the turn of the millennium. The revived interest has been tied closely to the problem of international terrorism, because of the fear that terrorists might acquire and use nuclear or other deadly weapons (so-called weapons of mass destruction or WMDs), a concern important enough that the 2006 National Security Strategy of the United States intoned, "There are few greater threats than a terrorist attack with WMD."

The current emphasis on WMDs has two basic sources that culminate in the possibility of terrorist acquisition and use of proscribed weapons. The first has to do with the countries that might acquire such weapons, and it focuses currently on countries such as the Democratic People's Republic of Korea (DPRK, or North Korea) and Iran. The second source of concern is the various types of WMDs that might be acquired. Ultimately, the WMDs that most matter are nuclear weapons because of their enormous destructive capacity, but other forms such as biological and chemical weapons are of importance as well, as the Syrian crisis has demonstrated.

This case study seeks to clarify and apply the problem of proliferation. It begins with a discussion of the general problem as it has evolved through scholarly and policy concerns, including the nature of the problem and how the international system has attempted to deal with it. Proliferation is a real and vital current problem, and the case then applies the general principles to one of the most important current potential nuclear proliferators, the DPRK, looking at both attempts to prevent North Korea from joining the nuclear club and the dynamics that have made such conformance impossible to achieve. Some references to the same dynamics regarding Iran are introduced as additional examples of and as a foundation for the discussion in Chapter 7.

THE PROLIFERATION PROBLEM

Proliferation is a delicate international problem, in large measure because its underlying aim is both discriminatory and condescending to those at whom it is aimed. In the modern context, the desire to limit possession of nuclear and other proscribed weapons has come from countries that already possess those weapons and is aimed at those who do not possess them. Thus, current efforts to prevent countries like North Korea from obtaining nuclear weapons are made most loudly by countries like the United States, Britain, and even China, which already have them.

The delicacy of the situation comes from rationalizing why it is all right for some states to have nuclear weapons whereas other states should not. Such assertions and arguments are, of course, inherently discriminatory, and the question that must be answered is, why some but not others? Invariably, the answer to that question comes back to an assumption regarding responsibility: Those who have the weapons, it is argued (usually by those countries that have them), can be trusted to act responsibly with the weapons (which basically means they will not use them). Others, however, are not necessarily so trustworthy and, by definition, have no track record of responsible possession. This logic is convincing to the countries already possessing the weapons but not necessarily to those that do not, which feel that the assertion is inherently, and from their vantage point, unjustifiably condescending. This dynamic is a major conceptual barrier to enforcing proliferation policies.

The proliferation problem is also complex. To understand and be able to analyze current cases such as the DPRK, one must look at the structure of the problem. This will be done by raising and trying to answer three questions: What is the nature of the problem? Why is it a problem? And what can be done about the problem? The answers collectively form the context for analyzing the case application to North Korea.

What Is the Nature of the Proliferation Problem?

The roots of the contemporary proliferation problem lie in the Cold War. The major purposes were to prevent the spread of nuclear weapons to states that did not have them, and also to limit the size and destructiveness of the arsenals of possessing states. These two intents were related to one another. In addition, there was concern about the destabilizing impact of burgeoning nuclear possession, which in turn spawned two additional concerns. One was about the kind of capability that countries were attempting to proliferate (what forms of WMD), and the other was the mechanics of how proliferation could occur (and thus what steps had to be taken to prevent it from happening).

Two basic forms of proliferation were identified and targeted during the Cold War: vertical and horizontal. Vertical proliferation refers to incremental additions of a particular weapons system by a state (or states) that already has the weapon. It is a concern both because additional increments of weapons add to the potential deadliness of confrontations and because those increments can spawn arms races in which additions by one side cause the other to build more, resulting in an arms spiral that was potentially destabilizing. Efforts to control vertical proliferation generally aim at curbing or reducing levels of particular arms and are the traditional object of arms control. Most of the nuclear arms treaties negotiated by the United States and the Soviet Union during the Cold War (the Strategic Arms Limitations Talks—SALT—and the Strategic Arms Reduction Talks—START—are examples) were attempts to limit vertical proliferation.

Contemporary proliferation efforts center on horizontal proliferation: the spread of nuclear or other weapons to states that currently do not possess them; generally, when the term *proliferation* is used in contemporary discussions, it is shorthand for horizontal proliferation. The two forms are linked because many of the calls for limiting horizontal proliferation have come from states (like the United States and the former Soviet Union) that have been engaged in vertical proliferation (nuclear arms races) that made their entreaties to others to self-abnegate attempts to gain the weapons seem disingenuous and created demands to link the two (see the following discussion of the NPT).

The kinds of capabilities being proliferated were also a concern that led to independent efforts to curb each kind of capability. The kinds of weapons that may be proliferated are (and were) WMDs, which generally are categorized into three groups captured by the acronym NBC: nuclear, biological, and chemical weapons. Though all are of concern, the dangers they pose are different. Nuclear weapons are arguably the only unambiguous weapons of mass destruction, because of the size and destructiveness of nuclear explosions. Biological (or agents of biological origin, ABO) and chemical weapons can cause large numbers of deaths that are often particularly hideous, but their extensiveness of destruction is more limited. On the other hand, biological and especially chemical weapons are much easier to construct than nuclear weapons. In an era when terrorist possession and use is a major concern, chemical and biological weapons take on added importance because they are the kinds of weapons that terrorists are more likely to be able to obtain (or make) and use than nuclear weapons. Efforts to contain proliferation have centered on nuclear weapons, although they have been extended to other forms of WMDs. In addition, there is also concern about how WMDs might be delivered to targets. The most dramatic form of WMD (and especially nuclear) delivery is by ballistic missiles, because at present there are no reliable means of engaging in highly effective defenses against ballistic missile attacks.

The mechanics of producing and avoiding the production of these capabilities have also been a matter of major concern, centering particularly on nuclear weapons and ways to get them to target. The problem of nuclear weapons production is straightforward and has two components. The first is the knowledge of how to fabricate a nuclear device. Nuclear physics has been taught openly for over 60 years now in the world's (and notably American) universities, so that knowledge is widely available both to most governments and undoubtedly to many private groups. The knowledge genie is clearly out of the bottle. The other requirement for building nuclear weapons is possession of adequate supplies of weapons-grade (i.e., highly enriched) isotopes of uranium/plutonium, which generally are byproducts of nuclear reactions in certain types of power generators and the like (which is why many concerns are raised about the kinds of nuclear reactors potential proliferators have or propose to build). Access to such materials is highly guarded and restricted, and aspirants to nuclear weapons either have to come into possession of nuclear reactors that produce weapons-grade materials or they must purchase or steal such material from those who possess it. Nonproliferation efforts have been concentrated on denying access to weapons-grade material to potential proliferators.

The other, somewhat less publicized, aspect of nuclear proliferation surrounds the ability of proliferating states to deliver those weapons to targets—specifically to targets in the United States and other Western countries. Terrorist horror scenarios center on clandestine shipment of assembled bombs via cargo ship and the like to places like New York or the dispatch of so-called suitcase bombs (small nuclear devices contained in luggage or other parcels) or dirty bombs (conventional explosives coated with radioactive materials dispersed with detonation of the bomb). More conventional analyses deal with the ability of nuclear pretenders to build or buy ballistic missiles to deliver these weapons, because a country that can deliver weapons over only a short distance creates much less of a problem than a country that can deliver the same weapon over intercontinental ranges. The question of ballistic delivery systems has been a particular problem in dealing with the DPRK.

Why Is Proliferation a Problem?

The short answer to this question is that one has much less to fear from a weapons capability that one's actual or potential adversaries do not possess than from a capability that they do possess. In the classic, Cold War seedbed of thinking about nuclear proliferation, the problem was conceptualized as the difficulty of keeping additional sovereign states from achieving nuclear capability. The more such additional countries obtained the weapons, the more "fingers" there would be on the nuclear "button," and thus as a matter of probability, the more likely nuclear war would be. That problem remains central to the contemporary problem, but is augmented by the fear that some of the potential proliferating states might share their capabilities with terrorist nonstate actors, who would allegedly be more difficult to dissuade from using those weapons than would state actors.

In classic terms, the problem of the spread of nuclear (or other) weapons to nonpossessing states is known as the $N+1$ problem. The idea is straightforward. In the formulation, N stands for the number of states that currently possess nuclear weapons and refers to the dynamics among them. $+1$, on the other hand, refers to the added problems that would be created for the international system (notably the states that form N) by the addition of new $(+1)$ states to the nuclear club.

The problem is that the current members (N) and potential proliferators $(+1)$ see the problem essentially from opposite ends of the conceptual spectrum. The current members generally believe that the current "club" represents a stable, reliable membership (even if earlier members opposed the addition of some current members before they "joined"). Viewed this way, the emphasis of the club is on the problems that will be created by new members, and the criterion for concern is the likelihood of destabilization of the system created by new members. Looking from this perspective, it is not surprising that members of N tend to look for and find sources of destabilization that should be opposed and want to restrict membership to existing levels.

Members of +1, however, see the problem differently. The nonmember does not see his own acquisition of nuclear weapons as destabilizing and is righteously indignant at the notion that his acquisition would have a detrimental effect on the stability of the system. The accusation of destabilization is a backhanded way of suggesting that the new member would be a less responsible possessor than those who already have the weapons. Put more bluntly, the imputation that a new state would destabilize amounts to accusing such a state of a greater likelihood of using the weapons than those who already have them and have refrained from doing so. If you are a member of the government of North Korea, for instance, you would like an explanation of exactly why the United States, which maintains over 28,000 troops and numerous nuclear warheads on the soil of your next-door neighbor (South Korea), should be treated as more responsible with weapons of mass destruction than you are. It is not an easy sell.

Indeed, in the current context, nonpossessors are more likely to make the argument that their membership in the nuclear club will actually stabilize their situations, because it is a fact (even if the causality is arguable) that no state that possesses nuclear weapons has ever been the victim of an aggression against it. Indeed, one of the arguments that both the Iranians and North Koreans (among others) have made in recent years is that gaining nuclear weapons capability is a useful—even necessary—means to avoid being attacked by an aggressive United States. Would, for instance, the United States have attacked Iraq if Iraq actually had, rather than being accused of trying to get, nuclear weapons? Some nonpossessing countries argue the American attack would have been less likely and that Saddam Hussein's major error was in not getting the kinds of capability that would deter the United States. Some even argue that had he not abandoned his nuclear weapons program, he might still be alive and in power.

There is a further irony that attaches to the N+1 problem—it is generally only viewed as such by the current nuclear club. A country that aspires to become a member (a +1 country) may be viewed as a problem before it gets the capability, but once it has and has demonstrated its "responsible possession" of the capability, it ceases to be a part of the problem and instead views other aspirants as part of the problem. Thus, for instance, when only the United States and the Soviet Union had nuclear weapons, they viewed the addition of the third member (Britain) as a potential problem. When Britain obtained the weapons, it ceased to be a problem, but viewed the addition of other countries (France, China) as destabilizing prospects. When those countries joined the club, they became part of N and thus looked at other prospective members as part of the problem.

The proliferation problem is by definition worse when there are more nuclear powers, but one obstacle to sustaining international momentum behind proliferation control has been that proliferation has not occurred at the pace that those who most fear the prospects have projected. The nuclear club was pretty well established by 1964, when China obtained nuclear weapons and pushed the number to five—in order of acquisition: the United States, the Soviet Union, Great Britain, France, and China. At the time, there were fears that the number, unless constrained, might jump to 20 or 30 or even more nuclear states, but that simply has not happened. Since the 1960s, five states have gained nuclear capability. One state (Israel) does not formally admit it has the weapons (it also does not deny it), one state obtained and then renounced and destroyed its weapons (South Africa), two countries openly joined the club in 1998 (India and Pakistan), and North Korea announced it had exploded a nuclear device in 2006. The total number of currently acknowledged nuclear states thus stands at nine, which is far less than the doomsayers predicted. In the current debate, three states have been mentioned with varying levels of likelihood of attempting to join the club: Iran, Iraq, and Syria. The American invasion of Iraq precluded that country's membership for the foreseeable future, and international pressures and internal chaos effectively curb any Syrian ambitions. That leaves Iran and North Korea as the current problems. They are different in that Iran has not yet demonstrated its ability to develop these weapons, whereas the DPRK has.

What activates the level of contemporary concern is thus clearly not the quantity of states that may join, but rather it is the quality of new aspirants. The DPRK's reclusive regime is regularly accused of being unstable and bellicose and raises fears on those grounds. Because it is desperately poor and in perpetual need of foreign capital, the fear that the DPRK will simply sell nuclear capability to some undesirable buyer is a continuing nightmare. The question thus arises of what can and should be done to try to control proliferation from occurring, particularly in light of the 2011 leadership succession in that country and changes in policy tenor that have accompanied the rise of Kim Jung Un.

What to Do About the Problem?

Because the roots of thinking about the control of nuclear weapons have their origins in the Cold War, so too does thinking about how to prevent proliferation. The key concept in dealing with nuclear weapons in the Cold War context was deterrence, and that concept dominates historic and contemporary discussions of proliferation as well.

The problem of deterrence has changed with the end of the Cold War system. In the past, nuclear deterrence existed among states with very large arsenals of nuclear weapons—principally the United States and the Soviet Union—and the dynamic of deterrence, captured in the idea of assured destruction, was that any nuclear attack against a nuclear-armed superpower would be suicidal, because the attacked state would retain such devastating capabilities even after absorbing an attack as to be able to retaliate against the attacker and destroy it, making any "victory" decidedly Pyrrhic (costing far more than it was worth). Because potential attackers were presumably rational (or at least not suicidal), the prospects of a counterattack that would certainly immolate them was enough to dissuade (or deter) an attack in the first place. The same logic applies to the continuing viability of the NPT, the major international regime on proliferation.

Deterring Proliferation in a Changed World. That situation has changed in two important respects. First, the possession of such large amounts of nuclear power is now unilateral: Only the United States has the unquestioned ability to launch a devastating nuclear attack against anyone in the world, and because of recent improvements in American capability and degrading of the capabilities of historic possible opponents, Kier Lieber and Daryl Press argued in 2006 that "it will probably be possible for the United States to destroy the long-range arsenals of Russia or China with a first strike." This means that the old system of mutual deterrence (i.e., the United States and the Soviet Union deterring one another) has disappeared or been seriously compromised. More important in the current context, the threats in the contemporary environment come from states that will, at best, have a small number of nuclear weapons at their disposal but may not be dissuaded by the same threats that deterred the Soviets during the Cold War. Thus, as Joseph Pilat puts it, "There are real questions about whether old, Cold War–vintage concepts . . . really address the needs of today."

What was the structure of deterrent threats that were available both to dissuade states from acquiring nuclear weapons and to convince states that had those weapons not to use them during the Cold War? Answering that question is logically a precondition to assessing whether such mechanisms will work in the current context.

In a text published originally in 1996, Eugene Brown and I laid out a reasonably comprehensive framework for categorizing types of mechanisms that could be used to deter unwanted nuclear behavior. Within this framework, arms proliferation can be dealt with in two ways, acquisition (or front-end) and employment (or back-end) deterrence. Acquisition deterrence, as the name implies, consists of efforts to keep states from obtaining nuclear weapons in the first place. The effort consists of two related and, for many purposes, sequential activities. Persuasion, or convincing states that gaining nuclear weapons is not in their best interests (often accompanied by the promise of related rewards for nonproliferation or punitive threats if compliance does not occur), seeks to cajole possible proliferating states into not doing so. In contemporary terms, efforts through the United Nations and the European Union to dissuade Iran from making a positive nuclear weapons decision fall into this category. If persuasion does not work, then coercion (threatening or taking punitive—including military—action to prevent proliferation) may occur. The attacks by Israel against an Iraqi nuclear reactor in 1981 and more recently against Syria are extreme examples of coercive options.

The success of acquisition deterrence has been mixed. These efforts were most successful during the Cold War, when the potential negative consequences of proliferation—the possibility of a general, civilization-destroying war—were greatest. In that circumstance, the leaders of the opposing coalitions could and did bring pressure on the states within their orbits to refrain from gaining nuclear weapons. The leading supporting members of the coalitions on both sides—Great Britain in the West and China in the East—did proceed with nuclear weapons programs, but they were the exceptions.

The current focus on proliferation has become the spread of nuclear weapons to countries—and especially unstable countries—in the developing world. The stalking horses of this concern were Israel and South Africa, both of which conducted highly clandestine weapons development programs that led to their acquisition of nuclear capability. Both countries developed their programs outside the Cold War context: Israel because of its fear its Islamic neighbors might destroy it; South Africa because of the alleged threat posed by neighboring black states (the so-called "frontline" states). When South Africa dismantled its apartheid system, it also destroyed its nuclear weapons. Israel continues to maintain, without publicly admitting it, its nuclear arsenal.

Israel and South Africa form a bridge of sorts to the present concern because both are instances where the attempt to restrain proliferation by the major powers was unsuccessful. Developing-world states have proven less prone to geopolitical constraint than were Cold War allies, and thus India and Pakistan ignored rejoinders and joined the nuclear "club" in 1998. One of the major commonalities of George Bush's 2002 Axis of Evil designation of Iraq, Iran, and North Korea was their aspiration to nuclear status.

The other form of dissuasion is employment deterrence. If efforts to keep states from gaining nuclear weapons fail, then one must turn to efforts to keep them from using the weapons they do acquire. Once again, there are two mechanisms that can be employed. One is the threat of retaliation against any nuclear possessor that may choose to use its weapons against another state (and particularly the United States). The threat is to retaliate with such devastating—including assured destruction—force that it would not only be suicidal for an attacking state to use its weapons (there is an argument that this deterrence could also apply to attacks with other forms of WMD) but the suicide would also occur without having inflicted comparable damage to the retaliating state. Thus, a possible future North Korean attack against the United States might consist of lobbing a handful of weapons against American targets and inflicting severe but not fatal damage; North Korea would be destroyed in the U.S. retaliation. The question that is raised about the extension of this form of deterrence in the current context is whether potential proliferating states' leadership are sufficiently rational (i.e., nonsuicidal) that this form of threat will be effective against them. The other form of employment deterrence threat is denial, the promise that if an attack is launched, it will fail because the potential attacked state has the capability to defend itself from an attack. The question here is whether the claim to be able to deny an attack is credible given the wide variety of means by which someone could attack, say, the United States with nuclear weapons.

Employment deterrence efforts have, to this point, been 100 percent effective, in that no state has used nuclear weapons in anger since 1945. Although one cannot state with certainty that deterrence threats have been the reason for this, nonetheless the record remains perfect. From a proliferation perspective, of course, keeping the number of states that could "break" this record as small as possible is the most compelling concern.

The mechanism by which nonproliferation has been enforced is the NPT. The NPT was negotiated in 1968 and went into effect in 1970. Most countries of the world are or have been members of the regime—Iran and North Korea, for instance—and the question is whether the treaty will remain a viable means to avoid more proliferation in the future.

The Role of the NPT. The NPT was, and still is, the most dramatic, open international attempt to prevent and reverse the spread of weapons of mass destruction around the world. Conventions exist banning the production, use, and sale of chemical and biological weapons and their components, and the Missile Technology Control Regime represents an effort by the major powers (it was initiated by the G-7 economic powers) to control the spread of missile delivery technology, and all have been reasonable successes. The crown jewel of proliferation control, however, has been the effort to prevent the spread of nuclear weapons in the world, and the instrument has been the NPT.

The NPT was not the first international agreement that addressed horizontal proliferation, but it was the first treaty to have proliferation as its sole purpose. In 1963, the United States, the Soviet Union, and Great Britain negotiated the Limited Test Ban Treaty (LTBT), which prohibited the atmospheric testing of nuclear devices, and this was supposed to have a secondary proliferation effect, because the technology at the time virtually required nuclear weapons aspirants to explode a nuclear device in the atmosphere to achieve adequate confidence such a device would work. As a proliferation action, accession to the LTBT effectively eliminated contracting parties' ability to acquire reliable nuclear weapon capability.

The same three states cosponsored the NPT. Its major purpose was to create a nuclear caste system on the basis of nuclear weapons possession. Nuclear-weapons-possessing states party to the NPT are allowed to keep their nuclear weapons, but agree not to share nuclear technology with nonpossessing states and to work toward disarmament of their arsenals. These provisions, one should quickly note, require very little action on the part of possessors, and are thus generally innocuous and painless. Nonpossessing states, on the other hand, incur real obligations, because they agree, as long as they are members of the treaty (and there are provisions to renounce one's membership), not to build or seek to build nuclear weapons. Among the nonweapons states that have signed the NPT, this creates a varying obligation. Some states (Sweden, for instance) have never had any intentions to build nuclear weapons and so could join the treaty regime without noticeable effect. Other states (most of the states of sub-Saharan Africa, for instance) lack the wherewithal to even think of developing the weapons, and thus they sacrifice little by joining either.

There is, however, a third category of states: countries that do not have nuclear weapons but might want the ability to exercise the option sometime in the future. For these states, the NPT creates a real potential problem, because ratifying it means giving away the right to exercise the nuclear option as long as one is a member. Although states can withdraw and thus free themselves from NPT restrictions, doing so is traumatic and would brand whoever did so as a potential aggressor. As a result, only one state that has signed NPT has ever left it (North Korea in 2003), joining Israel, Cuba, India, and Pakistan as nonmembers among the world's major countries.

States desiring to retain the nuclear option have two ways to deal with the NPT. One is not to sign it, thereby avoiding its restrictions. The most prominent states not to do so have included Israel, India, and Pakistan. Other states with potential nuclear aspirations have signed the agreement and either complied fully with it or have engaged in activities that come close to noncompliance but stop short of that level.

The nonproliferation enterprise remains a work in progress. Since the NPT was launched over a third of a century ago, there has been little overt nuclear weapons proliferation (India and Pakistan have been added, South Africa subtracted from the list). Yet, proliferation has emerged in the post–September 11 world as a major concern, fueled by the fear some rogue state—some member of the "Axis of Evil"—might acquire such weapons and either use them personally or through some terrorist surrogate. Whether this fear is real or fanciful is not the point; that this perception fuels international concern is the point. States like North Korea and Iran, however, retain interest in possibly gaining nuclear weapons status for different reasons that make the problem of proliferation an ongoing concern.

THE PROLIFERATION PROBLEM APPLIED: THE CASE OF NORTH KOREA

The general problem of proliferation gains meaning in the specific context of individual states that might or that are suspected of attempting to exercise the nuclear weapons option. The distinction of North Korea is that it has actually gone several steps through the proliferation process. It is, for instance, the only country physically to withdraw from the NPT, an action it undertook and completed in 2003. It is also the only potential new member of the nuclear club that has attempted to conduct actual nuclear weapons tests: in 2003, it attempted a small underground test, the success of which is disputed, and in 2009 seismic readings monitored in Japan indicated a seismic event consistent with a low-kiloton underground explosion in the DPRK. North Korea has also conducted medium-range ballistic missile tests with varying success, and it is actively working on a continental-range missile. It has not demonstrated the ability to wed nuclear weapons and ballistic missile delivery capabilities by testing a missile capable of delivering the weight payload of a nuclear weapon, and estimates vary about when it may achieve that status but are measured in years, not sooner.

The other states that have been mentioned prominently in proliferation concerns are Iran and Iraq, the two countries that joined the DPRK as members of George W. Bush's 2002 "Axis of Evil." All share several characteristics. First, they have or have had significant foreign policy differences with the United States (although of different natures and for different reasons) and have been categorized as among America's adversaries. Second, all three possess or have possessed the technology and expertise to produce nuclear weapons and either have or reasonably easily could have access to the weapons-grade plutonium necessary for bomb construction (this commonality separates them from other worrisome states). Third, all deny any interest or desire to build, and especially to use, nuclear weapons, claims that are widely disbelieved in policy circles, especially in the United States. Fourth, although they are or have been members of NPT, they are or have been deemed to be untrustworthy, rogue regimes whose word cannot be trusted at face value.

They are also different in an important respect already identified. Iran and Iraq are not currently nuclear powers, although Iran has active aspirations, as discussed in Chapter 7. There has never been verification that either has fabricated a nuclear weapon, and their regimes deny any interest in doing so. As such, they pose a problem of acquisition (or front-end) deterrence. North Korea is different. According to former assistant secretary of defense Ashton Carter and former secretary of defense William J. Perry (both under President Clinton) in a June 22, 2006, column in the *Washington Post*, the DPRK "openly boasts of its nuclear deterrent, has obtained six to eight bombs' worth of plutonium since 2003 and is plunging ahead to make more." A 2003 article in the *Bulletin of the Atomic Scientists* went so far as to state that "North Korea has apparently become the world's ninth nuclear power." Thus, the problem posed by North Korea is one of employment (or back-end) deterrence.

Background of the Problem

Although other ties between Iran, Iraq, and North Korea were tenuous (especially between the DPRK and the others) when Bush gave his Axis of Evil speech, they all shared a place on the proliferation agenda—especially the extent to which that agenda is affected, even dominated, by the United States. Each was an adversary of the United States, although the sources and nature of opposition varied. America's adversarial relationship with the DPRK was longest standing, dating back to the Korean War of 1950–1953, and its nuclear weapons program is normally dated back to the 1950s, when a nuclear-armed United States remained the occupying power in South Korea, a circumstance some argue helps explain the DPRK's perceived need for weapons of its own.

A common thread that runs through the North Korean and other cases is that the chief protagonist in the process has been the United States, which, of course, is the original N state, and it has consistently opposed almost all other attempts at proliferation. Great Britain's attainment of membership is the exception, and the United States has generally not been an overt opponent of the presumed Israeli program. Nuclear aspiration is one of the common attributes of the Axis of Evil states, and the long-standing animosity between the DPRK and the United States and the advanced status of the DPRK program give it especially poignant relevance for the United States. The location of the DPRK in East Asia, of course, makes the context different, a part of the East Asian power balance rather than the extreme volatility of the Middle East.

The proliferation problem posed by North Korea has ebbed and flowed. In the early 1990s it seemed to be settled. In 1994, the Clinton administration made a deal with the DPRK (the Framework Agreement), under which the

United States would furnish the North Koreans food, fuel oil, and light (nonweapons-grade) nuclear fuel in return for the DPRK abandoning its nuclear weapons program. That agreement held until the Bush administration, deeply suspicious and arguably ignorant of the North Koreans, threatened to and did renege on the deal. Cumings states the case regarding the Bush administration dramatically: "Bush combined utter ignorance with a visceral hatred for his counterpart in Pyongyang." This action led the North Koreans to remove themselves from the NPT in 2003 and to resume their nuclear program, the most recent chapter of which began in 2006.

The Continuing Problem

The proliferation problem regarding the DPRK is thus distinctive. North Korea, of course, poses a more advanced problem than the other pretenders, because of its presumed possession of a small number of nuclear weapons and its development of long-range missile systems. This means antiproliferation efforts must be based in employment deterrence or convincing the DPRK to disarm its arsenal, a less likely prospect.

The North Korean case is also distinctive in that it has been, at various times, in the process of being resolved through negotiation. After several years of off-again, on-again negotiations between the DPRK and the other countries involved in the so-called six-nations talks (the United States, Russia, China, Japan, and North and South Korea), a breakthrough occurred in summer 2008 that would, if fully implemented, result in North Korean disassembly of nuclear facilities capable of producing bomb-grade plutonium, destruction of nuclear bomb materials, and re-accession to the NPT. In return, the DPRK was removed from the U.S. State Department's list of terrorist states and the Axis of Evil, and some provisions of the American Trading with the Enemy Act pertinent to the DPRK have been lifted. Full implementation was interrupted in late 2008 by the apparent serious illness suffered by Kim Jong II, leaving DPRK leadership in limbo. Still, implementation of DPRK nuclear disarmament lags.

The rift between Pyongyang and Washington is far longer and deeper than it is between Tehran or Baghdad and Washington. The DPRK is the only country to withdraw from the NPT, and it has been much more recalcitrant about its weapons programs, including both nuclear weapons and ballistic delivery systems. Moreover, the Korean peninsula's location in the heart of East Asia gives it a great deal of geopolitical importance. On the other hand, North Korea has no oil, is one of the most destitute countries on the globe, and relies heavily on outside assistance to maintain its meager standard of living.

The DPRK's unique situation cuts both ways in terms of trying to deal with North Korea. The country's extreme poverty and lack of developmental prospects makes it receptive to outside assistance, as was part of the 1994 agreement. The regime is anxious to avoid letting the population know just how miserable their condition is and prospects are, particularly compared to the circumstances of surrounding countries like South Korea, but this is an ever-increasingly difficult condition to maintain, according to Lankov. More-over, as Lankov notes, the nuclear program serves to ameliorate some of the country's woes: "Pyongyang cannot do away with these programs. That would mean losing a powerful military deterrent and a time-tested tool of extortion. It would also relegate North Korea to being a third-rate country, on a par with Mozambique or Uganda."

The history of the North Korean nuclear program—and concerns about it—is long-standing and, as noted, is largely framed in terms of U.S.–North Korean relations. The United States and the DPRK have, of course, been antagonists since the Korean War (1950–1953) in which they were primary opponents. Aside from the general antagonism this confrontation created, it may have provided the impetus for North Korean nuclear pretensions. As Robert Norris put it in his 2003 *Bulletin of the Atomic Scientists* article, "The fact that North Korea was threatened with nuclear weapons during the Korean War, and that for decades thereafter U.S. weapons were deployed in the South, may have helped motivate former President Kim Il Sung to launch a nuclear weapons program of his own." Regardless of whether one accepts this expla-nation at face value, the North Koreans have been consistent over time that they need to maintain the option to develop nuclear weapons.

The genesis of the current crisis goes back to the Clinton administration. A May 1992 inspection of North Korean nuclear facilities by International Atomic Energy Agency (IAEA) inspectors headed by Hans Blix concluded the North Koreans might be engaged in weapons activity (converting spent nuclear fuel into weapons-grade plutonium). This precipitated a crisis in which the North Koreans threatened the until-then unprecedented step of withdrawing from the NPT in March 1993 (they had joined the treaty in 1984). At this point the Clinton administration intervened, entering into direct talks that produced a negotiated settlement to the problem, the Framework Agreement. Under its pro-visions (reference to the complete document is found in the suggested readings), the North Koreans agreed to freeze and eventually to dismantle their nuclear weapons program under IAEA supervision. In turn, North Korea would accept light water nuclear reactors to replace those capable of producing weapons-grade materials and would receive heavy fuel oil for electricity and heating purposes. In addition, Norris adds, "political and economic relations would be normalized, and both countries would work toward a nuclear weapons-free Korean peninsula and to strengthen the nuclear proliferation regime."

How well this arrangement worked was primarily a partisan political question in the United States. Republican critics—notably neoconservatives like John Bolton—of the Clinton policy underlying the Framework Agreement argued that the North Koreans were cheating on the letter and spirit of the agreement in terms of their handling of materials from their light water reac-tors, a claim vigorously denied by Selig Harrison in a 2005 *Foreign Affairs* article, who equates the intelligence reports of violations in North Korea to distortions similar to those coming out of Iraq in 2002.

At any rate, the current, ongoing crisis was precipitated when the Bush administration cut off the flow of heating oil to North Korea and terminated the Framework Agreement in December 2002. The DPRK responded by announcing on January 10, 2003, that it was withdrawing from the NPT, which it did after the mandatory 90-day waiting period following the announcement of intent. Following saber rattling on both sides in the ensuing months, six-party negotiations between the DPRK, South Korea, Japan, Russia, China, and the United States opened on August 28, 2003, at which point North Korea announced it was prepared "to declare itself formally as a nuclear weapons state" (which it did in December 2006) and added that it possessed the capability to deliver these weapons to target by ballistic means.

The North Koreans have always viewed the six-party format for negotiations (an American construct) as undesirable, preferring bilateral negotiations that the Bush administration refused to accept. On September 9, 2004, an explosion occurred at a nuclear site (Ryanggang) in North Korea that may have been a nuclear test, although the North Koreans denied that the test was of a nuclear device. The North Koreans announced on February 10, 2005, that they had developed nuclear weapons for self-defense purposes and suspended participation in the six-party talks. In a direct reversal that illustrates some of the flavor of the ongoing relationship, the six-party talks resumed in September 2005 and produced an agreement whereby the DPRK agreed to dismantle its nuclear weapons program in return for economic assistance. In June 2006, as the Taepodong crisis (tests of North Korean Taepodong missiles, some of which flew over Japanese territory) unfolded, critics Carter and Perry declared that "the six-party talks . . . have collapsed."

The summer 2006 brouhaha over North Korean missile tests emerged from this context. North Korea has for some years had a missile development program, and its potential ability to deliver WMDs by ballistic means distinguishes the DPRK from other proliferators, as noted. The previous missile crisis occurred in 1998, when the DPRK tested a Taepodong 1 missile that passed over Japan and created an international incident. The Clinton administration had exacted a moratorium on missile testing from the North Koreans in 1998, which, according to a June 21, 2006, *Los Angeles Times* report by Barbara Demick, it renewed in 2002. The North Koreans, in keeping with their nuclear tradition of denying they are engaged in WMD activities while asserting their right to do so if they choose, maintain that more recent Taepodong 2 tests are intended to see whether North Korea can insert a satellite into space. At the same time, they argue they retain the right to develop military missiles.

Was the missile dispute just another round of U.S.–North Korean bickering or something more serious? Carter and Perry, who were officials during the 1990s when agreements were reached with the DPRK, believed the crisis was real and that the United States should have considered a preemptive strike against the missile launch site if the North Koreans fail to decommission the missile. Alarm was raised because the Taepodong 2, especially if equipped with a third boost stage—which the purported test did not include and which the North Koreans have never done successfully—could reach targets in the United States (purportedly the current version could hit Hawaii, Alaska, and possibly parts of the West Coast of the United States). On the other hand, the

Taepodong series of missiles uses old technology, very vulnerable liquid-fuel rockets that take literally days to fuel at above-ground launchers and could hardly be used for a sneak attack against the United States or anywhere else. They are also very vulnerable to being attacked and destroyed during the fueling process, as Carter and Perry admit. "The multi-story, thin skinned missile filled with high-energy fuel is itself explosive—the U.S. airstrike would puncture the missile and probably cause it to explode." There is no reliable public information available on the accuracy of such missiles; presumably, they are fairly inaccurate.

One is left with what to make of the North Korean nuclear "threat." If, as they imply, North Koreans are nuclear-capable, the question is what would keep them from using their weapons? It is difficult to conjure reasons why North Korea would launch an offensive, preemptive nuclear strike against anyone, given the certain response would be its own utter and certain destruction. Using the nuclear weapons most observers say they have—and that the North Koreans do not strongly deny—may make little sense, but possessing such weapons may make sense if North Korea believes they help deter the United States from attacking the DPRK. The idea that the United States needs to be deterred may seem outlandish to most Americans, but not to the North Koreans. As Cumings puts it, "it seems irrational for Pyongyang to give up its handful of nukes when the United States still threatens to attack." In February 2007, both sides in effect "blinked." The DPRK agreed in the six-party talks to suspend its nuclear weapons program in return for the same kinds of incentives offered in 1994 by the United States.

The resumption of six-party talks (this time under Chinese chairmanship) resulted in the agreement announced in June 2008. It was an agreement from which both sides benefited. Those concerned with proliferation saw North Korea join South Africa as countries that have joined then quit the nuclear club, although some issues remained (whether the DPRK had actually constructed bombs and provided nuclear aid to Syria, for instance). In return, the DPRK succeeded in removing international sanctions against it that have prevented badly needed assistance from flowing to it (food and fuel, for instance). As President Bush said on June 27, 2008, "if, it [the DPRK] continues to make the right choices it can repair its relationship with the international community."

Mutual distrust and American concentration on Iraq and Afghanistan left the details of implementing these agreements uncompleted when Barack Obama became president in 2009. At one level, the prospects for agreement seemed improved; Obama lacked the Bush administration's intense hatred of the DPRK, and Obama had suggested his willingness to negotiate with adversaries, including the North Koreans. At the same time, the DPRK leadership clearly believes maintaining the nuclear option is in their best interest as their main sources of international stature and leverage. As a result, Cumings concludes that "it seems unlikely that the North can be coaxed into negotiating another nuclear agreement." Moreover, Lankov contends, "the United States and its allies have no efficient methods of coercion at their disposal." The DPRK proliferation problem is not, in other words, going to go away anytime soon.

A further twist in this ever-changing saga began on December 17, 2011, when DPRK leader Kim Jung-il died of a heart attack while on board a train. His health had been fragile for some time, and in 2010, one of his sons, Kim Jung Un, was declared the "Great Successor," a position to which he ascended on his father's death. The third-generation inheritor of power was, at that point, the world's youngest head of government at age 28. His youth has added to concern about relations on the peninsula and notably about DPRK nuclear intentions.

Under his leadership, the DPRK has continued and even accelerated its nuclear program, notably through the testing of medium-range ballistic missiles which, if upgraded, could eventually pose some threat to the American West Coast, as well as Alaska and Hawaii. Kim June Un has made increasingly bellicose statements toward the United States, including threats of nuclear war during the 2013 crisis. Although it is unclear whether these statements were actually part of a more warlike personal stance or an attempt to bolster his standing with the hardline North Korean military, this more aggressive stance has increased tensions on the peninsula. Both weapons and delivery systems progress have occurred since his rise to power. Whether these have been the result of efforts he initiated or the outcomes of programs initiated by his father is unclear, but at a minimum, the young leader has certainly sought to exploit them. One effect has been to make the nuclear proliferation problem worse, not better in East Asia.

CONCLUSION

The North Korean case study stands as a potential harbinger for other proliferation cases. The DPRK defied the proliferation regime and paid a price in terms of international sanctions, but international knowledge of its nuclear program and its nuclear weapons provided it with leverage that allowed it to maintain control of its nuclear fate and thereby to preserve the advantages North Koreans believe nuclear weapons provide them. Iraq lacked such leverage and it was flattened; Iran faces the international community exposed but weaponless, and its fate is uncertain. Is there a lesson here for future proliferators?

No one, except potential proliferating countries that are part of +1, argue that the spread of nuclear and other weapons of mass destruction to nonpossessing states is in principle a good idea that should be encouraged. On the other hand, the empirical evidence of the impact of individual proliferations (when individual countries joined the nuclear weapons "club") hardly provides incontrovertible proof of the most dire perils that have been predicted. What is the evidence, for instance, that the world is a less stable place because Israel, India, or Pakistan possesses the bomb? One can contend it would be better if they did not, but the peril remains theoretical, not demonstrated.

How should future proliferators view the scene? Should they conclude that their attempts to attain nuclear weapons status will be viewed as internationally dangerous and destabilizing, prompting an international response that will reduce their security if they do not eschew proliferation? Or will they decide a positive nuclear weapons decision will protect them—provide them a deterrent—from attacks by predators, thereby increasing their security?

Nuclear-possessing states have one answer to that question, but recent experience may offer a different interpretation. When they ask themselves (as the North Koreans apparently have) if Saddam Hussein would have been immune from an American invasion had he not stopped pursuing nuclear weapons, many believe he made the wrong choice. At the same time, its nuclear weapons may have won the DPRK a ticket off the Axis of Evil by presenting the world (and especially the United States) with a threat that harsh rhetoric alone could not solve. At a minimum, recent experience does not unambiguously tell potential proliferators not to pursue the nuclear option, and the experience of the DPRK in attracting world attention during the 2013 crisis with South Korea and the United States demonstrates that "going nuclear" still provides some leverage and has some attraction in international politics.

SUGGESTED ACTIVITIES AND QUESTIONS

1. What is the basis of the current international concern for nuclear proliferation? How does the DPRK exemplify this problem?
2. Why is proliferation a "delicate" problem? Distinguish between types of proliferation, including what kinds of materials and capabilities are being proliferated and what difference each makes.
3. What is the $N+1$ problem? Define it and explain why it suggests the delicacy of the proliferation problem. Why is it so difficult to resolve?
4. What means are available to deal with proliferation? Distinguish between acquisition and employment deterrence. How does each work?
5. What is the Nuclear Non-Proliferation Treaty (NPT)? How does it work? What categories of states are there in regard to the treaty? How are they different?
6. Define the DPRK in proliferation terms. What is its status? How has it evolved to where it is? How serious is it to international stability, and what can be done about it?
7. How has the success of the six-party talks changed the proliferation situation regarding the DPRK? Who gets what from the agreement?
8. Put yourself in the position of a country contemplating nuclear proliferation. Does recent experience suggest that pursuit of the nuclear option will enhance or detract from your security? Why?
9. If you were representing a country contemplating gaining nuclear weapons but in an adversarial relationship with the United States, how would that fact influence your decision process? Elaborate.

SUGGESTED READINGS AND RESOURCES

Arnoldy, Ben. "How Serious Is North Korea's Nuclear Threat?" *Christian Science Monitor* (online), August 27, 2003.
Bluth, Christoph. "North Korea: How Will It End?" *Current History* 109, 728 (September 2010), 237–243.
Carter, Ashton B. and William J. Perry. "If Necessary, Strike and Destroy." *Washington Post*, June 22, 2006, A29.

Cha, Victor D. and David C. Kang. *Nuclear North Korea: A Debate on Engagement Strategies.* New York: Columbia University Press, 2008.

Cumings, Bruce. "The North Korea Problem: Dealing with Irrationality." *Current History* 108, 719 (September 2009), 284–290.

Demick, Barbara. "Few Moves Left with N. Korea." *Los Angeles Times* (online), June 21, 2006.

Harrison, Selig S. "Did North Korea Cheat?" *Foreign Affairs* 84, 1 (January/February 2005), 99–110.

Lankov, Andrei. "Changing North Korea." *Foreign Affairs* 88, 6 (November–December 2009), 95–105.

Lieber, Kier A. and David G. Press. "The Rise of U.S. Nuclear Supremacy." *Foreign Affairs* 85, 2 (March/April 2006), 42–54.

Mendelsohn, Jack. "The New Threats: Nuclear Amnesia, Nuclear Legitimacy." *Current History* 105, 694 (November 2006), 385–390.

The National Security Strategy of the United States of America. Washington, DC: The White House, March 2006.

Norris, Robert S. "North Korea's Nuclear Program, 2003." *Bulletin of the Atomic Scientists* 59, 2 (March/April 2003), 74–77.

Onishi, Norimitsu and Edward Wong. "U.S. to Take North Korea Off Terrorist List." *New York Times* (online), June 27, 2008.

Perkowich, George. "The End of the Proliferation Regime." *Current History* 105, 694 (November 2006), 355–362.

Pilat, Joseph F. "Reassessing Security Assurances in a Unipolar World." *Washington Quarterly* 28, 2 (Spring 2005), 59–70.

Sigal, Leon V. "The Lessons of North Korea's Test." *Current History* 105, 694 (November 2006), 364–365.

Snow, Donald M. *Cases in American Foreign Policy*, 1st ed. New York: Pearson, 2013, especially Chapter 4.

_____. and Eugene Brown. *The Contours of Power: An Introduction to Contemporary International Relations.* New York: St. Marin's Press, 1996.

Specter, Arlen and Christopher Walsh. "Dialogue with Adversaries." *Washington Quarterly* 30, 1 (Winter 2006/2007), 9–26.

Winner, Andrew C. "The Proliferation Security Initiative: The New Face of Interdiction." *Washington Quarterly* 28, 2 (Spring 2005), 129–143.

WEB SITES

North Korean Weapons Program Summary (Wikipedia): http://en.wikipedia.org

Text of U.S.-DPRK Agreed Framework of 1994: http://www.kedo.org/pdfs/AgreedFramework.pdf

Pivotal States: Confronting and Accommodating Iran

PRÉCIS

Although the theory of sovereign equality makes all states equal, their influence within the international system is variable. At one extreme are the most powerful states, the great powers or superpowers, and at the other end are more minor states, whose power is less. Between them are a number of regional powers that, by virtue of history, size, and a number of other measures, are powers whose interests must be taken into account within their parts of the world. In this case study, these states are referred to as pivotal states. In the contemporary international system, one of the most important pivotal states is Iran, making it the subject of this case. Pivotal states become important when their interests and those of the major powers come into conflict, and this aspect of the pivotal state phenomenon is explored through an examination of U.S.–Iranian contemporary relations.

There is a category of states in the international system that falls somewhere below the most important powers (what used to be called *major powers* and during the Cold War *superpowers*) but above the "rank and file" of states in the system. Major states, especially the most powerful superpowers, wield predominant influence on the international scene and are its most influential members. Generally, their reach goes beyond the physical region in which they are located and has an impact on other countries around the world. At the other extreme are the mass of states that are comparatively weak, have some limited regional influence at best, and generally can be influenced by the major powers and more important regional states.

The category in between these extremes is composed of a limited number of states. They lack the comprehensive power and influence to play a major role globally, but are substantially powerful enough that they cannot be manipulated easily by the major powers and generally can influence the behavior of other states and thus events in their regions. Moreover, even though the power such states possess may compare unfavorably with that of the major powers on a broad array of measures (military might or economic size, for instance), they may be capable of frustrating the designs of more powerful states, at least within their particular regions. Although their ability to influence global politics may not compare favorably to the capabilities of the most powerful countries, they are nonetheless consequential within the range of their influence. One way to think about states in this category is as regional powers; another is as *pivotal states*.

The effects of pivotal states can be benign or problematical, depending on circumstances and who is affected by their actions. Brazil, for instance, is clearly a pivotal state in the Western Hemisphere (with arguable aspirations to major power or even superpower status) that, most of the time, is not a negative factor in the politics of its region and lacks the global reach to make it a major world power despite its aspirations. It does, however, provide an occasional obstacle to the interests of its hemispheric superpower, the United States, in areas such as the expansion of a free trade association within the region (the Free Trade Area of the Americas proposal). At the same time, Brazil is the largest country in Latin America in size and population, making it the predominant regional actor south of the American–Mexican border. In Asian affairs, the impact of Brazil is not generally critical; within the Western Hemisphere, its interests cannot be ignored.

It is when pivotal states come into conflict with the major powers that their influence becomes problematical and their presence and status become controversial. Particularly to the largest powers like the United States, each region of the world is one theater of its global interests, and it prefers an order in the region congruent with its worldview. The American foreign policies of globalization in the 1990s and democratization in the 2000s are examples. In each case, the United States has seen the success of its foreign policy in the success or failure to bring countries in different regions either into Clinton's circle of market democracies or Bush's expanding circle of democracies. When that vision comes into conflict with the regional interests of the most important state or states in a particular region, then the prospect for conflict emerges. The superpower may have greater global resources to apply to achieving its ends worldwide, but because those resources must be parsed across the globe, this does not necessarily translate into resources with which to confront successfully the contrary interest of the pivotal state in a given place. In addition, the regional pivotal state's interests are likely to be more important to it within a region than the major power's interests in that region are to it, and although the major state may have greater power than the pivotal state, the pivotal state's power is more proximate and may be easier to apply than that of the major power.

In the contemporary international system, no state better exemplifies the roles of a pivotal state than does Iran, which Nasr and Takeyh identify as the aspiring pivotal state in the Middle East in a January/February 2008 *Foreign Affairs* article that was an inspiration for the theme of this case study.

Iran is arguably the pivotal state in the Middle East as a whole and certainly in its oil-rich section, the Persian Gulf. The world's second oldest existing state (after China), Iran—or Persia, or the Persian Empire—has been a major power in the Middle East for centuries, dating back at least to 1500 B.C. When that part of the world was at the center of the world system, it was one of the world's major powers, a superpower of its time. The inheritors of the Peacock Empire are well aware of their heritage and their place in the global politics of the oil-rich Middle East, and it is a past status to which many Iranians cast a wistful eye. Iran views itself as *the* most consequential state in the region, and on the basis of that perception, it believes its interests are of paramount importance in the region and even beyond.

Iran and the United States have been engaged in a superpower–pivotal state struggle since 1979, when the pro-American Iranian government of Shah Reza Pahlavi was overthrown and replaced by a stridently anti-American, theocratic Islamic Republic of Iran. As a result, the existence and actions of the pivotal state of Iran became particularly vexing for the United States, as American interests and those of the regional pivotal state came into conflict across a range of issues affecting the region to the point that a U.S. Secretary of State, quoted in Nasr and Takeyh, has declared that "Iran constitutes the single most important single-state challenge to the United States and the kind of Middle East we seek." And this conflict has been intensified by Iran's nuclear weapons program, which Iran denies exists. Major powers are used to getting their own way most of the time and are particularly frustrated when the actions of supposedly lesser powers—and notably the pivotal powers—provide an effective obstacle to achieving those interests. In the Persian Gulf region, Iran poses the primary barrier to outside influence, and its challenge is increasing. As Milani puts it, "Iran now rightly considers itself as an indispensable regional player." The United States' relationship with Iran is an absolutely classical example of the clash between a superpower and a regional pivotal state.

This case study serves two purposes. The first is to explore the nature of the pivotal state, using Iran as the primary example. The second is to examine the problems that pivotal states can create for the international system. This in turn requires looking at what makes pivotal states important and thus provides them with power and leverage and also at the frustrations that major powers have in both understanding and coping with recalcitrant pivotal states. The enormous frustration of American foreign policy makers in their attempts to control the behavior of Iran serves as the prime example of superpower–pivotal state relations problem.

IRAN: A PIVOTAL STATE

Iran occupies a unique place in the world. It has been a major part of world civilization through most of recorded history, and it has been a central actor whenever its region has been the focus of the international system. As a result, it has seen its place in the international sun wax and wane, and it clearly aspires and is actively working to seeing it rise again. Part of the basis for this ambition is its physical presence, including, most prominently in the contemporary setting, energy resources over which there is a growing global competition (see Chapter 2). At the same time, Iran has a unique history and historical legacy that is both a part of and simultaneously apart from the rest of the region. Its unique attributes help explain its contemporary evolution and Iran's place in the contemporary international system.

The Physical Setting

Iran is a large country. It has a land area of 631,659 square miles (slightly larger than Alaska and about three times the size of Arizona), which makes it the largest physical state in the Middle East and the world's second largest state in area (after Indonesia) with a Muslim majority. With a population of 78,868,711 (2012 estimate based on *World Almanac and Book of Facts 2013* figures), it is the third most populous Muslim state (following Indonesia and Egypt) in the world. Its economy ranks 20th among world countries in overall size, the highest of any Islamic country, and its per capita gross domestic product is at $12,300, making it globally a middle-range economy.

It is also a resource-rich country. Iran is one of the world's leading exporters of oil, selling 2.52 million barrels per day internationally out of a total daily production of 4.15 million barrels in 2006. Its proven reserves of oil are the world's third largest at 132.5 billion barrels (after Saudi Arabia and Canada). Its natural gas reserves are among the largest in the world, at an estimated 26.37 *trillion* cubic meters. Taxes on oil revenues currently account for over 80 percent of governmental revenues.

Iran's renaissance as a world power is directly related to the growing importance of petroleum energy in the last century. Due to its central location, Iran is a pivot in the burgeoning traditional global oil competition of which neighboring China and India will be growing players in upcoming years, as pointed out in Chapter 2. So will Russia. As Baktiari puts it, "China and Russia . . . are wrapped up in Iran's energy sector. China is aggressively pinning down future sources around the world, and Russia is assisting Iran in the construction of a civilian nuclear reactor in Bushehr." Aside from Iran (Iraq is a partial exception), the oil-rich states of the region happen also to be relatively small, underpopulated, and possessed of limited military resources with which to protect themselves. Iran is *the* major power, in potential and reality, in the Persian Gulf region, and it will hold that position as long as the world appetite for fossil fuel energy remains unrequited. Dependence on oil is, however, a double-edged sword for the Iranians, as it is for all the countries whose economies depend on oil revenues. As long as demand and price remain high, the fact that, according to Vaki, "the oil sector is vital for the government's export earnings, 80 percent of which are oil-related," is tolerable. Should trends such as greater reliance on shale gas and oil make traditional oil revenue become less central, the Iranian economy will become vulnerable unless the economy is diversified. Indeed, some analysts like Chadar argue that economic factors may become the pivot of potential economic stability and demands for political change.

In several ways, Iran's physical location also contributes to its pretension as a pivotal power. It sits astride the vital Persian (or Arabian) Gulf, through which most of the region's petroleum moves to the marketplace, and its coastline on the Gulf includes one of the world's major maritime choke points, the Straits of Hormuz. The possibility, raised periodically by the Iranians themselves, that Iran might menace the flow of oil to the West is the basic reason for a large American naval presence in the Persian Gulf region. At the same time, Iran is located strategically near the oil-rich Arab states of the Persian Gulf littoral (Saudi Arabia, Kuwait, and Iraq) and the potential oil-producing giants of Central Asia and the Caspian littoral. Iran also is not far from both Russia and China, and the result is that good relations with the regime in Tehran are important for both countries.

Iran as a Unique State

Iran stands at odds with the other states of its region. It is not "just another" Middle Eastern country that can be lumped conveniently with others in the region. Two ways in which Iran differs from other aspects of the Middle East–region conflicts are worth mentioning: its historical significance and its ethno-religious status. Each contributes to the uniqueness of Iran and why it is misleading and potentially distorting to consider Iran within the context of other regional states.

The second oldest continuous state in the world, Iran was known for most of its history as Persia; the name changed in 1935 to Iran. Its history dates back at least to 549 B.C. when Cyrus the Great declared the Persian Empire and, among other things, restored Jerusalem to Jewish rule. Through its history, the central location of Persia/Iran made it attractive to foreigners, and the result has been a history marked both by independence and greatness and also by occupation. Persia was conquered by Alexander the Great in 333 B.C. and the Turks and Mongols in turn ruled Persia from the eleventh into the sixteenth centuries. In more modern history, the Russian and British empires competed for influence in Iran in the nineteenth century, and in 1941, the British and Soviets forced the abdication of the first Shah of Iran (Reza Khan, the father of Shah Muhammad Reza Pahlavi) because of his suspected Nazi sympathies and the likelihood he might deliver Iranian oil to the fascist powers in World War II. Iranian independence was restored with the ascension of Muhammad Reza Pahlavi as Shah of the Iranian (Peacock) Empire in 1941, and it has remained independent ever since. Persian/Iranian civilization's status is among the oldest in the world, creating a sense of nationalism and identification that is much stronger than in other states in the region.

Iran also stands out from its neighbors in ethno-religious terms in ways that have become familiar to many Americans because of connections made between the Iranians and Iraqis during the American-instigated war and occupation of Iraq. Of the major (and especially oil-producing) states of the Middle East, Iran is both the only non-Arab major oil producer and the largest Shiite state in the region. Both characteristics create major distinctions between

Map 7.1 Map of Iran

Iran and its neighbors. Without understanding these differences, it is impossible to appreciate the nature and extent of Iranian participation as the region's pivotal state and why that status is opposed not only by the United States but also by other regional powers.

Although Iran is a multiethnic state, its core population is Persian. Persians make up just over half of the Iranian population. Ethnically, they are Aryan as opposed to Arab, the ethnic designation of most of Iran's neighbors, especially to the west and south. The Kurds of Iran, Iraq, and Syria share Aryan lineage, as do several other minor ethnic groups in the region. Historically, the relationship between the Persians and the Arabs has been antagonistic, including mutual histories of conquest and occupation. Indeed, Islam arrived in Persia as a result of its conquest by the Arab Empire. In addition to the dominant

Persians, Azeris (mostly in the northwestern province of Azerbaijan adjacent to the former Soviet Republic and current state by the same name) constitute an additional 24 percent of the population, and other ethnic groups each with less than 10 percent of the population include Kurds, Arabs, Turkmen, and Baluchis. This composition leads Bradley to suggest that Iran is "not so much a nation-state as a multinational empire dominated by Persians."

Iran is also distinguished from surrounding states because almost 90 percent of its population belongs to the Shiite sect of Islam. Shia Islam is a minority sect within Islam overall (only about 15 percent of Muslims are Shiite, although their proportion is growing). Sunni Islam is the sect to which the majority of Muslims in most neighboring states (Iraq, with a 60 percent Shiite majority, is a notable exception) belong. Sunnis and Shiites have been in conflict since the two sects split apart in the aftermath of the death of the Prophet Mohammad in the seventh century A.D., and they view one another as political rivals within Islamic countries and internationally. Acceptance of Iran as the region's pivotal state is thus denied or decried in the region both because the Iranians are Persian and because they are Shiite.

The result of these distinctions is to complicate the Middle East and to muddy Iran's place in it. With a population of over 78 million people, Iran dwarfs the rest of the Persian Gulf states and is, on purely geopolitical grounds, the most consequential and thus pivotal state in the region. Were Iran an Arab, Sunni state, there is little question that it would be accepted as the most important regional power. The fact that animosities between Persians and Arabs date back to biblical times (between Persia and Mesopotamia, for instance) and are overlaid with sectarian differences within Islam keeps the Sunni Arab states from accepting Iranian leadership and, indeed, most other regional states see Iran as a rival, if not an outright enemy. This division between Persian, Shiite Iran, and its Arab, Sunni neighbors has particular significance in shaping regional, as well as global, suspicions about Iran's nuclear weapons plans, as discussed later in this case.

This wariness is especially evident in Iranian relations with two countries, Iraq and Israel. The Iraqi connection is most obvious: Arab Iraq and Persian Iran share a long common border that includes, at its southern reaches leading to the Persian Gulf, the oil-producing regions of the Iraqi Basra and Persian Khuzestan oil fields and the refining capacities along the Shatt al-Arab, the waterway created by the confluence of the Tigris and Euphrates rivers that flows into the gulf. The two counties are, in important respects, the successors of Persia and Mesopotamia, and they have had a turbulent past, most recently demonstrated in the Iran–Iraq War between 1980 and 1988.

The current role of Iran in the politics of Iraq has become particularly problematical since Iraq resumed full sovereign independence in 2011. Common Shiite roots give Iran an automatic interest in and influence over how Iraq emerges from the American occupation. Iran has involved itself in Iraqi politics, providing support for virtually all the Shiite movements both inside and outside the al-Maliki government, and the American command in the country accused the Iranians, principally through its Quds force, of providing military hardware that is used against both American and Iraqi forces. Vaki describes Iranian policy in Iraq as "controlled chaos, in essence a stealth strategy designed to undermine American initiatives while strengthening Iran's regional position." At a minimum, the Iranians hope to influence the new Shiite-dominated post-American government in Iraq; how much more they desire is problematical. The major factor limiting the extent of Iranian influence is the fact that the Iranians are not Arabs like the Iraqis.

Iran has also had a unique relationship with Israel. Through its creation and support of Hezbollah, which is dedicated to the elimination of the Israeli state, the Iranian position appears to be one of total antipathy toward Israel, a useful position among Muslim states in the region. Over time, however, the relationship has been more complicated. As already noted, Cyrus the Great did return Jerusalem to the Jews, and under the rule of the Shah of Iran from the end of World War II until 1979, Iran was a major supplier of oil to Israel in the face of the antipathy of its neighbors. The militant revolutionary regime that succeeded the Shah after the Iranian Revolution has been steadfastly anti-Israeli, making Western countries like the United States that support Israel even more leery of the Iranians.

The Evolution of Contemporary Iranian Politics

Modern Iranian politics has been schizophrenic, and part of its changeability has been a result of the relationship that Iran has had with the United States. In essence, the political history of contemporary Iran can be divided into two polar-opposite periods: the period of rule by Muhammed Reza Pahlavi, the Shah of Iran, and the period since his overthrow, the Iranian revolutionary period. The first period is marked by close collaboration and relations between the United States and Iran; the latter has been distinguished by sometimes bitter enmity between the two countries.

As noted, the Shah of Iran came to power originally in 1941 as the successor of his father, Reza Khan; he was briefly removed from office in 1953 by the democratically elected government of Dr. Mohammad Mossadeqh over a dispute about the nationalization of Iranian oil, but the Shah was returned to power with the aid of the Central Intelligence Agency late in that year (an American action that remains a major source of anti-Americanism in Iran to this day). The Shah remained in power until 1979, when he was forced into exile by the Iranian Revolution.

Reign of the Shah. The major theme and goal of the Shah's rule was the restoration of Iran—the Peacock Empire—to its former glory among the countries of the world. It was a highly nationalistic appeal to a people who had spent 200 years under foreign domination before the rise of his father, and it had been heavily influenced by the European powers in the years surrounding World War II. To restore Iran to its historic place among the world's powers, the Shah tied Iran's oil wealth to an ambitious program of economic and social modernization and westernization that sought to create a modern Iranian state that would be a worthy successor to the Persian Empire. To help him accomplish that goal, the Shah found a ready ally in the United States. In return for American assistance in modernizing Iran's economy and society (and, not coincidentally, its military), Iran served as the guarantor of oil supplies flowing from the Persian Gulf, thereby obviating the need for a direct American military presence in the region to ensure the supply of petroleum to the United States and its allies.

The principal vehicle of this transformation was the *White Revolution*, a series of economic and political reforms that underpinned Iran's transformation. Among other things, the reforms created a modern industrial society, including the creation of a technocratic middle class and military officer corps largely educated and trained in the West (especially the United States) that became a major vehicle for social westernization. In addition, the Shah introduced reforms that led to a massive movement of people from the countryside to urban centers like Tehran that were unequipped to absorb the influx. This demographic change also undercut much of the traditional power of the religious community—nationalizing land holdings and reforming the judicial system to exclude the clergy from its historic role in areas commonly thought of as civil law in the West.

This transformation came with costs that gradually accumulated. For one thing, the supporters of the Shah became a highly visible, affluent, and westernized elite that flaunted its status through conspicuous consumption (alcohol usage, gambling, Western dress, for instance) that offended the sensibilities of the extremely conservative Shiite majority. The society became highly stratified, and members of the westernized middle class came to realize that they lived under a glass ceiling limiting their upward-status mobility. At the same time, the vast majority of Shiite peasants lived in poverty, even squalor, in the urban slums created by forced urbanization or in the countryside. The religious hierarchy, stripped of much of its power but forming the natural leadership of the peasants, seethed at their displacement and vowed holy revenge.

The contradictions of the White Revolution began to boil to the surface in the early 1970s. The lightning rod of discontent was a Shiite religious figure, the Ayatollah Ruhollah Khomeini. The recognized leader of Iran's Shiites, Khomeini was forced into exile first in Iraq (where most of the holiest shrines of Shia Islam are located) and later, after the Shah brought pressure on the Iraqi regime, to Paris. From his Parisian exile, the Ayatollah advocated the overthrow of the Shah's regime, a cudgel taken up by the mullahs (religious teachers) who opposed the Shah.

The movement against the Shah grew as the 1970s progressed. Initially, the Shah employed his hated and feared secret police, SAVAK, to suppress dissidence, but by the middle of the 1970s, anti-Shah protests grew, aided by two unrelated phenomena. First, the United States elected Jimmy Carter president in 1976, and one of his principal themes was the promotion of global human rights enforcement. Iran was one of the worst offenders in the human rights area, and the administration came down especially hard on the Shah's government to improve its record. The Iranians complied by restraining SAVAK, and the result was largely to decrease its coercive ability and thus to loosen control on the dissidents. Second, the Shah was diagnosed with the cancer that eventually killed him, and when critical decisions had to be made about how to deal with the dissenters in the late 1970s, the Shah was apparently so physically debilitated that he was unable to reach critical decisions about how to control the growing unrest.

Matters reached a head on January 16, 1979, when the Shah and his family left the country on what was officially a foreign visit but that everyone recognized was an abdication. Within two weeks, Khomeini and his entourage returned from exile, and the process of revolutionary change was begun. Leaders of the middle class and the religious hierarchy vied initially for power, but it became increasingly clear that the religious majority would consolidate power to itself. The country's name was changed to the Islamic Republic of Iran as symbol of the change. On November 4, 1979, Iranian "students" overwhelmed the American embassy in Tehran and took its occupants hostage. The resulting crisis lasted until January 20, 1981, when the hostages were released in an atmosphere where newly inaugurated U.S. President Ronald W. Reagan threatened dire military action if they were not. The era of U.S.–Iranian collaboration was ended.

Revolutionary Iran.   Since 1979, a highly antagonistic, theocratic regime has ruled Iran. It is a highly disruptive and bedeviling force in the region and particularly toward the United States. The details of the operation of Iranian politics since the overthrow of the Shah are byzantine and beyond capture in the limited space available here. The essence of that evolution can nonetheless be described.

The Iranian Revolution was both a religious and a political event. At one level, it was a revolt against the policies and person of the Shah and his entourage and particularly against the repression that had been part of the Shah's way of dealing with dissidents from the White Revolution. This opposition was based both in the vast underclass of Iran and also in the middle class adversely affected by limits on their upward mobility. The other level of the revolution was religious, the revolt of the Shiite majority, led by the religious hierarchy that is a feature of Shia but not Sunni Islam. This aspect of the revolution was both revivalist and fundamentalist in the classic Muslim tradition of religious purification and return to Quranic purity, a strand also present in Sunni Islam (the Wahhabi sect of Sunnism that dominates Saudi Arabia arose originally as a revivalist movement opposing dilution of Islamic purity, for instance). These two strands coalesce and blend together in the theocratic framework that is particularly strong among Iranian Shiites and their religious leadership.

These two strands of the revolution are not and have not been totally in agreement with one another in terms either of the revolution or the Iran the revolution has created. In the months after the departure of the Shah, there was, indeed, a competition between those who supported one or the other emphasis. The middle class, by and large, saw the revolution as a vehicle to remove the tyranny of the Shah and his instruments of repression and to replace it with some more participatory, democratic political system. In this desire, they owed a common heritage with the Mossadeqh tradition. As a well-educated and sophisticated segment of the population, they viewed themselves as the logical inheritors of political power and assumed that the lower classes and their religious leaders could be brought to heel in support of their claim to leadership. Iranians from this tradition form much of the core of the potential dissonance that periodically resurfaces, as in the case of demonstrations protesting the outcomes of the 2009 presidential election.

The religious elements, whose appeal was based in Shiite fundamentalism, had different visions, and they prevailed. The vast mass of discontented peasants saw westernization and modernization as both the vehicle of their repression and as an abomination before Allah, and they supported the religious hierarchy that promised a return to Quranic virtue. With Ayatollah Khomeini acting as their spiritual symbol (Khomeini never held any political office, even though he was the de facto political leader of the country), the religious conservatives successfully overwhelmed the middle class and rapidly took over and consolidated control of the country. Their principal vehicle for doing so was through the actions of the Revolutionary Guards and Courts, originally vigilante bodies who identified opponents of religious revivalism and suppressed both these heretics and anyone else associated with the Shah's regime. Gradually, this element has been incorporated as a major part of the government.

The result has been a militantly religious Islamic Republic of Iran that has been an increasingly important element in the politics of the Middle East. Its political system operates at two different levels. The real seat of power remains in the firm control of the religious hierarchy. The Supreme Leader of the country is Ayatollah Ali Khamenei, who operates the system of revolutionary guards and courts through something known as the Guardian Council (which, among other things, selects candidates for formal political office). Parallel to this structure is the democratically elected government, consisting of a parliament (the Majlis) and an executive branch, the top elected official of which is the president. The first president was Mohammed Khatami, described as a "moderate" cleric, who gained office in 1997 and was viewed in the West as someone who would lead Iran back to a more conventional place in the hierarchy of countries.

Khatami was replaced in 2005 by Mahmoud Ahmadinejad, who has become a well-known figure in the West and the lightning rod for American concern about the direction of Iranian international politics. Ahmedinejad, the former mayor of Tehran, was initially elected in 2005 and reelected in 2009. He had been one of the six candidates allowed to run for office by the Guardian Council in 2005 and is known as a conservative, savvy politician. He has been particularly anti-American because, as Takeyh explains, the president "understands that the carnage in Iraq, the stalled Israeli–Palestinian peace process, and the inability of Arab rulers to stand up to Washington have created an intense anti-Americanism throughout the Middle East" that he hopes he can exploit to his own and Iran's advantage. Ahmedinejad was replaced in 2013 by Hassan Rouhani who, among other things, has voiced an interest in reducing tensions between the United States and Iran.

The United States serves as a useful foil in Iranian politics. As Milani describes it, "For decades, the Iranian regime has used anti-Americanism to crush its opponents and expand its power abroad." The association of the "Great Satan" with the Shah and the White Revolution makes the United States a useful displacement object to arouse scorn and to obscure the very real weaknesses of the current regime's performance. The great hope that the United States has for inducing change in Iran derives from the nascent desire for political freedom that is most strongly voiced by Iranian students, and it is associated with the middle class and the Mossadeqh days. The middle class is less anti-American than are the supporters of the revolution, and many of the ideas and demands they have are for reformed conditions not dissimilar to the goals of the White Revolution. Anti-Americanism, however, remains a strong influence-limiting factor in Iranian politics.

DEALING WITH IRAN

Iran is an important and pivotal state with its own unique place in the world, and it is a prominent member of the Middle Eastern equation that cannot be ignored. The current Iranian government sees its interests very differently than did the Shah of Iran, and almost all of the changes from pre- to postrevolutionary Iran have caused increasing antagonism between the United States and Iran. Iran sees itself as the logically dominant state in the Persian Gulf region— the pivotal state, a status it covets and that has important regional ramifications. As Ehteshami puts it, "Given Iran's significant weight and influence in the broader Middle East, developments in that country will cast a shadow over everything else."

U.S.–Iranian relations have become a textbook example of the sometimes fractious relations between a major power (the United States) and a pivotal regional power (Iran) in the pivotal state's region. Based upon a comparison of gross power along virtually any dimension of power, the United States is clearly the more powerful state, and the comparison would suggest that the United States should prevail in a struggle over those interests. That, however, has not been the case, and the result is an Iran that both frustrates the United States by not conforming to its wishes and continues to pursue policies the United States opposes. The interaction demonstrates the importance of pivotal states in the international order.

The most visible source of U.S.–Iranian disagreement focuses on Iran's nuclear program. Former Secretary of State Condoleezza Rice deemed Iran a major menace because of the prospect that Iran might use what it says is a peaceful nuclear power program to produce nuclear weapons, a prospect that multiple American politicians have said is absolutely unacceptable and about which there have been dire warnings issued. This issue is closely entwined with disagreement over Iranian policy toward Israel—the connection being Israel's unadmitted but universally accepted possession of nuclear weapons. The conflict extends to the regional power balance in the Persian Gulf region, in turn focusing on Iranian actions and intentions toward Iraq. McFaul, Milani, and

Diamond summarize these areas of disagreement, adding American interests in Iranian domestic politics: "limit Iran's assertiveness in the region; halt Tehran's support for terrorism, promote Iranian democracy and human rights; and stop Iran from obtaining nuclear weapons."

The Nuclear Weapons Issue

The Iranian nuclear program is the lightning rod of U.S.–Iranian enmity. The United States maintains that Iran's nuclear program is intended to produce nuclear weapons, an outcome it opposes in nonproliferation principle and because it fears the radical Iranian regime might use any weapons it obtains irresponsibly, including possibly sharing them with terrorists or attacking Israel. The disagreement between the two countries is a classic $N+1$ problem as discussed in Chapter 6. The 2006 *National Security Strategy of the United States* puts the implications most dramatically: "We face no greater challenge from a single country than from Iran." The Obama administration has repeatedly reiterated that emphasis. The Iranians, on the other hand, deny any intention to develop and possess nuclear weapons and argue that their program is fully in compliance with international atomic guidelines.

Why would Iran want to obtain nuclear weapons? There are at least three possible reasons. The first is as a demonstration of Iran's place of prominence in the world, a matter of prestige. Although the designation has a Cold War aura about it, one way to distinguish the most powerful countries in the world from one another and from lesser powers is through nuclear weapons possession. As Baktiari explains, "Iranians tend to support the nuclear program as a matter of national pride. The conservatives in Iran's government are successfully using the nuclear issue as a means to cement their own power through nationalist fervor." He adds a touch of irony: "In this, they have been unwittingly assisted by President Bush," whose objection to the program simply makes it more popular in Iran. Moreover, as Chadar adds, "Tehran has effectively turned U.S. opposition to its program into a nationalistic cause," as well as "an effective bargaining chip."

There are two other possible motivations for the Iranians. One, which Pollack argues is their primary motivation, is to deter an American attack on them. "From an Iranian perspective," he asserts, "possession of nuclear weapons makes sense for purely defensive reasons. If you have nuclear weapons, the United States will not dare use force against you, but if you do not, you are vulnerable." This motivation reflects a perception that many people in the Middle East share that the primary mistake Saddam Hussein made in the years leading to his overthrow was in abandoning his nuclear weapons program under international pressure, as noted in Chapter 6. In the eyes of McFaul, Milani, and Diamond, this motivates the Iranian program: "In large measure, Iran's leaders seek nuclear weapons to deter a U.S. attack." Even if one questions this motive, there is a more practical motivation, according to Maloney: "No regime is likely to bargain away its deterrent capability as long as it believes that the other side's ultimate objective is its own eradication."

The nuclear weapons possibility thus provides a basic part of its foreign policy, as stated by Milani: "Tehran has responded to Washington's policy of containment with a strategy of deterrence."

This argument is based, in other words, on Iran's sense of insecurity in the face of what it views as capricious U.S. policy and actions in the Persian Gulf region. It does not matter that the American public overwhelmingly opposes military action against Iran; the invasion of Iraq and American intransigence toward Tehran create an atmosphere where the nuclear program serves as a useful hedge against the "crazy" Americans. In addition, the historic unwillingness of the United States to negotiate unconditionally with the Iranians may add fuel to their perceived need for possessing nuclear weapons. Waltz further argues that Iranian possession will create a more stable military balance in the region and will thereby reinforce stability, not instability.

The other possible motivation in Iran's eyes is Israel. If one discounts Pakistan as regionally marginal, the only state in the Middle East that has nuclear weapons is Israel, and since 1979, relations between Iran and Israel could hardly be worse. One major aspect of this antagonism is Iranian creation of and continuing support for Hezbollah, which has the destruction of the Israeli state as one its major goals. Anti-Israeli and anti-Semitic rhetoric by Ahmadinejad (questioning whether the Holocaust really occurred, for instance) have only fanned the fire of Israeli–Iranian antipathy.

This antagonism is reciprocal. Israel has been among the loudest doomsayers about Iranian intent and especially the nuclear program. The Israelis have the precedent of having attacked an Iraqi nuclear reactor to destroy its weapons program in 1981, and took similar actions against Syria in 2006. Part of the reason the Iranians have greatly dispersed and hardened elements of their nuclear capacity underground is to discourage a reprisal against them. Because of Israeli antipathy, Donovan argued a decade ago that "the Israeli nuclear arsenal will continue to drive Iranian . . . WMD acquisition efforts in the foreseeable future."

Israeli–Iranian antagonism may prove to be the most combustible aspect of the Iranian nuclear program. Israel clearly feels more threatened by Iranian nuclear weapons than anyone else (given its small size and population concentration, as well as proximity, Israel is quite vulnerable to attack) and has repeatedly threatened to take preemptive action to prevent the Iranian program from reaching fruition. The fear of a possible Israeli preemptive decision may, in turn, push Tehran toward a nuclear decision to gain a capability to deter such an attack. Iran's Sunni Arab neighbors are also suspicious of the Iranian program, however, and Iran's attainment could spur some of them such as Saudi Arabia to similar action. As Ehteshami argues, "Israel's nuclear monopoly could end in rapid proliferation."

For the time being, the standoff between the United States and Iran over the latter's nuclear weapons program remains a stalemate. Iran denies any intentions to convert its program to nuclear weapons acquisition, but it could do so in the future. The United States and especially Israel question the sincerity or the truthfulness of the denials. For now, Iran argues that the development of a peaceful nuclear power capability is the purpose of its nuclear efforts, and that those efforts are clearly allowed under international norms. Thus, the Iranian nuclear program is perfectly legitimate in its eyes, and there is little international disagreement. Moreover, Iranians believe they have every right, as a pivotal state, to pursue nuclear technology. As Kodmani puts it, "Iranians are almost unanimous in believing that their country has a sovereign right to enrich uranium. They want international acknowledgement of their country's importance in the region." The United States, reflecting both its own and Israeli concerns, worries more about the ability of Iran to "break out" and redirect its program toward weapons capability, a situation it deems entirely unacceptable. At this point, the two sides are at loggerheads, and the United States, the great power, has been unable to force compliance with its wishes from the regional pivotal power. Why not?

The Limits of Power

The current impasse between the United States and Iran is frustrating, occasionally even infuriating, to American leaders, because of their inability to bring the Iranians to heel on a number of issues. The nuclear issue, including its Israeli component, heads the list of complaints, vying with the Iranian role in Iraq for primacy as an irritant. The Iraqi issue has partially defused itself with the American military withdrawal from Iraq, but continued Iranian meddling in Iraqi affairs remains a matter of concern in Washington.

Iran presumably shares this sense of frustration and remains obdurate in the face of American opposition. As the naturally most consequential state in the region (at least in its own eyes), it feels it operates from a position of strength on these matters of contention. It is, after all, by far the largest state in the region and cannot be bullied like the smaller, weaker states (including Iraq). Because it exports roughly 2.5 million barrels of oil a day, it gains leverage as well both from those it supplies and those whom it might supply (China, for instance) when sanctions are threatened against its export of energy. As Baktiari explains, "as long as oil prices stay high, Iranian leaders know that they will face little danger of an international oil embargo." Moreover, Iran does business with other powers (Russia, for instance, which is assisting its nuclear energy program), and the result is that it does not suffer from any kind of isolation in the world. As a result, Takeyh maintains, "The guardians of the theocratic regime do not fear the United States; they do not relate to the international community from a position of strategic vulnerability. Tehran now seeks not assurances against American military strikes but an acknowledgement of its status and influence."

What options does the United States have for dealing with Iran? Basically, these options come in two categories, military and diplomatic. The problem is that one option (military force) is not meaningfully available to the United States, even though the threat of force (taking "no option off the table") is part of American rhetoric over Iran's nuclear program. The Obama administration has sought to reverse the Bush policy of isolating and ignoring Iran, but that policy change has yet to bear fruit, thereby reducing the potency of diplomatic tools. The result is that the Americans scowl at and curse the Iranians, who return the favor.

The possibility of using military force against Iran is tied principally to the Iranian nuclear program and historically to Iranian support for and supply of Iraqi Shiite forces operating in Iraq.

As the two largest countries in the region, Iran and Iraq have been the chief rivals in the Persian Gulf area for decades, and the inconclusive Iran–Iraq War of 1980–1988 demonstrated, among other things, that neither was clearly dominant. Iran, however, would clearly like to have primary influence in Iraq for both geopolitical and religious sectarian reasons, and the American war in Iraq has increased Iranian influence. As Nasr and Takeyh explain, "For close to half a century, the Arab world saw Iraq's military as its bulwark in the Persian Gulf." One result of the invasion was to disband the Iraqi military, and, according to Norton, "By crushing the regime led by Saddam Hussein, the Americans gave a geopolitical gift to Iran," by removing a hostile Sunni Arab regime and military force from its border. As a result, Baktiari contends, "It is Bush's policies that have put the Iranian regime in its present strong position. No one has benefited more from American blunders in the Middle East than the conservatives in Iran."

What can the United States do (or threaten to do) militarily to get Iran to abandon its nuclear program or to quit interfering in Iraq? To some, the answer is not much. Takeyh puts it bluntly: "the United States has no military option in Iran." The ability of the United States to deal politically with Iran was certainly compromised by the Bush administration's unwillingness to interact politically with the Iranians—at least in public. When Ahmadinejad visited the headquarters of the United Nations (UN) in 2007, he had no meetings with American officials, and when, in April 2008, Secretary of State Condoleezza Rice visited Amman, Jordan, for a regional meeting on Iraq, she pointedly prefaced her attendance with the assurance she would have no discussions with the Iranians. It is, of course, difficult to make diplomatic progress with someone to whom you will not speak. Barack Obama has tried to reverse the Bush policy, but with virtually no success. Early on in his first term, he repeatedly indicated a willingness to talk to Iran, a sign of possible change from the previous administration. That gesture has not been reciprocated in any public manner until recently, although the Iranians periodically hint at their willingness to engage in bilateral discussions. The initiatives by Rouhani and Obama about resuming talks that began when the Iranian leader visited the U.N. in September 2013 may represent a change in direction on both sides.

The withdrawal of the United States from Iraq loosens tensions with Iran on that dimension, but given Iranian influence with the Iraqi Shiite regime, it will not disappear altogether. The United States still wants an Iraq quite independent of Iranian influence, but is limited in its ability to bring this about. As a result, a short-run barometer of U.S.–Iranian relation is likely to center on Iraq (in addition to the nuclear weapons question). It seems unlikely that the United States can keep Iran from having some influence on a post-occupation

Iraqi government unless that government is not dominated by the majority Shiites. As the struggle for power in Iraq continues, the only thing the United States might do to limit Iranian influence would be to downgrade the power of those Iraqi elements it supports, but that is unlikely given Iran's penetration of the majority Shiites. The competition for ultimate political power in post-occupation Iraq is ongoing and the outcome indeterminate. The important geopolitical outcome will be the extent to which that result reinforces or detracts from Iran's status as regional pivotal state.

The post-occupation Iraqi–Iranian relationship thus represents the dynamics of pivotal state—great power relations in its purest form. The United States and Iran are far apart on the kind of Iraq the United States leaves behind. Despite policies that have had the effect of promoting Shiite rule in Iraq, the United States does not want a militantly Shiite regime to take hold after it leaves, whereas Iran is committed to helping the Shiites reign. Who will prevail?

Iran has the advantage over the United States in the region on both issues. American influence in Iraq has shrunk, and now that the Americans are no longer present in Iraq, it will likely shrink even more. The Iranians know this, and they do not suffer the same debility: Iran is a permanent part of the neighborhood. If Iranian influence over Iraq and the extent of Shiite dominance in Iraq are to be controlled, it will have to be because of the actions of regional forces that oppose such dominance (essentially the Sunni states of the region). The power of Saudi Arabia, Jordan, Syria, and the Gulf states are not as great as those of the United States, but they are more relevant. The shape of post-occupation Iraq and the extent of its ties to Tehran are simply more important to, say, Kuwait, than they are to the United States, and thus the role the United States is diminished now that it is no longer physically present in Iraq. Similarly, unless economic sanctions against Iran cause Tehran to halt its nuclear program, it is not at all clear what the United States can realistically do to prevent turning an acquisition deterrence effort into an employment deterrence situation. The other major geopolitical issue is, of course, the Iranian nuclear weapons program. It is a more complex issue because it combines both the $N+1$ dynamic of proliferation with intense regional feelings about a nuclear-armed Iran. The most public regional impact is Israel's fear that a nuclear-armed Iran would use its weapons to destroy Israel, and this prospect is so dire as to push Israel toward a preemptive military action to destroy the Iranian program. At the same time, many Sunni Arab states also dread a nuclear-armed Shiite Iran, and an Iranian attainment of nuclear status could spark an attempt by one or more Sunni Arab states to "go nuclear" as a counterweight. The United States opposes Iran's ambitions because of all of these factors.

The Israeli element adds a hamstringing political facet to efforts to reach out to Iran. Those American Jews who support the current Israeli regime are adamant not only in their opposition to Iran, but equate any diplomatic initiatives toward Tehran with abandonment of Israel. Whereas talking to one's adversaries—in this case the Iranians—might make sense in any other political setting, the entanglement of such initiatives with support or opposition to Israel fundamentally stymies these kinds of actions.

CONCLUSION

The role of pivotal states, and especially Iran in contemporary international relations, provides a limiting factor on the exercise of power within the international system and particularly for major powers like the United States. In one sense, the emergence of pivotal states as important, *independent* actors whose interests cannot readily be subjugated by the power of larger states is just another sign of the greater pluralization of the post–Cold War order. During most of the Cold War, after all, Iran was a loyal ally of the United States against Soviet communism, and even after the revolution of 1979, Iran did not make common cause with its Soviet neighbors. In an international order that is much less hierarchical than the Cold War order, there is greater independence for—or less restraint on—the actions of uncommitted states. Iran's actions in the Persian Gulf are but one prominent example of this freedom.

Iran also demonstrates the frustration that pivotal states provide for the great powers like the United States. American power is, for the most part, quite irrelevant to ordering its relations with the government in Tehran. The religious conservatives who rule Iran can—and do—snub the United States, and the United States resents that treatment and is frustrated by it. One can argue that this frustration caused the Bush administration to treat Iran with more pique than sound reason and made the relations worse than they otherwise would have been. The Obama administration in Washington has taken some tentative steps to try to improve that relationship, but its efforts have not been terribly successful and have largely been overwhelmed by the rhetoric of support for Israel against Iran's program.

Iran is not the only pivotal state in the world, only the currently most troublesome member of that genre, at least from an American vantage point. As the patina of the hierarchically dominated Cold War period fades into history and is replaced by a greater independence of states in the international order, pivotal states—from Brazil to India to South Africa—are likely to become more prominent parts of international relations.

SUGGESTED ACTIVITIES AND QUESTIONS

1. What is a pivotal state? How do pivotal states fit into the hierarchy of states in the international order? Why are they important and sometimes problematical?
2. Why does Iran qualify as a pivotal state? In general terms, discuss those attributes of Iran that contribute to this designation.
3. What is it about Iran that makes it a "unique" state? Discuss this uniqueness in both physical and historical terms.
4. Discuss the ethnic and religious demographics of Iran. How do they contribute to its special status in the Middle East region and the world?
5. Describe contemporary Iranian politics since the revolution of 1979. Who controls the country? How? Why is understanding this evolution critical to understanding the contemporary place of Iran in the international order?
6. How are U.S.–Iranian relations a "textbook case" of the relations between pivotal states and great powers? Elaborate.

7. What are the major foci of U.S.–Iranian political differences? Describe each. Why does the inability of the United States to compel Iran to change its policies on each issue demonstrate the limits of its power?
8. Is the Iranian position on the nuclear weapons option reasonable or outlandish? Depending on your answer, what should the United States attempt to do about that program? Why?
9. What is the Iranian position on post-occupation Iraq? Do you find it reasonable for Iran to try to influence Iraqi politics given its place in the region? Or is the Iranian position outrageous? Based on your assessment, what should the United States do about Iranian policy toward Iraq?
10. What must the new American administration do to repair relations with Iran? How important is Iran's status as a pivotal power to determining the direction of that policy?

SUGGESTED READINGS AND RESOURCES

Baktiari, Bahman. "Iran's Conservative Revival." *Current History* 106, 696 (January 2007), 11–16.

Bradley, John R. "Iran's Ethnic Tinderbox." *Washington Quarterly* 30, 1 (Winter 2006–2007), 181–190.

Chadar, Fariborz. "Behind Iran's Crackdown, an Economic Gap." *Current History* 108, 722 (December 2009), 424–428.

De Bellaigue, Christopher. "Think Again: Iran." *Foreign Policy*, May/June 2005, 18–26.

Donovan, Michael. "Iran, Israel, and Nuclear Weapons in the Middle East." *CDI Terrorism Project* (online), February 14, 2002.

Dreyfuss, Robert. "Is Iran Winning the Iraq War? *Nation* 286, 9 (March 10, 2008), 22–28.

Ehteshami, Anoushiravan. "The Middle East's New Power Dynamic." *Current History* 108, 722 (December 2009), 395–401.

Elliot, Hen-Tov. "Understanding Iran's New Authoritarianism." *Washington Quarterly* 30, 1 (Winter 2006–2007), 163–180.

Fuller, Graham E. "The Hizbollah-Iranian Connection: Model for Sunni Resistance." *Washington Quarterly* 30, 1 (Winter 2006–2007), 139–150.

Goldberg, Jeffrey. "The Point of No Return." *The Atlantic* 306, 2 (September 2010), 56–59.

Gonzalez, Nathan. *Engaging Iran: The Rise of a Middle East Power and America's Strategic Choice.* Westport, CT: Praeger Security International, 2007.

Jervis, Robert. "Getting to Yes with Iran: The Challenges of Coercive Diplomacy." *Foreign Affairs* 92, 1 (January/February 2013), 105–115.

Kaplan, Robert D. "Living with a Nuclear Iran." *The Atlantic* 306, 2 (September 2010), 70–72.

Kodmani, Bassma. "Clearing the Air in the Middle East." *Current History* 107, 709 (May 2008), 21–26.

Lindsay, James M. and Roy Takeyh. "After Iran Gets the Bomb: Containment and Its Complications." *Foreign Affairs* 89, 2 (March/April 2010), 13–42.

Maloney, Suzanne. "The US and Iran: Back to Containment?" *Current History* 106, 704 (December 2007), 440–442.

McFaul, Michael, Abbas Milani, and Larry Diamond. "A Win-Win Strategy for Dealing with Iran." *Washington Quarterly* 30, 1 (Winter 2006–2007), 121–135.

McInnis, Kathleen J. "Extended Deterrence: The U.S. Credibility Gap in the Middle East." *Washington Quarterly* 28, 3 (Summer 2005), 169–186.

Milani, Abbas. "U.S. Foreign Policy and the Future of Democracy in Iran." *Washington Quarterly* 28, 3 (Summer 2005), 41–56.

Milani, Mohsen M. "Tehran's Take: Understanding Iran's U.S. Policy." *Foreign Affairs* 88, 4 (July/August 2009), 46–62.

Nasr, Vali, and Ray Takeyh. "The Costs of Containing Iran." *Foreign Affairs* 87, 1 (January/February 2008), 85–94.

The National Security Strategy of the United States. Washington, DC: The White House, March 2006.

Norton, Augustus Richard. "The Shiite "Threat' Revisited." *Current History* 106, 704 (December 2007), 434–439.

Pollack, Kenneth M. "Bringing Iran to the Bargaining Table." *Current History* 105, 694 (November 2006), 365–370.

Reidel, Bruce. "The Middle East After Iran Gets the Bomb." *Current History* 109, 731 (December 2010), 370–375.

Ritter, Scott. "Notes from Iran: The Case for Engagement." *Nation* 283, 17 (November 20, 2006), 13–18.

Serwer, Daniel. "Iraq Untethered." *Current History* 111, 745 (December 2012), 344–349.

Snow, Donald M. *What after Iraq?* New York: Pearson Longman, 2008.

Takeyh, Ray. "Time for Détente with Iran." *Foreign Affairs* 86, 2 (March/April 2007), 17–32.

Trenin, Dmitri. "Travel to Tehran." *Foreign Policy*, January/February 2008, 72–73.

Vaki, Sanam. "Iran: Balancing East Against West." *Washington Quarterly* 29, 4 (Autumn 2006), 57–66.

_____. "Tehran Gambles to Survive." *Current History* 106, 704 (December 2007), 414–420.

Waltz, Kenneth N. "Why Iran Should Get the Bomb." *Foreign Affairs* 91, 4 (July/August 2012), 2–5.

Wood, Graeme. "Iran: Among the Mullahs." *The Atlantic* 305, 1 (January 2010), 15–16.

Zaborski, Jason. "Deterring a Nuclear Iran." *Washington Quarterly* 28, 3 (Summer 2005), 153–168.

Revolutionary Change: The Arab Spring

PRÉCIS

Revolution has been one of the ways in which political change has occurred throughout history both within and between countries. The exact way in which the extensive change associated with revolution occurs varies from place to place, but there is general scholarly agreement about when efforts at change reach or do not reach revolutionary proportions. The first part of this study looks at the dynamics of revolution, beginning by defining the term and then examining one of the most venerable descriptions of revolution put forward by the late Crane Brinton. The most prominent recent example of apparently revolutionary activity has been the uprising, or awakening, associated with the so-called Arab Spring, and the movements that have arisen since that began in late 2010 in Tunisia are examined in terms of the description of revolution.

Political change within and between states is one of the most fundamental characteristics of international relations. Sometimes change is
peaceful and evolutionary, allowing systemic response in an orderly,
peaceful manner, but that is not always the case. In some important instances,
change occurs rapidly, suddenly, and violently, and in cases where these
characteristics are present, the reaction is likely to be more difficult, both
for those societies that are undergoing change and for those members of the
international system that must deal with both the processes and outcomes of
revolutionary change. The Arab Spring, which began in late 2010 in and continues to evolve across the Middle East, is a globally prominent contemporary
example of the process of change.

The first popular depictions of the Arab Spring process have been to de-scribe it as "revolutionary." It began when a disgruntled Tunisian street ven-dor, Mohammed Bouazizi, doused himself with gasoline and burned himself to death in protest against the solicitation of a bribe by a local official, an event that went viral in the country and ignited a series of protests that brought down the long-standing regime of president Zine al-Abadine Ben Ali. Heartened by Internet-driven images of the successful "Awakening" (a term used throughout the region to describe the movement that has ensued), demonstrations spread to neighboring Egypt and then across the region to diverse locations that have included Libya, Yemen, Bahrain, and Syria. The movements that have arisen in various places have had very differing levels of success and are at very different stages of the change process. Their outcomes and whether the experience of the Arab Spring phenomenon to date represents a harbinger for other countries in the region remains very much up in the air.

The movements against regimes in the Middle East have been different in terms of their content, the kinds and effectiveness of resistance to them by various target regimes, and both interim and longer-term outcomes. Because of these differences, it is difficult to generalize about what has happened. The confusion begins with exactly what each of these uprisings and their totality ac-tually represent. The first reaction that Westerners displayed to these outbreaks was to treat them through the lens of the Western political experience and to treat them as Western-style movements that hopefully are leading to Western-approved outcomes, such as movements toward representative government, hopefully democratic. But is such an outcome realistic? In the Western tradi-tion, these movements seem revolutionary, and that is how they initially were depicted. As they have evolved, however, it is less clear that the language of political change that holds in Western democracies is exactly appropriate for describing these phenomena. If not, how are they similar or different? Are these movements truly revolutionary? If so, what does that mean in the context of a Middle East in which the underlying values may not be the same as those in the West? Where is the Arab Spring going or, for that matter, is it evolving in any coherent direction at all?

Specific questions about the outcomes of the various movements in the countries affected by the Arab Spring remain unanswerable in detail at this point, because they are still ongoing. What can be done, however, is to look at the basic underlying dynamics of violent political change of which they are apparent examples, and to see whether or to what extent those constructs are useful in understanding the Arab Spring phenomenon. To that end, the discussion begins with an overview of concerns that are typically raised regard-ing the phenomenon of fundamental political change—revolution in popular depiction—as it is understood in most Western countries. Using that discussion as a base, the various national movements associated with the Arab Spring will be examined to try to determine how well they conform to established ideas about revolution and, based on their histories to date, what the prospects for various kinds of outcomes may be.

THE PHENOMENON OF FUNDAMENTAL POLITICAL CHANGE

The concept of revolution is a good point at which to begin a discussion of political change. The term is useful partly because it is popular and a name that is attached to a wide variety of political and other phenomena—thus it is a "cover" concept that allows one to develop a fairly broad-ranging examination of political change. It is a concept the dynamics of which have long been fascinating to political scientists and other students of political change. In its most popular interpretations, however, it often connotes a rapidity of change that can be misleading regarding the fundamental, underlying changes associated with deep and politically transforming revolutions. True revolutions may be fundamental, but they represent a long, rather than a short, process.

Defining Revolution

The concept of revolution is often vulgarized in common usage, and the term is sometimes used to describe all sorts of change, from scientific revolutions to changes in men's and women's fashion. Dictionary definitions of the word *revolution* describe two distinct meanings of the term. First, there is the scientific definition, which is the rotation of an object on its axis. A single revolution of a sphere, for instance, refers to a rotation of that sphere one entire time around—or a revolution. Although this definition of revolution does not relate directly to the political and social phenomenon, it does suggest that the term is associated with basic change in the value of the object that is subject to rotation.

The second and, for present purposes, more relevant definition relates directly to the question of political or other social change. In most cases, there are two phenomena that are described in revolutionary terms. One of these, used most normally in the context of social or economic revolutions, is significant change. The *Collins English Dictionary* (10th ed., 2009), for instance, refers to revolution as "a far-reaching and drastic change," whereas *The Free Dictionary* defines this sense of revolution as "a sudden and momentous change in a situation." What is notable about both these definitions is that they do not specify how change occurs, who causes it to occur, and what kinds of change it entails. The emphasis in both cases is on the general outcome of a change process, not on the process itself.

Political definitions of revolution tend to be more process-oriented. The *Collins* definition of political revolution thus is "the overthrow or repudiation of a regime or political system by the governed," whereas *The Free Dictionary* defines it as "the overthrow of a government and its replacement by another."

The *Columbia Encyclopedia* (2007 edition) brings the social and political definitions together and goes a bit further with the designation that a revolution is a "fundamental and violent change in the values, political institutions, social structure, and policies of a society." This definition combines both the process by which a revolution is designated and the kind and extent of change that is associated with the term. It is also a much more restrictive use of the term if one assumes that all of the criteria it lays out must be met for a political movement to be deemed revolutionary. In the process, it also lays out some of the basic dimensions and disagreements about what does and does not constitute revolution or some other phenomenon.

The essence of revolution is change, which can occur in a variety of forms and by a variety of means. The most obvious manner of differentiation is a dichotomy between nonpolitical and political change. Economic and social revolutions are aimed not so much at the political unit and the people who run it as they are at the social and economic policies the system creates and enforces on its citizens, and particularly as those policies that disadvantage some people. The political system is often the indirect object of social and economic demands for change, as the conditions that these movements seek to change are created and enforced by political authorities. As a result, one method that social and economic "revolutionaries" often adopt is the attempt to unseat particular individuals in power, at which point such revolutions become at least partly political.

Ultimately, of course, the two forms can be related. Because economic and social changes have political ramifications in terms such as wealth distribution and social stratification or leveling, they are normally accomplished or at least accompanied by political actions. Such actions may precede and codify these changes: progressive taxation legislation that has the intent or effect of redistributing wealth or social policies that make discrimination in housing illegal are examples. Sometimes, these actions are preceded by politically oriented actions: the Occupy Movement in the United States in 2011, a political movement, had economic policies at its base, for instance. At other times, political actions may follow social or economic movements: the codification of civil rights legislation followed years of civil rights demonstrations in the United States during the 1950s and early 1960s.

As the definitions of revolution suggest, political revolutions have more fundamental political change as their primary objective. Although the definitions do not specify *how* political change can or should occur, they share the traumatic nature of the action: the term *overthrow* occurs in all definitions cited, and the *Columbia Encyclopedia* adds that such actions involve "violent change." What they share is that the objective is to remove a particular set of political actors and replace them with others, and normally this action is accompanied by some structural, constitutional change as well, presumably to help ensure that the *ancient regime* does not return to power. The intent and impact of political revolutions, in other words, has as its basic purpose the transfer of political power from one group of individuals in one institutional setting to another group, usually in some altered institutional context.

Those who occupy political power almost always relish their status and are reluctant to relinquish their positions to pretenders. Their motives for wanting to retain power and authority vary greatly, from the narrowly self-interested (power to guarantee their status and well-being) to the more broadly based self-perception that their reign is "good" for the population as a whole. Depending on why they believe they should remain in power, they can be expected to cling as tenaciously as they can to retain the status quo from which they benefit. The tenacity of their determination to stay in power will help determine whether those who seek their removal and replacement will find the recourse to violence necessary to attain their ends.

It is not universally true that all movements that produce revolutionary political change are violent, although there is certainly a coincidence between the desire for revolutionary change and violence. That revolutionary events can be either violent or nonviolent is exemplified by the twentieth-century history of Russia/the Soviet Union, a country that underwent two fundamental revolutions within a period of slightly over 70 years during the last century. In 1917, the Bolshevik Revolution swept through the country, pushing aside the imperial tsarist regime and replacing it with a new communist dictatorship. Because the tsarists would not have relinquished power willingly, the revolution was very bloody, and it served the purposes of removing both the old regime (the tsarists) and replacing it with a new ruling elite (the communists) and in transforming the monarchical government of the empire with a new form of authoritarianism based in Leninist interpretations of Marxism (technically, of course, there was a democratic inter-regnum between the tsarists and communists between March and October 1918, but it was transient enough to omit from the narrative). The impact was also profoundly social and economic, as both the imperial social structure and the economic system were replaced. The Russian Revolution, as it is universally known, was a classic example of a "fundamental and violent change in the rules, political institutions, social structure, and policies of a society."

The collapse of the Soviet Union that began with the disintegration of communist rule in Eastern Europe and culminated in the formal demise of the Soviet Union was an event every bit as revolutionary in effect as the 1917 uprising, but it is generally not described as revolutionary, because it was accomplished with essentially no violence. The change was certainly revolutionary: the communist system and those who ruled under it were jettisoned and replaced by new, nominally anti-communist personnel who produced a constitution that was broadly democratic for the new, physically reduced Russian Republic. A variant of Western-style capitalism replaced the Marxist economic structures that underlay the Soviet system, and the communist *nomenklatura* (the communist bureaucracy) was displaced socially by the new entrepreneurial class and even the *Mafiosi* as the wielders of social power and prestige. Although the new Russian system continues to evolve politically and otherwise, it is clearly not like the system it displaced, and this transformation was accomplished without the widespread recourse to political violence specified in some definitions of revolution. The point is that all events with revolutionary effects are not violent. Nonetheless, most revolutions, and certainly most of the movements in the contemporary world that are given that label, at a minimum pass through some violent phase.

Thinking About Revolutionary Violence and Change

Why do political revolutions occur? The definitions of the term offer part of the answer, which is to change the people and institutions that hold political power. The underlying motivation for such action arises from some form of grievance that part of the population feels. Writing in the early 1970s, the political scientist Ted Gurr described this process as one of "relative deprivation," by which he meant that movements that eventually came to desire to overthrow and replace governments begin when some portion of the population feels that they cannot succeed in achieving their legitimate goals because of the way the political system is structured by those in charge rather than because of the validity of their claims. Put a different way, rigging a game only becomes a problem when those losing recognize that the game is rigged. In other words, the urge to revolution begins with the perception of being mistreated unfairly (deprivation), and further, that this deprivation is discriminatory: some groups succeed and others prosper because of the advantages they are afforded by the political system (their deprivation is relative to their place in society). When this realization is combined with the knowledge that there may be ways to rectify the problem through political action, the seeds of potential revolutionary activity may be activated.

In the contemporary political environment, there are two basic purposes for which revolution may be contemplated. The first, and by far the most frequent, is the rearrangement of power (people and institutions) within an existing political unit, and it is this purpose that is common to the various movements that have so far emerged as parts of the Arab Spring. These kinds of revolution do not normally question or raise the integrity of the state unit against which they may be directed, but rather seek to rearrange internal power to their own advantage. The other purpose is to break apart and create a new political unit wherein the revolutionary group's interests can be achieved. During the breakup of the European colonial empires during the second half of the twentieth century, many of these kinds of revolutions were wars of independence with the purpose of breaking away from colonial domination. Another variant is wars against existing states the purpose of which is for some part of a country to break away, or secede, from an existing state and to create a new entity. Wars of secession are comparatively infrequent but can be particularly brutal and bloody. They also raise a whole series of other issues, such as whether the "right" to secede exists, and as a result, Chapter 15 is devoted to the phenomenon of secession and its application in South Sudan. The instances examined here are wars with regime change as the basic purpose.

Revolutionary war is the dominant form of political violence in the contemporary world, far eclipsing conflicts between sovereign states and reflecting that most of the grievances fundamental enough to lead to violence are domestic in origin. These conflicts in turn tend to have at least two salient characteristics that both define them and provide a context within which outsiders (including those who may feel some interest in influencing their outcomes) can view what goes on, where it is likely to evolve, and whether interference is meaningfully possible.

The first and most obvious characteristic is that these kinds of conflicts tend to occur in the developing world, a blanket designation that encompasses parts of Africa, Asia, and Latin America. Within each of these regions, there are differential levels of political and economic development and thus levels of satisfaction with ongoing political structures and personnel. The potential for revolutionary violence is generally thought to be greatest in areas where developmental levels are sufficiently low that not all can prosper and in which there is likely to be relative deprivation among some segments of the society. Normally, the roots of disagreement among groups are difficult and intractable, and are often overlaid with ethnic, religious, historical, or other burdens as well. The point is that the roots of revolutionary violence are generally domestic, are difficult to resolve short of violence, and are likely to be misunderstood by outsiders who view them. Internal conflicts also tend to be particularly desperate, because they pit existing governments and their personnel against insurgents in a zero-sum game where there are clear winners and clear losers and where the stakes involved may include the personal survival of those who those who do not prevail.

The second characteristic is that the violence that is the most visible sign of developing world revolutions is likely to be asymmetrical. Most post–Cold War revolutions have featured very well-armed government forces being confronted by a rag-tag opposition that is, on the face of it, no match for the national armed force it confronts. In this situation, the resistance faces the options of fighting unconventionally or being annihilated and chooses to fight in a way that maximizes its possibilities first of survival and eventually of success, in other words, it fights asymmetrically in terms developed in Chapter 5 because that method is the only way bywhich it can hope to win. The fundamental objectives and asymmetries in physical armaments can lead to violence that is quite deadly and that can extend to nominal civilian populations with very deadly effects that attract a great deal of negative world publicity. Moreover, as asymmetrical wars in terms of conduct, these kinds of conflicts tend to be very protracted and their outcomes ambiguous and problematical. The civil war that has been raging in Syria since 2011 is a contemporary example.

Patterns of Revolution

All revolutions are unique in details, but they also share some common characteristics, the study of which allows one to examine how different revolutions evolve and to place different revolutions along the spectrum of revolutionary activity. Trying to sift through the complex dynamics has been an active scholarly endeavor for many observers, some of whose work is cited in the bibliography at the end of the chapter.

One of the most venerable and durable constructs to describe revolution was devised by the American historian Crane Brinton. His seminal book, *The Anatomy of Revolution,* was published originally in 1938 and was revised and reissued in 1952 and 1965. The basis of Brinton's study is a comparative analysis of four classic, thoroughly Western revolutions, the English Revolution of the 1640s, the American and French Revolutions of the late eighteenth century, and the 1917 Russian Revolution. The study examines each event and seeks to generalize conditions common to revolutions. The study looks exclusively at revolutions in Western countries with common underlying social and cultural values (Russia may be a partial variant in this regard), and some deviation from the patterns Brinton found are not totally surprising in applying his observations to revolutions in non-Western societies such as those in the Middle East in the early twenty-first century.

Recognizing that the Brinton framework may be somewhat culturally biased and affected by the historical period in which it was based, its general contours are still relevant and can form the basis for examining contemporary revolutions. The terms used here are not exactly the same as Brinton's, but they convey the same general meaning. For this purpose, one can view revolutionary violence as a three-step process: the prerevolutionary phase leading to the "fall of the old regime" (designations in parentheses are Brinton's); the evolution of the revolution itself ("revolutionary regimes"); and the outcomes of the revolutionary process ("lasting results"). Following a brief description of each stage, the discussion will move to an attempt to apply the framework to the Arab Spring.

Prerevolutionary Phase.   What triggers some countries to revolt against their leader, whereas others do not? The first thing to note is that revolutions generally arise not in the poorest, most destitute, and backward places, but in countries that have experienced some societal progress. In the poorest places, there may be a sense of wretchedness and deprivation, but except for contrasts with the situations a few members of the elite, the condition is likely to be universal enough not to cause a sense of comparative, or relative, deprivation. Gurr's relative deprivation is triggered when there has been some improvement in conditions that is interrupted for some people, leaving parts of the citizenry feeling not only deprived but discriminated against. For revolutionary instincts to be aroused, the source of the resulting frustration has to be blamed on the government, whose personnel must be considered incapable or unwilling to rectify the situation that is deemed unacceptable.

The source of frustration may be social or political, but in the Brinton framework, it is most often economic; his examples include "government deficits, more than usual complaints over taxation, conspicuous governmental favoring of one set of economic interests over another," and these are reinforced by a perception of the incompetence and indifference of the government to deal with these problems. When the government is confronted with demands for change, it fails to respond out of ineptitude or resistance, and this triggers further demonstrations against it. Acting out of a sense of frustration, the government may lash out at those demanding change, including the use of force, and these actions may reinforce the resolve of those demanding change and even broaden their appeal. At some point, if reconciliation does not occur, then revolutionary violence may become the method by which resistance is manifested.

Brinton emphasizes that most of the conditions that may provide the seedbed for revolution tend not to be radical when they are first articulated, and those who voice them are not classic radicals in terms of their places in society and their backgrounds. The people who emerge in positions of revolutionary leadership tend to be reasonably moderate with middle-class or even upper-middle-class backgrounds. The early leaders of what became the American Revolution, after all, were largely New England businessmen, and the earliest resisters to the Bourbon throne in France were lower-level nobility (the *parlements)* who objected to the imposition of taxes against them to pay for the king's foreign adventures, including his support for the American revolutionaries a decade earlier. This pattern has largely held since: Fidel Castro, for instance, was a lawyer, and Alexander Kerensky, who led the movement that initially overthrew the Russian tsar before the revolution was taken over by the communists, was also a lawyer. Radicalization occurs as the revolution unfolds.

The period leading to the actual overthrow of the government is, according to the definition, prerevolutionary, and only after the government has been overthrown and replaced by a different structure can there properly be said to have been a revolution. Movements that never reach the stage of overthrowing the government or that are unsuccessful in doing so are something other than revolutionary, even if their intent is revolutionary. Such movements can, for present purposes, be thought of as uprisings, a designation that encompasses several of the movements that have comprised the Arab Spring.

Evolution of the Revolution. Movements that are successful in upending and replacing existing governments typically go through some or all of several distinct stages in terms of who governs and how, and the outcome of a particular revolution depends to a large degree on how far through the process a particular event evolves. Brinton identifies three steps through which the revolution may move: the rule by the "moderates and dual power," "the reigns of terror and virtue," and "thermidor." They are connected and sequential.

Revolutionary atmospheres tend to attract groups with a variety of interests and causes they want served, and an early part of most revolutions is sorting out which groups will prevail and which will not. Revolutions tend to begin with a short "honeymoon" period following the overthrow of the old government. It is a period of self-congratulation that gradually turns to the question of which faction representing which interests will ultimately prevail. In the classic kinds of revolutions that Brinton studied, there is a tendency for "dual power" centers to emerge, a moderate government that controls the reins of legitimate governance, and a more radical alternative power structure outside the formal institutions of government. The 1979 Iranian revolution very much followed this pattern, with moderates, many of whom followed the legacy of Mohammad Mossadeqh, initially gaining control of the Iranian parliament, while the Revolutionary Guards and Courts, associated with the radical Shiite clergy, formed an alternate center of power.

A power struggle normally emerges between these two alternate power sources, and in most cases, the radicals prevail. Brinton lists five reasons that this may occur. First, the moderates tend to be a loose configuration of middle-class figures, whereas more radical forces tend to be "better organized, better staffed, better obeyed." Second, the radicals can act more forcefully because they have "relatively few responsibilities," in contrast to the moderates who are trying to operate the governmental structures of the old regime and thus end up assuming "some of the unpopularity" of that regime. Third, because the moderates are not extremist in attitude, they also tend not to be extremist in their actions, including actions against former colleagues "with whom they have recently stood united," whereas more radical elements lack such compunction. Fourth, the moderates tend to find themselves sandwiched between the disgruntled conservatives from whom power has been taken and the "confident, aggressive extremists" who offer an alternative to them. In the process, the political center tends to shrink as the moderates are blamed from both ends of the spectrum. Fifth, because they are moderate, the leaders of the moderate forces tend to be "poor" leaders in terms of activating their base and prove unable to provide the discipline" and "enthusiasm" needed to maintain power.

When the extremists prevail in the struggle with the moderates, the result is the "reigns of terror and virtue." This term was originally derived from the French Revolution (the modern use of the term *terrorism* originates in this period) and refers to the emergence of the most radical and self-righteous elements within the revolutionary spectrum. The basic dynamic of this phase is the decline of the moderates and the ascension of the most radical elements in the revolutionary spectrum. In the cases that Brinton studied, the radicals were generally leftist in political orientation, although some of the policies associated with at least some of them are highly puritanical and more closely "virtues" that are more clearly rightist and conservative in modern calculations.

The seizure of control and subsequent actions by the radicals is often the bloodiest and most hideous stage of revolution. Terror often comes in the form of suppression, even violence and execution of anyone seen as an opponent of the revolution's more extreme views, and the virtues that most often are promoted and enforced tend to be puritanical, seen as righting the perceived degradations of the old regime. The radicals who enforce this "reign" are often a fairly small minority, but they are highly organized and fanatically committed to their mission. Because opposition to them is usually seen as a sign of counter-revolutionary sentiment with which the terror will deal, dissent tends to be muted by fear of the consequences. This phase of revolutionary activity also often becomes evangelical, seeking to spread its principles to other countries.

The length of this phase will vary considerably among revolutions, with factors such as the level of fanaticism of the radicals, their numbers and resources, and levels of resistance acting as variables affecting the reign. In most cases, the period will be bounded and relatively short, but in others it can virtually become institutionalized. A prime example of this is the continuing sway of the Revolutionary Guards and Courts in Iran, which arguably continue to enforce terror and virtue on an Iranian population that has seemed unable or unwilling to bring this period to an end. It is the fear of a similar open-ended rise of the radicals in the form of Islamists that constitutes many of the qualms that outsiders have toward the evolution of the various movements associated with the Arab Spring. Will they ever move past the reign of terror and virtue?

The level of energy, even fanaticism, associated with the reign of terror and virtue is generally not inexhaustible, and it usually followed by a period of what Brinton describes as "convalescence" that he calls the "thermidor" period. The term itself is borrowed from the period after Robespierre's reign of terror and virtue during the French Revolution. Thermidor is a general reaction to the excesses of the preceding period and, in Brinton's observation, tends to have some combination of several characteristics. One of these is "establishment of a tyrant," what Brinton refers to as "an unconstitutional ruler brought to power by revolution." The appeal of this leader tends to be in restoring order after the relative chaos of the radical phase and is often supported by the institution of government that most values public order, the military. Once in power, the dictator will generally act conservatively, seeking to restore many of the prerevolutionary values that were upset by the more excessive phases of the revolution, including its most puritanical practices. As well, in some cases the "missionary spirit" to spread the revolution is replaced by an "aggressive nationalism" that may include territorial aggrandizement. During thermidor, in other words, there is a return to older, preexisting forms of nationalism.

The PostRevolutionary Phase.   It was Brinton's general observation that the outcome of revolutions was generally disappointing in terms of the long-term, beneficial changes that they produced. Although all four of Brinton's revolutions met the general criterion of regime overthrow and replacement with an alternative government (which was presumably one reason he chose his cases), they were not so successful in implementing the "fundamental changes" that some definitions suggest as parts of revolution. Although the long-term result was the furtherance or establishment of political democracy in three of the four cases he studied (Russia is the exception to this point), such evolution was not the immediate result of the formal revolution except in the United States. Indeed, it was Brinton's general conclusion that the societal effects of nonviolent, nonrevolutionary events such as those associated with the Industrial Revolution, Kemal Ataturk's reforms of Turkey, or the post–World War II transformation of Japan under the American occupation (the examples are Brinton's) produced more democratic, "progressive" outcomes.

THE ARAB SPRING

There are several reasons to view the related but distinct movements in several Middle Eastern Islamic states known collectively as the Arab Spring within the framework of traditional conceptions of revolution. The most prominent of these is that the Arab Spring movements are generally typified in these terms, and the designation creates some expectations and fears that may or may not be warranted. Are these movements in fact revolutions, or are they something else? The underlying fear that tends to accompany such depictions is that they will evolve in the same way and with the same generally negative results (at least from a Western perspective) as the Iranian Revolution of 1979. That revolution, however, is certainly not exemplary of the phenomenon of revolution as described thus far in the chapter, apparently stuck as it is within the reign of terror and virtue stage. Will other movements associated with the Arab Spring be more like those described in the Brinton model, or are these movements in non-Western settings sufficiently different from similar processes in the West that they defy prediction?

The short answer to questions about the equitability of the phenomena that collectively comprise the Arab Spring is that it is not possible to predict how they will turn out, individually or collectively. They have all arisen in conditions that are roughly those that Brinton describes as prerevolutionary: movements against long-term dictatorships that had ignored or suppressed the majority of their populations and in which there were significant economic difficulties. When such conditions result in revolt in Western societies, a movement to overthrow the government is almost expected; the same reaction in Middle Eastern societies was viewed by many as surprising because it was uncharacteristic of societies with a supposed greater tolerance for illegitimate regimes. Maybe that was not the case.

One of the apparent commonalities among the Arab Spring countries has been a contagion effect caused by the electronic revolution. When demonstrations broke out in Tunisia and enjoyed success, most of the Arab world followed this progress electronically and, in many cases, were encouraged by it. Writing when he did about the examples he examined, Brinton could not include such an influence in his observations. That it has acted as a catalyst for particularly young people in other Islamic states seems a certainty in all cases, however.

None of the countries that have been part of the Arab Spring has yet proceeded all the way through the stages of successful revolution, although Tunisia seems more advanced through the process than the others. In some cases (Syria and Bahrain, for instance) forceful government resistance to revolutionary change has been successful in preventing the overthrow of the old regime, and in the others (Yemen, Egypt, and Libya), the old regimes have been overthrown but the revolution remains stuck in the revolutionary process. Because none has been entirely successful, it is tempting to think of most of these movements as *uprisings* rather than as formal revolutions, although some or all of them may evolve into full-scale revolutions.

Experts in the region make a distinction between the dynamics that have underlain the movements in various countries and the more general regional causes of unrest. Each level of analysis yields ample sources of stress: bad political and economic conditions in individual counties, and overall regional social and religious disorders and schism, for instance. Despite these trends, the emergence of resistance movements came as a surprise to many observers, and there was a consensual agreement of why uprisings were unlikely in the region. As Brownlee summarizes this consensus: "The middle classes are too weak, the repressive agencies are too strong, the ruling elite is too insecure and, in some cases, too wealthy to enable genuine liberalization." Despite this common wisdom, the region has been experiencing what Hudson calls "explosive demographic growth" that has created a youth bulge in the population (a high percentage of citizens under 25 years of age), and the "young people in search of political freedom and economic opportunity" (Ajami) have formed the catalyst against regimes resistant to change. It is not at all coincidental that this demographic is also the part of the general population most adept and comfortable with the electronic revolution and both its information-providing and communications utilities.

In the longer view, what these movements may cumulatively represent is a more fundamental trend, what Ajami refers to as the third Arab awakening of modern times. As he explains it, "The first, a political-cultural renaissance born of a desire to join the modern world, came in the late 1800s. . . . The second awakening came in the 1950s and gathered force in the decade following." The second awakening was primarily nationalistic in nature, reacting to foreign domination and control, and it was led by people like Gamal Nasser of Egypt and resulted in the installation of modern authoritarian regimes in many countries of the region. The heart of the third awakening has been a reaction to this authoritarianism and an apparent desire to move toward some form of more popular control. The exact form that political control might take in individual countries and regionally is not clear, and it may not be Western in a strictly Western sense.

The awakening is clearly a work in progress. It has not been uniform in the sense that it is not geographically universal, nor has it been uniformly successful. Most of the oil-rich countries, at least partly because they are protected by the "oil curse (a great deal of oil wealth that allows regimes effectively to "buy off" the population), have avoided the Arab Spring. Oil has the dual effects of creating comparatively high standards of living but political repression as its cost. As Jones points out in a 2013 assessment, oil riches and authoritarian (including monarchical) governance coexist in a number of countries, and rulers have used their wealth to dampen desires for change, essentially buying off the populations. Ross adds, "The citizens of countries with little or no oil generally have more freedom than those of countries with lots of it." The exception has been tiny Bahrain, where religious division is also a factor. Although instances of the awakening have dotted the map of the Middle East (an arbitrary designation made by Alfred Thayer Mahan in 1902 and rarely used by people in the region itself), there have been large gaps in terms of where it has and has not ignited into violent conflict.

The record to date has been spotty, and only in Tunisia have movements reached anything resembling a successful conclusion. In Tunisia, where it all started, some democratic consensus may be emerging, but it clearly is a work in progress. In Bahrain, the Sunni minority regime, with the considerable assistance of Saudi Arabia, has successfully crushed a resistance movement, buying off the Shiite majority that led the revolt with enough concessions to guarantee their acquiescence for a time. In Yemen, the movement was successful in removing President Ali Abdullah Saleh primarily through action by the Yemeni military. Change has not been significant in what Ajami argues is the "quintessential failed state," because, he argues, "The footprint of the government is light. The rulers offer no redemption, but there is no draconian terror." Yemen is mostly interesting to the world at large because remnants of Al Qaeda remain in the country (despite the assassination of Anwar al-Awlaki on Yemeni soil in 2011).

The other three stages on which acts of the Arab Spring have been playing out are Egypt, Libya, and Syria. Each of these instances has been distinctive, and each uprising is at a different stage of development. These three instances are worth examining separately because of the distinction of where they have occurred and the unique importance of each: Egypt because of its size and historical regional significance; Libya because of the scale of Western involvement and the fact it is the only oil-rich state in which a full-scale event has occurred; and Syria because of its geographic location, general regional importance, and especially the ferocity of government resistance to change.

Egypt

The Arab Republic of Egypt is the second major venue in which an Arab Spring uprising broke out, and it has, for most purposes, been the most prominent case. When demonstrations against the 30-year rule of Hosni Mubarak began on January 25, 2011, the world's attention was drawn to the demonstrators in Tahrir Square in Cairo, and global television followed the evolution of the demonstrations in great detail until Mubarak stepped down on February 11. A caretaker government headed by the Supreme Council of the Armed Forces (SCAF) was put in place with the charge of restoring order to the government and the economy, which went into free fall when the demonstrations began and private foreign capital fled the country.

The first stage of revolution was thus achieved with minimal bloodshed with the resignation of the 82-year-old Mubarak, whose health had been enough in question before the uprising that many wondered if he could physically survive an election campaign, much less another term in office. Reaction to the military assuming interim control was almost entirely positive at the time, as the military occupies a position of great respect within Egyptian society.

All has not gone entirely smoothly since the SCAF gained control. The economy has continued to disintegrate, and joblessness, particularly amongst young urban Egyptians who were the heart of the original demonstrations, has increased. Unease with internal conditions has ground the Egyptian tourist industry, which is the backbone of much of the economy, to a virtual halt, and economic conditions are worse than they were before the uprising. There were new demonstrations in July 2011 at the slow pace with which the SCAF was moving toward a full return of power to civilian control, a sign of some tension between the military and democratizing elements that reflects the military's goal in terms of change. As Martini and Taylor argue, "The military ultimately wants an Egyptian government that does not threaten its position. It is attempting to build a system more democratic than Mubarak's but still beholden to its interests." Because a major variable in popular control of Egypt is the role that the Muslim Brotherhood and other Islamist elements may play via the ballot box, there was some natural hedge against a headlong, uncontrolled movement toward full participatory democracy that might turn against the military.

The fragile economic situation in Egypt makes the transition even more difficult. Were economic conditions and prospects better, prosperity might well grease the wheels of change, but it was, after all, economic deprivations that formed much of the basis of dissent in the first place. With the prospects of possible Islamist influence uncertain, foreign capital is unlikely to return to Egypt, meaning the cycle of deprivation that fueled the protests in the first place is unlikely to be relieved greatly in the short run. In Ajami's view, the result is a quandary of sorts. "Egypt lacks the economic wherewithal to build a successful modern Islamic order," he writes. "A desire for stability now balances the heady satisfaction that a despot was brought down."

The political situation is also in a state of some flux. The SCAF delayed holding full democratic elections until June 2012. When they were held, Mohamed Morsi, who has ties to the Muslim Brotherhood but denies an Islamist agenda, was elected in what international monitors say were fair elections. The record under Morsi has been mixed. Domestically, Morsi has attempted to wrest political power from the military, with some but not total success. Internationally, he has attempted an independent course, which has included criticism of the United States. This stance represents one of the sources of ambivalence the West has toward the Arab Spring. Jones explains: "The cold reality is that some democratic governments in the Arab world would almost certainly be more hostile to the United States than their authoritarian predecessors, because they would be more responsive to the populations of the countries, which are largely anti-American." A large part of that anti-Americanism, of course, stems from historic U.S. support for authoritarian regimes in the region. Military opposition to Morsi's style and quality of rule led to his overthrow in 2013, yet further evidence of the transitory nature of the situation.

Does Egypt's version of the Arab Spring represent a revolution in the true sense of that term? If one accepts the minimal requirement of the overthrow of a previous regime and its replacement with a different order, there was some prospect, depending on how elections of the president and parliament in 2012 evolved, that at least a new set of personnel would consolidate power, but Morsi's overthrow ended that speculation for now. If, on the other hand, the broader definition of revolution implying much broader and deeper economic and social change is the standard one chooses, then an Egyptian revolution has only begun. In this case, the SCAF caretaker government represented as close to a Brinton-style rule of the moderates as is available, and the radical stage has yet to come, possibly in the form of Islamist rule. If a thermidor-like condition is the ultimate outcome sans a radical phase, whether one considers what is happening in Egypt revolutionary or not is a question that cannot currently be answered.

Libya

The events leading to the overthrow and killing of former dictator and long-term despot Muammar Gaddafi were different from those in Egypt in several ways. The revolt against Gaddafi was certainly part of the more general set of responses begun in neighboring Tunisia, but within the context of an oil-rich country with a sparse population cleaved largely along tribal and regional bases. Among Gaddafi's distinctions was his tenure as Libyan leader; he had assumed power as part of a coup in 1969, meaning he held power for roughly 42 years, exceeding Mubarak by over a decade.

The pattern of the uprising in Libya was distinctly different than elsewhere, and as a partial result, so too are the prospects for the success of the diverse movement that began in the eastern part of the country, gradually moved westward toward the capital of Tripoli, and finally ended with the capture and killing of Gaddafi and one of his sons in September 2011. One of the themes of the Arab Spring that makes it difficult to generalize about it is indeed the idiosyncratic nature of the various places where it has occurred, making it necessary to note special circumstances in each country.

Libya is a regional outlier in several ways. It is the only state in northern Africa with large petroleum reserves, and the oil beneath its sands is particularly "sweet" (meaning it has low sulfur content and is thus relatively cheap to process). As a result, foreign buyers have always coveted Libyan reserves, giving leverage to a government famous for the erratic, often hostile behavior of its leader. European countries such as France and Italy have been especially good clients of the Libyans, and indeed, refining capabilities in both countries are designed to process the high-grade petroleum of Libya and cannot easily be adapted to higher-sulfur-content crude oil. Oil has always been the bedrock of the Libyan economy, with the double-edged effects of allowing a higher standard of living for Libyans than their neighbors but, due to the oil curse, meaning the bargain reached for such comparative affluence has been restrictions on the liberties of its citizens.

Petroleum created further effects in Libya. For one thing, it made possible the operation of what Friedman call a "petrolist" state where the regime had considerable leeway in how it governed and dealt with the outside world due to its ability to strike a Faustian bargain with the population (prosperity for political quiescence). The self-proclaimed Great Socialist People's Libyan Arab Jamahiriya was philosophically run on the basis of Gaddafi's bizarre version of Arab socialism (something he called the Third Universal Theory) and acted erratically in world affairs, including alleged involvement in terrorism and alleged ties to provocative international acts such as the bombing of Pan Am Flight 103 over Lockerbie, Scotland.

Libya is also a somewhat different country than the others demographically. It is physically a fairly large country, ranked 17th in the world in size (a little larger than Alaska) but with a quite small population of about 6.7 million. Most of Libya is the sands of the Sahara Desert, and as a result, the vast majority of the population lives in a string of cities and towns along the Mediterranean coast. Reflecting the fact that Libya was not a unified political unit until the period between the world wars, the country has traditionally been divided into eastern and western regions. This geography was part of the uprising against Gaddafi, breaking out initially in the eastern city of Benghazi and gradually spreading westward, to the areas from which Gaddafi hailed and into tribal regions where his support was greatest. As a movement, the forces that succeeded in overthrowing Gaddafi were an ad hoc coalition united mainly by their opposition to the Gaddafi dictatorship. Whether these armed groups can make a transition to stable postconflict rule, or whether there are further revolutionary steps remains a question for the government elected in July 2012. These elections represented what Jones call a "remarkable achievement" given the country's chaotic political past.

Another distinguishing characteristic of the Libyan revolt is that it elicited an active military response from outside the country in the form of Allied intervention in the form of a no-fly zone over Libyan territory that simultaneously kept the Libyan air force out of the air and monitored and interrupted the movement of Libyan ground forces against rebel positions. Gaddafi and his military forces (most of whom were recruited from tribes loyal to the dictator) would probably have engaged in the kind of bloody suppression that marked the regime's reaction to the uprising in Syria. International public sympathy for the rebels was also enhanced by extensive electronic media coverage of the fighting, and especially at government action against rebel-held municipal areas.

The same kind of interim assessment as that for Egypt must be made regarding whether the uprising in Libya constituted a revolution or something more modest. As in Egypt, the rebels succeeded in toppling the traditional authoritarian government, although doing so required considerably more bloodshed than was true in Egypt. The interim political substitute was the TNC, which by organizing and conducting the 2012 elections, was a moderating force. The new government faces daunting problems. These include tribal and sectional divisions as well as Islamist extremists who could interrupt an orderly succession to democratic rule. It is thus hard to place Libya within the Brinton categories of progression beyond the first stage of revolution. The prospects for moving toward a thermidor effect seem greater in Libya than in some other places because, as Ajami points out, "Wealth, a sparse population, and foreign attention should see Libya through."

Syria

The Syrian variant has also been distinctive. It shares with Egypt and Libya a long period of rule by a single family, the al-Assads. The patriarch of the Syrian autocracy, Hafez al-Assad, ruled the country from 1971 to 2000, when he died, and he was succeeded by one of his sons, Bashar al-Assad. Bashar had lived extensively in the West, where he received a medical education, and it was hoped that Bashar would be a reformer who would loosen the tight reins by which his father had ruled and engage in popular reform of the country.

These hopes were gradually dashed. The politics of Syria are highly tribal, overlapped with confessional implications, and the Assad rule has rested on the support of a minority tribe, the Alawites, who are loose members of the Shi'a sect of Islam. The Alawites have traditionally dominated the Syrian military. Although Syrians are overwhelmingly Arab, they are divided by tribal allegiance and religion, with the Sunni majority in particular opposition to Alawite rule. Sunnis have been the most prominent targets of the violence against civilians. It is against this backdrop that the first spin-off demonstrations in Syria broke out in a series of Syrian cities (which are, by and large, the redoubts of the Sunnis), in March 2011.

What has distinguished the evolution of violence in Syria is the intensity with which the regime has dispatched the Syrian military to put it down and the ferocity of the repression that has ensued. Much of the most fervent fighting—and most notable accusations of atrocity—have been in Syria's third largest city, Homs, which is also heavily Sunni (reportedly two-thirds Sunni, one-quarter Alawite, and the rest Christian). The magnitude of Syrian armed forces' actions against urban populaces was widely covered by samizdat media coverage and elicited broad international condemnation of the Syrian government actions. Numerous countries, notably the United States and its closest allies, demanded removal of the Assad regime, and tight economic sanctions were placed on the regime. Syrian repression was condemned in the United Nations, but Russian support for Syria prevented the enactment of decisive Security Council actions. International pressure, including sanctions against the regime and even assistance to various insurgent groups opposing it, has been steady and ongoing, but the Assad regime has been remarkably resistant to attempts to bring it down. Part of this resistance may be the result of harsh likely treatment of those who supported the regime's activities if the revolution succeeds. The international pressure is described in Chapter 3.

The Syrian example's distinction to date has been the comparative success that the regime has had in maintaining itself in power. Because of its tribalism and resulting fragmentation, "the regime does not feel threatened enough to cede power, or to offer far-reaching reforms that might assure its peaceful sustainability," according to Moubayed. The constancy of international pressure on the Assad regime will thus be a critical factor in whether the Syrian uprising manages to achieve the first step in the revolutionary process of removing the old regime. There is general agreement that Assad may eventually be forced out, but no consensus about what happens next. Because there has been no real organized opposition to the regime for years, it is not clear what would evolve in Syria should the regime be overthrown. It could be no better than the current regime, and it even could be worse.

CONCLUSIONS

None of the movements that have arisen from the awakening known as the Arab Spring has achieved the shape or proportions of full-blown traditional revolutions as that phenomenon has developed in the Western world. Why is that the case? One reason may be that it is simply too early to reach a judgment. Full-fledged revolutions take time to unfold, and it is often easier in retrospect to distinguish their progression than it is at the time. The violent phase of the American Revolution, after all, took over six years, and it was not until 12 years after the shots heard at Lexington and Concord produced a U.S. constitution that completed the revolutionary process from British colony to full democratic independence. The French Revolution, if one includes its evangelical phase as the French Empire, lasted for over a quarter-century. The movements of the Arab Spring are still only two years old or less. Deciding whether they constitute full-blown revolutions may simply be premature.

It is also possible that the concepts of revolution described by Brinton and others are bound by time and place, limiting their applicability to the contemporary situation. As has been noted, all the examples that Brinton used as the basis for his model are Western (or Western-influenced) events, the most recent of which (the Russian Revolution of 1917) was nearly a century ago. It may be that modern revolutions are simply different and that the concepts and dynamics surrounding traditional conceptions simply do not fit as well or even apply at all to contemporary examples. It is hard, for instance, to classify the breakup of the Soviet Union within Brinton's terms, even if the results have been as clearly revolutionary as the events earlier in the century in that country. Whether the revolts associated with the awakening will have similar outcomes or not remains to be seen, and if they prove significantly different than the instances from the past, it may be the models that need revising.

One of the consequences of a media-driven view of world events is to expect rapid and decisive outcomes to accommodate the 24-hour news cycle and audience impatience and attention loss over long periods. History suggests that revolutionary change takes considerably longer than the two years since the Arab Spring began to take place. Within the confines of modern expectations, there is also a tendency to rush to judgment and to seek definitive outcomes prematurely. In the January/February 2013 edition of *Foreign Affairs*, for instance, two views are put forward. One, articulated by Jones, is pessimistic: "The prospects for future democratization have dimmed," he maintains. Writing in the same issue, Berman demurs: "The widespread pessimism about the fate of the Arab Spring is almost certainly misplaced." Berman argues her position on historical grounds that assessments are premature. Both may be right: prospects are now dim but will brighten with time. Both may also be wrong.

It is almost certainly premature to render a verdict about how to categorize the Arab Spring movements. One positive effect of placing these events within the framework of traditional revolutions is to suggest that one should not jump to superlative descriptions of events that are still ongoing and whose outcomes are, as Ajami summarizes, "in the scales of history. It has in it both peril and promise, the possibility of prison but also the possibility of freedom."

Those limits in mind, Hudson offers some interim judgments about the awakening. The awakening will change the nature of and perceptions about the region, proving "that its people share values widely held in the rest of the world" and that the revolts "will lead to a bigger role for public opinion in Middle East governance." Additionally, he believes there will be a spillover effect that suggests "Arabs in various countries share identity and values more than had been imagined." He concludes with a note of caution that is almost certainly appropriate for an interim assessment of the Arab Spring movement. "The Arab Spring has only just begun," he writes. It "may produce a long period of uncertainty and turbulence." Berman concurs: "The toppling of long-standing authoritarian regimes is not the end of the process of democratization but the beginning." Such a period is a hallmark of the Brinton model and other depictions of revolution. One can only wait and see if history will judge the Arab Spring as revolutionary or not.

SUGGESTED ACTIVITIES AND QUESTIONS

1. Define revolution. What are the different forms of revolution, emphases, and requirements of different senses of the term? Why are such distinctions important when dealing with and trying to describe modern violent political change?
2. What is the Crane Brinton model for describing revolutions? Describe each stage of the model. Based on the historical examples on which he bases his explanation, what are possible sources of bias when trying to apply the model to contemporary situations?
3. What is the Arab Spring? Where did it begin, how did it spread, and where have instances of it occurred? What is the third Arab awakening, and how does it relate to the phenomenon? What similarities and differences do the various instances seem to display?
4. The most prominent examples of Arab Spring–induced and –related change have been in Egypt, Libya, and Syria. Briefly describe the evolution of each of these to date (including updates of the text where appropriate), with particular attention to how each is distinctive and has evolved.
5. Are the various movements that are part of the Arab Spring revolutions or something else, such as uprisings or revolts? Where do they fit on the Brinton model? How does the application of the model to these situations help clarify what they are and what they may or may not become in the future?

SUGGESTED READINGS AND RESOURCES

Ajami, Fouad. "The Arab Spring at One: A Year of Living Dangerously." *Foreign Affairs* 91, 2 (March/April 2012), 56–65.

Anderson, Lisa. "Demystifying the Arab Spring." *Foreign Affairs* 90, 3 (May/June 2011), 2–7.

Arendt, Hannah. *On Revolution.* New York: Penguin Classics, 2006 (originally published in 1963).

Berman, Sheri. "The Promise of the Arab Spring: In Political Development: No Gain Without Pain." *Foreign Affairs* 92, 1 (January/February 2013), 64–74.

Bradley, John R. *Inside Egypt: The Land of the Pharaohs on the Brink of Revolution.* New York: Palgrave Macmillan, 2008.

Brinton, Crane. *The Anatomy of Revolution.* New York: Vintage Books, 1965.

Brownlee, Jason. "The Transnational Challenge to Arab Freedom." *Current History* 110, 739 (November 2011), 317–323.

Bynum, Daniel. "Terrorism After the Revolutions: How Secular Uprisings Could Help (or Hurt) the Jihadists." *Foreign Affairs* 90, 3 (May/June 2011), 49–54.

Cook, Steven A. *The Struggle for Egypt: From Nasser to Tahrir Square*. Oxford, UK: Oxford University Press, 2011.

Daalder, Ivo H., and James G. Stavridis. "NATO's Victory in Libya: The Right Way to Run an Intervention." *Foreign Affairs* 91, 2 (March/April 2012), 2–7.

Eisenstadt, S. N. *Revolution and the Transformation of Societies: A Comparative Study of Civilizations*. New York: The Free Press, 1999 (originally published in 1978).

El-Sharif, Ashraf. "Islamism After the Arab Spring." *Current History* 110, 740 (December 2011), 358–363.

Gelvin, James L. *The Arab Uprisings: What Everyone Needs to Know*. New York: Oxford University Press, 2012.

Goldstone, Jack A. "Understanding the Revolutions of 2011: Weaknesses and Resilience in Middle East Autocracies." *Foreign Affairs* 90, 3 (May/June 2011), 8–16.

Gurr, Ted Robert. *Why Men Rebel*. Princeton, NJ: Princeton University Press, 1973.

Hudson, Michael C. "The Middle East in Flux." *Current History* 110, 740 (December 2011), 364–369.

Jones, Seth G. "The Mirage of the Arab Spring: Deal with the Region You Have, Not the Region You Want." *Foreign Affairs* 92, 1 (January/February 2013), 55–63.

Martini, Jeff, and Julie Taylor. "Commanding Democracy in Egypt: The Military Attempt to Manage the Future." *Foreign Affairs* 90, 5 (September/October 2011), 127–137.

Moubayed, Sami. "Letter from Damascus: Will Syria Descend into Civil War?" *Current History* 110, 740 (December 2011), 339–344.

Norton, Augustus Richard and Ashraf al-Sharif. "North Africa's Epochal Year of Freedom." *Current History* 110, 736 (May 2011), 201–203.

O'Neill, Bard. *Insurgency and Terrorism: From Revolution to Apocalypse*. Washington, DC: Potomac Books, 2005.

Ottoway, Marina, "The Rise and Fall of Political Reform in the Middle East." *Current History* 109, 731 (December 2010), 376–382.

Ross, Michael I. "Will Oil Drown the Arab Spring?" *Foreign Affairs* 90, 5 (September/October 2011), 2–7.

Shehata, Dina. "The Fall of the Pharaoh: How Hosni Mubarak's Reign Came to an End." *Foreign Affairs* 90, 3 (May/June 2011), 26–32.

Snow, Donald M. *Distant Thunder: Third World Conflict and the New International Order*. New York: St. Martin's Press, 1993.

———. *UnCivil Wars: International Security and the New Internal Conflicts*. Boulder, CO: Lynne Riener Publishers, 1996.

Trager, Eric. "The Unbreakable Muslim Brotherhood." *Foreign Affairs* 90, 5 (September/October 2011), 114–126.

International Political Economy

One of the most dramatic and heralded characteristics of the contemporary international system has been the increasing rise of economic activity across national boundaries, a process often referred to as globalization. The increasing economic interdependence arising from globalization has been viewed by some as a tool for increased international peace and stability. Globalization became an international force in the 1990s, but it remains a very complex and uncertain work in progress. The chapters in this part portray a sequential view of the heart and evolution of globalization.

Chapter 9, "Free Trade," examines the post–World War II birth and evolution of the idea of free trade, the basic international dynamic of globalization. It traces the various efforts culminating in the creation of the World Trade Organization (WTO) in 1995. It also raises questions about the desirability and inevitability of free trade and its future as a key element in international relations.

The first post–World War II economic integration effort began in war-torn Europe and has evolved into the European Union (EU), globalization on a regional scale and in its most evolved manifestation. Chapter 10, "Regional Integration," explores the evolution of the EU from its beginnings as a limited-scope free trade arrangement to its present level of economic and political integration. It also explores future directions and problems of the union, principally through the debate between those who seek to maximize the size of its membership (wideners) and those who seek a more complete integration of its present members (deepeners), and more specifically in terms of the so-called "sovereign debt crisis" that is a current source of controversy within the EU and has implications for the wideners–deepeners debate.

Three of the most successful states in adapting to a globalizing world have been China, India, and Brazil, the subject of Chapter 11, "Rising Economic Powers." These three countries, along with Russia, form the so-called BRIC states, historically developing countries that are challenging the most developed states economically. The phenomenon of countries challenging the established world power structure (rising powers) is not a new aspect of international relations, but countries challenging the existing order primarily at the economic level is.

Chapter 12, "Globalization and Development," looks more specifically at the entire question of economic development since World War II. It has been a shibboleth of the last 60-plus years that a major component of increased global stability is the need to engage in the systematic development of the less developed world, a process intended to raise standards of living and satisfaction and thus to contribute to world peace and stability. This case examines the bases and development of these concepts and applies them to the currently highly differential world situation, including the process of change that is uplifting some states and areas more than others.

Free Trade: From ITO to WTO and Beyond

PRÉCIS

Free trade is, and for a long time has been, a controversial concept, as has its institutionalization in the form of an intergovernmental organization. This case begins by looking at the question of promoting free trade historically, from before the early post–World War II advocacy of an International Trade Organization (ITO) through the creation of the World Trade Organization (WTO) in 1995. Globalization is the most obvious manifestation of free trade, but while the process of freeing trade continues, so too have there been ongoing objections to it. Because of controversy surrounding the concept, one must ask the question of whether free trade is a good idea. This in turn leads to breaking the question into two aspects argued by advocates and opponents: the desirability of free trade as an idea and phenomenon, and what kind of institutional structure is most desirable for promoting and enforcing free trade. The case concludes by combining the two aspects and comparing them in the current economic climate.

T rading goods and services has been one of humankind's oldest forms of interchange with other peoples and communities, and it is at the heart of the contemporary emphasis on economic globalization. In ancient times, the purpose of trade was generally to acquire goods that either did not exist, grow, or could not be produced locally, such as exotic fabric like silk, spices, or precious metals. As the ability of political communities to span greater distances in shorter periods of time increased, trade expanded both in extent and in terms of what was and was not traded. The modern issue of trade probably congealed over whether to import goods and services that were also produced domestically. That question is near the top of the agenda in contemporary discussions of trade and is manifested in most disagreements on the subject, from questions of barriers to trade to environmental impacts of importation versus domestic production. Since the economic downturn of 2008, the contribution of trade to prosperity has been a particular point of concern, particularly in areas such as employment and fairness of competition in the United States and elsewhere. Despite accusations that the trade practices of some countries provided them artificial, unfair advantages during the difficult economic times of the past few years, free trade has transcended the crisis and continues to grow. It has become a virtually basic element of the contemporary global economic environment.

The debate over the impact of trade is not new, either internationally or in the United States. The emergence of the capitalist system first in Europe and then worldwide pitted global traders against what are now called protectionists in the form of mercantilists seeking to protect new, infant industries from destructive outside competition. Historically in the United States, advocacy and opposition have been sectional and remain as part of the contemporary landscape. As Michael Lind explains, "From the eighteenth century on, the Southern plantation oligarchy was content for the United States to specialize in exporting agricultural goods and raw materials to more industrial nations, importing manufactured goods in return. Thanks to the dominance of the South and Southwest, what was once the foreign economic policy of the Confederate States of America has become the trade policy of the United States as a whole." In turn, he argues, this has caused the United States to lead "the campaign to reduce or eliminate tariffs worldwide."

Whether to allow the unfettered movement of goods and services internationally (free trade) or to place restrictions of one kind or another on that flow is a central element in contemporary international relations. The removal of barriers to trade emerged as the centerpiece of the economic globalization movement of the 1990s, one of the engines designed to draw countries into closer collaboration by entwining them in the global prosperity of that decade. The global economic downturn at the turn of the millennium and the rise of the global war on terror took some of the luster from the free trade issue and relegated it to a less prominent place on the international political agenda. Yet, while attention is diverted elsewhere, globalization continues, and proponents and opponents continue to fight over whether to expand or constrict free trade arrangements.

The basic poles in the free trade debate have been between those seeking to expand trade (free traders) and those seeking to restrict trade (protectionists). Nestled between the extremes are those who advocate freer, but not necessarily totally free, trade (who often portray themselves as fair traders). All three elements are vibrant parts of contemporary arguments.

While the Industrial Revolution was raging in Europe and later North America, the need to buffer nascent industries from outside competition militated toward restriction, largely under the intellectual banner of mercantilism. During the period leading to World War II, protectionism ran rampant in a Great Depression–riddled Europe, and economic restrictions were partially blamed for the bloodiest war in human history. The "lessons" of interwar economics, in turn, helped frame the international political debate and its institutionalization, the topics of this case.

The economic aspect of this debate has been, and is, asymmetrical, and proponents on one side or the other tend to talk past one another, meaning interchange often devolves into monologues. The arguments for free trade tend to be mainly abstract, impersonal, and macroeconomic. Free trade is said to be beneficial because it unleashes basic economic principles like comparative advantage that make overall economies (national or international) stronger and economic conditions within and between countries more vital. Advocates thus argue that arrangements promoting trade have had a net positive impact on the global economy.

Anti–free trade arguments, on the other hand, tend to be specific, personal, and microeconomic. Cries to restrict trade tend to be posed in terms of the adverse impact that opening up trade opportunities has on individuals. Trade is not about economic theories; rather, it is about peoples' jobs and livelihoods. Thus, opponents hone in on things like jobs lost by individuals in particular industries to make their points. Fair traders seek a compromise somewhere between the extremes, advocating selective trade reductions in conformance with the principle of free trade but seeking to minimize negative microeconomic impact. Frequently, fair traders emphasize the need for compensatory actions for those individuals adversely affected by what they basically see as the beneficial impacts from free trade.

The argument over textiles illustrates the asymmetry in this debate. To pro–free traders, moving clothing manufacturing overseas, where labor costs are lower, makes economic sense. Clothes are cheaper, and the economies of new textile producers are stimulated. Uncompetitive textile manufacturers can redirect their efforts to other production areas in which they can compete successfully (produce better products at lower costs). Moreover, all consumers benefit, because goods are produced at the lowest possible costs, and the savings are passed along to consumers. In the end, it is a macroeconomic win-win situation with the added benefit of drawing countries closer together, thus promoting greater cooperation and reduced international tension.

From the anti–free trade viewpoint, these abstractions are unconvincing, because moving textile manufacturing overseas costs textile workers their jobs. It is a concern centered on the impact on individuals, not on the systemic impact. Thus, when free traders extol the removal of barriers and anti–free traders deride that possibility, they are, in a very real sense, not talking about the same thing.

The debate is intensely political at both the domestic and international levels. At the level of American national politics, the asymmetry is reflected between branches of the federal government. Historically, the executive branch of government, more concerned with the overall health of the economy and somewhat more removed from the impact on specific individuals or groups (as opposed to the whole country), tends to be more free trade–oriented and macroeconomic. Members of Congress, whose constituents are the people whose jobs are endangered when foreign goods and services are allowed to enter the country more freely, tend to be more microeconomic and opposed.

At the international level, the debate tends to get muddled with preferences for the general orientation toward political interactions with the world. Broadly speaking, two positions have dominated the global argument. *Internationalists* generally advocate a maximum involvement in the international system, because such involvement is argued to be systemically beneficial, particularly in promoting cooperative interactions among states. Advocacy of free trade and globalization are the economic manifestation of that reasoning.

The other position, *isolationism,* advocates a much more restrained level of involvement in the world. This position reached its institutionalized zenith between the world wars, when "splendid isolationism" sought to keep the United States entirely separated from world, and especially European, politics, an economic exclusionary preference that spread to Europe during the 1930s. In its pure form, isolationists are also protectionist, because protectionism limits international economic interactions.

The terms of the debate are not purely economic. Pro-trade advocates of the 1990s, for instance, argued that the globalization process of which free trade is an underpinning produces political as well as economic benefits. As noted in Chapter 11, one of the major reasons for promoting trade with China is to draw that country more intimately into the global political system. At the same time, anti–free trade arguments have expanded to include strictly noneconomic concerns ranging from environmental degradation to compromises of sovereignty, as well as politico-economic arguments about the effects on different groups within societies, all arguments that also arise in the China context.

This introduction frames the structure of the case, which has three purposes. The first, and major, purpose is historical, tracing the process whereby free trade has been institutionalized in the international system since the end of World War II. That process has crystallized the principal reasons for advocating and opposing free trade, a discussion of which supports that evolution and is the second purpose of the case. Finally, it will attempt to apply this institutional framework and the positions of the two sides to the current, ongoing debate on the issue.

INSTITUTIONALIZING TRADE

The genesis of the contemporary debate over free trade was the period leading to World War II, the traumatic impact of world history's bloodiest war, and the determination to attempt to do a better job than had been done at the end of World War I to restructure the international system so that those circumstances would not recur. One major reason for the war was economic conditions that had arisen during the Great Depression and had produced economic chaos that worsened conditions and facilitated the descent into the maelstrom of global war.

Economic nationalism and protectionism were deemed to be among the chief culprits for this situation. As the Great Depression took hold across Europe and North America, governments scrambled to minimize the effects on their own economies and peoples. One solution was to protect national industries from ruinous foreign competition by erecting prohibitively high trade barriers to keep foreign goods and services out and thus to keep domestic industries (and the jobs they created) alive. The erection of tariff and other barriers spawned retaliation and counter-retaliation that brought European trade to a virtual standstill. At the same time, currency fluctuations and devaluations became commonplace as a means to prop up failing enterprises. The resulting destabilization was felt strongly, especially in Germany, which faced stiff reparations requirements exacted at the Versailles Peace Conference that ended World War I. Unable to meet reparations schedules with foreign exchange from trade that had dried up, the German economy spun out of control as the depression hit that country harder than any other. The horrible economic privations that these practices created fueled the animosities and hatreds that made the slide to war easier. In that atmosphere, Adolf Hitler arose, promising, among other things, to restore prosperity.

The process of rebuilding the world after World War II began early during the war itself, largely through British and American collaboration. The purpose was to ensure that the mistakes made in 1919 were not repeated and that the structure of postwar peace would prevent a recurrence of another global war. Politically, this collaboration produced thoroughly internationalist constructs such as the United Nations Charter and the North Atlantic Treaty Organization (NATO). Economically, it produced a series of agreements known as the Bretton Woods system.

The Bretton Woods System and Free Trade

Encouraged and cajoled by the governments of Great Britain and the United States, representatives of 44 countries met in the White Mountains resort town of Bretton Woods, New Hampshire, in July 1944 to plan for the postwar economic peace. At Bretton Woods, the conferees hammered out a series of agreements that produced international economic institutions that have endured into the twenty-first century and have become staple parts of the system of globalization.

The conferees agreed that the heart of the 1930s economic problem was protectionism, manifested in international financial and economic practices such as large fluctuation in exchange rates of currencies, chronic balance-of-payments difficulties experienced by some countries, and prohibitively high tariffs. All of these practices had contributed to restriction of international commerce, and the conferees agreed that a major antidote to these practices was the encouragement of much freer trade among countries. This explicitly free trade preference was held most strongly by the U.S. delegation to Bretton Woods (the British, seeking to protect the series of preferences for members of the Commonwealth through the Imperial Preference System, sought a more restrained form of trade restriction reduction). This preference, coming from the Roosevelt administration, had some opposition domestically from some conservative members of Congress and from private organizations like the

U.S. Chamber of Commerce (a close ally of American businesses that benefited from protectionism).

The Bretton Woods process was more successful in confronting some of its priorities than others. Two international organizations were created, the International Monetary Fund (IMF) and the International Bank for Reconstruction and Development (IBRD, or World Bank). The IMF was originally chartered to deal with the problem of currency fluctuations by authorizing the granting of credits to shore up weak currencies, thus contributing to economic stabilization. The IMF has gradually widened its purview to a variety of other economic matters. The World Bank, on the other hand, was to assist in economic stabilization by granting loans originally for reconstruction of war-torn countries, and later for the development of the emerging Third World.

The priority of freeing trade did not enjoy as successful a fate. Although Bretton Woods produced two organizations, it failed to see the third pillar of its vision institutionalized, an international organization devoted explicitly to the promotion of free trade. Instead, that process was gradual and convoluted, not reaching fruition until the 1990s.

The Road from Bretton Woods to the WTO

Although there was a clear sentiment for institutionalizing a free trade–promoting international organization at Bretton Woods, there was enough opposition to the idea both internationally (British misgivings about infringements on its Imperial Preference System relationship with the Commonwealth, for instance) and domestically in the United States to keep such an organization from being part of the Bretton Woods package. The American position was crucial because the United States dominated the early postwar international economic system so thoroughly as to have an effective veto over economic matters. The problem was that the proposal to create a free trade–promoting entity ran into the familiar ambivalence of American politics relating to foreign affairs. For nearly half a century, the United States found itself alternately championing and opposing the creation of an organization to promote free trade, depending on whether free trade or anti–free trade elements held sway in the domestic decision process.

During and shortly after the war, the idea of the International Trade Organization (ITO) largely existed within the executive branch of the American government, and more specifically the U.S. Department of State. When Harry S. Truman succeeded Franklin Delano Roosevelt as president in 1945, he adopted the ITO as his own project. The Truman administration took the leadership role in proposing a United Nations Conference on Trade and Development (UNCTAD) in 1946, a major purpose of which was to draft a charter for the ITO. That proposal was, however, opposed by powerful elements in the U.S. Congress, and as a result, a meeting was held in Geneva, Switzerland, in 1947 to lay out the principles of a General Agreement on Tariffs and Trade (GATT), as an interim, partial solution to the free trade issue. The proposal for GATT was to be a temporary "fix," while the treaty to create the ITO was being honed and perfected. A meeting was scheduled for Havana, Cuba, in 1947 to formally propose the ITO.

Then American domestic politics got in the way. The ITO, like other free trade institutions since, would have done two things of varying controversy. The first was to provide an institutional basis for promoting the reduction of barriers to trade. Although there were objections to the proposal on this basis from protectionists and others, it was the less controversial aspect. The second, and more divisive, purpose was to create an instrument with jurisdiction and authority to enforce trade agreements, including the capability to levy enforceable penalties against sovereign governments. Opponents of the ITO and its successors complained that this enforcement provision represented an unacceptable infringement on American sovereignty, a position that resonated with both opponents and some proponents of the principle of free trade.

The ITO proposal was undermined by political actions in the United States in 1948. A coalition of powerful elements in the Congress led the way. The major players in this array against the ITO included conservative Republicans backed by protectionist agricultural and manufacturing interests seeking to protect American goods from foreign competition, liberal Democrats who viewed the ITO document as too timid an approach to promoting free trade, and conservatives who feared the sovereignty infringement that ITO enforcement provisions represented.

This congressional array faced a Truman administration that favored ratification of the ITO statute but that was unwilling to expend scarce political capital in the process. Competing on the foreign policy agenda was the North Atlantic Treaty Organization (NATO) proposal. As an initiative to create the first peacetime military alliance in American history, NATO was also controversial. The Truman administration reasoned that it could muster support for one but not both of the treaties, and that of the two, NATO was the more critical (the Cold War was heating up at the time). At the same time, 1948 was a presidential election year, and underdog incumbent Truman feared that spirited advocacy of a controversial idea like the ITO could become a negative campaign issue. Thus, the Truman administration backed away from its advocacy of the ITO, and the proposal died. The United States had, not uncharacteristically, both enthusiastically endorsed and helped develop the charter for the ITO and then destroyed it.

The demise of the ITO elevated GATT to a prominence and permanence that those who had originally proposed it had not envisioned. GATT survived as the flag bearer for international free trade from 1948 until the WTO came into existence in 1995. Those who oppose free trade in principle or effect were unenthused by GATT, but felt less threatened by it than by the ITO.

The reason GATT was less objectionable than the ITO was that it lacked the second characteristic of the ITO, an enforcement capability. GATT, in effect, was not an organization at all, but rather a series of negotiating sessions (called "rounds" and normally named after wherever a given round's first session was held) among the sovereign members. These sessions created international agreements on different free trade issues, but they were less threatening than the ITO. For one thing, GATT was not an organization and thus lacked more than a modest staff; therefore, it had no investigating capability. Moreover, GATT was never granted any enforcement authority, and all of the agreements reached during GATT negotiations had to be ratified by all participating countries before its provisions affected them. Thus, those who feared institutionalizing free trade on sovereignty grounds had little to fear from the GATT process.

Although it lacked the foundation of a permanent international organization, GATT was not useless. Indeed, the outcomes of the various rounds did produce a series of principles and practices that have been incorporated into the WTO. At heart, the principal thrust of GATT action was centered on the *most favored nation* (MFN) principle: the idea of providing to all trading partners the same customs and tariff treatment enjoyed by a country given the greatest trade privilege—the most favored country. Thus, if one country lowers its tariffs on a particular good to another country, it should extend that same tariff treatment to all GATT members.

The last, or Uruguay, round of GATT included among its proposals the establishment of the WTO. In a very real sense, the WTO is the ITO reincarnated, because it combines the two basic elements of the ITO again within a permanent international organization: the promotion of free trade, *and* mechanisms to enforce trade agreements and the legal authority to penalize members of the organization that violate international trade agreements.

When the WTO was first proposed in 1993, it did not produce the same volume of objection that the ITO did in 1948. The same basic opposed interests, if with different representatives, were against the WTO in the United States. Protectionists disfavored the principle of free trade; in 1948, these were mostly business-related Republicans, but in 1993 they were mostly union-supporting Democrats. Some again objected on the grounds that the organization was too timid—in this case the objectors were principally environmentalists concerned that the WTO would not aggressively protect the environment. Others raised objections on the grounds of infringements of national sovereignty. The WTO statute was ratified by the U.S. Congress on December 1, 1994. It was not submitted as a treaty (requiring the advice and consent of two-thirds of the Senate), but instead as an economic agreement under the provisions of so-called *fast track* procedures (also known as trade promotion authority). Treating the WTO as an economic agreement meant it had to pass both houses of Congress, but with only a simple, rather than a weighted, majority. Designating it under fast track (a provision to facilitate the passage of trade agreements) meant there were limits on congressional debate on the matter and that it could only be voted up or down in its entirety (the authority to amend it was removed). The date is important because it came after the November 1994 off-year elections but before the newly elected Congress was inaugurated (qualifying it as a lame duck session). Critics wailed at the timing and procedures (some maintained, for instance, that had WTO accession been presented as a treaty that it never would have gotten a two-thirds majority), but their cries of "foul" were in vain. Nearly 50 years after its principles were first proposed, institutionalized free trade became reality in 1995.

The WTO has now been in existence for over almost two decades. Its membership has increased from approximately 70 in 1995 to 159 as of March 2, 2013 (according to its Web site). In addition, 30 nonmember countries participate in the organization (observers have five years to apply for full membership), including Russia, Iraq, Iran, and Afghanistan. According to the WTO home page, the membership does 97 percent of world trade. The headquarters, including the secretariat, are located in Lausanne, Switzerland. The WTO has established itself as a leading international economic organization in the process.

Its brief tenure has also been filled with controversy and a great deal more visibility than functional international organizations (those that deal with a specific policy area rather than generalist organizations like the United Nations) usually attract or desire. In some ways, the acceptance of or opposition to the WTO reflects the status of globalization, whose central principle of free trade it exemplifies. When the charter came into effect in 1995, globalization was at its apex and the new WTO only activated its most ardent opponents. After 9/11, international attention shifted to the problem of terrorism, taking the spotlight off globalization and the WTO. Free trade has continued to grow. How it fares through the economic crisis that began in 2008 remains problematical as the global recovery progresses. Many of its basic values are by now so ingrained in international economics, however, that the whole process is probably impossible to reverse, even if one wished to do so (which hardly anyone does). Whether that continued momentum is good is still a matter of some contention.

IS INSTITUTIONALIZED FREE TRADE A GOOD IDEA?

This is really two separate but related questions, and there is disagreement on both of them. One question has to do with whether free trade itself is a worthy goal, and it has as a subtext the question whether free trade *as it is currently defined and being pursued* is a good idea. One can, for instance, believe that the general principle of removing barriers to trade is a good idea, but disagree that the overarching implementing principle of removing "barriers to trade" should override other principles, such as the promotion of human rights. The other question is whether free trade advocacy and implementation should be institutionalized, and that question has the subtext of whether the WTO *as it is currently organized and with the authority it has* is a good idea. Many who believe that free trade is a good principle and accept the idea that it needs some institutional base, for instance, disagree with the current structure of the WTO and advocate a more open, democratic structure for the organization. Clearly, those who oppose free trade (in principle or in its present guise) oppose the WTO as well.

The WTO has become a lightning rod on the free trade issue. Those who oppose free trade, generally on the basis that its effects are not as desirable for individuals or societies as its advocates suggest, clearly oppose an advocating institution, and especially one with mandatory authority to impose its values on individuals and countries. Proponents of free trade generally support the idea of an institutional base from which to promote their advocacy, but may or may not like the structure that exists. To make some reasonable personal assessment on the issue of free trade requires unraveling and analyzing each aspect.

Free Trade or Not Free Trade?

The generalized defense of free trade rests on the macroeconomic benefits it brings to countries and the microeconomic benefits it accords to individuals and groups. Both benefits are controversial. Free trade is the international application of the Ricardian principle of comparative advantage. The argument asserts that removing barriers to the movement of goods and services across national boundaries, the most efficient producers of goods and providers of services will come to dominate the markets in the areas of their advantage, to the benefit of consumers who will receive the best goods and services at the lowest prices from these providers. Presuming all countries can find products or services at which they have such advantages, all will find markets, and the result will be a general and growing specialization and prosperity. The application of free trade internationally is the handmaiden of the process of economic globalization, because the result should be the gradual widening of participation in the global economy, as more and more countries find and exploit areas in which they have or can develop a comparative advantage.

Freeing trade has the added benefit of promoting a more cooperative, peaceful environment, according to its champions. The major conceptual vehicle for this dynamic is *complex interdependence,* the idea that as countries become increasingly reliant on one another for essential goods and services, their ability and desire to engage in conflict, and especially war, becomes more remote—either because the desire to fight is decreased by proximity and acquaintance, or because the intertwining of economies makes it impractical or impossible to fight.

This macroeconomic argument is abstract and intellectual, and its dynamics are not universally accepted. It argues that free trade improves the general lot of peoples, and thus increases the prosperity of individuals: "a rising tide lifts all boats," to borrow a phrase that advocates often invoke. As an abstract matter presented in this way, it is difficult to argue with the virtue of free trade, although some do. At a slightly less abstract level, proponents of free trade also point to largely macroeconomic indicators, especially from the mid-1990s, to demonstrate growth in the global economy and within individual countries, phenomena they attribute to free trade–driven globalization. Despite these arguments, when these statistics are applied at more specific levels—to those of individuals or even sectors of economies within countries—the case is not as clearly positive.

The major objections to free trade come not over these abstract principles, but from the way they are applied. In the current debate about free trade, many of the objections go back to the conjunction of free trade and the values of market economics in fact if not in theory. It is the effects of the kind of free trade that the advocates put forward that present the problem.

A key element in opposition arises from the presumption that all countries (or whatever entities are part of a free trading arrangement) will in fact find areas of production at which they have a comparative advantage. This is not always the case, and countries lacking comparative advantage (generally the least developed countries) thus tend not to be WTO members. It also presumes that areas of uncompetitive production undercut by free trade can find compensatory equivalent areas of comparative advantage that will replace uncompetitive enterprises, and it is central to microeconomic objections to free trade that this is also not always the case.

This contrast in macro-level versus micro-level benefits helps explain why free trade is more popular among economic elites than the general population and why the issue becomes a flash point in economic debates during political campaigns. The economic elites—investors, entrepreneurs, and the like—are all more likely to be insulated from negative micro-level impacts but more affected by broader, macro-level effects like the overall impact on the stock market. If globalization indeed produces benefits to members of the broader economy, then they are likely to benefit personally and thus to be supportive. Negative micro-level effects have a direct impact on the jobs of individual voters, and candidates for public office are likely to reflect the suffering that displaced individuals and industries feel. Thus, it is not surprising to see opposition to globalization in areas where globalization has produced declines in noncompetitive industries, from the textile workers of the Carolinas to automobile workers in Michigan or steelworkers in Pennsylvania.

An international example of negative effects is the impact of institutionalized free trade on the economic development of poor countries. Because the basis of free trade is the most favored nation (MFN) principle, opponents argue that poor countries are in a disadvantageous situation. Because they are at a comparative disadvantage at producing nearly everything (a major reason they are less developed), they are vulnerable to a flooding of goods and services across the range of economic activity if they are part of a free trade system. Their inability to protect nascent economic activities means that indigenous development will be systematically undercut by participation in the free trade regime and thus development will be retarded. The net impact of being exposed to MFN has thus been, according to critics, to contribute to greater economic inequality between the rich and poor countries, the very opposite of what the proponents of free trade argue.

For the "turtles," as Thomas Friedman labels the countries that cannot compete in the free trade environment, there are two options, as the example suggests. One is to stay outside the WTO framework, as its principles and rules only apply to members. Thus, almost all the countries that have not joined the WTO are extremely poor, and although the WTO has tried to develop outreach programs to these nonmembers, they have not been entirely successful at overcoming these objections. The other alternative is to join the WTO and suffer the consequences of assault on the domestic economy in the hopes that doing so will help "lift" the national boat.

The policies that implement free trade can have similar effects. Joining the free trade–driven globalizing economy requires adopting both macroeconomic and microeconomic policies that require individual privation and thus engender popular political opposition both to the policies and to the governments that advocate them. Such policies are easier to digest in economic good times that they are in periods of economic privation, when free trade is raised into greater question.

The WTO: Problem or Solution?

The WTO is the final fulfillment of the dreams of the Bretton Woods planners, but is it the answer to the free trade question, or the problem? Assessing whether the WTO helps or hinders the progression of free trade can be broken into three separate concerns. The first is the kind of free trade that the WTO advocates. To its opponents, the WTO is little more than a handmaiden to the large multinational corporations (MNCs). Global Exchange, a Web-based research organization that is very critical of the WTO, calls it an "unaccountable, corporate-based government" that reflects the values of the MNCs at the expense of virtually everyone else. At least to some extent, this should come as little surprise. The globalization process of which free trade is an implementing device is based in the promotion of capitalist, free market economics, of which corporations are a prominent core part. Moreover, much of the economic resources on which the spread of globalization is based comes in the form of foreign direct investment (FDI) by private sources, and entities like international banks and multinational corporations provide most of the FDI. Because they do so out of a profit motive and not from a sense of philanthropy, it follows that these entities would have an interest in helping to shape the philosophies and policies the WTO promotes. As indirect evidence of the success of the MNCs in this regard, it might be remembered that corporations within the United States were major opponents of the ITO because of protectionist motives, but have by and large been equally strong supporters of the WTO.

The advocacy of free trade and the promotion of its implementation through the WTO thus includes two substantive judgments. One is whether there is an alternative economic philosophy that could be attached to free trade that would make it more palatable to those who oppose the idea or its consequences. Is there some alternative to a market-economy-based, free trade–driven, globalized economy? The second judgment flows from the first: If there is no acceptable alternative underpinning, are the positive outcomes of institutionalized free trade better or worse than the absence of such a system? The analogy of the rising tide and the boat is sometimes used to frame this question. Pro–free traders admit that not everyone benefits equally from free trade, but that everyone does benefit to some extent and thus everyone is better off under a free trade regime (the tide lifts all boats). Opponents argue that the benefits are so inequitably distributed that gaps are actually widened to the point that some are left relatively worse off (some boats get swamped).

The second disagreement concerns the structure of the WTO itself. The WTO, after all, has two basic functions: the promotion of free trade and the enforcement of free trade agreements. The enforcement mandate is and always has been the more controversial aspect of the WTO. The mechanism for enforcement was agreed on during the Uruguay round of GATT in the form of the Dispute Settlement Understanding (DSU). Under the DSU, the WTO is authorized to establish and convene the Dispute Settlement Body (DSB). *The Geneva Briefing Book* describes the considerable authority of the DSB, "which has the sole authority to establish such panels to adjudicate disputes between members and to accept or reject the findings of panels and the Appellate Body, a standing appeals body of seven independent experts. The DSB also . . . has the power to authorize retaliation when a member does not comply with DSB recommendations and rulings."

These powers are not inconsiderable and include the power to identify alleged violations; to convene and prosecute those alleged violations; and then to issue binding rulings and penalties and to enforce those penalties, ostensibly without recourse to an outside, independent source of appeal (all appeals are internal to the process). The membership of these panels is chosen by the WTO itself, and, according to Global Exchange, "consist[s] of three trade bureaucrats that are not screened for conflict of interest."

To critics that span the ITO–WTO debate, a chief objection to this arrangement is its effect on national sovereignty. The rulings of the DSU process have the effect of treaty law on the countries against which they are levied, which means that governments cannot unilaterally overturn the effect of those laws. This is particularly a concern in the United States where, as noted, there is particular sensitivity over intrusions on state sovereignty. In the specific case of WTO rulings, these have disproportionately affected the United States. According to the *Geneva Briefing Book*, "From the advent of the WTO, in January 1995, until October 1, 2003, the United States has been a party in 56 out of 93 WTO dispute settlement panel reports and 36 out of 56 Appellate Body reports." The source does not indicate how many of these involved judgments against the United States, but it is likely at least some of them did.

The third concern regards what unforeseen consequences the institutionalization of free trade has had, and whether those consequences are acceptable. As one might expect, most unforeseen outcomes that have been identified are negative and are expressed most vocally by opponents of the process and its outcomes. Two in particular stand out as examples: the alleged antilabor bias of the WTO, and its negative environmental impacts. Unsurprisingly, these two arguments have been raised by two of the most prominent and visible opponents of the WTO, and neither of these groups was evident in the 1940s but both are today. Both touch on the dual questions of whether free trade itself or the way it is institutionalized is the problem.

Objections to free trade on the basis of being antilabor contain both elements of objection. Free trade is, of course, the culprit among those people working in industries and services that do not enjoy comparative advantage and can only compete if protected by some form of trade barrier. The textile industry cited earlier is a prime example. Labor unions also contend that the way in which the WTO operates to remove barriers to trade and provides incentives for corporations to move their businesses to places that engage in unfair labor practices (everything from low wages and benefits to child labor), thereby creating an unfair environment within which to compete. Moreover, they believe that the corporatist mentality they say reigns supreme within the WTO encourages foreign direct investors to nurture and create these unfair practices as ways to create and sustain comparative advantage. These allegations are parallel to older domestic arguments about union busting and scab labor practices, and in the United States, to so-called "right-to-work" laws that restrain organized labor activity and jurisdiction. Because these are extremely emotional issues among trade unionists, it helps explain the depth of their animosity toward the WTO and the prevalence of trade unionists in anti–free trade, anti-WTO activities.

Environmentalists' objections to free trade and the WTO are parallel. The need to establish conditions of comparative advantage drives some countries to rescind environmental regulations that add to the cost of production (e.g., dumping hazardous chemicals used in processing materials into the environment rather than rendering these chemicals harmless before release), thereby making their industries more competitive than industries in the United States that must meet environmental standards that add to production costs. Critics cite cases in Latin America (especially Mexico) in which environmental standards have indeed been relaxed or done away with to attract industry. More recently, China has become a major object of this criticism, as it generates much of its energy cheaply (thereby contributing to its comparative advantage) by burning coal that pollutes the atmosphere disproportionately and contributes in a major way to global warming.

The environmentalist objection is also applied directly to the WTO. Environmentalists contend that most corporations resist environmental restraints philosophically and only accede to environmental regulation reluctantly and unenthusiastically. Because the WTO is alleged to be largely controlled by corporate interests and reflects corporate values, they are thus predisposed to be suspicious of the organization on those grounds. Environmentalists are also generally conspicuous at demonstrations against the WTO.

CONCLUSION

Whether to advocate or oppose free trade and its institutionalization is not, nor has it ever been, an easy or straightforward proposition. At the abstract, theoretical level of international macroeconomics, the case for free trade is very convincing, and it is not surprising that many of the defenses of free trade spring from these theoretical arguments. At the applied level of the impact of free trade on individuals and groups (the microeconomic level), the proposition creates more ambivalence. Certainly, individuals as consumers benefit when comparative advantage produces goods and services at lower cost and higher quality through free trade rather than from less efficient, protected domestic industries. Imagine, for instance, the impact on Christmas gift spending if all goods made in China were eliminated. At the same time, removing protection can terminate employment for those in the less efficient industries. Although the theory of comparative advantage says that people so displaced should find alternative employment in more competitive fields, accomplishing that task is almost always easier said than done. When these dislocations affect large portions of a society, there may also be a negative political reaction both to the phenomenon of globalization (and hence free trade) and to those politicians who are supporters of free trade.

The question of institutionalizing free trade is related but not synonymous, because one can reasonably take one of three positions on the desirability of free trade per se: one can favor free trade unconditionally, one can oppose it equally unconditionally, or one can favor free trade with some restrictions, the fair trade position. For the "pure" positions, the answer to whether some organization should be established to promote and enforce free trade is fairly straightforward. If one believes free trade is comprehensively desirable, then a free trade–promoting institution is clearly a desirable instrument to that end (although the kind and extent of enforcement capability may be debatable). Conversely, if one opposes free trade across the board, then it would be nonsensical to support any instrumentality that promotes or enforces a rejected idea.

That leaves the "fair traders," who support expansions in trade through the reduction of barriers to trade, but who believe there should be exclusions or limitations on the extent and degree of trade promotion. Such an advocacy attempts to finesse the dichotomy between free trade and protectionism by advocating some of both, depending on the context. This position is generally politically tenable as well, because it allows support for free trade (which, in the abstract, most people favor) with restrictions to protect politically significant victims of free trade.

The advocacy of freer trade leads to three questions that can be applied to the dual thrusts of free trade and its institutionalization. The first is, "How free should trade be?" The general criterion for answering the question is how much of the benefits and costs of free trade is one willing to bear, and one's answer will, in turn, vary with the level of personal benefit one (or one's group, or country) derives from various levels of free trade.

The second question is, "What kinds of values should underlie a free trading system and, especially, the institution that supports and promotes it?" If the current free trade–based system of globalization is based on the values of market-based, capitalist economics, as it at least partly is, it leads to a form of organization based on pure economic competition in which the less government regulation exists, generally the better. If, as alleged, the WTO is dominated by people with these values and interests, then the *kind* of free trade system that evolves and is institutionalized will reflect those values. On the other hand, if one enters values such as equity (fair trade) and social consciousness (environmentalism) into the values underlying a free trade system, it probably looks different than the current system.

The third and final question is, "What kind of enforcement mechanism is most desirable?" The answer, of course, begins with the level of enthusiasm one has about free trade in the first place: The more enthusiastic one is, the more enforcement one is likely to favor or tolerate. But the answer also incorporates how one has answered the second question: One's enthusiasm for enforcement may depend on what kinds of values are being enforced and whether one supports those values. In a favorite example cited by critics of the current system, the American ban on tuna fishing using mile-long nets that also ensnare and kill dolphins was overruled in a judgment by the WTO. In an action brought by Mexico, the WTO said the law, when applied to American territorial waters, was a barrier to trade. Does a free trade regime need to lead to that kind of conclusion?

The free trade movement has apparently weathered the economic storm created by the worldwide economic crisis that emerged in 2008. Despite economic conditions that could give rise to protectionist efforts to shield individual countries from vagaries like high unemployment, such solutions were not seriously proposed. If anything, the crisis was viewed as an indication of the need for more, rather than less, globalization. As one of the crown jewels of globalization, that meant continuing, even growing, support for free trade as well. Naim summarizes the impact: "Globalization is such a diverse, broad-based, and potent force that not even today's massive economic crash will dramatically slow it down or reverse it. Love it or hate it, globalization is here to stay." If that bold assertion is true, then free trade, as a prime pillar of globalization, will be enduring as well.

SUGGESTED ACTIVITIES AND QUESTIONS

1. What is free trade? Why is it an issue, both historically and in the contemporary context? What are the basic disagreements about the desirability of free trade? What basic positions do people take on the trade issue?
2. Describe the process of institutionalizing free trade from the Bretton Woods conference of 1944 to the ratification of the World Trade Organization in 1995. Why did the International Trade Organization fail to come into existence in 1948 but the WTO succeed in 1995? What was the role of the General Agreement on Tariffs and Trade in this evolution?
3. What are the principal arguments for and against free trade? How do the disputes over intellectual property rights and the impact of free trade on development of the poorest countries illustrate this debate?
4. What are the major controversies surrounding the WTO? What values does it promote? What powers does it have? How do labor and environmental objections illustrate this controversy?
5. Answer the three questions posed in the conclusion: How free should trade be? What kinds of values should underlie a free trading system and, especially, the institution that supports and promotes it? What kind of enforcement mechanism is most desirable? After determining your personal answers to these questions, do you consider yourself a free trader, an anti–free trader, or somewhere in between (a fair trader)? Why?

SUGGESTED READINGS AND RESOURCES

Barshefsky, Charlene. "Trade Policy in a Networked World." *Foreign Affairs* 80, 2 (March/April 2001), 134–146.

Bauman, Zygmunt. *Globalization: The Human Consequences.* New York: Columbia University Press, 1998.

Dierks, Rosa Gomez. *Introduction to Globalization: Political and Economic Perspectives for a New Era.* Chicago, IL: Burnham, 2001.

Dregner, Daniel W. *U.S. Trade Strategy: Free Versus Fair.* New York: Council on Foreign Relations Press, 2006.

Friedman, Thomas L. *The Lexus and the Olive Tree: Understanding Globalization.* New York: Farrar, Straus and Giroux, 1999.

_____. *The World Is Flat: A Brief History of the Twenty-First Century.* New York: Farrar, Straus, and Giroux, 2005.

Landau, Alice. *Redrawing the Global Economy: Elements of Integration and Fragmentation.* New York: Palgrave, 2001.

Lind, Michael. *Made in Texas: George W. Bush and the Southern Takeover of American Politics.* New York: New America Books, 2003.

McBride, Stephen and John Wiseman, eds. *Globalization and Its Discontents.* New York: St. Martin's Press, 2000.

"Measuring Globalization." *Foreign Policy*, March/April 2004, 46–53.

Naim, Moises. "Think Again: Globalization." *Foreign Policy*, March/April 2009, 28–34.

O'Connor, David E. *Demystifying the Global Economy: A Guide for Students.* Westport, CT: Greenwood Press, 2002.

Panagariya, Arvind. "Think Again: International Trade." *Foreign Policy*, November/December 2003, 20–29.

Park, Jacob. "Globalization After Seattle." *Washington Quarterly* 23, 2 (Spring 2000), 13–16.

Ricardo, David (R. M. Hartwell, editor and Introduction). *On the Principles of Political Economy and Taxation.* New York: Penguin Classics, 1971.

Rothgeb, John M. J. *Trade Policy: Balancing Economic Dreams and Political Realities.* Washington, DC: CQ Press, 2001.

Schaeffer, Robert K. *Understanding Globalization: The Social Consequences of Political, Economic, and Environmental Change.* Lanham, MD: Rowman and Littlefield, 2003.

Shah, Anup. "Free Trade and Globalization." *Global Issues* (online), July 25, 2009.

World Trade Organization. *The Geneva Briefing Book.* Lausanne, Switzerland: World Trade Organization, 2004.

WEB SITES

Critical views of the World Trade Organization: Global Exchange at http://www.globalexchange.org/campaigns/rulemakers/topTenReasons.html
The home page of the World Trade Organization: http://www.wto.org

Regional Integration: The European Union and the Sovereign Debt Crisis Face the Future

PRÉCIS

The process of economic integration is both global and regional. Within the context of the post–World War II world, the process began in Europe shortly after the war through the establishment of a small group of institutions that have evolved into the European Union (EU). They represent a geographically limited (but physically expanding) area but have achieved a far greater degree of integration than global schemes and proposals. The EU has moved from being a limited-scale free trading arrangement to a true economic union with strong political implications, controversies, and problems. It is also, however, an extremely dynamic competitor in the world economic system. The evolution of the EU offers some reasonable precedents about at least one way in which the movement toward globalization may evolve. The case will concentrate on the growing physical size of the EU and the challenge to its continuing growth and vitality represented by the sovereign debt crisis. It will also examine how the resolution of that crisis will affect the further development of the EU as an experiment in integration.

The European Union celebrated its 55th birthday at the beginning of 2013, marking the longevity of an organization that came into being with the implementation of the Treaty of Rome in 1958. Regional economic integration of the nature and on a scale such as the European Common Market, as it was known then, was unprecedented, and it had both political and economic purposes. The frank underlying political goal was to create a Europe in which a repetition of the events leading to the century of warfare centering on Germany and France would be eliminated, and the precursor institutions that became the core of the EU had this purpose fully in mind as they sought an institutional setting in which war between the major European powers would become impossible. Economically, the process proposed to stimulate the economies of its members through an integration that would apply the principles of the theory of comparative advantage to the continent.

The history of the EU has not been one of smooth sailing. The ambitious idea of international integration was controversial at the time the Treaty of Rome was negotiated. The steps along the way to further integration, of which the current sovereign debt crisis is the most recent example, have been controversial as well. Still, the EU has been an enormous success. A Europe devastated by World War II, in a state of economic doldrums after its conclusion, was rapidly transformed into an economic force in the world that could compete on a global scale with the United States and Japan and as a political equal to the Soviet Union. Moravcsik recently called it "the most ambitious and successful international organization of all time." The EU has grown over its 50 years physically and in its extent of integration from a free trading arrangement between six adjacent continental states to an evolving economic union of 27 states, with more waiting in the queue for inclusion. At the same time, the attendant process of political integration and the extension of the EU to countries unlike the original membership have created a crisis of sorts within the EU that is a source of concern as the organization moves further into the twenty-first century.

Strains have emerged between the more and less prosperous members that reflect the economic heterogeneity that has accompanied expansion. Northern European countries like Germany possess the most stable, prosperous status in the EU, and they have been called upon with increasing frequency to cover economic deficiencies and excesses in the less prosperous members' economies. These problems have been most glaring in a number of Mediterranean countries like Greece, Italy, Spain, and most recently Cyprus (but also in Ireland), which form the core of the current EU debt crisis.

Globalization represents the process of economic integration on its grandest scale, incorporating the entire world or at least those parts of it willing and able to participate into the globalization process. The EU has been its most positive regional symbol. As Foroohar put it in a 2013 article, "The E.U. is perhaps the most benign example of globalization. As a global phenomenon, this process maximizes the number of states that participate in globalization but not the depth or extent of participation that EU does." The EU is thus an important symbol of how far global integration can proceed on a regional basis, making the fate of the EU important for gauging the prospects for globalization in the worldwide context.

All economic integration schemes are not the same. Rather, they differ on at least two salient characteristics. One is the *physical dimensions* of the unit under consideration. In the evolving history of globalization, there have been two major geographical foci of economic integration: regional approaches and worldwide applications. In Chapter 9, the discussion centered primarily on the broader global level, as represented by the concept of globalization and institutionalized through entities such as the World Trade Organization (WTO). The EU is the original and by far most advanced regional approach to economic integration.

The second dimension is the *extent* of integration being sought. Although the averred purposes of economic integration schemes have the removal of economic barriers and the promotion of trade among participating units as their major purpose, there are inevitably political consequences and goals involved as well. The admixture of economic and political purposes tends to grow as the extent of the integrating unit expands, and in some cases, political integration may even be the coequal or overriding purpose of the economic integration effort.

Extent of integration goes beyond the incorporation of political integration, and indeed, most economists viewing the process tend to downplay the political implications and instead look at the extent of economic integration that is proposed. In rough terms, integration spans a range of ever-closer association and commitment that begins with the establishment of free trade among the members and moves through stages such as a customs union, a common or single market, a monetary union, and a true economic union. Most of the global schemes have proposed no more than a free trade area–level of integration, as have some regional organizations (the North American Free Trade Agreement [NAFTA] and the Asia-Pacific Economic Cooperation [APEC] are examples). The EU is unique in that it has traveled through all the steps of economic integration.

Because it has traversed more fully the path of economic integration than any other contemporary economic set of institutions, the EU provides the best available precedent for judging the desirability, opportunities, and pitfalls associated with regional attempts at integration that go beyond free trade arrangements to a much deeper and more pervasive form of integration. To understand the dynamics of the regional economic integration process, we will begin with a general discussion of the dynamics and forms of regional integration and how the political and economic dynamics intertwine. These observations will then be applied to the evolving case of the EU. The travails of the EU are particularly important for this process because, as Foroohar puts it, "If it (EU) fails, that has big consequences."

THE REGIONAL INTEGRATION PROCESS

Regional integration—binding together the economies of physically proximate states within a geographical area—is simultaneously simpler and more difficult than global approaches to integration. It is simpler because of smaller geographical reach and jurisdiction and because regional groupings are likely to contain peoples of similar culture and history with some understanding and history of interaction among them. The Germans and the French, in other words, have known each other for a long time. This very familiarity can, however, breed contempt and animosity among regional actors that make their cooperation more rather than less difficult. One reason Germans and Frenchmen know each other so well is that they have been fighting so long. Within regions, there may be dissimilarities between potential members (the United States and Mexico within NAFTA, for instance) that create unique problems and circumstances.

Although it may be difficult, even misleading, to try to generalize on the regional integration process, it is possible to describe it. The discussion will be centered on two major benchmarks surrounding integration, both of which are applicable to the global and regional levels but are particularly poignant when dealing with a highly integrated regional structure like the EU. One is the degree of integration involved in any particular proposed or existing scheme. A taxonomy of gradually increasing levels of integration will be laid out. The other concern is the degree of political and economic integration and controversy involved, and the relationship between existing or potential economic and political goals. As a general rule, the more complex and extensive an economic association is, the more political concerns either arise or underpin the effort. Because familiarity can breed both attachment and contempt, however, even deepening association can also accentuate points of difference and conflict.

Forms of Integration

The process of economic integration, whether pursued at global or regional levels, can produce greater or lesser degrees of interdependence and interpenetration among parties. In the general discussion of globalization, most goals are stated in terms of the pursuit of *free trade*, as introduced and discussed in Chapter 9. Agreements like that creating the WTO or regional arrangements like the APEC have the promotion of free trade as their primary, even sole, focus. The principal objectives of free trading arrangements are to encourage greater trade among members by reducing barriers to trade—tariffs, quotas, and the like—among the members. Such arrangements represent the initial, and least binding or formal, means to approach greater economic—or political—integration.

There is a series of increasingly entangling forms of economic integration that go beyond free trade arrangements. These can be placed in a sort of hierarchical order of greater complexity and commitment to the form of integration. The ultimate expression is economic union, of which the EU is the sole example.

The next step beyond a free trade area is a *customs union*. In this form of arrangement, the members adopt a common external tariff toward all goods and services entering any of the member countries. In a free trade area that is not also a customs union, the various members all have their own external tariffs. The effect is that import duties are not uniform among members for different goods and services. If there is a free trade agreement in force, high duties on goods and services imposed by one member can be circumvented by importing that good or service into a country where there is a lower barrier, then moving that good or service through the free trade area into the country with the higher tariff, thereby avoiding the original high tariff through indirect importation. The old European Free Trade Area, composed of early nonmembers of the European Common Market (or European Economic Community), was of this nature, and it did not work terribly well.

When a free trade area and customs union are created for the same physical area, the result is the creation of a *single* or *common market*. The goal of a common market is to create the free circulation of goods, capital, people, and services within the geographic constraints of the common market region. This is done by reducing, preferably to zero, all trade barriers among the members (the basis of a free trade area) and by creating a common external barrier against goods and services imported anywhere within the region (a customs union). The result is to create an economic area that maximizes the flow of goods, services, capital, and people within the single market area while excluding or making more difficult the entry of items produced outside the area at lower costs. This was the original form that the European Economic Community assumed in the 1960s and beyond, and it was a huge success in stimulating the economies of the member states and in attracting the interest of other states that wanted to join the process. It is a form of association that goes far beyond most current conceptions of integration beyond Europe.

A common market's level of integration, however, is circumscribed if its members maintain their individual currencies, because this means that commerce is slowed by the necessity of establishing and enforcing exchange rates, and translating transactions from one currency to another. The solution to this barrier to further integration is the establishment of a *monetary union*, a financial institution that can issue a common currency and make monetary policy that is binding in all the political units. The EU has established a monetary union, but it is, as will be shown, one of the most controversial aspects of the EU, because a monetary union requires a common monetary policy among the members, and this requires a political body that has the authority to make such policy. This "power of the purse" comes at the expense of national legislatures and is, in some cases, a major source of political concern on sovereignty grounds. One way to attenuate the dilution of national sovereignty created by a monetary union is to leave the setting of fiscal policy (such as taxation) under national control, as is done in the EU. As Gros explains, "Monetary union was not intended to lead to a transfer of power in the fiscal field." The euro is the most visible manifestation of the monetary union, and resistance to adopting the euro in countries like Great Britain is a symbol of the controversy. Some observers believe that the lack of a central mechanism for setting common, mandatory monetary policy has been a major contributor to the current crisis of the EU.

The ultimate form of economic integration is the *economic union*, an arrangement that combines a single or common market and a monetary union. This is the form of association that was created originally by the EU in 1993, and it remains one source of controversy surrounding the organization. At the purely economic level, the creation of an economic union is the culmination of the process of economic integration, because the formation of the monetary union removes the last barrier to economic activity across political boundaries created by the necessity of exchanging currencies when transactions occur. If economic integration is the goal, economic union is its zenith.

The movement toward an economic union, however, also has the strongest possible political reverberations. Economic and political unions are, in theory, separable, because one deals with what can be viewed as purely economic consequences and benefits, whereas political union implies an arrangement or rearrangement of political authority in the proposed unit. Economic associations at whatever level and form have tended to be less controversial, because their economic benefits tend to overwhelm political concerns and implications. Certainly that has been the case throughout most of the process of European economic integration; the current controversy over the political implications of the NAFTA in areas like immigrant flow is a contrary example. The movement to an economic union has stronger political implications for the EU than previous steps short of the creation of an economic union per se.

Political and Economic Integration

Separating politics and economics in any real situation is always difficult. The realm of politics is authoritative (normally governmental) decision making. I have elsewhere defined politics as "the process by which conflicts of interest over scarce resources are resolved." The definition is fairly conventional and suggests politics is both a process (a set of rules for making authoritative allocations of resources) and a substantive concern over those resources being allocated (the conflicts of interest over scarce resources). Although there are many scarce resources that may require allocation, one of the most common and prominent is economic resources, the subject of economic integration schemes.

Economic resources are so important that deciding how they should be divided may become a major concern in deciding who can make political decisions. One such concern, for instance, is what political authorities have the right to levy taxes and spend money, and who has what authority certainly influences which resources are allocated for what purposes (fiscal policy). In the case of the movement to an economic union, a major political question is what political authority will have the jurisdiction over matters such as monetary policy (including currency regulation). Because of the centrality of monetary policy to the overall operation of any political or economic unit, what political authority has control over that function is fundamental to the political equation. Because national governments have possessed and continue to covet autonomous power over monetary policy, a transfer of that authority to a central entity like the EU is a highly controversial and strongly resisted step.

The reasons for entering into economic associations have a more or less political underpinning as well. At the most obvious level, economic associations are supposed to stimulate economic activity and create prosperity, and those who propose and construct those associations expect political support for having done so. When the European Common Market was first instituted, for instance, it was wildly successful and overwhelmingly popular; part of the underlying purpose of forming the organization was indeed to strengthen governments as a way to discourage support for communism among populations in Western Europe.

Political and economic aspects of economic schemes may be so inextricable as to be impossible to disaggregate altogether, and the EU is a prime example. The roots of what has become the EU go back to World War II and the attempt to reconstruct the international system—and specifically Europe—after the end of the second European-based world conflagration in less than 40 years. For planners who were intent on producing a more peaceful world order, the UN system was the general solution for matters of war and peace. The more specific problem, however, was what most believed to have been the root cause of the world wars—Franco-German rivalry for control of Europe. World War II, in effect, was the fourth violent round in that competition that began with the Napoleonic wars and came forward through the Franco-Prussian War of 1870 and World War I. The first four rounds had proven inconclusive, and there was a strong desire to avoid the possibility of a fifth round. But how?

The answer, devised through allied consultation during the war in which the Frenchman Jean Monnet played a very prominent role, was to make future warfare between Germany and France functionally impossible. The planners began from the assumption that modern, symmetrical warfare of the kind practiced by Europeans rested on the ability to produce steel and thus the implements of war. If a country could not independently produce steel, it could not go to war. Thus, the planners sought to see if they could create an international political unit that would deprive France and Germany of the ability to produce the wherewithal of war independently of one another. The result was the European Coal and Steel Community (ECSC) of 1951, the first institution in what evolved into the EU.

For many planners during the war, the movement leading to the EU thus had both distinctly political and economic intents that have become impossible to disentangle over time. The great successes and support for the movement have been economic and seen in expanding economies and prosperity and the impatient demands of European countries outside the association to be included. At the same time, the political intents have never been far below the surface. Those who planned the progression of the EU recognized that economic integration would create increasing pressures for political unification as well, and this was the intention of the earliest planners of the regional economic integration that the EU represents. For Monnet and many others, a *real* underlying goal was political integration of the European continent into something like a United States of Europe (an American depiction, of course), with the fruits of economic integration providing the impetus and demand for that evolution.

This political goal was mixed with a more politically tinged economic goal. As noted already in Chapter 9, most of the planners in the aftermath of World War II agreed that economic policies had played a large role in the form of economic nationalism that caused the breakdown of commerce among European states and fueled animosities leading to conflict. The Bretton Woods institutions were clearly intended to respond to this perceived problem, but so was the movement toward European economic integration. A Europe that was politically united could not be economically divided, and vice versa.

Much of the history of the EU thus has been an attempt to maximize the economic benefits that provide the popular base for integration while deferring or trying to soften political consequences that were viewed as being equally necessary but that might rouse political opposition. Most of the potential political opposition was based in the dilution of national sovereignty that an expanding integration movement created. Common policies inevitably require common political institutions that transcend national boundaries and encroach upon purely national political prerogatives. That movement has always been controversial and thus it has been a matter not to be confronted directly by the organization. An approach that emphasized economic benefits while downplaying political costs was possible until the fateful step was taken to create a full economic union; since that step was taken in 1993, the *politics* of European regional economic integration have largely been about how to deal with the political implications of union. The final ratification of the Lisbon Treaty in 2009 (discussed later) represents an important step in that process.

The synergism between economic and political dynamics works in both directions. The momentum and support for greater integration has always been driven by the increasing benefits that integration has produced, and support for political integration has largely derived from and followed economic success. Economic setbacks, as have become so prominent since the economic downturn of 2008, have thus had the reverse effect of raising questions about political support for the EU in a number of member countries. This reversal has been particularly evident in the ongoing debt crisis.

Because of these overt and important political implications, the EU stands apart from other efforts leading toward the general goal of globalization or economic integration. In the current debate over globalization, none of the proposed or actual forms have gone beyond proposals for free trade areas, which can be and are negotiated by national governments that retain control under them. If countries involved in globalization (or other regional approaches) seek to expand beyond a status as free trade areas to some more advanced form of economic integration, the experience of the EU as both an economic and a political institution may prove instructive.

THE EUROPEAN UNION EXPERIENCE

By any measure, the EU is by far the most successful experiment in cross-national economic integration. It began modestly in 1951 as an association of six continental states, France, Germany, Italy, and the Benelux countries

(Belgium, the Netherlands, and Luxembourg), with a limited agenda and limited integration goals. From its very beginning, it was wildly successful and popular, consistently exceeding expectations in terms of the amount of growth and prosperity it created. The very success the process enjoyed in turn led to demands for expansion in two simultaneous directions: horizontally in terms of the accession of new members and vertically in terms of greater integration of the economies of the member states. These two directions have been reflected in the longest existing debate within and outside the organization, between so-called *wideners*, who believe the primary focus of regional integration should be to bring as much of Europe under the EU umbrella as possible (widening membership), and so-called *deepeners*, who believe that primary energy should be placed on maximum integration of the economic systems of the members (deepening relationships between existing members).

From its modest beginning, the EU has grown to a membership of 27 states that incorporates most of Western and Eastern Europe, except only most of the former republics of the old Soviet Union and a few, largely less economically developed states on the physical fringes of the continent. At that, most of the states in or contiguous to the EU have sought membership because of the perceived economic boost such membership would bring. The result of that growth has been to make the EU a major competitive force in the world's economy with a size, economic strength, and market rivaling that of the United States. According to the *CIA World Factbook* for 2013, for instance, the population of the EU today stands at 504 million (July 2012 estimate), compared to about 317 million for the United States. The gross domestic product (GDP) per capita of EU members is $34,500 (2013 estimate); the comparable figure for the United States is $49,800. The physical area of the EU is a little less than half that of the United States.

The EU is a unique phenomenon. It is the most far-reaching of all the attempts at international economic integration. Moravcsik summarizes its achievements as of 2010: "The EU has enjoyed an astonishingly successful run: It has completed the single market; established a single currency; created a zone without internal boundaries; launched common defense, foreign and internal security policies; promulgated a constitutional treaty; and most importantly, expanded from 12 to 27 members." The uniqueness of the EU goes back to its birth in the crucible of the immediate post–World War II world and the mandates for change the times created. The fact that the European continent was a more homogeneous cultural, historical, and developmental area than other parts of the world has undoubtedly contributed to a degree of success that would be much more difficult or impossible in more diverse, heterogeneous regions. If, however, the EU experience is ever to be translated on a parallel or larger scale, one must first assess its unique evolution.

Birth and Early Evolution

At the end of World War II, Europe, which had been the primary battlefield of the conflict, lay in tatters. It had been the center of world civilization for over 300 years, but the two great wars left the major European powers prostrate.

To the east, the Soviet Union stood as a giant military and ideological opponent that had also been devastated economically by the war but retained a huge armed force with which it occupied most of Eastern Europe and menaced the rest. To the west, an ideologically compatible but upstart United States stood as the only country physically strengthened by the war. In between was Europe.

The question was how to revive Europe, to make it strong enough to withstand Soviet military power, and prosperous enough to rebuff the ideological blandishments of communism. Militarily, the North Atlantic Treaty Organization (NATO) formed in 1949 to provide an American-led bulwark against Soviet military expansion, and in that same year, the first political association of Western European states—the Council of Europe—formed to link the countries culturally, socially, and economically.

The process leading to European economic integration began in 1950. At the suggestion of Monnet, French Foreign Minister Robert Schuman proposed the pooling of French and German coal and steel resources. This initiative, known as the Schuman Plan, formed the basis for negotiating the first European Union institution, the ECSC, in 1951. With the six core members (France, Germany, Italy, and the Benelux countries), the ECSC began operating in 1952, and it was so successful that it spawned interest in a wider form of association. The result was the negotiation of the Treaties of Rome in 1957, which created the European Atomic Energy Community (EURATOM) and, more important, the European Economic Community (EEC) among the six members of the ECSC. The EEC expanded the previous degree of economic cooperation among the ECSC by creating both a common or single market and a customs union. Thus, the integration process was begun toward both the free circulation of goods, services, people, and capital among the states of the EEC area and a common external tariff for the rest of the world.

The Rome Treaty was the platform from which the EU evolved. It has followed two basic tracks already raised. One has concerned membership. The primary emphasis of the wideners (and their most ardent outside supporters, notably the United States) has been to expand EU membership to more countries than it originally represented. Its current membership is 27 countries, and there is a waiting list of aspirants. The momentum toward expanded membership is now overshadowed by the debt crisis, and there is little prospect that new members will be admitted until that crisis is surmounted. The other form has been deeper integration of the membership, through movement to the economic union that was created by the Treaty of Maastricht in 1992 and more deeply implemented by the Lisbon Treaty. How much further the EU will progress toward a full political union has been a matter of considerable contention since the original days of the EEC and remains a source of major difference within the EU.

Ongoing Processes: Widening

Increasing EU reach into new member countries has been a major priority since the process began. The wideners believe that the EU (and the rest of the world) is best served by extending membership, drawing as many of the formerly contentious states and regions of Europe under the common banner of the EU as possible and thereby reducing as much as possible the prospect of renewed conflict in Europe. In addition, many wideners have seen widening as an *alternative* to creating deeper institutional bonds that restrict national sovereignty and, for some, sacrifice aspects of national identity. As Rachman puts it, "the wideners believed that the larger the EU was, the more diverse it would become, and the more difficult it would be to achieve the deepeners' goal of a united Europe."

The process of increasing the membership of the EU has occurred through a series of what the organization calls rounds. To date, there have been five identified rounds of membership accretion, taking the organization from its core of six members to its current complement of 27. This membership process is summarized in Table 10.1.

The table requires a little explanation. Rounds 1, 2, and 4 consisted of single actions on membership in a single year (1957, 1973, and 1995). The other two rounds consisted of actions in more than one year. Thus, the first accession of Round 3 was Greece in 1981, followed by the addition of Portugal and Spain five years later. Round 5 also has consisted of actions in two different years, with 10 states admitted in 2004 and two in 2007.

The pattern of membership growth reflects the debate about who should be members of the organization. Through the first two rounds, all the countries were essentially similar: market democracies of relatively long standing, Western in their political and security orientations, with vibrant, similar levels of economic development (Ireland at the time was a partial exception). Thus, there was little economic or political controversy or much need for adjustment when adding the three new members in 1973.

Round 3 introduced more explicitly the question of who should be allowed into the union. Greece had a long tradition of political democracy that had been interrupted by authoritarian interludes, and it was not as developed

TABLE 10.1

Membership Growth in the EU

Round 1 1957	Round 2 1973	Round 3 1981	Round 4 1995	Round 5 2004	Round 5 2007
Belgium	Denmark	Greece	Austria	Cyprus	Bulgaria
France	Ireland	1986	Finland	Czech Republic	Romania
Germany	United Kingdom	Spain	Sweden	Estonia	
Italy		Portugal		Hungary	
Luxembourg				Latvia	
Netherlands				Lithuania	
				Malta	
				Poland	
				Slovakia	
				Slovenia	
6	3	3	3	10	2

as the other members, meaning there would have to be a development effort by the existing members to bring the Greeks up to the economic standards of the rest. Portugal and Spain represented this same problem even more starkly, as both had just begun the process of movement toward full political democracy. As a result, their membership applications were delayed.

The introduction of new kinds of states and the end of the Cold War caused the EU to formalize what it believed to be the bases for new membership. In 1993, the union adopted the so-called Copenhagen criteria (so named because they were agreed to in the Danish capital). There were four criteria established that are interesting, because it is neither clear how strictly they have been applied since adoption nor how they will be applied in the future. The four criteria for a new member are as follows:

1. It must be a stable democracy.
2. It must demonstrate respect for human rights and the rule of law.
3. It must possess a functioning, market economy.
4. It must be willing to accept all membership obligations.

The first accession under these rules occurred in 1995 and was relatively straightforward. The three new members (Austria, Finland, and Sweden) had all been, by virtue of history and geography, Cold War neutrals which, had they joined earlier, might have caused Cold War consternation because of their proximity to the Soviet Union.

The fifth round is in some ways the most interesting and most indicative of the problems the EU will face in the future. A total of 12 states have been added over two accessions in 2004 and 2007. Most are formerly communist states that were either members of the old Warsaw Pact (the Czech Republic, Hungary, Poland, and Slovakia in the first accession, Bulgaria and Romania in the second), former Soviet republics (Estonia, Latvia, and Lithuania) or parts of Yugoslavia (Slovenia), or Mediterranean island countries (Cyprus and Malta). None unambiguously meet the criterion of long-standing political democracies, and most have economies far less vibrant than those of the older, more traditional members. In most cases, their accession is difficult to justify in purely economic terms, suggesting that more political, even geopolitical, considerations have become more prominent in the membership process.

Not all states of Europe are members. Two states, Norway and Switzerland, have declined the invitation to join. Switzerland's reasons include its long tradition of neutrality (the Swiss have not been combatants in a foreign war since 1515) and the possibility that membership in the organization would subject the Swiss banking system to international regulation, thus undermining its unique and sometimes controversial place in the world. Norway voted down membership in 1994 because of the fear that its national identity would be compromised (Norway is a relatively young European state, having broken away from the Kingdom of Sweden in 1905), and many Norwegians were unwilling to forfeit their hard-won national independence. Three other countries have candidate status for membership: Croatia, Macedonia, and Turkey. In the past, all states that have been candidates have become full members;

the application of Turkey has, however, been controversial for some time. In addition, a number of former republics of the Soviet Union (notably Ukraine) and western Balkans states (former parts of Yugoslavia—Serbia, Bosnia and Herzegovina, and Montenegro, for instance) are still in the queue for membership consideration.

The worldwide economic crisis that engulfed the global economy in 2008 did not spare the countries of the EU, and one impact has been to raise questions about the continuing pace of membership expansion. As Cohen explains, because of the economic downturn, "EU elites and publics have been forced to revisit whether they can afford the costs of both EU enlargement and a more centralized and activist union." Some even wonder about the continuing viability of the EU as an institution. The possibility of membership in EU remains, in Moravcsik's words, "the most powerful policy instrument Europe possesses" in its dealings with the world, and despite the debt crisis, it is highly unlikely it will abandon it.

Ongoing Processes: The Sovereign Debt Crisis and EU Deepening

Although hardly anyone within the EU area opposes the economic impacts of the economic union, the political implications of increasing levels of integration do raise opposition. The problem is straightforward: the more deeply the economies of the members of the union become intertwined, the greater the need for common political decision-making bodies to make political decisions on economic issues. Policies regarding common monetary policy may be economic in content, but they are political decisions derived through political processes. For a common policy to be arrived at and enforced in the most efficient and effective possible way, the political body that makes that decision must be coequal in authority to the physical area for which it is making policy. A union-wide set of policies thus requires a union-wide political set of institutions with union-wide authority. Because policies made by such a body would override, even replace, the same kinds of decisions made by national political bodies, the result is a loss of national political power. That means, in turn, the loss of sovereign political control by the member states to the union. For those whose primary allegiance is to the state, the trade-off of political power for economic advantage becomes an increasingly more questionable proposition.

This is not a new problem for the European integration movement. The British, for instance, opted out of participation in the process until 1973, when economic considerations seemed to overcome political objections. But these concerns have made the British supporters of widening rather than deepening since 1973 because widening slowed deepening (the Tony Blair Labor government was a partial exception). Even France, one of economic integration's firmest supporters, bridles when movement seems to be providing a perceived threat to French sovereignty and thus French nationalism.

The sovereign debt crisis in several EU member states is the latest source of strain. The EU institutions have not yet evolved to the point that a number of economically consequential and politically sensitive decisions have come under its auspices because they remain under national control. Among those abilities is budgetary control that includes the capacity to incur national indebtedness, or sovereign debt.

What is sovereign debt? The term is more imposing than its meaning, probably because the adjective "sovereign" is attached to it. As the *Financial Times* points out, however, sovereign debt is "debt that is issued by a national government." All governments incur some level of sovereign debt to some extent, borrowing money whenever their current assets do not adequately cover obligations that must be met. Borrowing is a universal phenomenon, and as the *Financial Times* further states, "It is theoretically considered to be risk-free, as the government can employ different measures to guarantee repayment, e.g., raise taxes or print money."

Sovereign debt is ubiquitous in the international economic system, but it has been elevated to the level of a "crisis" within the EU and elsewhere in recent years. The stimulus for concern has been the *amount* of debt that some states have incurred and the negative impact increasing levels of debt have on the economies that are running them up. Although the adjective "sovereign" is rarely appended to describe it, the ongoing debt debate in the United States is illustrative of both the issues and especially controversies and disagreements that surround the debt issue.

In the American microcosm of the global debate that has wracked the EU, the issue has had at least two facets that are also reflected in the EU debate. One is the amount of debt that annual deficits are accumulating. Among the most dramatic and publicized indicators of the debt accumulation is debt as a percentage of the size of the national economy expressed as a percentage of gross domestic product (GDP). Generally speaking, the lower the ratio between debt and GDP (the lower the percentage of debt compared to GDP), the healthier the economy is thought to be. Within the United States, concern became great when the ratio achieved unity (debt equaled GDP), which occurred in early 2013. To critics, this unity represented a kind of tipping point indicating that the debt problem had reached critical proportions. Other economists argued this symbolic event lacked such great significance, and the *Economist,* in an assessment in January 2013, argued that "economists do not know how much debt is too much."

The second concern is with the ability of government to honor the debts they have. Can the issuing government cover the obligations it incurs with lenders in terms of repayment, and what can be done to improve that situation? This dimension is both physical and psychological. The physical inability to process debt can lead eventually to government default on its debts, with consequences that investors who have bought debt can lose their investments. Questions about the ability or willingness of governments to repay have the psychological effect of making potential purchasers of future debt reluctant to invest further. To deal with these kinds of perceptions, states have to make the terms of the bonds and the like they issue more appealing, for example, through higher interest rates. These incentives may make the problem of debt service (paying for debt incurred) even greater.

The most pernicious effects of both aspects of the debt problem create the sovereign debt crisis in the EU. Countries that are members of the "euro zone" (the countries that use the euro as their currency) are required to maintain a debt-to-GDP ratio of 60 percent (debt is no more than three-fifths of GDP). Many states have long since exceeded that ratio, and many members of the euro zone and elsewhere have passed unity (debt exceeds GDP), so that standard itself is not a major concern.

What does raise concern is when the ratio greatly exceeds unity. Although, as the *Economist* points out, "Many countries may be able to afford to have significantly higher ratios of government debt to national income," there is also general agreement that the ratio can become too high. There is no consensual agreed point where the ratio is intolerable: fiscal conservatives begin to worry before the ratio reaches unity, whereas more liberal economists are comfortable with higher ratios. There is agreement that a "too high" or "too much" point exists, but not where it is.

The basis of concern is familiar to anyone who has followed the American variant of the debate. At some point, a growing debt raises concern about the ability of a government to repay it. Debt ratios tend to be highest in countries with relatively weak economies. This characterization is not universally true: Japan, for instance, has a very high debt ratio. Nevertheless, a combination of a weak economy and growing debt raises questions about the ability of states to use traditional tools such as taxing or printing more money to service current debt, and thus raises potential lender concern about buying additional debt from the offending country. At some point, confidence in the solvency of a country may collapse to the point where no one will lend the country more at a time when government spending still exceeds revenue and it is too politically difficult to impose fiscal austerity. At this point, a crisis emerges in which insolvency and even discussions of national bankruptcy emerge. All these elements have been raised in discussions about the current U.S. situation.

This is the frightening point at which the euro zone has found itself, notably in Greece and Cyprus and potentially in places like Spain and Italy. The only recourse at this point is an artificial injection of capital from other countries into the ailing economy—a bailout in popular, if pejorative, terms. That prospect is particularly irksome to some countries—which are generally prosperous and have maintained debt ratios below unity—that must provide the funds to underwrite the bailouts of those whose fiscal policies have caused the crisis. Within the contemporary EU, most of the countries in crisis are Mediterranean states, while the potential saviors are from northern Europe.

Germany is the linchpin, and its patience and willingness to continue propping up weak euro zone economies is being tested by the ongoing sovereign debt crisis. As Foroohar puts it, the Germans "feel they have done everything right—worked hard, liberalized their economy, kept debt and unemployment low—why should they support spendthrift southern European nations?" Beyond that arguably self-righteous vantage point is the more basic question of what they can do to keep the problem from recurring. The current answer is not very much, which brings the discussion back to the issue of EU deepening.

The reason there are large economic problems in some EU countries but not in others is that the monetary union has not progressed to the point of being able to legislate and enforce common fiscal policies (such as levels of government spending) across the membership. The basic reason such authority has not been transferred to the EU reflects the ambivalence the members have always had toward deepening toward a full political union. Creating a full union swamps national sovereign decision-making power over policies regulating the lives of citizens, and ultimately threatens national identity. Those who seek such authority to eliminate what they view as profligate spending do not necessarily have such insidious underlying motives or intents, but their proposed intrusions raise suspicions that they do, or that diluting national sovereignty will be an outgrowth of such policy changes. Indeed, when the Germans and others impose stringent, politically stressful fiscal authority requirements on bailouts, the worst of those suspicions about deepening are aroused. The result is further resistance to deepening.

Seen in this light, the sovereign debt crisis is the latest substantive example of the dilemmas of deepening. The debt crisis and its solution are part of the same cloth. As the *Washington Post* explained it in a March 2013 editorial, the current EU "is a currency union absent the usual political, legal, and regulatory infrastructure. Until that inherently confusing and unstable situation changes, Europe's policy-makers will continue to make it up as they go." Ad hoc solutions are almost certainly not the best answer to the debt crisis, but creating a comprehensive, union-wide authority that could solve them in an orderly way requires resolving the deepening disagreement, a solution that remains elusive. Yet, until Europe can decide it wants to be a full union, there will almost certainly continue to be crises like sovereign debt that periodically threaten the whole union.

CONCLUSION

The sovereign debt crisis also brings together the problems of widening and deepening. The crisis has placed the membership expansion question on hold, as countries of the EU have turned to the sovereign debt question and its deepening implications. Until the debt crisis is at least temporarily solved, the idea of new membership, which faces its own unique problems (including the inclusion of additional fiscally suspicious members) remains in limbo.

The problem has considerable resonance because the two strands are strongly interrelated. The sovereign debt issue is a new membership concern because almost all the candidates for admission have less robust economies than those of the core members like Germany. These candidates can thus be viewed as potential additional crises waiting to happen, and if they are EU members, there seems little the EU can do but to bail them out if it is to avoid a major structural crisis that might threaten the viability of the entire enterprise. This prospect is sufficiently frightening that it creates a paralyzing inhibition on admitting new members.

There is a solution to this problem that extends the discussion to further structural integration, or deepening. That solution is to take the next—some would argue ultimate—step of creating EU-wide monetary and fiscal institutions that could override national monetary and fiscal policies, in other words to create a full monetary union. Had such institutions been in place a decade ago, they might have imposed restrictions on decisions in places like Greece, Italy, and Cyprus that would have nipped what became the sovereign debt crisis in the bud. They might also have undermined and even destroyed Greek, Italian, and Cypriot national sovereignty.

The EU is by far the most comprehensive, successful experiment in economic integration in the contemporary world. It has been a far more ambitious effort than any other attempt to transcend national boundaries economically, and it has moved much further along than other proposals and actions, none of which has moved past the initial stage of forming free trading areas. The EU has marched through free trade status to customs union, to single market, and now to full economic union with strong political implications. It has done this on a regional basis among countries that share a common civilization and were in common economic straits after World War II. Its uniqueness reflects partly the circumstances in which it was born and in which it has subsequently strived. Whether the lessons of the EU have value for future similar endeavors aimed at economic integration must be measured by comparing the experiential universe in which the EU was born and has flourished with the parallel circumstances of other places and times.

What kind of future does the EU have? It can develop in two directions—economically or politically—but will it do both, or either? The economic dimension involves the completion of the economic union process, which means the inclusion of all members within the currency union and the inclusion of all new members into all aspects of the union. Because a number of the members admitted under Round 5 (to say nothing of candidate members and other aspirants) have economies that are substantially less developed than those of the pre-expansion core of Western European states, pulling off the latter requirement will be no small feat. If completing this dimension is the most important business the EU sees for itself, the argument of the deepeners would seem to be made stronger.

A political perspective leads to different problems. Essentially, there are two political questions. The first is the political evolution of the EU itself: will the EU move toward becoming a full political union? Progress has floundered on this question, and reaction to the Reform Treaty suggests this concern has not disappeared. In the past, countries that very much favored and enjoyed the benefits of further integration became very skittish when the political consequences of moving forward had potentially erosive effects on national identity and prerogatives.

The resolution of these dilemmas will certainly influence the ultimate potential impact of integration on the global system. The EU is at its ultimate crossroads where it must decide if it will become a full political and economic union or remain a somewhat looser institution wherein its members retain sovereign control over their countries. It is a question that Europeans have been asking themselves and one another since the process began in 1958, and they have not reached an EU-wide consensus. The answer to this point, in American political parlance, has been to "kick the can down the road," fashioning Band-Aid solutions to periodic crises while avoiding the larger and more profound underlying questions. The sovereign debt crisis is the latest manifestation, with cosmetic solutions like underwriting the bailouts of the Greek and Cypriot economies.

Eventually, of course, Europeans will have to decide on the basic question of integration. They can maintain the status quo that retains sovereign state control of important monetary and fiscal functions but that virtually guarantees that crises like the current imbroglio over sovereign debt continues. They can create a true monetary union that effectively becomes a political union, in the process undermining national sovereignty and threatening national identity. To this point, the members have been unwilling to forfeit or threaten their national identities, as nationalism remains a stronger force than economic efficiency. As long as that is true, one can expect crises like that associated with sovereign debt to continue.

SUGGESTED ACTIVITIES AND QUESTIONS

1. On what bases do economic integration schemes differ? Discuss the differences. Where does the EU fit in these schemes?
2. What are the forms of economic integration? How does each stage build on the others? How does the balance between economic and political aspects change in various steps in the process? Describe the evolution of the EU in these terms.
3. How have the birth and evolution of the EU been influenced by both economic and political motives? Elaborate.
4. Discuss the process by which the EU came into existence and the steps in its development, including the steps and dynamics of its membership growth.
5. What are "widening" and "deepening?" Apply this distinction to the evolution of the EU.
6. What is sovereign debt? What is its nature, and when does it become a "problem"? Why is the European situation described as a debt "crisis"?
7. How is the sovereign debt crisis related to the widening and deepening process within the EU? Explain.
8. How does the current crisis in the EU symbolize the deeper and more fundamental kinds of ambivalence many Europeans feel about the entire integration process? How are resolution of the sovereign debt crisis and those choices related to one another?

SUGGESTED READINGS AND RESOURCES

Alesino, Alberto and Francesca Giavazzi. *The Future of Europe: Reform or Decline.* Cambridge, MA: MIT Press, 2006.

Algieri, Franco. "A Weakened EU's Prospects of Global Leadership." *Washington Quarterly* 30, 3 (Winter 2006–2007), 106–115.

Bache, Ian and Stephen George. *Politics in the European Union*, 2nd ed. Oxford, UK: Oxford University Press, 2006.

Cohen, Lenard J. "Detours on the Balkan Road to EU Integration." *Current History* 108, 716 (March 2009), 124–130.

Dinen, Desmond. *An Ever Closer Union: An Introduction to European Integration*, 3rd ed. Boulder, CO: Lynne Rienner Publishers, 2006.

Finan, William W. Jr. "Wrestling with Euro-Islam." *Current History* 106, 698 (March 2007), 140–142.

Foroohar, Rana. "Continental Commitment Issues." *Time*, April 1, 2013, p. 16.

Gordon, Philip and Omer Taspinar. "Turkey on the Brink." *Washington Quarterly* 29, 3 (Summer 2005), 57–70.

"Government Debt: How Much Is Too Much?" *Economist* (online), January 2, 2013.

Gros, Daniel. "The Dogs That Didn't Bark: The EU and the Financial Crisis." *Current History* 108, 716 (March 2009), 105–109.

Hay, Colin and Hakan Karlsson. *Changing Atlantic Security Relations: Do the U.S., EU, and Russia Form a Strategic Triangle?* New York: Routledge, 2006.

"In Cyprus, Making a European Solution on the Fly." *Washington Post* (online), March 26, 2013.

James, Jackson and Stephen Szabo. "Angela Merkel's Germany." *Current History* 106, 698 (March 2007), 106–111.

Kauppi, Niilo. *Democracy, Social Resources, and Political Power in the European Union*. Manchester, UK: Manchester University Press, 2005.

McCormick, John. *Understanding the European Union: A Concise Introduction*. New York: Palgrave Macmillan, 2002.

Miguet, Arnauld. "France's Election-Year Disquiet." *Current History* 106, 698 (March 2007), 112–116.

Moravcsik, Andrew. "Europe, the Second Superpower." *Current History* 109, 725 (March 2010), 91–98.

O'Brien, James C. "Brussels: Next Capital of the Balkans?" *Washington Quarterly* 29, 3 (Summer 2006), 71–88.

"Q&A: The Lisbon Treaty." *BBC News* (online), February 5, 2010.

Rachman, Gideon. "The Death of Enlargement." *Washington Quarterly* 29, 3 (Summer 2006), 51–65.

Shepherd, Robin. "Romania, Bulgaria, and the EU's Future." *Current History* 106, 698 (March 2007), 117–122.

"Sovereign Debt." *The Financial Times Lexicon* (online), February 2, 2013.

Taspinar, Omer. "Turkey's Fading Dream of Europe." *Current History* 106, 698 (March 2007), 123–129.

Watts, Duncan. *The European Union*. Edinburgh: Edinburgh University Press, 2008.

Wood, David M. and Birol A. Yesilada. *The Emerging European Union*. New York: Longman, 2004.

Wood, Steve and Wolfgang Quaisser. *The New European Union: Confronting the Challenges of Integration*. Boulder, CO: Lynne Rienner Publishers, 2007.

WEB SITE

The official EU Web site: http://ec.europa.eu

Rising Economic Powers: China, India, and Brazil

PRÉCIS

One of the ways in which the international system has changed historically is through the emergence of new major powers, called "rising powers." China, India, and Brazil, the most prominent members of the so-called BRIC countries, are poised and apparently ready to assume that role in the contemporary world. China was a consequential country during the Cold War, but its significance increased after the 1970s with its adoption of different economic policies that have raised its status among world powers. India's entrance as a rising power is more recent, dating essentially to the 1990s, as is Brazil's. World politics is never static, and one major source of its dynamism is the relative prominence that different states have in the world order. The idea of new states arising to challenge the existing power order is not new, but in the contemporary world, it has been based more on economic factors than in the past. It is the impact of these rising powers that forms the concern of this chapter.

One of the constants of international relations is change in the relative nature of the members vis-à-vis other members. In particular, the ability of some states to influence others—in other words, to exercise power—is a variable in interstate relations. In the state system, some states become more powerful while others experience a relative decline in power. Those on the ascendancy are sometimes known as "rising powers."

There is certainly nothing that is new about the rising state phenomenon. If one looks back a century to the eve of World War I, the major powers were the countries of the old European Balance of Power (Britain, France, Germany/Prussia, Russia, and the Austro-Hungarian Empire), and the major rising power was the United States. Prodded by World War II, the traditional powers declined, and from the rubble, the United States and the Soviet Union rose to primary status, a position both occupied until the Soviet Union imploded in 1991. During most of this period, military power was the major criterion by which power was measured.

With the demise of the Soviet Union, the United States was for a time the unchallenged world superpower, and the bases of its dominance were both military and economic. No other state has arisen to challenge American military strength, and the absence of deep politico-military division in the system has reduced the relevance of military strength as the major instrument of power. There are few conceivable situations where massive systemic war—the major American forte—seems likely. Economic competition has become the playing field on which power competition occurs.

The United States entered this redefined basis of power competition with a sizable advantage. Immediately after World War II, the United States sat astride an international economic system in ruin from the war. The American economy accounted for close to 40 percent of world activity (measured as gross domestic product, or GDP), but that proportion fell as other areas (notably the European Union and Japan) recovered. Still, the United States remains the world's economic giant. Rising powers thus ascend in comparison to the American economic system. Before assessing that change, however, it is necessary to look at the general phenomenon of "rising powers."

RISING POWERS

One of the most certain things one can say about the dominant powers of any period of international history is that eventually their dominance will be eclipsed by the emergence of some different country or countries. The contemporary situation is no exception. Although the United States has been *a* dominant power since World War II and *the* dominant power since the end of the Cold War, this observation is undoubtedly true for the United States as well.

What does it mean to be a "rising power"? In the most general sense, a rising power refers to a country that, by virtue of increased military, economic, or other power, is or has the potential to play a more prominent role in the international system than it has heretofore played. As noted, the United States was such a rising power in the late nineteenth and early twentieth centuries, as was the Soviet Union during the middle of the twentieth century. Countries like China, India, and Brazil are candidates for this status today.

The impact of rising powers is important. At the level of the international system, rising powers change the relative power balance between the major powers, with ripple effects throughout the system, often in ways that are controversial and difficult to predict. Will, for instance, a rising China eventually challenge American international predominance and lead to a transformation from an essentially unipolar to a bipolar or multipolar balance? Would such a transformation be stabilizing or destabilizing? What is the impact of the Indian challenge in areas like technological and scientific leadership on American world leadership? Will an increasingly dominant Brazil challenge

American preeminence in the Western Hemisphere? If so, how and to what degree will this challenge occur?

The degree and extent to which rising powers challenge the given order depends to a great degree on the areas in which the rising power seeks to influence the existing order and establish its own place. Traditionally, for instance, world power comparisons have largely been at least implicitly military in content. "Power" and "military power" were used more or less synonymously, and the most certain way for a rising power to assert a challenge to the existing order was by building and flexing its military muscle.

It is clear that power status is not so unidimensional in a globalized world. Economic capability has increasingly become a benchmark of global importance, and it is the primary claim China, India, Brazil, and some other countries have about rising power status. China, of course, is also a military power whose military might requires some concern, India's military prowess is almost exclusively devoted to ensuring its place on the Asian subcontinent, and, militarily, Brazil is clearly a regional power. As powers with global aspirations, however, the primary claim of all three states is largely concentrated in the economic realm.

The impact of rising states creates foreign policy questions for countries affected by the rising power. The basic question is whether the impact will help or hinder the realization of interests of the affected power. Will the rising power be a looming threat to those interests or a global partner assisting in their accomplishment? Or will it be both? Like the systemic impacts, these changes are never entirely clear in advance, leading to speculation and disagreement. Europe worried about the impact of an industrially gigantic United States, and the United States worried about the impact of a militarily powerful Soviet Union. The United States ended up a strategic partner of Europe, and the Soviets emerged primarily as a threat. Where do the current aspirants fit?

Another characteristic of periods where powers rise in their importance within the system is that who will rise and how are somewhat unpredictable and thus the subject of some disagreement before they have arisen. In the nineteenth century, as it struggled to occupy a continent and self-flagellated through a bloody, destructive civil war, it was undoubtedly questionable that the United States would rise to be the dominant power of the twentieth century. Projections are much more accurate in hindsight than before the fact, a useful rejoinder to viewing the current rising power phenomenon.

The contemporary period is no exception, for a least two reasons. One is that judgments about rising states are based mostly upon economic projections, and these are inherently difficult and uncertain. As Sharma illustrates regarding current trends, "forecasts typically took the developing world's high growth rates from the middle of the last decade and extended them straight into the future. . . . Later returns are throwing cold water on the extravagant projections." Despite what some economists would assert, economic prediction is much more art and much less science that its enthusiasts are prone to admit.

The second source of uncertainty is that the current crop of rising powers is drawn from the vast, heterogeneous developing world. There are multiple states in the developing world that can and do make a case for their emergence as more important powers. Many of these states are either of recent vintage, the results of European colonies breaking up (see Chapter 12), or are states that have no recent history in the global spotlight. As a result, how they will handle increased affluence internally and how they will project expanded status on the world stage are uncertain.

Much recent speculation has centered on the so-called BRIC countries (Brazil, Russia, India, and China). The acronym was the invention of Goldman Sachs analyst James "Jim" O'Neill in a 2001 paper in which he sought to describe countries poised to or making an increased impact on the global economy. The acronym caught on as a way to describe rising states in the international economic order. The BRIC countries have adopted the idea and now meet as a group to discuss economic policies.

The BRIC concept has evolved in the years since it was coined. New states have been added. In 2010, with Chinese sponsorship, South Africa was added to the list, so that the acronym has formally expanded to BRICS. Because it is the world's fourth largest country in population and has a growing economy, Indonesia is sometimes added to potential membership in the group (expanding the acronym to BRICSI), as is Mexico (creating the more awkward acronym BRIMCSI). The point is the fluidity of the list, as well as the abundance of candidates for rising state status.

For present purposes, three rising states from the BRIC list, China, India, and Brazil, have been chosen as examples of rising states. The entire notion of the BRICs has been the subject of some criticism on the basis that, as Sharma points out, "other than being the largest markets in their respective regions, the big four emerging markets have never had much in common." Russia is a traditional European power that has been a major power, arguably falling from that perch in the 1990s and now attempting to reassert its past status. It is more of a reemerging than a rising state and thus unlike the others in that way, thereby justifying its exclusion from the percent discussion.

CHINA, INDIA, AND BRAZIL AS RISING POWERS

Although the Sharma quote about the dissimilarities between the three selected states has truth, there are also some interesting commonalities. The most obvious is sheer size: by most measures, the three countries join the United States (and for some purposes, Russia) as the world's largest countries. In sheer population terms, of course, China and India dwarf everyone else, but size is nevertheless a commonality.

Table 11.1 captures some of the relevant comparison between the three selected countries and the United States, data on which is provided for comparative purposes. Figures in parentheses are rankings compared to other countries.

TABLE 11.1

Comparisons of the United States, China, India, and Brazil on Selected Indices

	U.S.	China	India	Brazil
Physical				
Population	316 mil (3)	1.349 bil (1)	1.220 bil (2)	201 mil (5)
Area (sq. mi)	3,794 (3)	3,705 (4)	1,269 (7)	3,257 (5)
Economy				
GDP (trillion $)	15.66 (1)	12.38 (3)	4.78 (4)	2.4 (8)
GDP/Capita	49,800 (15)	9,100 (122)	3,900 (166)	12,200 (100)
GDP Growth	2.2 % (134)	7.8% (18)	6.5% (34)	1.5% (a5a)
Military				
Spending (bil $)	697 (1)	76 (2)	30.9 (9)	33.4 (8)
Active Duty				
Troops (thousands)	1,569 (2)	2.285 (1)	1,325 (3)	318 (18)

Source: *CIA World Factbook 2013* for economic and physical data; *World Almanac and Book of Facts 2013* for military figures.

What is immediately striking about the four countries is that they are among the world's largest by virtually any measure. The United States has the world's largest economy, spends more on defense than any of the others, has the second largest armed forces, and has the world's third largest population and land area. China possesses the world's largest population (a distinction it will soon cede to India) and size of armed forces, the world's third largest economy (the *CIA Factbook* classifies the EU as a country for ranking purposes), and the world's fourth largest landmass. India is a step behind as the world's second largest population, ninth largest in defense expenditures (but their largest forces), fourth largest economy, and seventh largest landmass.

Brazil is a bit behind, which is why it is a recent addition to the list. Its population and landmass are the world's fifth largest, and its economy ranks eighth globally, as does its level of military spending. It has a much smaller active duty military, ranking 18th worldwide, although its reserve forces are the world's fifth largest.

There are apparent anomalies in the economic comparative rankings. The United States, for instance, is only 15th in per capita GDP, which reflects the fact that a number of smaller states with modest GDPs but even smaller populations prosper by dividing population into GDP; Lichtenstein leads the list at number one. Likewise, China's growth rate is at 18th, the highest in the group. The sheer size of the leaders' economies, however, ensures that a smaller percentage increase can mean larger absolute growth.

Each of the three rising powers has arrived at its status by different routes, and each has a different set of prospects, including barriers to continued growth. As a result, the discussion moves to a country-by-country overview.

China

China's emergence on the world stage has been the most spectacular of any of the BRICs. The world's oldest continuous civilization began to reemerge as a world power after the country was taken over by the Communist Party in 1949, but its meteoric ascent to a world economic—and potentially military—giant began in the late 1970s. Since then, China has become the greatest threat to American economic primacy, and virtually all economic predictions suggest that China will pass the United States on important measures in the near future. At the same time, China has some economic and other problems that may cloud the rosiest projections.

China has reached the global forefront against the backdrop of a turbulent past. China endured a "century of humiliation" during the nineteenth and early twentieth centuries that reduced it to a semicolony. The situation resulted from the loss of creativity; corruption and resistance to reform within the imperial court; the obsolescence of its emperor-based political system that relied on a corps of bureaucrats chosen for their mastery of Confucian classics rather than their command of modern ideas; and the numerous unequal treaties imposed on it by foreign powers since its defeat in the Opium War with Great Britain in the 1840s. Westerners roamed throughout China. Merchants, adventurers, diplomats, and missionaries all enjoyed special privileges placing them beyond Chinese authority, a situation that was humiliating to all Chinese.

Layered atop all of China's other discontents was a split between two centers of political and military power, each of which was determined to unify, govern, and strengthen China. The Guomindang—or Nationalist—forces led by Chiang Kai-shek were generally supported by the United States. Beginning in the 1920s, an initially small upstart group of communists led by Mao Zedong articulated its own vision of mobilizing mass support to overthrow China's antiquated social order and restoring unity to the country.

As the two forces began their titanic struggle in earnest, China endured yet another devastating blow, this time from Japan's exceptionally brutal aggression, first in its invasion of Manchuria in 1931 and then throughout its bloody drive through China proper from 1937 to 1945. The defeat of Japanese forces by the United States in 1945 renewed the violent conclusive phase of the internal battle to control China between Chiang Kai-shek's Nationalist forces and Mao Zedong's communist followers.

By the autumn of 1949, China's communists emerged victorious and drove Chiang's forces to the island refuge of Taiwan. China was at long last unified under a strong central authority, and foreign intervention in its internal affairs would no longer be tolerated. Beyond unification and the reclamation of China's sovereignty, it was Mao's abiding passion to create within China a radical, egalitarian society. In so doing, China remained largely outside the international community, and terribly repressive within, with its people mired in poverty throughout his rule from 1949 to 1976, when Mao died.

Mao's death created a scramble for power among China's ruling elites. Within a year, Deng Xiaoping had effectively consolidated governing authority within his own hands. Purged three times during Mao's reign and standing less than 5 feet tall, Deng appeared at first glance a physically unlikely ruler of the world's most populous state. Deng soon implemented his famous "Four Modernizations" campaign, a bold series of reforms designed to advance China beyond the revolutionary dogma of Maoism and to create instead a stronger, more modern country by loosening the reins of state authority; more fully embracing economic globalization in search of foreign markets, technology, and investment; and accepting income differentials in a society that had so recently been singularly animated by radical egalitarianism.

The Four Modernizations—agriculture, science and technology, industry, and military—began in the countryside, home to three-fourths of all Chinese. Gradually, socialist-style communal farming was phased out, and explicitly, peasants were now allowed to lease land individually from the state. Without quite admitting it, Deng's regime injected market—that is, *capitalist*— incentives by allowing peasants whose production surpassed their obligatory quotas to the state at fixed prices to sell any surplus that they could produce for as much money as they could get for it.

The older norm of imposed egalitarianism was quietly shelved in the process. What the regime today calls "Socialism with Chinese Characteristics" took its place. With the passage of time this slogan has simply become a euphemism for capitalism with state supervision, but with less direct central control. Gradually, the limited market system begun in the countryside spread to the cities. Individuals were allowed to open restaurants, shops, and factories. Workers could be hired and fired, something that had been utterly unthinkable under Mao's "people's" regime. The wheels of a more market-driven economy were thus set into motion.

The second and third modernizations—industry plus science and technology—inherently required China's leaders to turn outward to the most advanced industrial countries for investment capital, markets for Chinese goods, scientific know-how, and the most modern production technology and management skills. Four Special Economic Zones (SEZs) were established in southeastern China in which foreign corporations were allowed to form joint ventures with Chinese partners and thus transfer their leading-edge technological, manufacturing process, and managerial expertise to initially quite limited enclaves of capitalist experimentation.

Economic Growth, but Questions. China's economic results have been the most dramatic. Riding a boom powered by foreign capital inflows and an aggressive export strategy, China's economy grew at an average annual rate of around 10 percent from the 1980s into the 2000s. Not all Chinese specialists accept these astounding government-promulgated growth statistics at face value, but, there is no denying that China's economy has grown dramatically during the past quarter century. In critical consumer sectors such as clothing, shoes, toys, and other low-technology products, China dominates world markets. As dramatic evidence of this rise, China became the world's leading producer of manufactured goods in 2008 with 17 percent of world production compared to 16 percent for the United States.

China's dramatic economic ascent is conditioned by a litany of domestic woes that, taken together, raise the alarming possibility of widespread unrest. Its internal preoccupations include a mounting political crisis of regime legitimacy in what Minxin Pei describes as the "Chinese neo-Leninist state," severe environmental degradation, immense population pressures, official corruption, a growing gap in urban versus rural incomes, high unemployment, a steady loss of arable land, a diminished social safety net for the poor and displaced, scarcity of resources like water and petroleum, and secessionist movements in Tibet and in the westernmost province of Zinjiang. Gilboy and Read concur, stating "Beijing faces serious challenges in maintaining sustainable growth and social stability, eliminating corruption, and improving government effectiveness in a one-party system."

China's rise as an economic power is thus paradoxical. China has made great strides as an industrial power, but it has done so within the confines of a political and social system that places serious constraints on the ability of China to expand, especially into a world power, if that is its desire. Thus, individually and collectively, what do these trends and problems mean, and how do they affect an assessment of China as a rising power?

Assessing China's Economic Rise. Does China's economic and technological rise pose a threat to the world power balance? The sheer potential size of an economy energized by one-fifth of humankind raises concern: If China were to become competitive structurally with the world's most advanced economies, would that size not pose a danger of simply overwhelming the global economy and establishing itself as the "800-pound gorilla" that everyone else would have to treat with care and deference?

Opinions vary on this subject, based on differing assessments of the nature of the Chinese economy and the impact on the Chinese political system. Analysts critical of the notion China poses a threat often point to factors in Chinese development that limit the threats China could pose. In a recent *Foreign Affairs* article, for instance, David and Lyric Hughes Hale identify three of what they call the "dragon's ailments." The first is demographic and points to the extremely uneven character of Chinese development. There are, they point out, "great disparities between the integrated, largely urban coastal areas in the eastern part of the country and the fragmented, rural economies in the western part." In addition, there is a substantial unemployment problem, especially in western China, that results in considerable migration to the industrialized areas. China also faces the need "to find a way to support its rapidly aging population," a dilemma shared by many industrialized countries. The Chinese population is also aging, meaning a reduced workforce (particularly of young workers willing to toil for very low wages) and a greater burden caring for older citizens.

That is not all. Much of the prosperity associated with the SEZs is the result of foreign collaboration and investment that limit future independence for the Chinese economy, and thus potentially threaten further development. In the July/August 2004 issue of *Foreign Affairs*, Gilboy accentuates how this attenuates the threat posed by Chinese growth. "First, China's high-tech and industrial exports are dominated by foreign, not Chinese, firms. Second, Chinese industrial firms are deeply dependent on designs, critical components, and manufacturing equipment they import from the United States. . . . Third, Chinese firms are taking few effective steps to absorb the technology they are importing." Huang and Khanna, writing in *Foreign Policy*, agree, pointing out that "[f]ew of these products are made by indigenous Chinese companies. In fact, you would be hard-pressed to find a single homegrown Chinese firm that operates on a global scale and markets its own products abroad. The Chinese economy has taken off, but few local firms have followed." In fact, most of the collaboration is between foreigners and the notoriously inefficient state-owned enterprises (SOEs). Minxin Pei adds that the private sector is no more than 30 percent of the overall Chinese economy.

The energy crisis raised in Chapter 2 is also part of the mix. A growing economy has an increasingly voracious appetite for energy, and most of the energy generated by China comes from the burning of highly polluting coal, and this in turn makes the air pollution problem in the country severe and growing worse. China is also a growing importer of traditionally extracted petroleum, adding a further cost and burden on the economy. The exploitation of China's vast shale gas and oil reserves is a potential answer to both of these problems, but it is a solution that is somewhere in the future.

The result is a mixed message about the Chinese economic challenge. China's economy has clearly expanded to the point of rivaling the economies of the world's major powers in sheer size, and this impact is growing. There are, however, limits to China's current growth. Most of that growth has resulted from manufacturing consumer goods that require little scientific contribution from China, and much of it is based on artificially controlled low labor costs used to achieve comparative advantage. The result has been large surpluses from foreign sales that allow further expansion, but it does not add to the vibrancy of China's innovative sector, which lags behind but is critical for long-term economic health. At the same time, the huge Chinese labor pool will eventually have to be addressed in terms of things like human services, and this will produce a significant burden, as suggested earlier.

How China will continue to evolve economically remains the major point of contention. Will China become a "normal" state whose economy and political system gradually become more and more like those of the rest of the world? Or will China use its growing muscle to challenge the current order? The answers are, of course, speculative. Positively, China has taken a place at the G-20 forum of world economic powers. There are, however, barriers to the continuation of the trends of the recent past. Sharma cites them as follows: "The even bigger story in the global economy . . . will be the three to four percent slowdown in China, which is already underway," he asserts.

"China's population is simply too big and aging too quickly for its economy to continue to grow as rapidly as it has."

India

The Indian experience stands in some contrast to that of China. Both are very large, populous countries with long histories, but their trajectories toward rising power status are distinct. China began earlier, whereas India's is more recent. China's rise economically has been tied to its growth as a manufacturer of consumer goods, whereas the Indian education system (at least for some of its citizens) has allowed it to challenge the leaders of the world economy closer to the cutting edge of technology.

Particularly in recent years, India has been portrayed as the "poster child" of globalization, the country where the values of globalization are clearly in place, are spreading, and are bringing with them the benefits that globalization can promise for improvements in the human condition. The explosion of India onto the global scene was, for instance, the inspiration for globalization enthusiast Thomas Friedman to reexamine globalization in his 2005 book *The World Is Flat*, because it is the Indian entrepreneurship that has provided much of the evidence of how technology generation has spread globally, thereby "flattening" both access to and the ability to produce technology. Fareed Zakaria, in his 2008 best seller *The Post-American World*, reinforced this positive direction.

Led by its aggressive adoption of the values of globalization and fueled largely by its preeminence in high technology, the statistics of Indian growth are substantial. As *Newsweek* reported in its March 6, 2006, edition, for instance, India had the world's second largest growth rate over the previous 15 years. The result has been an unprecedented growth both of personal income and entrepreneurial activity that has helped increase the size of the middle class in India to over 300 million, and this group has the second highest consumption rate in the world, trailing only the United States. Projecting from current trends (always a risky proposition), India's economy will be larger than that of Italy in 10 years and of Great Britain in 15 years. By 2050, the Indian economy could be five times that of Japan. Even if the details of these projections are overinflated, the fact that India has experienced and is likely to continue to have high continued growth that could make it one of the world's future superpowers is clear.

The question is what has caused India to become such an active and successful partner in globalization? India is such an enormous, diverse, and complicated place that simple explanations do not capture its dynamics. It is, for instance, about one-third the physical size of the United States, but it has a population more than three and a half times the American population. It is enormously ethnically, linguistically, and religiously diverse (there are, for instance, sizable numbers of adherents of all the world's major religions in the country). In addition to English and Hindi, there are 14 additional officially recognized languages in the country. The 300 million estimated members of the Indian middle class (the largest in the world) are matched by at least that number who fall below the world's standard for destitution, surviving on less than $2 a day, although there are efforts under way to reduce that total. Ethnic divisions have resulted in open or smoldering violence in places as diverse as the Tamil lands in the south to Kashmir in the north. The country is also beset by one of the few remaining active Marxist wars of national liberation conducted by a small but persistent Maoist guerrilla movement. All of this diversity occurs within the framework of the world's largest political democracy.

India's growth has been fed by policy reforms reminiscent of the Reagan–Thatcher initiatives of the 1980s. Under the leadership of Indira Gandhi, state control of economic activity had effectively stifled economic growth. When she left office, deregulation and privatization permitted the growth of entrepreneurial activity that is transforming India's place in the world. The situation truly changed in 1991. As Feigenbaum explains, "In 1991, leaders in New Delhi pursued policies of economic liberalization that opened the country to foreign investment and yielded rapid growth." Whether the scale of deregulation–privatization can be kept in balance remains to be seen. The alternative may be many of the same difficulties that were revealed globally in 2007 in the West.

India's entrance into and place in the globalizing economy is largely the result of its prominence in the high-technology sector that helps define globalization's parameters. Many countries have embraced and become part of globalization by becoming essentially consumers and appliers of the growing economic possibilities that globalization provides. India does that, too, but its unique place comes from its position increasingly as both a consumer *and* a producer of technology.

The city of Bangalore has become the symbol of India's evolving place in the globalization system. Often referred to as India's Silicon Valley, it has become synonymous with the country's entrance into the global economy and serves as a gathering spot for the large number of scientists and engineers produced by India's educational system. They come to this modern, cosmopolitan city to engage in the kinds of technological innovation and entrepreneurial activity associated with the San Francisco Bay area and other American concentrations of high technology. Bangalore serves as both technological innovator and consumer, as it is also the location in which much of the highly publicized "outsourcing" of lower-end technology jobs from the United States (e.g., telemarketing, service contractors) is found.

Several factors are often cited about why India has succeeded in entering the globalized economy. One is that India emerged from an economically repressive past that left the country poised for a leap forward in activity once the opportunity arose. As numerous analysts have pointed out, the country had a closed, protectionist economy with scarcely any foreign goods, especially consumer goods, available for public consumption, because tariffs on imported goods were among the highest in the world and combined with extremely progressive tax schedules that effectively stifled entrepreneurial activity, and, according to Feigenbaum, barred "foreign investment in many sectors." This was particularly true under Indira Gandhi, who espoused a kind of socialist economic philosophy that "the Indian upper-middle class perceived . . . as a straitjacket," and was continued by the government of Rajiv Gandhi. Those reforms opened the country to outside investment and influence and came as a significant reaction to prior overmanagement of the economy. What has become increasingly an Indian economic "miracle" dates to these reforms, although they are hardly complete (India retains relatively high tariffs against certain classes of goods).

Several other influences have helped stimulate the Indian transition. One is that India has a societal structure amenable to economic growth. That structure includes, according to *Newsweek*, "a real and deep private sector, a clean, well-regulated financial system and the sturdy rule of law." India also has a largely democratic political culture that, when combined with an entrepreneurial work ethic, results in what Max Singer and the late Aaron Wildavsky refer to as a "quality economy" (one that has the requisites for growth because it provides the economic and political incentives for people and groups to work hard and to innovate significantly).

India has at least two other advantages. One is the Indian commitment to quality education. At least for those classes that have access to it, India has some of the best schools and colleges in the world in science and technology. Feigenbaum and others note this opportunity is far less than universal, and "a UNESCO index recently ranked India 102 out of 129 countries on the extent, gender balance, and quality of its primary education and adult literacy." The Indian Institute of Technology, for instance, is a global leader in the field, and its graduates are heavily recruited worldwide, including in the United States. Many Indians have gravitated historically to the United States for the opportunity to use their economic tools, but now they are increasingly staying in or returning to India. They do, however, become Americanized during their time in the United States, which helps explain why the Indian people are among the most pro-American in the world.

India's headlong plunge into globalization has not been entirely smooth or devoid of criticism, although the level of opposition remains minor. The major criticism is that globalization may indeed increase the prosperity of the country as a whole, but that improvement is not uniform for all people. The anomaly of growing inequity has already been suggested in Indian demographics: India has both the world's largest middle class and number of desperately poor. Due to the tradition of social castes in India's past, this disparity has not produced a sizable backlash, as the dispossessed have not—at least yet—asserted effectively the unacceptability of their meager existence. The result is a debate within India that is currently largely confined to the upper classes of Indian society. Defenders of globalization make an argument familiar to Americans: That the benefits of economic growth will "trickle down" to the poor eventually and that efforts to redistribute wealth will cut off that trickle altogether. In more extreme cases, the poor are even blamed for their condition, because, among other things, they have too many children. Pal, quoting Indian columnist Dilip D'Souza, counters, "Proponents of globalization say wait ten years.

But the poor can't wait. They have waited 53 years (since independence). We have to have urgent measures to help them." Activism, however, is weakened because the poor are also politically weak and disorganized, and as long as they remain so, macroeconomic justifications of globalization will overwhelm and swamp their microeconomic woes.

Like China, India's path as a rising power is still partly undefined. To date, it has largely been confined to the economic sector, with particular emphasis on the technological edge that the educational system produces. Whether that growth will continue in anything like a linear fashion is not so certain. Sharma, for instance, is skeptical. As he pointed out at the end of 2012, India's annual growth rate has fallen from 9 percent to closer to 6 percent, and he believes that the nature of economic cycles that have produced gaudy predictions for India will also slow the Indian "miracle" as well.

Brazil

Brazil, the South American giant, is a more recent entrant to the category of rising powers in the world. Brazil is, as Table 11.1 points out, a formidable state, with the world's fifth largest population and landmass, as well as the eighth largest economy. It dwarfs the rest of South America, with a landmass that has a boundary with all but two continental states (Chile and Ecuador) and a population greater than the rest combined. Although acknowledged as a dominant regional state (a *pivotal power* using the term introduced in Chapter 7), the fact that it is a former Portuguese colony and thus Portuguese-speaking country takes away from its appeal as regional leader of its Spanish-speaking neighbors.

Geography and historical perception add to why Brazil has not, until recently, been considered a major world player. Its location in the Western Hemisphere places it under the perceptual shadow of the hemisphere's grudgingly acknowledged leader, the United States, and South America has also been historically considered outside the geopolitical mainstream. There is also a historically negative perception about the country and its aspirations to major power status. To paraphrase an old saying, "Brazil is the country of the future . . . and always will be." The first half of the saying reflects the great potential Brazil possesses; the second half derides Brazil's consistent failure to realize its potential, from which the gloomy prediction follows that Brazil will likely never live up to its promise.

Much of the reason for historic pessimism has been economic. Brazil, like most of Latin America, has historically followed protectionist economic policies designed to shield the country from being swamped by the "colossus of the North." The result has been economic inefficiency and lack of competitiveness in world markets. This situation began to change in the mid-1990s, when two remarkable Brazilian presidents, Fernando Henrique Cardoso and Luiz Inacio "Lula" da Silva, began the process of making the economy competitive in ways reminiscent of changes that occurred in China and India. Dilma Rousseff, who succeeded Lula in 2011, has continued this process, and the result has been sustained growth that made Brazil a BRIC country and a rising power. According to Shifter and Combs, these changes include "a commitment to growth through fiscal discipline, a significant concern for poverty reduction, and a deepening of democracy."

Much of Brazil's profile in international economic terms arises from its position as a commodities producer and exporter. In Rohter's words, "Brazil is blessed with vast expanses of fertile land and abundant supplies of minerals, water, and other resources." Brazil is a major food exporter and provides natural resources to commodity-dependent countries—notably China. The discovery of large traditional oil reserves off its coast and its possession of the world's ninth largest reserves of shale gas and oil means, according to Shifter and Combs, Brazil is "poised to become a major energy power."

This emphasis on commodities is not an unmixed blessing. For one thing, being so resource-blessed has facilitated an overexploitation of resources like those in the Amazon Basin in the apparent belief that there will always be another resource once one is depleted. Rohter explains this by quoting a Brazilian proverb: "God repairs at night the damage man does by day." At the same time, a reliance on commodity exports leaves the country vulnerable to fluctuations in the commodities market. The slowing of Chinese growth, for instance, is currently hurting revenues from Brazil's largest customer and resulting in a current account deficit (a negative balance between export revenues and import expenses), according to Roett.

Whether Brazil is on course to remove the "always will be" from its claim as a major power will soon be symbolically evident on the world public stage. In a manner not unlike the 2008 Beijing Olympics, the country will host the 2014 World Cup soccer championships and the 2016 Olympics. Both events will test a historically questionable Brazilian infrastructure of roads, bridges, railroads, and air services that the government has vowed will be in place before the arrival of the vast influx of fans for these world events. Brazil's success—or failure—will be a clear public indicator of just how far Brazil has and has not come.

CONCLUSION

The exact nature and impact of rising powers is always somewhat difficult to project. It is always tempting to state the challenge in dramatic, even apocalyptical terms, but these descriptions are likely to overshoot the mark, and Menon argues this is likely to be the case today. As he puts it, "those who expect a quick emergence of coequal partners to the United States are mistaken in their view. But so are those who see a future of unchallenged, open-ended American dominance." The recent experiences of China, India, and Brazil exemplify this caution.

To some extent, the existing powers generally have some role in the emergence of new challengers to their dominance, even if that contribution is unintentional. Capital from British banks in the nineteenth century, for instance, was critical in American expansion westward and the emergence of the United States as a global power in the twentieth century, and there is little evidence the British either realized or nurtured that outcome consciously. As Menon explains, the same is true today. "Dominant powers—by providing security, exporting capital, selling goods and services, and creating new technologies—unwittingly enable the rise of new centers of strength. They also stir envy and the desire to emulate. The United States has done all these things."

The question that remains is what does the rise of new powers mean for the United States and for the rest of the world? Certainly, their evolution will have a continuing impact on the structure and operation of the global economy, as discussed in the next chapter. Beyond that, each country will, in all likelihood, make its own individual, if not entirely predictable, impact as well.

China is unquestionably a rising power, and it has already ascended to a position of world economic leadership. The consequences of this ascent, however, remain uncertain and subject to varying, even diametrically opposite, interpretations. No one can reliably look into the future and know for certain how it will be: Whether China will increasingly be a looming threat, a global partner, or some of both. No one knows for sure.

Uncertainty surrounds India's rise. India got a later start than China in the globalizing business, and it is thus at an earlier stage of evolution. Major obstacles remain to its growth, two of which are worth noting here. One is education, an area that cuts both ways. The Indian educational system is excellent for those who can avail themselves of it, but access is restricted, and that means a substantial part of the population (especially women) remains uneducated or undereducated.

The second, and obviously related, example is massive poverty. India has, in Mukherji's words, "more poverty than any other nation in the world," which has very difficult consequences. This means there is a future responsibility to uplift the population that cannot be deferred indefinitely—at great expense. It also means a large part of the population neither contributes to nor benefits from the globalization phenomenon. As Mukherji concludes, "the benefits of rapid economic growth trickle down too slowly in India."

Brazil's trajectory is even more conjectural. Brazil is growing, it has already begun to attack a sizable legacy of income inequality, and it is posed to become a world leader in energy production and export. Its promise, however, must be balanced against a past that has consistently failed to produce the kinds of positive results that have formed a potential that never seems to be realized.

Rising states are a natural and inevitable feature of global development. States decline in their relative power and importance within the international system, and other states arise to supplant them. The BRIC countries are the latest aspirants to rising power status, and they may continue their ascent—current trends and the sheer size of each country certainly point in that direction. At the same time, there are other aspiring states in the wings ready to mount their own challenges and become rising states themselves.

SUGGESTED ACTIVITIES AND QUESTIONS

1. What is a rising power? Why is the concept important in understanding the nature of international politics and changes in the balance of power? As suggested in the introduction, rising powers arise periodically. To get some flavor of the process and why it is confusing and controversial, put yourself in the position of being a European in the late nineteenth century trying to assess the impact the United States would eventually have. Would you view the United States as a looming threat or a global partner? Why?

2. A primary source of China's rise is economic. Although China's economy has indeed expanded greatly, there is disagreement about the nature of that growth and what it means. Try to construct two arguments, one that points to the emergence of China as a major competitor and rival, and one that suggests Chinese economic development is less ominous. Compare the two arguments. Where do they agree and disagree?

3. India's rise has been different than China's. How and why has this been the case? Compare the two countries' experiences in terms of their status and the direction of their rise.

4. Both India and China have positive and negative influences on their present and future growth. What are the distinctive positive and negative impacts on both, with special emphasis on the situation in India?

5. Speculate on the impact that China and India as rising powers will have on the next 10, 25, and 50 years, and how that impact will affect the United States. Explain the reasoning underlying your projections.

SUGGESTED READINGS AND RESOURCES

Abdelal, Rawi and Adam Segal. "Has Globalization Reached Its Peak?" *Foreign Affairs* 86, 1 (January/February 2007), 103–114.

Biaian, Zhang. "China's 'Peaceful Rise' to Great Power Status." *Foreign Affairs* 84, 5 (September/October 2005), 18–24.

Blinder, Alan S. "Offshoring: The Next Industrial Revolution." *Foreign Affairs* 85, 2 (March/April 2006), 113–128.

Brzezinski, Zbigniew. "Make Money, Not War." *Foreign Policy,* January/February 2005, 46–47.

Bush, Richard C. and Michael O'Hanlon. *A War Like No Other: The Truth About China's Challenge to America.* New York: John Wiley and Sons, Inc., 2007.

Deng, Yong and Thomas G. Moore. "China Views Globalization: Toward a Great New Power Politics?" *Washington Quarterly* 27, 3 (Summer 2004), 117–136.

Dickerson, Bruce J., Bruce Gilley, and Dali L. Yang. "The Future of China's One-Party State." *Current History* 107, 701 (September 2007), 243–251.

Feigenbaum, Evan A. "India's Rise, America's Interest: The Fate of the U.S.–Indian Partnership." *Foreign Affairs* 89, 2 (March/April 2010), 76–91.

Fravel, M. Taylor. "China's Search for Military Power." *Washington Quarterly* 31, 3 (Summer 2008), 125–141.

Friedman, Thomas L. *The Lexus and the Olive Tree: Understanding Globalization.* New York: Farrar, Straus, and Giroux, 1999.

———. *The World Is Flat: A Brief History of the 21st Century.* New York: Farrar, Straus, and Giroux, 2005.

Gifford, Rob. *China Road: A Journey into the Future of a Rising Power.* New York: Random House, 2007.

Gilboy, George J. "The Myth Behind China's Miracle." *Foreign Affairs* 83, 4 (July/August 2004), 33–48.

——— and Benjamin J. Read. "Political and Social Reforms in China: Alive and Walking." *Washington Quarterly* 31, 3 (Summer 2008), 143–164.

Gill, Bates. *Rising Star: China's New Security Diplomacy.* Washington, DC: Brookings Institution Press, 2007.

Hale, David and Lyric Hughes Hale. "China Takes Off." *Foreign Affairs* 82, 6 (November/December 2003), 36–53.

Huang, Yeshing. "The Next Asian Model." *Foreign Policy*, July/August 2008, 32–40.

Jisi, Wang. "China's Search for Stability with America." *Foreign Affairs* 84, 5 (September/October 2005), 39–48.

Kaplan, Robert D. "India's New Face." *The Atlantic* 303, 3 (April 2009), 74–81.

Lapton, David M. "The Faces of Chinese Power." *Foreign Affairs* 86, 1 (January/February 2007), 115–127.

Legro, Jeffrey W. "What China Will Want: The Future Implications of a Rising Power." *Perspectives on Politics* 5, 3 (September 2007), 515–533.

Mahbubani, Kishore. "Understanding China." *Foreign Affairs* 84, 5 (September/October 2005), 49–60.

Menon, Rajan. "Pax Americana and the Rising Powers." *Current History* 108, 721 (November 2009), 253–260.

Mukherji, Hahul. "A Tiger Despite the Chains: The State of Reform in India." *Current History* 109, 726 (April 2010), 144–150.

The National Security Strategy of the United States of America. Washington, DC: The White House, March 2006.

Pei, Minxin. "Dangerous Denials." *Foreign Policy,* January/February 2005, 54–56.

———. "The Dark Side of China's Rise." *Foreign Policy*, March/April 2006, 32–40.

Roett, Riordan. "Toodle-oo, Lula: Brazil Looks Forward to Dilma. *Current Histoey* 110, 733 (February 2011), 43–48.

Rohter, Larry. *Brazil on the Rise: The Story of a Country Transformed.* London: Palgrave Macmillan, 2012.

Segal, Adam. "Practical Engagement: Drawing a Fine Line for U.S.-China Trade." *Washington Quarterly* 27, 3 (Summer 2004), 157–173.

Sharma, Ruchir. "Broken BRICs." *Foreign Affairs* 91, 6 (November/December 2012), 2–7.

Shifter, Michael, and Cameron Combs. "Shifting Fortunes: Brazil and Mexico in a Transformed Region" *Current History* 112, 751 (February 2013), 49–55.

Singer, Max and the late Aaron Wildawsky. *The Real World Order: Zones of Peace, Zones of Turmoil* (revised edition). Chatham, NJ: Chatham House, 1996.

Wolf, Martin. "Why Is China Growing So Slowly?" *Foreign Policy*, January/February 2005, 49–52.

———. *Why Globalization Works.* New Haven, CT: Yale University Press, 2004.

Zakaria, Fareed. "India Rising." *Newsweek,* March 6, 2006, 24–42.

———. *The Post-American World.* New York: W. W. Norton, 2008.

WEB SITES

A general overview of China: http://www.insidechina.com
A compendium of Chinese foreign affairs position papers
State Council Information Office: http://www.china.org.cn
Ministry of Foreign Affairs at http://www.fmprc.gov.cn
Systematic overview prepared by the Federal Research Division of the Library of Congress, "China, a Country Study": http://memory.loc.gov/frd/cs/cntoc.html
Yale Global Online: http://yaleglobal.yale.edu

Globalization and Development: Extending the Prosperity

PRÉCIS

The benefits of and participation in globalization are not currently universally enjoyed, and thus a major question is whether and how to extend globalization more globally. Part of the answer involves the current status and dynamics of globalization and how the development of the less developed nonparticipants in globalization is tied to globalization. At the same time, extension is also a major aspect of the debate and dynamics of economic and political development at both the moral and geopolitical levels. After introducing these concerns as context, the case moves to a focus on the evolving institutional structure within which the question of extension of globalization is contested. The highlight of that institutional development is the evolution of the Group of Seven (G-7) to the Group of Twenty (G-20).

Throughout most of its existence, the term *globalization* has been misleading. The implication is that the process is global, suggesting a universality of application that has not really occurred in any systematic way to all reaches of the world. Globalization does reach and have an impact on virtually every corner of the globe, but its impact varies considerably from locale to locale. Globalization and its merits and rewards are enjoyed by some but not by all.

Another way to approach and describe the places that have and have not experienced globalization is in terms of development. This concept has both political and economic aspects, but because the focus here is on the economic dimension, it is that aspect on which the discussion will focus. Broadly speaking, development refers to the process and resulting condition where economies have moved from a fairly primitive level of productivity that is incapable of providing prosperity to a level of greater productivity and at least the potential to create prosperity for all or most of its members (to the extent the prosperity is widely shared). Developed societies are those that have attained a greater level of productivity and prosperity. In the contemporary world, development is associated with the successful practice of Western, capitalist-style economics. Less developed (or developing) societies fall short of that structure or level of attainment.

The developmental gap between the most and least developed economies is considerable. While some parts of the world enjoy affluence, other parts languish in the most miserable poverty—a large part of humankind subsists on $2 a day or less. The evidence suggests that this condition is not self-remediating; the developing world requires help to become more prosperous.

The question is what can or should be done to narrow the gap. There is no consensus on either question. How to develop the economies of the less developed countries has been the subject of enormous thought, research, and theorizing by academics and policy practitioners since the end of World War II. Although there has been success associated with some—mostly massive—developmental efforts, there is no "formula" for aiding development that everyone agrees is foolproof. At the same time, there is also disagreement about what, if any, priority should be assigned to the developmental enterprise. Part of the skepticism arises from the absence of a clearly effective approach that leaves some suspicious that resources devoted to development are likely to be wasted. Another part questions whether aiding development is even a worthwhile exercise for outsiders to undertake.

The development movement must be put in context for it to gain full meaning. The movement, even the interest, in extending globalization is not universal, and there is no universal agreement on how to bring it about. Extending globalization to the benefit of the maximum number of people is a social and political value, and as such, it is a concern about which purely economic approaches, including theories of globalization, are neutral. The partial exception is that spreading globalization is "good business," but approaches to globalization are steeped in capitalist economics that are conspicuously welfare valueless.

There is also disagreement on how extension, to the extent is can be induced, should occur. Globalizers are not so much anti-extension in the sense of seeing spreading prosperity as a desirable or undesirable value as they are "a-extensionist." Advocacy goes beyond their theoretical reach (which tends to be value-neutral), and many see extension as a social as well as an economic benefit. The question is how to go about extending the benefits. Here the arguments become value-laden, mixing advocacy of economic and political development and globalization. A prominent criticism of globalization, after all, is that it shares the economist's lack of concern with social equity. It cares that the boats rise, but not whose boats rise more, to extend the analogy introduced earlier.

These remarks help to frame the complex relationships surrounding development and the extension of globalization to the developing world as a way to facilitate the development goal. It begins by examining the dynamics and controversies involved in development and globalization as its tool. What exactly is development? What is globalization, and why is it a controversial way to approach the task of development? That discussion leads to a focus on development. It begins by examining the developmental process: what does it entail? It then moves to a consideration of the "whys" of engaging in development along two frequently used lines of argumentation. One of these is that the developed world has a moral obligation to assist the process; the other is that spreading the prosperity is in the enlightened self-interest of the developed world. The discussion then moves to institutionalized efforts to bring about greater convergence through the expansion of the G-7 process to the G-20.

DYNAMICS AND CONTROVERSIES

Although most analysts believe that globalization is desirable in a general sense, exactly what it means, how it is reached, and—most important to this chapter—how it is extended to places that do not currently enjoy its fruits are not matters so universally accepted. Unraveling the question of extending globalization thus begins by placing it in the context of the debate about development and looking sequentially at controversies surrounding globalization. In the process, the discussion reveals some of the primary underlying dynamics of the process and the effective "rules of the road" by which aspiring nonparticipants can join the prosperity.

The Roots of the Development Movement

In his Inaugural Address on January 20, 1949, President Harry S. Truman (quoted in Latham) made the case for what became a policy emphasis on development, a term he used synonymously with modernization. "More than half of the people of the world are living in conditions approaching misery," he said. "Their food is inadequate. They are victims of disease. Their economic life is primitive and stagnant. Their poverty is a threat both to them and to more prosperous areas." Their situation, he continued, was both unacceptable and dangerous to everyone, including Americans. As a result, he concluded, the United States would "embark on a bold new program for making the benefits of our scientific advances and industrial progress available for the improvement and growth of the underdeveloped areas."

This pledge, known as "Point Four" of Truman's foreign policy (along with support for the United Nations, the Marshall Plan, and the North Atlantic Treaty Organization) threw down the gauntlet for developmental efforts ever since. It also gave those efforts a particular cast with three distinct elements. First, it identified the process as American-centered, a reflection of American economic preeminence at the time (see Chapter 9). Second, it established development as a security concern in the emerging Cold War—a way to make areas impervious to communist blandishments. Third, it established the moral imperative of helping to improve the situation of the less developed world. The second and third elements remain central to the ongoing debate over development.

The context and need for development were largely artifacts of the post–World War II process of European decolonization. Prior to the war, almost all of Africa, large parts of Asia, and smaller areas of the Western Hemisphere were under the colonial rule of one European state or another. The developmental gap between the colonial masters and their colonies was enormous, and it was never a priority for the colonial rulers to narrow it except where developmental efforts (building roads or deepening ports, for example) would directly benefit their exploitative efforts. Indeed, nurturing political or economic development was counterproductive, as it would likely encourage independence movements demanding an end to colonial rule.

World War II changed the equation. Most Europeans overlords on both sides were exhausted by the war and had neither the energy nor wherewithal to resist postwar independence movements in their colonies. The result was a steady, growing stream of former colonies demanding and being granted their national freedoms. By the end of the 1970s, the old empires had all but disappeared.

Independence, however, carried its own set of difficulties. In the developmental realms described by Truman, there was a gaping chasm between the most developed countries, distinguished after 1960 by their membership in the Organization for Economic Cooperation and Development (OECD), and the new developing world. This new set of countries—mostly very poor and politically unstable—quickly became a competitive ground in the Cold War, as the Soviet-led communist bloc competed with the American-led Western coalition for the allegiance of these areas. In the process, the geopolitical rationale for development was born and nurtured.

The manner by which the developing world was "born" also underpinned the moral dimension of the ongoing debate about development. The simple facts were that the European colonialists had done little intentionally to develop their colonies and thus left a huge developmental disparity behind when they departed. The question raised at the time and frequently repeated since was whether the Europeans had some moral obligation to assist in the uplifting of their former dependents.

The whole idea of development has been and is controversial. As it has evolved, serious deficiencies in theories of development have been revealed, fueling a growing suspicion that much of the movement is a chimera. At the same time, the end of the Cold War has removed some of the geopolitical necessity of engaging in developmental efforts.

The spread of globalization has created a new developmental avenue that is evident in phenomena such as the movement of labor-intensive manufacturing and other industries to developing countries. The globalists lack either the sense of geopolitical mission or moral guilt of the original developmental advocates, and their interests are largely defined in terms of what some would argue are sterile economic calculations. This change of orientation and motivation, in turn, contributes a whole new dimension to controversies surrounding development.

Controversies

A number of sources of controversy surround globalization as the primary method for inducing development. Seven will be discussed because of their relevance to the question of extending globalization and the impact of that extension on development. All reflect, to some extent, the difficulties of grafting the economic model of the developed world onto parts of the world where that model is foreign, even alien.

The first is that globalization is a distinctively Western construct, based on theories of economic activity that are Western at base and that reflect Western economic and political preferences and practices. The symbol of globalization has been something called the *Washington consensus*, which represents a set of rules of economic practice that govern participation in the globalized economy. These rules reflect strongly Western economic and political values, and are especially heavily influenced by the United States, which has been the leading apostle of globalization since it began to emerge in the 1990s. In order to become a full-fledged member of the globalization system and thus to reap the primarily economic benefits that it promises (largely reflections of the material prosperity of the West, and especially the United States), countries have been effectively required to adopt the values and practices of the Washington consensus, which some countries and areas find inconsistent with their own values and situations and which are not uniformly practiced by the countries that espouse them.

The other sources of controversy flow from the intrusiveness of the Western model. The second controversy surrounds the cultural impacts of embracing the Washington consensus. Becoming part of the global system inevitably entails becoming *like* the countries that are members of the system: capitalist, consumer-oriented societies that eventually adopt both the cultural aspects of the West and many of its outward trappings. A prime necessity of membership in the globalization system is opening societies to outsiders for economic purposes, including foreign investment. Foreign investors in turn bring with them preferences for how things should be done that their money helps them to influence: If you become part of the globalization system, the friendly arches of McDonalds are likely not to be far behind.

This opening and cultural assault is of greater or lesser import from region to region of the world. The trade-off it requires—sacrificing established values and practices that are dysfunctional in a globalized society for values that are compatible with globalization—is more acceptable in some places than in others. The Islamic Middle East, for instance, has been more reluctant to make this bargain than other parts of the world, but even in places like parts of Latin America that initially embraced globalization, there has been a backlash against some of its effects. These values have been most readily accepted in Asia, as the cases of China and India highlighted in Chapter 11 demonstrate.

The third and fourth sources of controversy are related to one another. The third is the difficulty of making the transition from a noncapitalist economy to the capitalist economy implicit in globalization. In general terms, the model requires putting in place macroeconomic and microeconomic practices that are difficult and that can require considerable sacrifice and even privation during the transition process. As an example, one macroeconomic requirement is reduction of government expenditures in order to create something like a balanced budget that will create a healthy economic condition for low inflation and investment, among other things. Such practices may make good long-term economic sense, but they also generally entail reductions in benefits to citizens and thus cause economic privation and political opposition to the process. Political and economic criteria often collide, and the process of reconciliation can be both painful and difficult.

This description suggests the fourth source of controversy, already raised in Chapter 9, which is the differential macro- and microeconomic impact of globalization. Most arguments made in favor of globalization are macroeconomic in character, referring to the overall benefits to societies that become part of the globalization system. Although in theory such benefits accrue to individual members of the society as well (the "rising tide that lifts all boats"), those benefits are highly differential (some boats are raised more than others), and there are individuals whose boats are not only not raised but may also be swamped and sunk in the process. Although its champions argue that globalization overwhelmingly produces winners (people become better-off), it also produces losers, and those losers become the opposition. If their numbers become large enough, the result may be political shock waves that raise the controversy to significant levels.

The dynamics of these third and fourth controversies have led, especially in Asia, to a debate over the optimal political setting for inducing—or, where incentives are inadequate, forcing—change. Conventional wisdom has suggested that the authoritarian environment is a more efficient setting for economic change, but the recent startling expansion of the Indian economy has raised questions about these assessments.

The fifth controversy surrounds whether the debate is purposive. The heart of this controversy is whether the process of globalization is inevitable and whether there are meaningful, non-self-destructive choices that can be exercised as to whether one participates in globalization or not. In some parts of the world, globalization has been almost wholeheartedly embraced and the question is moot. In other parts of the world, however, the question is lively, because there is reluctance to embrace the core values of globalization and, by extension, broad-based societal development. In places like the Islamic Middle East, this reluctance may be the result of indecision about adopting the basic rules of globalized societies (free-market capitalism or transparent banking laws, for instance) or because the secondary and tertiary effects of globalization and development (secularization and Westernization) are deemed undesirable. At the same time, the transition to globalization may be politically or economically so difficult that some societies believe it should or needs to be avoided, either in principle or because preliminary experience with globalization has been disillusioning.

The sixth controversy is over accessibility to globalization. Because of its capitalist underlying premise, the private sources of capital that provide the enabling condition for productivity and thus participation are drawn to those places where they can maximize their profits and are repelled from places where they cannot. The latter assessment is most likely to occur in the poorest, least developed countries that lack both the human (e.g., educated people) or physical (e.g., transportation, power facilities) infrastructure to be attractive to those for whom profit is the primary motive. Infrastructure enhancement, in turn, normally requires public investments that fall outside the conceptual parameters of globalization beyond insisting on austerity to self-finance the development of such capabilities. The result may be simply to lock some societies out of the globalization process. The process of development is thus a factor.

A seventh controversy has arisen more recently and has influenced the willingness of developing countries to adopt the strictures and privations the developed world has created for entrance into the global economy. That factor, simply put, is the apparent hypocrisy of the developed countries requiring neophyte members to adopt policies and restrictions the developed countries are unwilling to impose upon themselves. The reduction of governmental deficits and debt, a prime value of the Washington consensus, is illustrative. The unwillingness or inability of Western governments to swallow the political costs of the budget reductions they seek to impose on others has made aspiring globalizers wary of this advice. The sovereign debt crisis in the European Union (EU) and the difficulty the EU is having in resolving it (Chapter 10) is a prime example. The moral suasion of the Washington consensus has also been eroded by the persistent inability of the United States to resolve its own debt problem.

THE DEVELOPMENTAL DIMENSION

The desirability of extending globalization to places currently untouched by it or receiving less than its optimal benefits is ultimately a value question that goes beyond strictly economic theories of growth. How globalization spreads addresses the question of where it extends only indirectly, arguing that extension essentially will occur in places that either have or can develop some form of comparative advantage and that it will bypass or ignore places that do not. Questions of equity, justice, or moral and political desirability of expansion to some places but not to others simply is not part of purely economic discussions.

The extension of globalization cannot, however, be divorced from those value concerns, because it impinges upon and affects the patterns of interaction between those states that are currently part of and helped by globalization—the wealthier states of the developed world and ambitious and successful developing world states—and the generally poorer states outside the general prosperity of the most prosperous—the so-called developing states. The extension of globalization implies raising some states out of the economic morass of the developing world and into the more rarified atmosphere of globalization. As a result, extending globalization is part of a more general discussion of development.

Globalizers generally do not like to phrase the process of globalization in these terms for several reasons. First, it removes the process from the supposedly more objective level of the application of the capitalist model applied internationally to the "softer" realm of economic and social equities, and economic analysis is uncomfortable with these kinds of distinctions. Second, because developmental efforts generally have a prominent public component, moving the extension of globalization into the development framework moves the discussion more toward the role of government in economic affairs, a question for which most globalizers has a negative answer. Third, the equation of globalization and development has strong international political implications in the area of most general conflict between the developed and developing worlds—the obligations of the developed to the developing world. For all these reasons, many supporters of globalization would object to the very inclusion of development in a discussion of globalization.

Nevertheless, the developmental question needs to be addressed, because it is a part of the ongoing debate and especially a major part of the underlying dynamic about the evolving international institutionalization of globalization. One of the primary reasons for expanding the globalization system is to include members of the developing world that have become globalizers into world economic councils, and one of the agenda items they add to the mix is that of development.

The Process of Globalization and Development

These two concepts are clearly related to one another but are by no means identical or, in some cases, even compatible with one another. For countries to "qualify" for membership in the globalization system, they must first achieve some level of development to make themselves attractive to globalizing concerns—multinational corporations (MNCs) that make things or do business in multiple countries, for instance. Generally, this means at least some development of the country's infrastructure of human and material resources—education, transportation, and power facilities, for instance.

Textile manufacturing is an "entry-level" enterprise for joining the globalization system, because it is a labor-intensive business where the availability of abundant cheap labor is a major attraction as a means to lower the cost of goods. Even the least developed countries have people who can sew and for whom even modest wages are more than they can earn otherwise. At the same time, even an industry like textiles requires some development in the infrastructure, such as electricity to powering sewing machines and transportation facilities to move finished goods to consumers in developed markets.

Infrastructure requirements increase as the sophistication of economic activity increases. Whereas textile manufacturing does not require a particularly well-educated population, more complex manufacturing and service industries do, and this points to an important—arguably the critical—element in the relationship between globalization and development. Although the fruits of globalization can help underwrite the greater development of a developing country's economy, there must be some basic level of development in place in a country before it becomes attractive to the globalizers in the first place. Globalization spreads to the developing countries—those countries that have achieved enough infrastructure to make them competitive for some economic activity at comparative advantage—but not to the poorest and least developed countries, where environmental conditions are not conducive to any form of investment by globalizing concerns. The globalizing enterprise has no interest in financing rudimentary development itself, because building a road or a power plant is a business expense that does not yield a profit measurable in quarterly or annual earnings reports. Its incentive is to find and exploit situations that are "ripe for the picking," not to grow the fruit trees from seeds.

This dynamic has two important consequences. First, it means the relationship between the two phenomena is sequential: at least some development must precede globalization. Those places that have not undergone some infrastructure development are simply outside the interests of the globalization process and remain outside as long as that lack of development continues. Driven by the profit motive, the forces of globalization are simply not interested in or motivated to become the drivers or facilitators of development.

Second, this means the process of development is largely independent of the globalizers, at least at the early critical stages that allow initial entry into the globalizing world. Infrastructure development is simply beyond the purview and structure of interests of the globalizers, because most infrastructure development cannot be translated directly and accountably into profits, which is the base value of the globalization system. This in turn means that the forces of globalization may contribute to the *continued* development of developing countries by providing wealth that can be invested in further infrastructure development, but it will never be the basic force behind such development.

The reason for this dynamic arises, quite obviously, from the different basic values underpinning development and globalization. Development reflects economic values of attaining comparative advantage, but it also includes social and political values that are not included in purely economic calculations. Ultimately, the goal of development is societal *effectiveness*, the extent to which economic and other dynamics contribute to the more effective creation and delivery of a better way of life than in its absence. Globalization, however, is almost solely directed by questions of *efficiency:* how activity is channeled to maximize comparative advantage and profit. They are simply different criteria reflecting different values.

The two values sometimes clash, as the tragic textile factory fire in Bangladesh in May 2013 illustrates. Textile manufacturing occurs in that country because of its comparative advantage in the cost of labor, and the foreign clothing firms whose products were manufactured in the factory that burned, killing over 1,100, were primarily motivated by keeping costs minimal to maximize profits. Although efficient, the process neglected the kinds of safety regulations that might have made the facility safer and thus more effective for its workforce. That the efficiency of globalization trumped the effectiveness of societal development was best illustrated by the slow and reluctant pace by which manufacturers responded to the tragedy.

Because development is driven by different, broader values than those of globalization, the question is what incentives underlie providing the resources necessary for development to be sparked. One set of arguments suggest a kind of moral obligation on the part of the developed world to assist the process. Another set of arguments is that development produces stability and is thus in the geopolitical interests of the developed world. In turn, these rationales affect approaches to development.

Why Development? The Moral Obligation?

There are two lines of argumentation generally invoked to assert a moral obligation to assist development, and it should come as no surprise that the developing countries are the strongest advocates of asserting this obligation on the developed countries as a way to gain assistance in their development. One line of argumentation arises from the colonial experience, asserting that colonialism both created the appetite for development and suppressed its achievement, a situation the colonizers are obligated to rectify. The other argument, largely a product of the post-1945 environment, argues a humanitarian basis for assistance, in essence contending that all humans have a moral imperative to relieve the misery of other members of their species.

The problem of economic and political development is indeed an artifact of the dissolution of the European worldwide empires after the end of World War II. As noted, the process began in the later 1940s in places like the Asian subcontinent and effectively culminated when Portugal granted independence to its remaining African colonies in the middle 1970s. The result of decolonization was an explosion of new sovereign states that nearly quadrupled the number of such states in 1945. The Bretton Woods conference, as noted in Chapter 9, consisted of 45 states; the current number of independent entities is close to 200.

One of the characteristics that almost all of the newly independent states shared was a lack of economic development. Their poverty stood in stark contrast to the conditions of their former colonial rulers after those countries recovered from World War II. This disparity created an understandable desire on the part of the formerly colonized countries to emulate the prosperity of their former rulers, and development thus became the major agenda item in the relations between the developed and developing worlds. It is a problem that now spans over a half-century and remains vital and cogent.

The task of raising the economic standards of the former colonies to those of the rich countries required a difficult, expensive process for which the developing states lacked adequate resources of their own, meaning such resources would have to come from elsewhere for development to occur. The obvious candidates were the rich countries—and especially the colonial powers that had held them in bondage. The developing states, however, lacked much effective leverage to extract necessary resources—principally money and expertise—to encourage development. If the developed states refused requests or demands for assistance, what could the developing states do to force them to comply? The general answer was, "not very much."

One response to this situation was to phrase the question in moral terms: the rich states had a moral obligation to uplift the poor states. The moral basis of this argument was the immorality of colonialism and the perversity of its effects. Colonial rule was often harsh, inhumane, degrading, and reprehensible (see George Orwell's *Burmese Diaries* for a personal, vivid description), and the former oppressors thus "owed" the formerly oppressed restitution for these indignities. More to the point, colonialists were economically exploitive (appropriating natural resources in the colonies and forcing subjects to consume products from the ruling country, for instance), and the exploitation inhibited economic development in the colonies. While this latter claim was arguable, it did serve as an explanation for both why there was disparity and why the former oppressors were obliged to do something about it.

The other argument is of more recent vintage. It was first expressed in founding United Nations principles regarding the universal rights of all people, including economic entitlements only available in a situation of some development. The recognition of great, sometimes human-caused privation and suffering noted by Truman has broadened that appeal in the past couple decades to encompass the idea of "humanitarian vital interests" universal to all people. Because at least some of the privations involve qualities and standards of living, this concern becomes a part of the moral content of advocacies of development, asserting in essence that, as human beings, everyone has a moral obligation to help make the conditions of their fellow humans better.

The moral arguments are "soft" entreaties based on abstractions and ideals not always present in global affairs. One result has been for developmental advocates to search for "harder," more "realistic" reasons to impel developmental help. Because moral suasion does not always carry the day in questions about the allocation of scarce resources—in this case funds for development—the result has been to find a firmer ground in geopolitical reality.

Why Development? Geopolitical Self-Interest?

Resources that can be devoted to developing less developed countries must compete with many other political priorities and demands within the donor countries. In most of the developed world (including the United States), the calls for developmental assistance based in moral, humanitarian appeals receive a polite but lukewarm reception and ended up toward the bottom of the list of funded priorities. Humanitarian concerns generally lack a sense of immediacy for donor publics, particularly compared to international conditions that pose a real or potential threat to national security. Advocates of developmental assistance thus have turned to more national-security, threat-oriented reasons on which to enhance the appeal of their advocacies.

The resulting arguments assert that assisting countries in the developmental process is in the enlightened geopolitical self-interest of the donors. The arguments are both general and specific. The general argument is centered on the idea that development leads to economic and political stability, conditions generally deemed desirable for the reduction of international turmoil and violence. A contemporary variation is the notion that stability also enhances the attractiveness of these countries to the globalized economy, thereby enhancing everyone's prosperity. The more specific claim used to be based in making target societies prosperous enough to allow them to resist the appeals of communism. More recent emphases have been on making states prosperous enough that they will not become sanctuaries or recruiting grounds for terrorists.

Long before the term *globalization* became popular, development was a key concept regarding the emerging former colonies of the so-called Third World. It became a shibboleth within academic circles in the 1940s and 1950s, as academics and some policy makers sought to mitigate the enormous economic and political gulf between the rich, OECD countries of the First World (the communist states formed the Second World) and these new, impoverished countries. Much of the basis of concern was captured in documents like the United Nations Declaration of Human Rights of 1948, which asserted that all humans were entitled to a "standard of living adequate for the health and well-being of himself and his family" (Article 25), conditions clearly not present in much of the developing world. Moreover, the result of wretchedness was increasingly instability and violence within some of these new states, which sometimes affected the rich state adversely.

For the first 40-plus years of the post–World War II period, instability translated into a perceived vulnerability of the developing world to the appeal of global communism. Development was viewed as an antidote to this allure, and this formed much of the rationale for developmental assistance. Because unstable countries are also unattractive places for foreign investors, development has more recently been argued in globalization terms.

The more contemporary substitute for communism has been terrorism. The national security tie-in between terrorism and development arises from the observation that terrorism both thrives and receives safe haven in the most underdeveloped, failed states. Somalia, Yemen, and Afghanistan are the most frequently cited examples of this confluence. The relationship emerges from the assertion that raising developmental levels will relieve the "misery index" in these kinds of societies and make them less fruitful both recruiting and staging grounds for terrorist activity. Some terrorism experts (see Chapter 16) refer to this process as "draining the swamp" of terrorist-friendly environments, where the "swamp" refers to the levels of material deprivation in these places and "draining" refers to alleviation of the misery in which terrorism is said to "breed."

Approaches to Development

There are essentially two basic approaches to obtaining and applying the resources necessary for development. One, which has been historically dominant, is through the application of public sources of funds—what is generally referred to as developmental assistance or foreign aid. The other, and more recent, is the application of private-sector resources, an approach that has become associated with globalization. At the application level, the two approaches are frequently applied in tandem.

The most basic developing world economic problem is infrastructural underdevelopment (many developing countries have multiple additional difficulties such as corruption as well). Infrastructure, of course, refers to the basic human and physical building blocks on which development of a more sophisticated and productive economic system is premised and includes basic physical elements such as roads and railroads, power generation facilities, and urban areas that can accommodate a working-class population. Human resources can include an educated, trained workforce, political stability, and congenial economic policies. The absence of these conditions makes countries unappealing to the kind of private investment that is the core of globalization.

The question for developing countries is how to develop the infrastructure necessary to ascend the world economic ladder. The answer—and in some ways the rub—is that the very economic resources these countries lack are the enabling mortar to cement the building blocks on which prosperity is based. But where can and should these resources come from?

The two broad potential sources are public and private. Particularly from the vantage point of the developing states themselves, foreign public sources have great appeal. For one thing, there is the matter of entitlement: the rich former oppressors "owe" help to the poor they oppressed. The other appeal of public resources arises from the nature of infrastructure investment in economic terms. Borrowing from the vocabulary of developmental assistance, many (even most) infrastructure development is not "self-liquidating," meaning that regardless of the benefits of a particular infrastructure project, it does not directly generate the revenue to pay for itself. Schools are a particularly clear example. They are clearly necessary parts of the human-infrastructure needs on which a productive economy is based, but their direct contribution cannot be measured so that the "profits" from their activities can be used to pay off the costs incurred to build and operate them. There are a number of other elements of the infrastructure that are of a similar nature in virtually all societies that are treated as publicly supported public goods.

The globalization question revolves around the sources from which public funds should come. The traditional answer from the developing world has been the transfer of resources from the developed to the developing world on a government-to-government basis (foreign aid). The developed states have never formally repudiated this approach, but they have generally been unwilling to honor it at levels anywhere near what is needed to meet the demands of the developing states. Resource transfer has been a perpetually inadequate source for the development demands of the developing world.

Globalization encourages a movement toward an alternative source of public funding: internal resources. To produce the wealth needed to underwrite economically non-self-liquidating infrastructure development, the globalization response is fiscal and monetary austerity to wring developmental resources from the developing countries themselves. Developing countries find shifting the emphasis to this ground objectionable on three grounds. First, it shifts the debate away from the moral grounds of a developing-world obligation to assist in the developmental process. Second, it is an approach that is too politically dangerous for Third World countries to embrace. Austerity, which is at the heart of much of this approach, means enforced savings at the expense of current consumption, which is politically unpopular. Moreover, the insistence by developed states is to some extent hypocritical, as it demands that developing states adopt and enforce odious restrictions that the states demanding them often lack the political courage to enforce on themselves. Third, it is not clear that the adequate domestic resources are available in many countries even if a maximum husbanding effort is undertaken. The paucity of developmental resources is, after all, the very problem that developmental efforts seek to change. Reliance on this method is intolerably slow under the best of circumstances and impossible physically at the worst.

No real consensus exists about either the most appropriate sources or methods of development. Differences are based both in empirical questions about what works and in sometimes ideological differences about whether such assistance should come from public or private sources. The questions are most difficult to answer for the most desperately underdeveloped states, and it is not unfair to say that no one has devised a satisfactory solution for the most destitute societies.

The situation is less grim for states that are at least partially developed and are therefore less distant from entrances into the globalized world. These states have developed their own advocacy mechanisms (such as the Group of 77) and other entities like the Brazil, Russia, India, and China (BRIC) construct and the expansion of the G-7 to the G-20. These latter mechanisms are allowing movement into the global economy and are addressed as the major case application of the relationship between development and globalization in the next section.

INSTITUTIONALIZING EXTENSION: FROM G-7 TO G-20

Reconciling the problems and contradictions within the global economy to the mutual satisfaction of all or most of its members remains a work in progress. There are fundamental disagreements about how the system should be organized and to whose benefit and advantage. Historically, the discussions have been dominated largely by the wealthiest countries, which had an adequate stranglehold on resources to be able to dictate the context and outcomes on such important matters as development. The developing world was left on the outside looking in.

Globalization is changing the equation of these discussions. Newly powerful states like the BRICs have broken the monopoly once concentrated in

North America, Europe, and Japan. The result is new faces and voices with different messages demanding a seat and voice at the economic table. Their appeals for inclusion are increasingly proving ineluctable.

These changes are increasingly being manifested institutionally. The original framework devised at Bretton Woods (see Chapter 9) produced a structure of institutions like the International Monetary Fund (IMF) and the International Bank for Reconstruction and Development (IBRD) that continue to be dominated by the traditional powers. This pattern was continued in developed world-dominated forums like the Organization of Economic Cooperation and Development (OECD) and culminated in the formation of a kind of executive directorate in 1985, the G-7.

While all this was congealing, the developing world emerged from colonialism and brought with it the developmental agenda, which was first formally articulated and came to center on forums like the G-77 and the G-20 developing states (an organization separate from the G-20 that is the focus of the study). Developing-world demands, however, fell on at least partially deaf ears until the process of globalization began to move the center of economic power away from its traditional mooring to a broader and more inclusive base. The culmination of that process to date was the late 2009 announcement that the G-7 would supplant itself with the more broadly based G-20, a body the G-7 created.

This case application looks at the history and dynamics of this significant change in global economic development. It begins with a brief overview of the historical evolution of a maze of institutions on both sides of the developmental divide. It then moves to the changing world economy and how those changes have militated toward a shift in institutional arrangement that is currently captured in the movement from G-7 to G-20.

Economic Institutions Since World War II

A major concern of post–World War II planners was how to avoid another calamity resembling the economic conditions of the 1930s. Their major goal was economic stabilization, first among themselves and later toward emerging parts of the world, and the original Bretton Woods institutions, the IBRD and the IMF, were designed for this purpose. Weighted voting formulas in each based on the initial subscriptions of the founding members (in the case of the United States, about one-third of the funds and thus votes) guaranteed control by the rich states.

From an operational standpoint, the solidarity of the developed world on economic issues falls to the OECD. This organization was originally instituted in 1948 as the Organization of European Economic Cooperation (OEEC) at American insistence to dispense Marshall Plan assistance to war-torn Europe. In 1960 it was reconstituted as the OECD with the aim, stated on its Web site, to act as a "forum of countries committed to democracy and market economies." The headquarters of the 30-member organization include the three major states of North America, most of the countries of the European Union, and several important Pacific rim states (Japan, South Korea, Australia, and New Zealand), and Turkey. All members of the G-7 are OECD members, and because the European Union is the 20th member of G-20, most other OECD members are part of G-20 as well.

A parallel group of organizations emerged among the members of the developing world to champion their position in the economic order. The original meeting of developing world states expressing what became the developmental agenda was the Bandung Conference of 1955. This movement did not gain momentum until 1964, however, when the first United Nations (UN) Conference on Trade and Development (UNCTAD) adjourned on June 15 in Geneva, Switzerland, with 77 developing country participants declaring the formation of the Group of 77 (G-77). This organization, whose membership has swollen to 130 states, held its first meeting and declared itself a permanent organization with the Charter of Algiers (the site of the meeting) in October 1967. The G-77 now meets annually at the beginning of each regular session of the UN General Assembly.

The purpose of G-77 is to further the developmental agenda of its membership, which encompasses most of the developing world. As stated on its Web site, the G-77 provides a "means for the countries of the South to articulate and promote their collective economic interests and enhance their joint negotiating capacity." In 2003, the G-77 was joined by the creation of the G-20, or group of 20 developing states, an organization including 23 members in 2008. The organization was spearheaded by Brazil, India, and South Africa, whose foreign ministers brought it into existence on June 20, 2003, with the Brasilia Declaration. Other prominent members include Argentina, China, Indonesia, and Mexico, all members of the more prominent G-20 offshoot of the G-7.

The operation of the G-77 highlights the leverage problem the developing world has had in achieving developed-world status. In the 1970s, the G-77 issued a call for a New International Economic Order (NIEO), the most prominent feature of which was a call for the developed countries to transfer 1.5 percent of their annual wealth to the developing world each year to facilitate the developmental process. This figure was wildly in excess of the amount the developed countries were willing even to contemplate. In 2009, for instance, the gross domestic product/purchasing power parity (GDP/PPP) of the United States stood at $14.3 trillion, meaning a 1.5 percent transfer would have been over $200 billion; the U.S. developmental assistance budget is about 1/10 of that amount. Considerable moral exhortation by G-77 was unsuccessful in convincing the developed states to adopt the NIEO, which died a silent, unfulfilled death.

The G-7/G-20 Transition

The G-7 has existed since 1985, when a group of finance ministers from the countries that would form its membership met at the Plaza Hotel in New York to discuss mutual efforts to coordinate foreign exchange intervention to drive down the value of an overinflated U.S. dollar. From this meeting, G-7 evolved as a series of regular annual or semiannual meetings among what Elliott describes as the "rich G-7 countries." The membership of G-7 (and also G-20) and some of its pertinent characteristics are depicted in Table 12.1.

The G-7 countries are a homogenous lot. All are well-established economic powers with strong democratic traditions. Except for Japan, all are Caucasian with some colonial background (except for Canada). Their economic homogeneity is best shown through their uniformly high GDP/capita figures and low economic growth rates. All belong to the OECD and the Bretton Woods institutions.

When the G-7 was formed, its members arguably were the world's premier economic powers, the seven states including the North American economic giants, the core of the EU, and Japan. In terms of standards of living measured by GCP/capita, they remain at or near the top, challenged only by Australia

TABLE 12.1

G-7, G-20 Characteristics (2008)

Country	GDP/ PPP*	GDP Global Rank**	GDP/ Capita	Economic Growth
G-7 Members				
Canada	1.30 T	12	$39,300	0.6
France	2.1 T	8	$32,700	0.7
Germany	2.86 T	5	$34,800	1.3
Italy	1.82 T	10	$31,000	−0.7
Japan	4.34 T	3	$34,200	−0.4
United Kingdom	2.23 T	6 Tie	$36,600	0.7
United States	14.3 T	1	$47,000	1.3
G-20 Additions				
Argentina	675 B		$14,200	7.1
Australia	801 B		$38,100	4.7
Brazil	1.99 T	9	$10,100	5.2
China	7.8 T	2	$6,000	9.8
India	3.2 T	4	$2,800	6.6
Indonesia	916 B		$3,900	6.1
Korea, South	1.28 T	13	$26,000	2.5
Mexico	1.56 T	11	$14,200	1.4
Russia	2.23 T	6 Tie	$15,800	6.0
Saudi Arabia	583 B		$20,100	4.2
South Africa	490 B		$10,000	2.8
Turkey	906 B		$12,000	1.5
European Union	14.9 T		$32,900	−0.4

*GDP/PPP = gross domestic product/purchasing power parity.
**For countries with economies of over $1 trillion (U.S.).
Source: All figures from Infoplease, Economic Statistics by Country, 2008.

and a few oil-rich states that are otherwise economically unexceptional. In terms of gross size and pace of economic growth, however, the G-7 countries are no longer the unassailable world standard, and it is in partial recognition of changing economic importance that the shift from G-7 to G-20 is based.

The G-7 no longer encompasses the world's largest economies. Using that standard—reflected in the GDP Global Rank column of Table 12.1—three current members (France, Italy, and Canada) would no longer qualify, replaced by BRIC members China, India, and Russia. All three of these latter countries, however, are unlike the original G-7. Only India is meaningfully democratic, and all have significantly lower standards of living and higher growth rates than the G-7 countries. India and China in particular share the common characteristic of having been prominent members of the organizations that have advocated the developmental agenda *and* being states that have succeeded extravagantly in entering the globalization system. As noted in Chapter 11, Russia stands apart from the rest.

The G-20 is the creation of the G-7 at the group's meeting of finance ministers on September 25, 1999, at Cologne, Germany. Like so many economic institutions, it came into being as the result of upheaval, the financial crisis of 1997–1998, "to promote international financial stability" by broadening participation in the alleviation of the crisis. The first chair of the G-20 was Canadian finance minister Paul Martin, who said at the time that the new forum "will focus on translating the benefits of globalization into higher incomes and better opportunities everywhere" (quoted in Kirton). The G-20, in other words, would promote the globalization model of development.

The G-20 broadens the scope and heft of the G-7 considerably. According to the Global Partnership for Financial Inclusion (GPFI) Web site, "member countries represent 90 percent of global gross national product, 80 percent of world trade (including EU intra-trade), as well as two-thirds of world population." The countries added also make the G-20 entirely more diverse than G-7 in a variety of ways.

As Figure 12.1 shows, there are 19 countries that are members (the seven G-7 states plus 12 others); the 20th "state" member is the EU, which provides indirect membership for EU countries not otherwise represented in G-20. The 19 countries represented are all prominent economically but are not the 19 largest economies in the world. At $490 billion GDP/PPP, South Africa has the smallest economy of the G-20, a figure exceeded by at least three nonmembers: Iran at $842 billion, the Netherlands at $670 billion, and Poland at $667 billion (figures are from 2008 and are provided by Infoplease). The Dutch and Poles, of course, have indirect membership through the EU. Other economically prominent states that are not members include Pakistan ($453 billion), Egypt ($442 billion), Belgium ($390 billion), Malaysia ($386 billion), Nigeria ($381 billion), Sweden ($348 billion), and Venezuela ($338 billion).

The G-20 nonetheless adds enormous diversity to the G-7 and injects a significant number of proponents of extension of globalization into the ranks. At one obvious level, it corrects the anomaly of a G-7 that does not totally

Country	G-7	G-20 (developing)	OECD	G-77	WTO
Argentina		X		X	X
Australia			X		X
Brazil		X		X	X
Canada	X		X		X
China		X		X	X
France	X		X		X
Germany	X		X		X
India		X		X	X
Indonesia		X		X	X
Italy	X		X		X
Japan	X		X		X
S. Korea			X		X
Mexico		X	X		X
Russia					
Saudi Arabia				X	X
S. Africa		X		X	X
Turkey			X		X
U.K.	X		X		X
U.S.	X		X		X
EU					

FIGURE 12.1 G-20 Institutional Memberships.

represent the world's largest and most influential economies by incorporating not only the rising powers—China and India, but also the slightly smaller but increasingly important countries like Brazil, South Korea, and Mexico—among trillion-dollar-plus economies. It accomplishes this without depriving G-7 countries no longer at the top of their premier status.

The new membership includes two categories of states. The first group includes highly developed states that are members of the OECD but whose economies have historically been less central internationally than those of the G-7 members: Australia, Mexico, South Korea, and Turkey. These four countries are comparatively wealthy and developed, with relatively high per capita GDPs (higher for Australia and Korea, lower for Mexico and Turkey). None of the four are members of the G-77, and only Mexico is part of the G-20 developing-country group.

The other seven members of the G-20 clearly represent the developing world and its network of associations. All are members of both the G-20 developing countries and the G-77, and most have been vocal proponents of the developmental agenda. Generally speaking, they meet the economic criteria of aspiring developing countries: comparatively low standards of living (per capita GDP from $2,800 to $20,100) and comparatively high economic growth rates (2.8–9.8 percent). They vary considerably in size (China has the world's largest population and second largest economy, while South Africa has the 25th largest population and 20th largest economy) and thus geopolitical influence. What they share, beyond their aspiration to globalization prosperity, is a history of advocacy of the developmental agenda.

CONCLUSION

A truly global globalization process requires extending the developmental aspects of the system and its benefits to large reaches of the globe into which it has not yet protruded. Extension of globalization has occurred, but it has been limited, and it certainly has not spread to all the places that aspire to its status. The primary barrier to a greater dispersion of the prosperity is the lack of the kind of economic development that makes nonparticipating aspirants attractive to the globalizers. The globalized world is, after all, a rich man's club, and until outsiders gain the characteristics and values of the members, they are not going to be allowed to join.

Not all countries, of course, want to join. There is, for instance, little clamoring for inclusion within many Middle Eastern countries fearful of the westernization that is part and parcel of the process. Among those that do want to join, the problem is how to gain the resources to develop in ways that will make them attractive. The developed countries inside the globalized world and the developing countries on the outside have disagreed on how development should be financed. Because the globalizers have possessed the necessary resources, they have until recently been able to control the outcome.

The rising economic powers are changing the environment. Like the proverbial oasis camel, countries like China, India, and Brazil have poked their heads under the tent flaps symbolized by the G-7, and they have become full members of the discussions that will ensue. The G-20 is now *their* forum as well as that of the traditional powers, and they will add the developmental agenda to future discussions about extending globalization.

The G-20 has become a fixture of the landscape since its inception in 1999 as, in the words of the GPFI Web site, the "premier forum" for promoting "open and constructive discussions between industrial and emerging market countries on key issues related to economic stability." The decision by the G-7 countries to suspend regular meetings (while retaining the option of special ad hoc conclaves) and the convening of the G-20 "summit meeting" in Seoul, Korea, in November 2010 suggest the permanence of the institutional shift that has occurred.

Where all this will lead substantively in terms of the outcome of the process of development is, of course, anybody's guess. The institutional movement from the G-7 to the G-20 is both a recognition that change has happened and a platform and framework for future change. The platform itself is a dynamic, not a static, construct. It is only a matter of time until some of the emerging countries outside G-20 are admitted, and when they are, the structure and direction of the effort may shift as well.

SUGGESTED ACTIVITIES AND QUESTIONS

1. What is the concept of extending globalization? What is its place in the discussion of international economics, including development?
2. What are the dynamic bases of globalization? Describe them. How are these bases reflected in the Washington consensus?

3. Describe the process of globalization as a developed world–developing world competition. How has this been manifested in contending visions of how globalization should be extended?
4. What is the basic relationship between development and globalization? Why is it "sequential"? To what aspects of development does globalization contribute and not contribute?
5. Describe the developmental agenda of the developing world and why it has historically been less than successful.
6. Why is infrastructure development key to economic development and making developing economies attractive to globalizing forces? Why are private sources of funding reluctant to underwrite infrastructure development?
7. How has the institutional underpinning of the international economy evolved over time? How have the positions of the two sides in the debate over globalization been represented institutionally?
8. How does the shift from the G-7 to the G-20 represent an important shift in the institutional setting over the extension of globalization? Include in your response relevant comparisons and contrasts of the characteristics of G-7 countries and the countries added to forum G-20.

SUGGESTED READINGS AND RESOURCES

Abdelal, Rawi and Adam Segal. "Has Globalization Reached Its Peak?" *Foreign Affairs* 86, 1 (January/February 2007), 103–114.

Ahmia, Monrad. *The Group of 77 at the United Nations.* New York: Oxford University Press, 2006.

Blinder, Alan S. "Offshoring: The Next Industrial Revolution." *Foreign Affairs* 85, 2 (March/April 2006), 113–128.

Elliott, Larry. "G-7 Elite Group Makes Way for G-20 and Emerging Nations." *Guardian* (online), October 4, 2009.

Friedman, Thomas L. *The Lexus and the Olive Tree: Understanding Globalization.* New York: Farrar, Straus, and Giroux, 1999.

———. *The World Is Flat: A Brief History of the 21st Century.* New York: Farrar, Straus, and Giroux, 2005.

Kirton, John. "What Is G-20?" University of Toronto: Munk Centre for International Studies, November 30, 1999.

Latham, Michael E. *The Right Kind of Revolution: Modernization, Development, and U.S. Foreign Policy from the Cold War to the Present.* Ithaca, NY: Cornell University Press, 2011.

Orwell, George. *Burmese Days: A Novel.* London: Secker and Wartburg, 1986.

Singer, Max and the Late Aaron Wildawsky. *The Real World Order: Zones of Peace, Zones of Turmoil* (revised edition). Chatham, NJ: Chatham House, 1996.

Snow, Donald M. and Eugene Brown. *International Relations: The Changing Contours of Power.* New York: Longman, 2000.

Wolf, Martin. *Why Globalization Works.* New Haven, CT: Yale University Press, 2004.

Zakaria, Fareed. "India Rising." *Newsweek,* March 6, 2006, 24–42.

———. *The Post-American World.* New York: W. W. Norton, 2008.

WEB SITES

General sources: http://www.globalpolicy.org/globalization/globalization-of-the-economy-2-1.html; http://yaleglobal.yale.edu

CIA World Factbook: https://www.cia.gov/library/publications/the-world-factbook/index.html

G-20: http://www.g20.org/about_what_is_g20.aspx; http://www.g20.utoronto.ca/g20whatisit.html

G-77: http://www.g77.org/doc/

G-20 (developing countries): http://en.wikipedia.org/wiki/G20_developing_nations

WTO membership: http://www.wto.org/english/thewto_e/whatis_e/tif_e/org6_e.htm

Global economic statistics (Infoplease): http://www.infoplease.com/world/statistics/economic-statistics-by-country.html

Human Security

There are some international problems that affect people and their well-being across borders that cannot adequately or fully be solved by individual states acting on their own. Sometimes these kinds of problems are referred to as transnational or transstate issues. Because they have large implications for safety, sense of safety, and even survival of individuals, groups, and even states, they are lumped together as matters of human security.

The four chapters in this part address various aspects of this problem that are important in contemporary international relations. Chapter 13, "Global Warming," provides an overview and analysis of the global warming phenomenon and debates surrounding the existence or severity of the problem. Looking at the global effort to deal with the problem through the United Nations (UN) framework and the Kyoto Protocol, it seeks to extrapolate responses to the plans laid out in the 2007 Bali convention on climate change that were supposed to be formalized in Copenhagen in 2009. These efforts largely failed, and organized international efforts remain stymied. Chapter 14, "International Migration," looks at the global movement of people between countries, a phenomenon currently primarily associated with migration from the developing to the developed world. Current trends are likely to continue or even be accentuated by demographic change and globalization. The case study focuses on the U.S.–Mexico border as a prominent example of this phenomenon.

The final two chapters deal with more direct threats to human security and even existence. Chapter 15, "Secession and Self-Determination," deals with the desire and attempt by groups of people, usually regionally defined, to break away from an existing state to form a new political entity. The motives for doing so vary considerably, from claims of suppression and fear of genocide to economic exploitation. The "right" of secession is hotly contested in international law. The case of the establishment of the Republic of South Sudan, with examples from the American Civil War, examines the issue in detail. Chapter 16, "Terrorism," attempts to define and describe the problem of terrorism and, based upon that discussion, to find its solution. The chapter culminates in a discussion of possible future directions and possible termination of the so-called "war on terror" that has been the centerpiece of American and other efforts to suppress the problem.

Global Warming: Facing the Problem After Copenhagen

PRÉCIS

Global warming represents one of the clearest, yet most controversial, issues facing the world. It is clearly a problem that cannot be solved by the individual efforts of states, but must be done collectively if it is to be done successfully at all. It is controversial because there is substantial public, if not scientific, disagreement both about the nature and severity of the problem and over the structure and content of proposed solutions to climate change that is the clear byproduct of global warming.

This case study looks at the problem from two related vantage points. The first is an examination of the controversial process surrounding international efforts to deal with global warming. The lightning rod for this effort has been the Kyoto Protocol of 1997, which expired in 2012. Attempts to implement and move beyond the actions prescribed in that treaty have failed. The second is on the nature and extent of the problem and thus what does and does not require controlling. The two emphases are related because the nature of the problem has a clear relationship to the kinds and extent of remedies that are proposed for it.

The issue of global warming—the extent to which the earth's climate is gradually increasing in temperature due to human actions or natural processes—is one of the most controversial, divisive, and yet consequential problems facing international relations in the twenty-first century. No one, of course, favors a gradual or precipitous change in global climate because the consequences could be catastrophic. The issue contains a perceptual disconnect. Virtually all non-interested scientists (over 97 percent, according to a survey quoted in the May 16, 2013 *International Herald Tribune*) agree that the problem is real. Yet, as Helms points out, "the public gets more indifferent or even skeptical."

Whereas some question whether global warming exists at all, others predict dire consequences unless drastic measures are taken to curb the contributors to warming the earth, mostly the burning of fossil fuels, and especially coal, in support of a broad variety of human activities. The fact that fossil fuels are used to produce energy links global warming to the energy question, the subject of Chapter 2. There are significant differences on the parameters of the problem (exactly what will be affected and how much), and on the quality of the science underlying claims on either side. As might be expected, projections diverge most when extrapolations are made far into the future.

Regardless of how serious the problem is, global warming is clearly a classic, full-blown transnational issue. As Eileen Claussen and Lisa McNeilly put it, "Climate change is a global problem that demands a global solution because emissions from one country can impact the climate in all other countries." Global warming, in other words, will be curbed internationally or not at all.

The underlying dynamic, if not its seriousness, can be easily stated. Global warming is the direct result of the release of so-called greenhouse gases into the atmosphere in volumes that are in excess of the capacity of the ecosystem to eliminate them naturally. Although there are a number of these gases, the vast majority of the problem comes from the burning of fossil fuels such as petroleum, natural gas, coal, and wood, which releases carbon dioxide, methane, and nitrous oxide (what the Kyoto Protocol calls the "three most important" contributors to pollution) into the air in large quantities. The natural method of containing the amount of carbon dioxide and its ultimate damaging residue, carbon, in the atmosphere is the absorption and conversion of that gas in so-called carbon sinks, which separate the two elements (carbon and oxygen) and release them harmlessly back into the atmosphere. In nature, the equatorial rain forests have been where these sinks have historically done most of the work.

The problem of excessive carbon dioxide comes from both sides of the production and elimination process. The burning of fossil fuels, which are the source of much energy production and thus economic activity worldwide, has increased steadily over the last quarter century. Most of the added emissions have come from new contributors: countries entering the developed world by increasing production and their energy usage. China has been the most conspicuous example, both because of its geometrically growing need for and use of energy and its reliance on the dirtiest, most carbon-releasing fossil fuel—coal—to produce that energy. As a result, there is more carbon dioxide in the atmosphere than there used to be, and because carbon dioxide has a half-life of roughly a century, that which is emitted today will be around for a long time. At the same time, cutting down trees in the rain forests has reduced the number and quality of natural sinks, thereby reducing nature's ability to capture and convert carbon dioxide into innocuous elements.

The cumulative effect is that there is more carbon dioxide in the atmosphere than there used to be, and it acts as a greenhouse gas. What this means is that as heat from the sun radiates off the earth and attempts to return in an adequate amount into space to maintain current climate, carbon dioxide acts as a "trap" that retains the heat in the atmosphere rather than allowing it to escape. This blanketing effect keeps excess heat in the atmosphere, and the result is a warmer atmosphere and the phenomenon of global warming—net increases in atmospheric temperatures in specific locales and worldwide.

Responsibility for causing global warming and thus primary liability for doing something about it is also controversial. Significantly, the problem has become a mainstay of the global debate between the more industrially developed countries mostly located in the Northern Hemisphere and the less developed countries, many of which are located in the Southern Hemisphere. One aspect of this debate has to do with causation of the problem and hence responsibility. Fossil fuel burning is at the heart of warming; clearly, much of the problem was originally created in the North, which has already gone through an industrializing process for which fossil-fuel-based energy was and remains an important component. From the vantage point of developing countries that aspire to the material success of the developed countries, this creates two points of contention. On one hand, they view developed countries as the cause of the problem and thus believe those countries should solve the problem by reducing emissions. At the same time, developed countries ask them to refrain from the same kind of fossil-fuel-driven growth that they underwent, because doing so will simply make the greenhouse gas effect worse. The call for self-abnegation (under the banner of "sustainable development") by those countries that were fossil fuel self-indulgers strikes many in the developing world as hypocritical, to say the least. Currently, this aspect of the problem centers primarily on India and more particularly on China, which is now the world's second largest producer of carbon dioxide.

The recently expired Kyoto Protocol of 1997 (so named after the city where it was finalized) has been the most visible symbol of the global warming process and has become the lightning rod of the procedural and substantive debate over it. The protocol is a very technical, complicated document, the heart of which is a series of guidelines for the reduction of emissions almost exclusively by the developed countries in accordance with a timetable established in the document. The requirements of the agreement have raised controversy because of the differential levels of reduction they impose, especially in the United States. The Kyoto Protocol expired in 2012, creating a sense of concern among supporters of international attempts to control global warming through international regulation and a sense of relief among skeptics of global warming and opponents of provisions of the protocol. The process of modifying and extending the protocol began formally in Bali, Indonesia, on Kyoto's 10th anniversary on December 1, 2007, which laid out the principles to guide negotiations for a new, stronger accord in Copenhagen, Denmark, during December 2009. The Copenhagen summit failed to move the process forward, and the future of international attempts at global climate control are in limbo.

This introduction has laid out some of the basic underlying issues about global warming and the Kyoto Protocol as its symbol. The next section will briefly examine the process by which the international community moved to the formalization of the effort to contain and reverse global warming and where that effect appears to be heading. Because the urgency (or even the need) to engage in such a process depends on whether or to what extent the problem exists, positions on global warming are then presented. The case concludes by looking at the prospects for global warming and the institutionalization of efforts to contain it.

THE ROAD TO KYOTO—AND BEYOND?

Although the Kyoto Protocol has been the most visible symbol of global efforts to curb carbon emissions and thus to slow global warming, it was in fact an evolutionary step in a process that was begun well before the protocol was adopted and has continued to evolve since. Kyoto became the lightning rod for support or opposition because it provided the most comprehensive set of regulations and guidelines that had occurred to that point. Its expiration accentuates its symbolism. Since it lapsed, there is no international agreement that formalizes the effort to curb global warming. At the same time, a retrospective on the life of the protocol suggests it was hardly a success anyway. As critic Helm said bluntly in a 2013 interview, "Kyoto has had no effect whatsoever. Kyoto is fatally flawed."

Five points can be made about the road to Kyoto by means of introduction. First, concern about climatic change had been going on for a long time before the protocol was adopted, and the formal international process that resulted in the document began almost 20 years earlier. Second, the document and its requirements were highly technical, even arcane, to the point that only the truly committed really understood them. Third, the Kyoto process has been less than a ringing success. Its provisions produced some regional emissions reductions in the EU area, but they did not reduce or even particularly slow rising global emissions. Fourth, the United States has historically been the largest emitter, and thus has a special place in the process. Fifth, the 800-pound gorilla in the global warming equation is China, whose meteoric economic renaissance has also made it the major barrier to future progress on global warming.

The Kyoto Process

The chronology of global warming as a formal international concern is described by the United Nations Framework Convention for Climate Change (UNFCCC) Secretariat in a 2000 publication, *Caring for Climate*. According to that document, the first step in the process occurred in 1979, when the First World Climate Conference was held. That meeting brought together international scientists concerned with the effects of human intervention in the climate process and the possible pernicious effects of trends that they observed. This meeting also provided the first widespread recognition of the greenhouse gases phenomenon, which was largely known only within the scientific community before then.

The international momentum began to pick up in 1988 with two events. First, the United Nations General Assembly adopted a resolution, 43/53, urging the "protection of global climate for present and future generations of mankind." The resolution was sponsored by Malta. In a separate action, the World Meteorological Organization (WMO) and the United Nations Environmental Programme created the Intergovernmental Panel on Climate Change (IPCC) and charged this new body with assessing the scientific evidence on the subject. As requested, the IPCC issued its First Assessment Report in 1990, concluding that the threat of climate change was real and worthy of further study and concern. Also in 1990, the World Climate Conference held its second meeting in Geneva, Switzerland, and called for a global treaty on climate change. This call in turn prompted the General Assembly to pass another resolution, 45/12, which commissioned negotiations for a convention on climate change to be conducted by the Intergovernmental Negotiating Committee (INC). This body first met in February 1991 as an intergovernmental body. On May 9, 1992, the INC adopted the UNFCCC, which was presented for signature at the Rio De Janeiro United Nations Conference on the Environment and Development (the Earth Summit) in June 1992. The requisite number of signatures was obtained in 1994 and the UNFCCC entered force on March 21, 1994. The process leading to the Kyoto Protocol was thus officially launched.

One express feature of the UNFCCC was an annual meeting of all members of the Convention (which numbered 199 members and observers in 2010) known as the Conference of the Parties (COP). The first COP was held in 1995 in Berlin. The third COP was held in Kyoto, Japan; the result was the Kyoto Protocol.

The Protocol

The Kyoto Protocol is a complicated document (references to the whole treaty can be found in the Web sites section of this chapter), the details of which go beyond present purposes. Several elements can, however, be laid out that provide a summary of what the protocol attempts to do and, based on those purposes, the objections that have been raised to it.

The overarching goal of the protocol was reduction in the production and emission of greenhouse gases and thus the arrest and reversal of the adverse effects of climate changes caused by these gases. The protocol identifies six gases for control and emission reduction. Three of these gases are "most important": carbon dioxide (CO_2), methane (CH_4), and nitrous oxide (N_2O). This importance comes from the large relative contribution of these gases to the problem: Carbon dioxide accounts for fully half of "the overall global warming effect arising from human activities" in the UNFCCC's language, followed by 18 percent for methane and 6 percent for nitrous oxide. For the United States in 2002, for instance, the percentages were 83 percent carbon dioxide, 9 percent methane, and 6 percent nitrous oxide, according to David Victor. The other three specified categories, the "long-lived industrial gases," are hydrofluorocarbons (HFCs), perfluorocarbons (PFCs), and sulfur hexafluoride (SF_6).

The goal of the protocol was a global reduction in the production of targeted gases of 5 percent below the baseline year for measuring emissions,

1990, by the period 2008–2012. The baseline year established how much each developed country contributed to emission levels. These levels were then used for two purposes: to determine how much reduction each targeted country must accomplish, and to provide a measuring stick for determining when the protocol comes fully into effect. For determining these contributions, the protocol further divides the countries of the world into three different categories (what it calls Annexes) in terms of the obligations that are incurred.

The Kyoto accord created a complicated set of categories of states that included differential emissions reduction goals for each category. In essence, it placed the burden of reduction on the most developed countries, those members of the OECD with the largest economies, most productive industrial plants, and thus the greatest consumers of fossil-fuel-derived energy. Using 1990 baseline figures for CO_2 emissions as its yardstick, these countries are listed by the amount of emissions they produced and the percentage of the world's total emissions this amount represents. Leading the list by a wide margin is the United States, which was responsible for 36.1 percent of global emissions. Aggregated as a whole, the European Union followed with 24.2 percent, followed by the countries of the Russian Federation with 17.4 percent, and Japan with 8.5 percent (for a total of 86 percent of global emissions). The next largest polluter after these was Australia with 2.1 percent.

Most of the rest of the world was exempted from the reduction quotas or was required to make much smaller contributions. Most critically and controversially, some of the emerging developing states were excluded altogether on the grounds that they had historically not contributed to the problem and that they would learn from the pollution mistakes of the developed world and not follow in the polluting footsteps. That assumption provoked special controversy at the time and has proven almost totally false. China is the major example.

Critics argue that the structure of responsibility within the Kyoto Protocol doomed it to failure. Helm is a leading critic arguing the misplacement of priorities. As he puts it, under the protocol "the focus was on emissions in those countries where emissions were not growing very much—rather than on those countries where they were growing very rapidly."

The key country in the distortion created by Kyoto was China. It was excluded from emissions requirements, meaning it could—and did—vastly increase its fossil-fuel-produced energy greatly without becoming a violator. Attempts by others, notably Europeans, indirectly aided and abetted Chinese economic and pollution growth by transferring polluting enterprises to China. This process put Kyoto and China on a collision course with the United States.

The United States and China

Kyoto has been a growing source of contention between the United States and China. Although the United States was an early supporter of the Kyoto process during the Clinton years, it never signed the protocol, and the Bush administration was a leading global opponent of it. The heart of the

Bush objection was that Kyoto discriminated unfairly against the United States, and much of this assertion was based on the advantage that China had as a non-emissions reducer under its provisions. Although the movement toward shale-basis energy is changing the American national energy profile within the area of global greenhouse gas pollution, China's continued reliance on burning coal—the most polluting fossil fuel—makes it increasingly at the heart of the global problem.

The American position changed almost immediately after Bush took office. On March 13, 2001, he announced that he no longer favored U.S. participation in the Kyoto Protocol. In the process, the administration publicly stated that it would not send the treaty signed by Clinton to the Senate for ratification. As a result, the United States has remained the most important country in the world that was not a party to the protocol and thus does not consider itself subject to its requirements, although it remains a party to the UNFCCC.

Bush administration objections to the protocol, which reflected the views of opponents generally, tended to focus on two basic themes. The first is cost and burden to the United States. Although some other countries have higher percentage reduction quotas than the United States, treaty opponents argued that having to bear 7 percent of 36 percent of the total required reductions was too great a burden. In addition, U.S. emissions were already 15 percent above the 1990 level by the end of the millennium and, according to Victor, rising at 1.3 percent per year, thereby demanding even further reductions. Thus, the United States was being asked to do too much proportionately in comparison to the rest of the world. Compliance was viewed as economically ruinous in terms of the additional expenses of doing business and the loss of comparative advantage to industries in other countries that are not regulated by these requirements, notably China. American conformance to Kyoto standards that do not apply universally thus would unfairly imbalance the "playing field" of economic competition.

This leads to the second objection, which is the exclusion of developing countries from the requirements of the protocol. In most cases, this exclusion is innocuous, as most of these countries do not and will not contribute meaningfully to greenhouse gas in the foreseeable future.

The Bush administration directed its criticism of developing-world exclusion principally at two countries, China and India. China has become a major greenhouse gas emitter. It is already the second largest emitter in the world, and this situation will continue and intensify if China further develops. India does not pose quite as urgent a threat, but with a population roughly the size of China's and an emerging technological and industrial capacity, the sheer magnitude of the country's potential suggests it should be part of the solution before it becomes an overt part of the problem. One of the few signals of progress at Copenhagen was a joint Chinese–American accord to address this problem.

China is, however, the most pressing physical area of concern. China's economic rise (see Chapter 11) has been largely powered by burning coal, which supplies 90 percent of Chinese energy (see Chapter 2). As long as China continues to grow economically and to use coal to power that growth, it will be a persistent, growing part of the global warming problem. As Helm puts it, "Over the (Kyoto) period, the growth of emissions has been . . . based on coal and China and population." China is the epicenter of the problem, because of its commitment to growth for its huge population by burning coal. Ironically, the developing world has conspired inadvertently in this growing dilemma by transferring production to reduce its own emissions counts to a China that contributes even more intensely to the problem by burning coal.

A third, more contemporary objection to the protocol is that it is essentially dated. The argument here is the march of technology and change may have simply outgrown its provisions. John Browne, writing in *Foreign Affairs*, summarizes this argument: "First, Kyoto was simply the starting point of a very long endeavor. Second, we have improved, if still imperfect, knowledge of the challenges and uncertainties that climate change presents. . . . Third, many countries and companies have had experience reducing emissions that have proved that such reductions can be achieved without destroying competitiveness of jobs. Fourth, science and technology have advanced on multiple fronts. Finally, public awareness of the issue has grown."

Another source of technological obsolescence is the emergence of the American-led shale oil and gas revolution. The conversion of American power plants from coal to gas allows a 50 percent reduction in emissions for those plants and thus makes compliance with Kyoto standards attainable even in the absence of the protocol. Should China follow suit, it could contribute greatly to alleviating the problem as well, with or without a new accord.

There is a certain irony here. Shale gas is both less polluting and considerably cheaper than other gas sources to produce, thus providing the United States with a comparative energy cost advantage and allowing it to emerge as an emissions-controlling exemplar. Helm points out the irony in a 2013 interview: "Europeans put all this effort into global leadership on carbon emissions, and that has failed. And the Americans arguably have no sensible energy policy at all, and no climate change policy, and have done much better."

The flaws of the Kyoto Protocol—most prominently the exclusion of China from its dictates—have largely been responsible for the failure to renew it or to forge a modified follow-on agreement. It is at least arguable that until, or unless, China accepts the role as a leader in reducing rather than producing carbon emissions into the ecosystem, all efforts are doomed to fall short or fail altogether. Nevertheless, the process continues.

Bali, Copenhagen, and Beyond

The 10th anniversary of the Kyoto accords was marked by a major UNFCCC conference in Bali, Indonesia, in December 2007. Nearly 10,000 delegates attended the meeting, the purpose of which was to draft a follow-on agreement that would improve upon the results of the Kyoto Protocol. Gaining American participation and support was a major objective of the conferees.

The conference produced two documents of note. One, known as the Bali Road Map, laid out a process for finalizing a new, binding agreement in time for the 2009 meeting in Copenhagen. The other document was the Bali Action Plan, a set of principles to guide deliberations leading to the agreement.

Major issues introduced at the Bali meeting included future targets for carbon-dioxide-emissions reductions and the participation of countries excluded under the annexes of the Kyoto agreement, notably China and India. Mindful of Bush administration objections, the conferees agreed in principle (in the Action Plan) that deep cuts in global emissions will be required, but, according to Fuller and Rivkin, the plan "contains no binding commitments." The American delegation insisted that developing economies must likewise act, and China and India agreed to include alterations of their status in negotiations. These outcomes were sufficiently satisfying to the Bush administration that its delegation endorsed the Bali outcome.

Turning the general agreement into a specific, binding, and effective accord proved to be the hard part—the "devil in the details." Among enthusiasts of global warming control (which included President Obama), there were high hopes for the December 2009 Copenhagen summit. Technically, the Copenhagen conclave was a series of meetings, most prominently the 15th meeting of the Conference of Parties of the UNFCCC (COP15) and the 5th convening of the Meeting of the Parties of the COP members of the Kyoto Protocol (COP/MOP5). The summit was attended by 115 heads of state and generated much anticipation prior to its beginning on December 8.

The Copenhagen summit was a failure. It neither formally proposed nor enacted any binding, mandatory agreements to supersede Kyoto after its 2012 expiration, nor did it succeed in creating the framework for a global treaty by 2012, the goal specified by the Bali Road Map. As the meeting wound down threatening to produce no agreements at all, a group of major countries, including the United States, China, India, Brazil, and South Africa, convened what the UNFCCC Web site called an "Informal High Level Event" on December 18, the day before the summit was to adjourn. The result was something called the Copenhagen Accord calling for a goal of no more than a 2-degree-Fahrenheit increase in global temperatures. This accord was noted but not adopted by the conference.

The process has continued to sputter along since Copenhagen and the expiration of the Kyoto Protocol. The Doha economic summit of late 2012 agreed to extend the Kyoto principle to 2020, when a more comprehensive agreement is supposed to be put into effect, but the prospects for a follow-on agreement remain debatable. A meeting held in Durban, South Africa, in 2011 to draft standards that were not set at Copenhagen was, in Helm's estimate, "a disaster," and the institutional process seems hopelessly stalled, despite the fact that the underlying problem remains unsolved.

WARM AND GETTING WARMER: BUT HOW MUCH?

The urgency and importance of a new global warming accord depends vitally on the urgency and importance of the problem. The debate over global warming is contentious. At least three related factors make a calm, rational debate over the extent and consequences of global warming difficult to conduct. The first is the absence of immediate consequences of whatever change is occurring. Over the past quarter-century or more, climate change in the form of warming has indeed been occurring worldwide, but the effects have been so gradual and generally small that either they have gone unnoticed by most people or have not been definitively attributable to the phenomenon. Were there dramatic events that could be associated with climate change (or equally convincing absences of predicted changes), it would be easier to make the case one way or the other. Certainly global warming is blamed for a number of contemporary events, from the melting of polar ice caps to recent patterns of violent weather, but there is disagreement about whether the man-made global warming that underlies them is the culprit. Superstorm Sandy's effects, for instance, were almost certainly made worse by a rise in sea levels along the Jersey shore, but can that impact be traced to and blamed on global warming?

Second, there are abundant scientific disagreements about the parameters of the problem and its solution. Some of the disagreement is honest, some possibly self-interested, but for every dire prediction about future consequences, there is a rebuttal from somewhere. This debate often becomes shrill and accusatory, leading to confusion in the public about what to believe. In this confusion, the citizenry has a difficult time making reasoned assessments and consequent demands on policy makers to adopt standards.

Third, almost all the projections have until recently been sufficiently far in the future to allow considerable disagreement and to discourage resolution. One can argue that the scientific evidence to date is very strong one way or the other on various consequences of warming; the actual consequences are distant enough, however, that the extrapolation is subject to sufficient variation that scientists can take the same data and reach diametrically opposed conclusions. These extrapolations are often 50 or even 100 years in the future, when most of the people at whom they are aimed will not even be alive to witness or be held accountable for them. Attempts to add urgency to the issues by public figures like former U.S. vice president Al Gore reinforce those who already believe in the problem, but they do not convert skeptics.

The often acrimonious debate over the melting of polar ice caps provides an example of this disagreement. There is no disagreement that ice caps are melting; the disagreement is about why and what this means. Those most worried about global warming argue that the burning of fossil fuels is the culprit, and the consequences include rising ocean levels (mostly from melting in Antarctica) and ecological change (especially in the Arctic). Critics contend there is little evidence that the changes are not natural and dispute the notion of an accelerated rise in sea levels.

Getting Too Warm?

That global climate is changing is not contested on any side of the debate over global warming. The Intergovernmental Panel on Climate Change (IPCC) has investigated the extent to which this has happened in the past and has concluded that the average surface temperature of the earth increased by about 1 degree Fahrenheit during the twentieth century and "that most of the warming observed over the past 50 years is attributable to human activities." (Much of the IPCC material in this section is from the 2001 report of Group I–III of the IPCC, cited in the suggested readings.) Extrapolating from trends in the last century, the IPCC predicts additional warming between 2.2–10 degrees Fahrenheit (1.4–5.8 degrees Celsius) in this century. The primary culprits are the greenhouse gases cited in the Kyoto Protocol that result from deforestation (and its destruction of carbon sinks), energy production from the combustion of fossil fuels (natural gas, oil, and coal), transportation (primarily cars and trucks, but also trains and other modes), cattle production (methane gases), rice farming, and cement production.

A variety of effects have been observed and attributed to these changes. In some areas, birds are laying eggs a few weeks earlier than they used to, butterflies are moving their habitats farther up mountains to avoid lowland heat, and trees are blooming earlier in the spring and losing their leaves later in the fall. Any of these changes can be dismissed as of low relative concern, but there are more fundamental changes alleged with more obvious consequences. Warming, the IPCC II reports, shows that snow accumulation is decreasing worldwide, as is the global supply of ice pack. At the same time, glaciers are retreating worldwide (some of the most dramatic American examples are in places like Glacier National Park in Montana), sea levels and ocean temperatures have risen, and rainfall patterns in many regions have changed as well. In addition, there is evidence that permafrost is thawing in the polar regions, that lakes are freezing later and thawing earlier, and that even some plant and animal species have declined and may disappear due to changes in climate.

Some of the most dramatic examples involve the effects on coastal regions. The projected problems arise both from the gradual rise of oceanic levels and the warming of ocean waters. Both are a concern because of the large and growing portion of populations residing in coastal locations (it is, for instance, a major demographic reality in the United States that the population is gradually moving out of the central parts of the country toward more temperate coastal regions).

The extent of these effects, of course, depends on the amount of change caused by global warming. IPCC II data project an average rise of between 6 and 36 inches in sea levels by 2100. Using the higher figure, the impact on some countries would be dramatic. A 36-inch rise would inundate territory in which 10 million people live in Bangladesh alone, forcing their relocation to scarce higher land. The same increase would cover 12 percent of the arable land of the Nile River delta in Egypt, which produces crops on which over 7 million people are dependent. Some estimates suggest the island country of Vanuatu in the South Pacific would simply disappear under the rising waters. Worldwide, it is estimated that 45 million people would be displaced.

Warming of ocean water could also have dramatic effects, for instance, by affecting ocean currents that now have an influence on climate in various parts of the world. The Atlantic Gulf Stream, for instance, could be affected by warmer water coming from polar regions, changing patterns for the coastal United States and Europe. As an example, Gulf Stream effects that tend to keep major hurricanes off parts of the American coast (e.g., the South Carolina Lowcountry) could be diverted, resulting in a new pattern of hurricane, tornado, and storm patterns. Large-scale changes in patterns of ocean circulation are possible worldwide. The cumulative effect, according to the IPCC, could be "a widespread increase in the risk of flooding for human settlements (tens of millions of inhabitants in settlements studied) from both increased heavy precipitation and sea level rise" (IPCC II).

Not So Fast

Some scientists—admittedly, a relative few—disagree with the accuracy of these projections and the direness of the consequences that they project. There is little disagreement about the historical record (e.g., the amount of climate change in the last century) because that is based on observable data that can be examined for accuracy. There is, however, some disagreement on the precise causes of change (e.g., scientists affiliated with the power industry tend to downplay the impact of energy production). There is also disagreement on projections of trends and effects extrapolated into the future. The main source of this disagreement is the fact that any projections are based not in observations of effects in a future that has not yet occurred, but are instead based on projections of historically grounded observations (and hence scientific inference) into a future the exact dimensions of which cannot be known or entirely predicted. Extrapolation becomes more uncertain the farther predictions are cast into the future, and thus there is an increased level of disagreement the farther into the future one goes. Because the deleterious effects of global warming are argued to be cumulative and thus more serious the farther into the future one makes projections, the basis for lively, at times acrimonious, discussions is thus built into the debate.

There tend to be three criticisms of global warming scientists that can be phrased in terms of questions. The first is the factual content of the warnings: How much effect will global warming have? A second, corollary question is how much those effects will accumulate under different assumptions about natural and man-made adjustments to these effects? Third, how difficult are the solutions?

The problem, of course, is that there is disagreement on these matters. Consider, for instance, the projections on how much average surface temperatures will increase in this century if action is not taken. Estimates range from 1 to 10 degrees Fahrenheit, and that is a considerable range in terms of the consequences to the world and humankind. If the actual figure is at the upper end of that spectrum, then things like snow pack, glacier, and polar ice cap melting will be considerable, with oceans rising at the upper limits of predictions (around three feet). Parts of Tampa Bay and New Orleans, among other places, will be under water unless levees are constructed to keep the water out, and Vanuatu may become the next Lost City of Atlantis (an analogy often made by global warming scientists). If the rise in mean surface temperature is closer to or at the lower extreme (a degree or so), however, the consequences are probably far less dire.

Who knows which part of the range is correct? The answer is that with any scientific certitude, no one does. The amount of warming is necessarily an extrapolation into a future that does not exist, after all, not an observation of something that does. Clearly, it is in the interests of those who either do not believe in the more severe projections or who would be most adversely affected by concerted efforts to reduce emissions to believe in the lower projections and thus to deny the more severe reactions. Because of the severity of the consequences of change at the upper levels of estimation, most climate change scientists tend to base their concerns on these possibilities rather than at lower levels of consequence.

The layperson is left up in the air. Because the effects are not immediate and unambiguous, the average person has little way to answer the second question: What does all this mean? Is the world headed for an environmental catastrophe if something is not done to slow, stop, or reverse global warming? The scientists on both sides of the issue are passionate and self-convinced, but they have not, by and large, made a case to the world's publics that is compelling, understandable, and convincing—one way or the other. In a world of more instantly consequential problems, it is hard to bring oneself to develop the passion that the advocates, regardless of scientific credentials, have on the issue.

This leads to the third question, which brings the concern full circle and returns to the Kyoto Protocol and beyond: What should be done about the problem? The immediate answer, of course, is that it depends on how bad the problem is. Most of the world has accepted the basic science of those warning about the more dire consequences of not solving the global warming problem, and the United States has until recently been prominent among major powers (and greenhouse gas emitters) in denying or downplaying the problem and resisting international solutions. The major source of historic U.S. objection is not the veracity of global warming science, but is instead directed at the differential obligations for solving it that Kyoto prescribes: reductions with economic consequences that would make the American economy less competitive and the exclusion of developing-world countries with large pollution potentials from regulation. In important ways, it is a U.S.–China problem.

There is, of course, a hedge in answering the third question that reflects a deep American belief that technology will somehow find a way to ameliorate the problem, either by finding a way to decrease the emission of greenhouse gases or to increase the ability to absorb and neutralize those gases and their consequences. That is the position often taken by the American energy and transportation industries, and it is an approach that has worked to solve other problems at other times. The revolution in shale gas exploitation in the past several years may be providing this technological "fix" by allowing the substitution of gas for coal burning. It aids both sources of the problem. It allows the United States to reduce carbon emissions without joining anything like the Kyoto system to which many Americans object, and because it accomplishes this at very low costs, it improves American economic competitiveness, thereby breaking the link between emissions control and economic disadvantage.

CONCLUSION

No one disputes that global warming is taking place or that its effects are not pernicious to some degree. There are no pro–global warmers. However, there is considerable reluctance to attack and eradicate the problem, and this has until recently been especially true in the United States, whose participation in the effort is absolutely critical to its solution.

The United States, along with China, is both the heart of the problem and its solution, or at least amelioration. American alienation from the international effort to curb global warming arose from what many Americans viewed as two unfair aspects of the Kyoto process: the imposition of crippling emissions reduction requirements that disadvantaged the country in the global economy and the exclusion of China from emissions requirements. The two objections were, of course, interrelated, as Chinese exclusion and American inclusion added to Chinese comparative advantage in a number of areas of production costs, largely at the expense of American competitors. The resulting American pique crippled the impact of the global accord but was also understandable in purely economic terms.

The tables have turned decisively. China is now well on its way to becoming the world's greatest polluter, and now it is reluctant to endorse a follow-on to Kyoto that would create the same requirements and disadvantages for it that the original Kyoto regime had for the United States. From an American standpoint, a virtuous circle is emerging. Thanks largely to the conversion of power plants from burning coal to gas, the Americans are now reducing emissions unilaterally and are even righteously proclaiming their intent to move unilaterally to the targets established using 1990 baselines. China, meanwhile, continues to produce 90 percent of its power from burning coal, the most polluting of the fossil fuels, making it even more the heart of the problem while the United States becomes part of something like the solution.

One obvious answer for China is the exploitation of its own massive shale formations—the largest in the world, as pointed out in Chapter 2. China lags far behind the North Americans in shale technology and would have to purchase much of that technology from the United States and Canada, a reversal in Chinese economic patterns. The Chinese have not yet bitten the bullet on this conversion, leaving this solution somewhere in the future.

Like world energy generally, shale gas (including the exploitation of methane hydrate from the world's sea beds) has the potential to change the dynamics of international global warming efforts, but essentially all scientists agree that it is an interim, not a permanent solution. Shale gas is, after all, still a fossil fuel, and it does emit carbon, if in smaller amounts than other fossil fuels like coal and petroleum. Ultimately, it allows the prospects of a "breather" of sorts in the process, but it only buys time for progress in the ultimate quest of a global energy system freed of dependence on fossil fuels and their emission of carbon residues. In that quest, the movement to renewable sources of clean energy remains the solution both to world energy needs and the scourge of global warming.

At the beginning of the case study, global warming was described as a true transnational issue, and one with unique aspects. That uniqueness has at least three significant emphases. First, global warming is truly a global issue that affects the entire planet and can only be solved by essentially universal actions by the countries of the world. Particular burdens fall on countries like the United States and China that contribute most to the problem. It is hard, arguably impossible, to see how these problems can be remediated without the active participation of both countries. Second, responding to global warming will have direct impacts on two of the most important motors of the global economy: energy production and use, and transportation. Disruptions to either or both of these industries could have catastrophic economic effects for the world generally. The problem of global warming, in other words, is important to everyone's well-being. Third, global warming is the only environmental change problem that intensifies or is intensified by other major environmental problems. Rising water levels affect the ability of the earth to produce food, and desertification is increased by warming, to cite two problems created. The effects of global warming are, in other words, pervasive.

How warm is the world getting, what does that matter, and what should or must be done or not done about it? These are the questions asked throughout this case study, and they are all questions that have potentially vital answers for the good of all of us, individually and collectively. Answering those questions satisfactorily is vital to the well-being of everyone living on the planet.

SUGGESTED ACTIVITIES AND QUESTIONS

1. Describe the global warming problem. What causes it? What are the short- and long-term consequences of global warming?
2. Describe global warming as a developed- versus developing-world political and climatic problem. Who bears responsibility for creating and solving the problem?
3. Describe the process leading to the Kyoto Protocol. What were the major provisions of the protocol? Which provisions were most controversial? Why have some argued that the protocol was fatally flawed?
4. Why does the United States have a unique place in the global warming and Kyoto Protocol process? What were the major U.S. objections to the protocol? Why can a similar or follow-on protocol not be effective without American participation in its implementation? Apply the same analysis to China.
5. The Kyoto Protocol expired in 2012. Discuss efforts to negotiate a follow-on agreement at Bali and Copenhagen. Why have these meetings failed to produce new accords? What are the implications for the future?
6. What are the major claims made by those who believe that global warming is a major worldwide problem? How do skeptics counter these assertions?
7. Explain the major dilemma of the global warming debate in terms of short- and long-term effects. Are the prospects sufficiently dire that you believe we should endure short-term sacrifices to guard against long-term dangers?
8. How does shale gas offer at least a temporary "fix" to global warming, especially for the United States? Why is it only a temporary solution?

9. How and why has global warming become a part of Chinese–American economic competition? Why is action by China crucial to approaching and solving the problem?
10. Why is global warming unique as a transnational issue? Explain.

SUGGESTED READINGS AND RESOURCES

Ackerman, John T. *Global Climate Change: Catalyst for International Relations Disequilibria*. PhD Dissertation. Tuscaloosa, AL: University of Alabama, 2004.

Anderson, Terry and Harry I. Miller, eds. *The Greening of U.S. Foreign Policy*. Stanford, CA: Hoover Institution Press, 2000.

Beyond Kyoto: Advancing the International Effort Against Climate Change. Arlington, VA: Pew Center on Global Climate Change, 2003.

Black, Richard. "Copenhagen Climate Summit Undone by 'Arrogance.'" *BBC News* (online), March 16, 2010.

Browne, John. "Beyond Kyoto." *Foreign Affairs* 83, 4 (July/August 2004), 20–32.

Claussen, Eileen and Lisa McNeilly. *Equity and Global Climate Change: The Complex Elements of Global Fairness*. Arlington, VA: Pew Center for Global Climate Change, 2000.

Crook, Clive. "The Sins of Emission." *The Atlantic* 301, 3 (April 2008), 32–34.

Diehl, Paul R. and Niles Peter Gleditsch, eds. *Environmental Conflict*. Boulder, CO: Westview, 2001.

Fuller, Thomas and Andrew C. Rivkin. "Climate Plan Looks Beyond Bush's Tenure." *New York Times* (online), December 16, 2007.

Gupta, Joyeeta. *Our Simmering Planet: What to Do About Global Warming*. New York: Zed Books, 2001.

Helm, Dieter. *The Carbon Crunch: How We're Getting Climate Change Wrong—and How to Fix It*. New Haven, CT: Yale University Press, 2012.

Intergovernmental Panel on Climate Change. A Report of Working Groups I–III. *Summary for Policymakers—Climate Change 2001*. Cambridge, UK: Cambridge University Press, 2001.

Luterbacher, Urs and Detlef F. Sprinz, eds. *International Relations and Global Climate Change*. Cambridge, MA: MIT Press, 2001.

Mann, Charles C. "What If We Never Run Out of Oil?" *The Atlantic* 311, 4 (May 2013), 48–63.

Michaels, Patrick J. and Robert C. Balling Jr. *The Satanic Gases: Clearing the Air About Global Warming*. Washington, DC: CATO Institute, 2000.

Palmer, Lisa. "Q and A: The Angry Economist (Dieter Helm)." *New York Times* (online in "Green: A Blog About Energy and the Environment), March 1, 2013.

Pirages, Dennis C. and Theresa Manley DeGeest. *Ecological Security: An Evolutionary Perspective on Globalization*. New York: Rowman and Littlefield, 2004.

Podesta, John and Peter Ogden. "The Security Implications of Climate Change." *Washington Quarterly* 31, 1 (Winter 2007–2008), 115–138.

Schelling, Thomas C. "The Cost of Combating Global Warming: Facing the Tradeoffs." *Foreign Affairs* 75, 6 (November/December 1997), 8–14.

Schuetze, Christopher F. "Ignoring Planetary Peril, a Profound 'Disconnect' Between Science and Doha." *International Herald Tribune* (online), December 6, 2012.

_____. "Scientists Agree Overwhelmingly on Global Warming. Why Doesn't the Public Know That?" *International Herald Tribune* (online), May 16, 2013.

Stern, Todd, and William Antholis. "A Changing Climate: The Road Ahead for the United States." *Washington Quarterly* 31, 1 (Winter 2007–2008), 175–187.

Victor, David C. G. *Climate Change: Debating America's Options.* New York: Council on Foreign Relations Press, 2004.

Vidal, John, Allegra Stratton, and Suzanne Goldenberg. "Low Target, Goals Dropped: Copenhagen Ends in Failure." *Guardian.co.uk* (online), December 19, 2009.

Whitty, Julia. "The Thirteenth Tipping: 12 Global Disasters and 1 Powerful Antidote." *Mother Jones* 31, 6 (November/December 2006), 45–53, 101.

Wirth, Timothy. "Hot Air over Kyoto: The United States and the Politics of Global Warming." *Harvard International Review* 23, 4 (2002), 72–77.

WEB SITES

Assessment of state of environment Yale Center for Environmental Law and Policy: http://epi.yale.edu/

Text of Kyoto Protocol: http://unfccc.int/kyoto_protocol/items/2830.php

Third Assessment Report of the IPCC: http://www.ipcc.ch

International Migration: The U.S.–Mexico Border

PRÉCIS

The movement of people across national borders to resettle—immigration—is a major international phenomenon, and one that dates back to the beginnings of humankind. People move for a variety of reasons, from the hope of economic betterment to the fear of political repression or extinction; the common theme is and has been the attempt to improve the human condition. Today there are roughly 200 million refugees worldwide, with the majority being people from the developing world (Africa, Asia, and Latin America) seeking new homes in the developed world (Europe and North America). The case study application of the movement of Mexicans and Central Americans across the U.S.–Mexico border illustrates the underlying dynamics of worldwide immigration, while adding some unique variables in the form of drug trafficking and terrorism.

M igration is one of the oldest and most enduring aspects of the human experience. According to the International Organization for Migration, there are currently 214 million people living as immigrants in countries other than those of their birth. If all of them were placed in a single political jurisdiction of their own, they would constitute the fifth most populous country in the world.

At some level of remove, essentially everyone is an immigrant or the descendant of immigrants; the only humans who can rightfully claim nonimmigrant status are direct descendants of the earliest humans from the Great Rift Valley in Africa (where the ancestors of today's human population are believed first to have emerged) who still live there. The immigrant label is especially true for North Americans: even those peoples to whom the appellation "Native Americans" is applied arrived here from Asia, probably walking across the then-existing land bridge between Asia and North America in the Bering Straits. Peoples moving from place to place are thus a very enduring part of history.

Immigration is a large, important, and controversial contemporary phenomenon. In 2005, the United Nations (UN) Department of Economic and Social Affairs reported that there were 191 million international immigrants (people residing in countries other than that of their birth). That figure fluctuates from year to year, as some immigrants are repatriated and others leave voluntarily or flee their native lands. The reasons they move are various and complicated, but the net result is a constant flow of people across borders. The arrival of these new peoples has always been a source of controversy of greater or lesser intensity depending on who was trying to settle where in what numbers and for what reasons. No two cases are identical.

The immigrant question has always been important for the United States. As the admonition to "bring me your tired, your huddled masses" on the Statue of Liberty heralds, the United States is a quintessential immigrant state, with waves of immigrants from various places arriving at different times in the country's history to constitute one of the world's most nationally and ethnically diverse populations. Sometimes the process of new immigrant waves has been orderly, open, and noncontentious, but as often as not it has been surrounded by considerable disagreement and rancor.

Immigration has become particularly contentious in the United States over the last two decades because of the large-scale movement of Mexicans and Central Americans across the U.S.–Mexico border. The actual numbers involved are difficult to estimate accurately, because many of the immigrants have been so-called "irregular" or illegal immigrants who, by definition, are unaccounted for when they arrive. Using the 2005 UN figures, it is estimated that about 20 percent of immigrants in the world are in the United States, over half of whom have entered across the U.S.–Mexico border, mostly illegally. The result has been an enormous political controversy in the United States over what to do about this problem, the dimensions and dynamics of which form the case application in this chapter.

Although the American situation is a current manifestation of concern over immigration, it is by no means the only place where the question sits on the public agenda. Europe, for instance, is host to a considerably larger immigrant population than the United States, especially in a few select countries like Germany. To understand the nature of the concern—and to place the current U.S. debate into a global context—it is necessary to look at the immigration question more broadly, which is the purpose of the next section.

PARAMETERS OF IMMIGRATION

Immigration is a normal, daily occurrence in much of the world. Some countries are more permissive about letting citizens leave (emigrate) or enter from other countries (immigrate), but some population movement is a regular part of international activity, and one that is arguably increasing in a globalizing world in which international commerce of all kinds is increasing. Employing an accepted definition used by Koser that an international immigrant is "a person who stays outside his usual country of residence for at least one year," the global total of immigrants today is over 200 million people, as already noted.

Immigrants are often subdivided into more or less controversial categories. Regular international immigrants consist of those individuals who have migrated to a country through legal channels, meaning their immigration is recognized and accepted by the host government. Countries allow immigrants into the country for a variety of reasons and in different numbers depending on the needs or uses they may have for such populations. Parts of Europe—notably Germany—have long admitted workers from places like Turkey to augment shrinking workforces as their populations age (see following discussion), and the United States has historically given priority status to people with particularly needed education and technical skills, such as scientists and engineers from developing countries like India.

There are, however, other categories of immigrants that are more controversial. In the contemporary debate (and especially the U.S.–Mexico case), the most controversial are so-called *irregular immigrants*. The UN Department of Economic and Social Affairs defines this class of people as "those who enter a country without proper authorization or who have violated the terms of stay of the authorization they hold, including by overstaying." Other terms for irregular status include illegal, undocumented, and unauthorized immigrants. As Koser points out, "there are around 40 million irregular immigrants worldwide, of whom perhaps one-third are in the United States." The most publicized and largest part of that total are irregular by virtue of illegal entry into the country; some of the most problematical, however, are individuals who have entered the country legally but have overstayed the conditions of their residence, as in not leaving after student or temporary work visas have expired. This latter category is troublesome because of possible connections to anti-American activities such as terrorism.

A special category of immigrants is refugees. Broadly speaking, refugees are the most prominent example of what the UN Commission on Human Rights (UNCHR) calls "forcibly displaced people," who, according to 2009 UNCHR figures, number about 42 million. The largest numbers of people within this category are refugees (displaced people living outside their native countries) at about 15.2 million, internally displaced persons or IDPs (refugees within their own countries) at about 26 million, and asylum seekers (people who have sought international protection but whose applications have not been acted upon), who numbered 827,000 in 2008. The Refugee Act of 1980 in the United States borrows its definition from the 1951 UN Convention Relating to the Status of Refugees (and its 1967 Protocol), saying a refugee is "a person outside of his or her country of nationality who is unable or unwilling to return because of persecution or a well-grounded fear of persecution on account of race, religion, nationality, membership in a particular social group, or political opinion." Those who seek refugee status often come from developing countries where human misery is both economic and political, meaning that it is sometimes difficult to determine why a particular refugee or group of refugees seeks to migrate. As Koser points out, "though an important legal distinction can be made between people who move for work purposes and those who flee conflict and persecution, in reality the two can be difficult to distinguish."

International and internal refugees are most prominently associated with conflict zones and especially civil conflicts. One of the world's most well-publicized instances of refugee dynamics is taking place in the Middle East, currently highlighted by the estimated 1.6 million refugees of the Syrian civil war in 2013.

The dynamics of immigration as a global issue requires looking at the phenomenon from at least three vantage points. The first is the motivation for immigration: Why do people emigrate from one place to another, and what roles do they fulfill when they become immigrants? The second is where the phenomenon of immigration is the most and least evident on a global scale. Although it is generally true that the global pattern is one of people moving from the developed to the developing world, the pattern is selective and regionally distinctive. The third concern is immigration as a problem, both globally and locally. Are there distinctive problems that are created by current, ongoing patterns, and are these likely to get better or worse in the future? The answers to these questions, in turn, help frame the context of the problems associated with immigration across the Mexican border into the United States.

Immigration Motivations and Functions

People migrate for a variety of both positive and negative reasons, and immigration is more or less positively received by the people of the places to which they migrate depending on the role and need the receiving country has for the particular migrants who are arriving. Both the motivations for migrating and the reactions to being asked to receive migrants are sufficiently numerous and complex that it is difficult to generalize across the board.

One way to think about the reasons for immigration is in terms of "push" and "pull" factors. Push factors are motives to leave a particular political jurisdiction—conditions that make people want to leave or that push them out. Pull factors, on the other hand, refer to perceived positive attributes to attract immigrants to particular destinations—or serve to pull people to different locations. When push and pull factors are in proximity, as is the case with parts of Central America and the United States and areas of North Africa and the Middle East and the European Union (EU) area—the immigration pipeline is particularly strong.

The most obvious—virtually tautological—push factor is to improve one's living conditions by relocation. People decide to leave for both political and economic reasons: politically to avoid conflict or discrimination in their homeland, and economically in the hope or promise of a materially better life in the country to which they immigrate. This basic statement of motivation has numerous variations, as Choucri and Mistree enumerate: "the most obvious patterns of international migration today include the following: migration for employment; seasonal mobility for employment; permanent settlements; refugees who are forced to migrate; resettlement; state-sponsored movements; tourism and ecotourism; brain drains and 'reversals' of brain drains; smuggled and trafficked people; people returning to their country of origin; environmental migration and refugees from natural shortages or crises; nonlegal migration; and religious pilgrimage."

History's most dramatic migrations have had political upheaval as an underlying theme. As Koser points out, "large movements of people have always been associated with significant global events like revolutions, wars, and the rise and fall of empires; with epochal changes like economic expansion, nation-building, and political transformations; and with enduring challenges like conflict, persecution, and dispossession." Although these dramatic kinds of events are still obvious in places like Syria, the current surge of immigration has a more subtle economic theme that is part of globalization and modern demographic changes in the world.

The economic motivation, to move somewhere where economic opportunities are better than those where one lives, is nothing new. As Choucri and Mistree summarize, "during good times people migrate to find better opportunities; during bad times people migrate to escape more difficult circumstances." In either situation, the motivating factor is opportunity, which is manifested in the availability of jobs because, as Choucri and Mistree add, "To the extent that population growth exceeds a society's employment potential, the probability is very high that people will move to other countries in search of jobs."

Demographics also enter the picture. Population growth rates are highest in developing countries, and that means the rising number of job seekers is greatest in these countries relative to the number of jobs available. In the developed world, on the other hand, population growth rates are much lower (in some cases below levels to maintain current population sizes), the overall population is aging, and thus the percentage of citizens in the active workforce is diminishing. Goldstone explains the consequence: "the developed countries' labor forces will substantially age and decline, constraining economic growth in the developed world and raising demands for immigrant workers." Indeed, there are estimates that the developed countries that will be most successful in the future are those that are best able to augment their shrinking workforces with immigrant labor. This simple dynamic dictates pressure for population migration from developing to developed countries globally, and that pressure is often in fairly dramatic excess of immigration quotas and the like that many developed countries (including the United States) have. The United States is the only major developed country with a direct land border with a developing country, making that interplay most obvious in the Mexican–American case.

The kinds of talents that immigrants can contribute come in different categories that make their acceptance more or less enthusiastic. The smallest and most welcome category of immigrants is what the United Nations refers to as "highly skilled workers." These workers, generally highly educated and possessing scientific or engineering expertise at the cutting edge of the global economy, are the subject of so-called "brain drains" in one direction or the other. Countries of origins of these individuals are often anxious to restrict their emigration or, for those who have moved, to encourage their return (reverse brain drains, a phenomenon introduced with regard to India in Chapter 12). Countries like the United States that have historically been the beneficiaries of the movement of the highly skilled people make special provisions to make immigration possibilities attractive for these groups (see Martin for a discussion).

The far more problematical category of economic immigrants is those who have comparatively low skill levels. They are a double-edged sword for the countries into which they move. On one hand, they provide labor when it is in short supply, and particularly in areas that are low paying or undesirable. Koser refers to these kinds of jobs as "3D jobs: dirty, difficult, or dangerous." He points out that "in the majority of advanced economies, migrant workers are overrepresented in agriculture, construction, heavy industry, manufacturing, and services—especially food, hospitality, and domestic services." Martin adds that these kinds of jobs are "the work magnet that stimulates illegal immigration."

Unskilled immigrants—especially irregular immigrants—pose a particular moral and practical dilemma for receiving states. These immigrants do jobs that the citizens are either unwilling to do or that they will not do at the lower wages that migrants will accept (especially irregular migrants). Thus, without a pool of such laborers, vital services either would not get done or would only be done at higher costs. The alternative to migrant labor is more expensive indigenous labor, which would demand higher wages (federal minimum wages in the United States at least), which would ripple upward through the wage system (there would be relatively fewer laborers for other jobs, making their labor more valuable). The dilemma is that quotas on legal immigration are often far too restrictive to produce an adequate-sized legal migrant pool to do the jobs migrants do, and if the current "underground" economy went above board and hired only legally registered immigrants, employers would have to pay them higher wages, provide benefits, and do other things that would raise the costs of their labor. The moral dimension is that this situation often leads to a public denunciation of irregular immigrants by those employers who most depend on them and who would be most economically damaged were there to be no irregular immigrants.

The acceptance or rejection of economic immigrants thus operates at two levels. Highly skilled immigrants are almost always welcome, because they augment the receiving country's talent pool and add intellectual or physical capabilities that might not otherwise be present in adequate numbers or at all. It is estimated, for instance, that fully one-half of the scientists and engineers practicing in the United States are of foreign birth. Under the Immigration Act of 1990, the United States allows 140,000 immigrants with needed skills into the country annually. The country's intellectual and technological base would be seriously compromised were they to leave or be evicted.

The system operates differently regarding less skilled immigrants, which, of course, includes most of the irregular immigrants. There is clearly some hypocrisy that taints the question of such economic immigrants. For the most part, the immigrants themselves are impoverished people fleeing great economic deprivation personally and motivated to improve the lots of themselves and their extended families. Indeed, remittances from these workers back to their relatives in their countries of origin are a significant part of the economies of some of these countries. The fact that these workers lack proper documentation, however, means they are illegal, and this fact triggers sentiment against them. At the same time, their status leaves them particularly vulnerable to unscrupulous employers who can pay them at very low rates because they have no leverage against exploitation. Complicating matters is that because illegal employment typically also means that wages are not taxed (they are paid on a cash basis), any demands that this category of people makes on community resources (health care and education, for instance) is not offset by taxes they have paid other than user taxes like sales tax. It is not clear whether the blame in this case lies with the workers or with employers that do not withhold and submit parts of earnings to appropriate government entities.

Refugees present a separate problem. Generally, they can also be divided into skilled and unskilled groups, with the skilled often constituting professionals from the country from which they flee, and the unskilled composed mainly of subsistence farmers and the like. The skilled parts of the population are more likely to be absorbed into the country to which they flee (although generally at much lower standards of living), whereas the unskilled generally cannot be absorbed and become a burden on the country or on international bodies like the United Nations Commission on Human Rights (UNCHR). Moreover, most refugees are from developing countries and flee to adjacent countries, which are also poor and thus lacking the resources to tend for their new citizens. Most of the Syrian refugees, for instance, have fled to adjacent countries like Turkey, Lebanon, Jordan, and Iraq, which have difficult political and economic problems already.

There is another category of generally irregular immigrants that should be mentioned: criminals who move to new countries in order to carry out illegal activities of one sort or another. Human traffickers and smugglers are one instance of this form of immigration. Another is the movement of drug traffickers into the countries in which they do business or through which they transit. This form of irregular immigration is a particular problem along the U.S.–Mexico border and the source of a disproportionate amount of the concern among anti-immigration forces. There is often not a great deal of effort within the anti-immigration movement to differentiate between criminal and purely economic immigrants.

The World Situation

There are two basic and overlapping trends in worldwide immigration. The first is that the burden of this immigration is shifting geographically from the developing to the developed world, and especially to Europe and North America.

(Asian migration is actually greater than migration to North America, but it is intra-developing-world movement.) The other trend is that immigration is increasing numerically: there are more immigrants worldwide than there have been. Part of this latter trend can be at least partially explained by the overall increase in world population. A significant element, however, is demographic, based in aging populations in the developed world and the consequent need to import younger workers both to sustain economic activity and to support an aging and unproductive population.

Immigrant destinations are geographically distinct. As the push–pull factors suggest, Europe and North America are the destinations of most of the immigrants to the developed world (not entirely surprising given that the two continents encompass most of the developed world). Europe bears the brunt of this migration, followed by North America. As the International Migration Review (IMR) summarizes, "the proportion of migrants living in North America rose from 18 percent in 1990 to 23 percent in 2005, and the share of Europe rose from 32 to 34 percent. In 2005, one in every three international migrants lived in Europe and about one in every four lived in North America." The growth rate of international migrants is greatest for North America, where the "migrant stock" rose by an annual rate of 3.2 percent between 1990 and 2005. Most North American immigrants come from Mexico and Central America, whereas immigrants to Europe come primarily from Africa and Asia.

These figures are particularly noteworthy for the United States, which has the largest number of international migrants of any country in the world (20.1 percent of the world total in 2005, according to the IMR). The U.S. Department of Homeland Security Office of Immigration Statistics provides estimates of the distribution and number of immigrants. For 2008, it reports that there were 1,107,126 immigrants with permanent legal resident status in the country, but also estimated that there were 11,600,000 "unauthorized immigrants." Slightly over 7 million of those residents were from Mexico, with approximately another 1 million each from El Salvador and Guatemala.

These trends are likely to increase in the future. As Goldstone points out, "the developed countries' labor forces will substantially age and decline, constraining economic growth in the developed world and raising the demand for immigrant workers." The rate at which populations are aging, and how governments respond to this problem, varies greatly, with different consequences. Japan, for instance, has one of the world's most rapidly aging populations and has, for cultural reasons, been very reluctant to allow non-Japanese immigrants into the country. This is already having two effects. First, it means that a shrinking portion of the population is part of the productive workforce that produces, among other things, the wealth needed to support older, retired Japanese. Second, it means a contraction in productivity and also population. The cumulative effect of these dynamics is the projection of a smaller and less economically prominent Japan in the future. In contrast, the American population is aging more slowly, and the effects have been attenuated by the influx of younger immigrant workers to do jobs that aging

Americans either cannot or will not do (3D jobs in particular). Europe also has this problem, which especially features low fertility rates, and is wrestling with acceptable rates or immigration to deal with it, a problem made more acute by the relatively high percentage of immigrants who are Muslim.

The scale of immigration, from the developing to the developed world, is not going to go away. If anything, it will increase in the future. As Goldstone suggests, "Current levels of immigration from developing to developed countries are paltry compared to those that the forces of supply and demand might soon create across the world." The degree to which this likely trend is a concern depends on whether one views immigration as a problem or not.

The Immigration Problem

Most popular discussions of immigration tend to focus on the problems associated with the phenomenon. The breaching of sovereign national borders is one manifestation of the concern many have with immigration, and underlying many concerns is a sort of "nativism" that seeks to protect the racial or other purity of particular countries from the polluting of countries by the outsiders. The desire to "secure" borders, one of the most frequent ways in which immigration opposition is voiced, also collides with the dynamics of globalization. Both these factors are present in the American debate about immigration from Mexico.

The question of migration needs to be put in some historical perspective, especially in the United States, where the debate has become particularly loud and shrill. The United States is, and basically always has been, an immigrant country, with different national groups arriving in waves during the over two centuries of the American experience. In the nineteenth century, for instance, much of the immigration was from Europe, as Europeans sought to flee physical (e.g., the Irish potato famine) or other economic and political distress (e.g., large Italian migration that, according to Martin, reached 285,000 in 1907 alone). Those immigrant waves have been selective and have provoked reactions: the National Origins Act of 1924, for instance, limited Italian legal immigration to 4,000 annually. The twentieth century saw the placing and then removal of bans or highly restrictive limits on Asian immigration. The current reaction to Latin American immigration must take into account that it is, in some important ways, part of a broader historical pattern of rejection and embrace of different immigrant groups.

Large-scale, and especially irregular, immigration does pose problems conceptually for governments. Although the instances of truly effective "Great Wall" of China solutions to keeping borders sacrosanct are historically few, high levels of border porosity do pose the question of national control of their own territory. As Choucri and Mistree put it, "perhaps in no other arena is countries' lack of effective control of borders and national access so striking as in the realm of international migration." According to Koser, this is particularly a problem with illegal migrants: "One legitimate risk is irregular immigrant's threat to the exercise of sovereignty."

The result is an essential ambivalence. Breaches of sovereignty are a matter of concern in principle among those to whom national sovereignty is a particular obsession, but it is also a practical concern if those who may breach sovereign boundaries are individuals—such as terrorists—about whom the country has legitimate concerns in national security of other terms. The problem, of course, is that creating boundaries that cannot be breached—the most extreme form of making boundaries secure—is probably impractical or impossible (the direct U.S.–Canada border, excluding the Alaska–Canada border, is over 3,900 miles long) and would have other undesirable consequences. Chief among these would be the effect of slowing or strangling the flow of goods, services, and people across national boundaries, the essence of globalization. Choucri and Mistree, once again, capture the basis of the problem: "the evident inability to regulate and control access across national borders is one legacy of the current phase of globalization."

This dynamic is most often overlooked in the debate over secure borders and immigration control. Restriction of movement across national boundaries is directly antithetical to the promotion of free trade, which, as pointed out in Chapter 9, is the heart of globalization. The movement of labor from places where it is abundant to places where it is not is indeed part of the globalization phenomenon, for instance. Goldstone argues that the two forces need not be at fundamental odds with one another, however. "Correctly managed, population movement can benefit developed and developing countries alike. . . . Immigration to developed countries can provide economic opportunities for the ambitious and serve as a safety valve for all."

The brunt of this discussion has been that international immigration is a large and complex phenomenon. The movement of people from one area to another began with the migration out of the Great Rift Valley that initiated human population of the globe, and it continues to this day. The growing size of the global population, the increased unacceptability of great disparities between people in the developed and developing worlds, and contemporary forces like those associated with globalization help shape the contemporary issue. Nowhere are these issues more poignant or prominent than in the case of the U.S.–Mexico border.

THE U.S.–MEXICO BORDER PROBLEM

Americans have always disagreed about immigration policy. One pole in the disagreement is and always has been the American self-image as a nation (and essentially a nationality) of immigrants who have escaped oppression from an otherwise tainted world and hold their arms open for others like themselves. The Statue of Liberty's welcome to the oppressed captures this popular sentiment. The other pole, however, suggests a more selective attitude, the idea that some peoples are more welcome than others. Immigrant nationalities as widely disparate as the Irish and Italians from Europe and the Chinese and Japanese from Asia have been the objects of exclusion and discrimination. In terms of the current controversy, it is symbolically significant that one of the derogations heaped upon Italian immigrants of the late nineteenth and early twentieth centuries was to refer to them as "wops," an acronym for "without official papers." In important ways, the current reaction against Mexican and Central American irregular immigrants (or "wops") is simply the contemporary manifestation of this historical strain.

The current U.S.–Mexico border crisis is also part of the global migration trend from the developing to the developed world. The basic dynamics that are causing a surge in African and Middle Eastern migration to Europe are present in the United States as well, and for most of the same reasons. The existence of an aging population that is not replenishing itself rapidly enough to sustain an adequate workforce to fill needed functions (especially 3D jobs) afflicts both North America and Europe, tying together immigration and prosperity in the process. The dictates of globalization, moreover, demand an increased flow of productive workers into the country if the national edge in the global economy is to be maintained.

The current situation also has its own unique, exacerbating characteristics. As a developed–developing world phenomenon, the U.S.–Mexico border case is intensified by the nature of the border. At 1,933 miles of mostly desolate, rural topography, it is a very long and difficult frontier to "seal," as its proponents advocate, without debilitating levels of resource expenditure that might prove inadequate in the most optimal circumstances. At the same time, the U.S.–Mexico boundary is the world's only direct land border between the developed and developing worlds. While G-20 member Mexico may chafe at its continuing designation as a developing world, the per capita income of Mexicans is only about 30 percent that of Americans statistically, meaning the economic lure of migration is present. Citizens from Central America migrate through Mexico and across the border, a more direct form of developing-world migration. Migrants to Europe, in contrast, have no equivalent of the U.S.–Mexico boundary as a symbol of obstruction to their entrance.

The U.S.–Mexico case is also distinguished by its sheer volume and the accompanying complexity of the problem. No one, of course, knows exactly how many irregular immigrants are in the United States, and those who voice the greatest concern would argue that official estimates of 11.6 million cited earlier are probably too low (one sees estimates ranging from about 10–20 million depending on the source). This is a larger number than for any other country, although there are several countries such as Germany that have a higher percentage of immigrants in the population than the United States. Moreover, the problem is geographically distinct within the United States: About one-quarter of all estimated irregular immigrants in the United States in 2008 were in California (2.85 million), followed by Texas (1.68 million), and Florida (840,000). The issue is also a complex one. The concern about the U.S.–Mexico border not only involves immigration, although it is certainly a central focus. In addition, however, the question of the integrity of the frontier has strong implications for the trafficking of illicit drugs into the United States. Indeed, it will be argued that much of the concern about criminality associated in the popular debate is not about immigration so much as it is about the U.S.

"war on drugs." In addition, the frontier is also important because foreign terrorists who are intent on doing harm to the United States must enter across the U.S. border from either Mexico or Canada. One irony of the current fixation with the Mexican border is that it may have the unwanted effect of making the Canadian border more permeable and thus more attractive for terrorists to penetrate than it was before.

This introduction suggests the direction of the rest of the case. The discussion will first move to describing the nature of the physical dimension of the American border and whether or how that border can be "secured." With that rejoinder in mind, the discussion will then move to the nature of the various prongs of the threat itself posed by a porous border: illegal immigrations, drugs, and terrorists. Each discussion will include some analysis of whether making the border more or less impermeable solves each aspect of the problem and what other forms of effort might be equally or more effective. One suggestion that will be raised is the possible hypocrisy of some claimed solutions.

The Physical Problem

Almost all the solutions proposed for the U.S.–Mexico border revolve around some better way to "secure" it, which means roughly to make it more difficult for unauthorized people to come across the border into the United States. The most extreme advocacies call for "sealing" the border, which generally equates to making it impossible physically for unwanted outsiders to intrude on American soil. Before examining the desirability of such a policy and what it would entail, it is necessary first to examine the physical problem posed by the unique nature of the American border.

Border security is, of course, a problem for all sovereign states. How much and what kind of a problem depends largely on two aspects of the problem: whether the border's function is to keep people from leaving (emigration) or entering (immigration), and the physical qualities of the border—its length and complexity, for example. Keeping émigrés from leaving the United States has never been a particular problem (except for criminals fleeing prosecution, for instance); the emphasis has always been on regulating who and how many people enter the country.

The territorial boundaries of the United States are among the most extensive, complex, and difficult to secure of any country on earth. These borders can be divided into sea and land boundaries, each of which poses different priorities and problems. Moreover, the land borders of the United States are shared with two contiguous neighbors, Canada and Mexico. Although the current dispute centers on the Mexican border, both are concerns: treating one as a problem and not the other is discriminatory and diplomatically untenable, and sealing the Mexican border but not the Canadian border runs the risk that some of the nefarious activity associated with a porous Mexican border would simple be transferred to the Canadian border (the entrance of terrorists or illicit drugs into the country, for instance).

The land and sea borders are extensive. The land border between the United States and Canada, for instance, is slightly more than 5,500 miles long (the boundary between Canada and the 48 contiguous states is 3,987 miles and between Canada and Alaska is 1,538 miles). Added to the 1,933-mile land border between the United States and Mexico, the total American land border is 7,358 miles. This is not the longest in the world (Russia's border with 14 other countries is approximately two-thirds longer), but it is nonetheless a very long and forbidding stretch of territory to secure. In fact, most of the U.S.–Canada border is hardly secured at all, particularly the extensive stretch between Lake Superior and the Pacific Ocean and the Alaska–Canada border. As a practical matter, it would be impossible to do so and, happily, for the most part such security is unnecessary.

The sea borders of the United States are even more extensive. Two measures are normally used to describe these borders: coastline and shoreline. The coastline generally refers to a line drawn along the intersection of the coast and the ocean, not allowing for bays, inlets, and other coastal features. The shoreline measures the topography of the coast, including the shores of bodies of water that empty into the oceans and seas. Using figures supplied by the National Oceanic and Atmospheric Administration, the coastline of the United States is 12,383 miles, and the shoreline is 88,633 miles. Almost 42 percent of the U.S. coastline (5,580 miles) and 35 percent of shoreline (31,383 miles) are Alaskan and have not been a major concern since the Cold War. The 1,350 miles of Florida coastline and 8,426 miles of its shoreline, however, are important security concerns regarding drugs importation and, to a lesser extent, the smuggling of irregular immigrants.

Effectively securing these borders is clearly a formidable task that is complicated by three other factors. One is the availability of assets to accomplish the task. The current effort concentrates on the 1,933-mile Mexican land border and two forms of security: a border fence and larger numbers of Border Patrol and other human assets to monitor activity. It is not clear where the funds are to meet both these demands, and expanding the effort to include the Canadian and sea boundaries of the United States beyond current (and quite limited) proportions would be a further drain on available resources.

A second problem is whether such efforts can be entirely effective against determined attempts to breach the boundary. Illegal entry across the Mexican frontier is already largely orchestrated by illegal agents (so-called "coyotes") who exact significant fees to sneak immigrants across the border, and the result of enhanced security efforts might simply be to increase their sophistication, as well as the expense and thus profit of their illegal enterprise. Moreover, it is not clear that an "immigrant-proof" solution is possible. As former New Mexico Governor Bill Richardson has been quoted as saying, "If we put up a ten-foot fence, somebody is going to build an eleven-foot ladder."

Finally, there is the question of unintended consequences of increased security. These are most marked in the case of the impediment to movement of goods and peoples across the borders, a question of the impact of border security on globalization, raised earlier. As Flynn has noted, an attempt to better control the border between the United States and Canada (especially the bridges between Detroit and Ontario) over a decade ago had catastrophic effects on U.S. productivity, and any serious attempt to screen effectively something as simple as truck traffic at major crossing points with either country would create an enormous economic dislocation. This, of course, is a major problem regarding both the land and sea borders, and one that is generally underemphasized in discussions of border security.

The Border Threats

The difficulty surrounding the U.S.–Mexico border is really more than one threat. Its most prominent feature has been the level and consequences of irregular immigration across the border, and that aspect will be most prominently examined. It is also, however, a question of the movement of illicit narcotics and the consequent criminal behavior they bring with them and of the possible penetration of the United States by terrorists. It is not entirely clear that the most extensive and most important of these threats are the same.

The Immigration Problem. Immigration is, and always has been, an integral part of the American experience. Although for most times and purposes, it has been one of the proud elements of the American heritage, it has had its dark side in the form of negative reactions to the migration of some people to the United States at some times. Throughout American history, what is now referred to as illegal immigration has always been a part of the pattern, and the history of immigration politics is largely an attempt to regulate both the quantity and quality (measured both in point of origin and skill levels) of immigration to the country. In the current context, the immigration problem along the U.S.–Mexico border is the most dramatic and contentious manifestation of a worldwide pattern of international immigration that appears likely to only increase in the future.

The sheer volume of irregular immigrants in the United States is the heart of the perceived problem in the American political debate. There is some minor disagreement about the terms of legal immigration into the country as it affects the flow of highly skilled and talented people into or out of the country, largely reflected in immigration quotas and the like. The heart of the debate, however, is about irregular immigration by Mexicans and Central Americans into the country in numbers that exceed 10 million and may be much higher. Efforts to secure the border are aimed at reducing or eliminating the flow of irregulars into the country; efforts to apprehend and deport irregular immigrants already in the country are aimed at reducing those numbers.

Why is this immigrant flow a problem? Generally speaking, two reasons are cited, which help illuminate the parameters of the concern. One concern is the criminality that is associated with illegal residents. Whether crime is greater in places where there are concentrations of irregular immigrants is contested, but those who hold this concern point particularly to greater incidents of violent crime in places where illegal immigrants are concentrated. Normally, most of these crimes are committed by members of the irregular immigrant population against other members of that community, but sometimes these spill over and affect the broader communities in which they are located. The other concern is the demands on social services (e.g., schools and medical facilities) made by irregular immigrants and their families, a concern accentuated by the fact that most irregular immigrants pay only user taxes (e.g., sales tax) but do not contribute to the Social Security fund or through payroll deduction, for instance.

These are two distinct problems that point to a basic division within the irregular immigrant population. There are, in essence, two groups that make up that community. By far the most numerous are *economic immigrants,* individuals who migrate to the United States in the same manner and for the same reasons that people in the developing world generally migrate to the developed world: the push and pull of providing a better life for themselves and their families. There is no systematic indication that their participation in or contribution to crime is any greater than that of the population at large; indeed, the knowledge that their arrest can lead to their deportation probably inhibits much criminal activity toward which they might be drawn. The other group is comprised of *criminal immigrants,* individuals who enter the country to engage in criminal behavior. Most prominent within this group are people engaged in narcotics trafficking in one way or another. This group brings with it the violent crime that has ravaged Mexico in particular, and is the source of virtually all the concern over the impact of immigration on crime.

Dividing the irregular immigrant community into these two categories helps in understanding the problem and what to do about it. One must begin by asking the question, why do immigrants come illegally to the country? In the case of the vast majority—the economic immigrants—the answer is economic opportunity: jobs. This should not be surprising, given the disparity of wealth between the United States and Mexico and Central America, but this is also why economic immigrants migrate worldwide. In the case of irregular immigration into the United States, one explanation of why this has occurred—and especially why it has occurred to the extent it has—is found in the impact that the North American Free Trade Agreement (NAFTA) had on Mexico. As discussed in the third edition of this book (Chapter 9, "Evaluating Globalization: The Case of NAFTA"), one of the perverse effects of that agreement was to flood Mexico with cheap, subsidized American corn, the price of which undercut Mexican peasant growers, bankrupting them and forcing them off their farms. Many of these displaced peasants have become part of the flood of irregular immigrants to this country. Before NAFTA came into effect in 1994, there were an estimated 4.2 million illegal Latin American immigrants in the United States, compared to current totals.

The irony of this situation is that NAFTA was supposed to have exactly the opposite effect: it was supposed to create jobs in Mexico that would reduce the need of Mexicans to come north seeking employment. As Governor Richardson put it, "The whole idea that NAFTA would create jobs on the Mexican side and thus deter immigration has just been dead wrong." In a 2005 Center for

Immigration Studies (CIS) report, Krikorian argues that what happened was virtually the result of American politics that forced acceptance of agribusiness-friendly farm subsidies (that included corn subsidies) as a part of gaining the acceptance of NAFTA. As Krikorian puts it, "the massive growth of immigration pressures was not a failure of NAFTA, but an inevitable consequence." Why? "Economic development, especially agricultural modernization, *always* sets people on the move, by consolidating small farms into larger, more productive operations. . . . The problem with NAFTA was that neither country did anything meaningful to make sure the excess Mexican peasantry moved to Mexico's cities instead of ours."

All of this, of course, took place within the context of the global economy of the 1990s and how that economy affected North America. Martin suggests the dynamics at work: "The economic situation in both countries in the 1990s—a boom in the United States, a very slow recovery from a 1994 bust in Mexico—led record numbers of Mexicans to enter the United States during the second half of the decade."

Without suggesting that NAFTA is the only reason that a large number of economic immigrants have entered the United States, nonetheless the vast majority of irregular migrants have been displaced Mexicans and Central Americans who have come to the United States in the pursuit of economic advancement, including the accumulation of enough money to send remittances back to their local communities and families at home, as already noted. Their migration is like economic migration everywhere, moving from where there is no economic opportunity (jobs) to where such opportunities exist.

The immigration problem and its solution take on a different complexion put in these terms. If there are jobs available that irregular immigrants fill, then there must be a labor need that these immigrants fulfill. Generally, this means low-skill, low-paying jobs, often with one or more of the 3D characteristics of being dirty, dangerous, or difficult. If there were Americans willing to do these jobs at wages that employers were willing to pay and that produced services at prices consumers would pay, there would not be jobs, and there would be no incentive for migrants to immigrate. That they have done so and continue to do so indicates not only that such opportunities exist, but that they have not been sated. That is simple supply and demand.

Moreover, the dynamics suggest that there is not only a market for immigrant labor but also a continuing market for irregular immigrant labor. Given the reaction against irregular immigration, this assertion seems anomalous, but it is nonetheless true. The simple fact is that illegal workers have advantages to employers over legal immigrants: They will work at lower wages (they have no bargaining ability on wages), they will work longer (they are covered by no labor laws or contracts), and they do not require employers to pay benefits like Social Security taxes or health insurance. For highly labor-intensive work like lawn care, roofing, or garbage collection, hiring irregular laborers has economic advantages for employers that allow them to maximize profits while minimizing costs to themselves and consumers. Moreover, if the kinds of jobs that irregular immigrants typically perform became part of the regular economy, labor costs would increase (to minimum wage, at the least), which in turn would drive up the costs of the services and the wages of other lower-end jobs. A large number of Americans would feel the impact in their wallets.

This places the problem in a different context than those who simply call for expelling irregular immigrants like to frame the question. Do all the advocates *really* want to get rid of irregular immigrants? Because they are doing jobs that either would not get done at all or only at higher labor costs otherwise, the answer is not clear. If all employees, including current irregulars in the underground economy, were to enter the mainstream, then suddenly these workers would be paying all taxes (rather than just regressive levies like sales taxes), thereby contributing to things like Social Security and Medicare/Medicaid and making themselves less of a social services burden. But doing so would mean employers would have to increase their own efforts and expenses, which they clearly are reluctant to do. As a result, some people publicly oppose illegal immigration but employ irregular immigrants.

If irregular economic immigrants are the heart of the border problem, then any solution aimed at reducing or eliminating them must begin with the incentives they have to migrate and to stay. That means an emphasis on the elimination of the illegal jobs in the underground economy that are the mainstay of and magnet for irregular immigrants. Assuming the country is willing to bear the consequences of such a policy succeeding (which is not clear), then the heart of border policy should have a significant component that seeks to reduce the numbers who seek to breach the border, in other words, to reduce the pull of immigration incentives to come to places like the United States. A core part of such a strategy necessarily involves reducing the availability of jobs that irregulars occupy. An avenue to do so already exists in American law and could be implemented simply by enforcing penalties against those who hire irregular immigrants. Reducing the number of available job opportunities would probably not, in and of itself, eliminate irregular immigration (it would, for instance, take a while for the word to circulate to potential immigrants), but it could reduce the flow, thereby making efforts to secure the border by other means more plausible.

This solution is so obvious that one wonders why it is not more prominently mentioned in solutions to irregular immigration. The reason at least partially reflects a certain degree of ambivalence, even hypocrisy, in the debate. Many people oppose irregular immigration and those who participate in it on the grounds that their actions are illegal, that they represent an assault on national sovereignty, and that they are a burden on social services. At the same time, however, many of these same people support the functions these same workers perform (3D labor at low costs), and some even benefit personally from the presence of these workers (primarily employers). It is particularly this latter group that may be enthusiastic denouncers of illegal immigrants but not want to prosecute those who hire them, as they are the lawbreakers.

There is some indication that the same demographics that combined to create the immigrant surge may also alleviate it with time. In a June 7, 2010, *Newsweek* article, Campos-Flores points out that fertility rates in Mexico have declined dramatically "from 6.7 children per woman in 1970 to 2.1 today," according to World Bank figures. The result will be a gradual reduction in the number of young people entering the Mexican labor market, from over 850,000 per year in the early 2000s to about 300,000 per year in 2030, a number the Mexican economy can more adequately absorb. Some of this is already occurring (projected new members of the labor force this year are down to 750,000), but with a rub: "Mexican migration will taper off further just as baby boomers begin retiring in 2012," according to Campos-Flores.

The other form of irregular immigration for which no one has official sympathy is *criminal immigration*, the movement of individuals into the country who are parts of criminal enterprises and whose reason for immigration is to further their criminal activities. In some cases, such immigrants may be associated with things like human trafficking, but the most prominent form that criminal immigration takes on the U.S.–Mexico border is the illicit drug trade, which is the second prong of the border problem.

The Narcotics Problem. The drug trade across the U.S.–Mexico frontier is both an immigration and narcotics policy problem. Most of the illegal drugs that enter the United States are shipped through Mexico and then across the border, making it a border issue. At the same time, many of those who carry drugs into the United States (so-called "mules") are irregular immigrants who are more or less reluctantly brought into the trade. As Shifter explains, "Mexico is the transit route for roughly 70 to 90 percent of the illegal drugs entering the United States. . . . Along the U.S.-Mexico border, the kidnapping trade, clearly tied to the drug trade, is flourishing." Andreas points out that increased American border security efforts exacerbate the drug problem: "adding thousands new Border Patrol agents has had the perverse effect of entrenching smugglers rather than deterring immigrants since the problem of breaching the border is more difficult and requires help for some immigrants"; some of that assistance is provided by drug traffickers. Moreover, the drug and immigration efforts come into conflict with one another, as they are conducted by different government agencies (e.g., the Border Patrol and the Drug Enforcement Agency) with different priorities and different cultures. Adding National Guardsmen to this mix, as was begun in 2010, only adds to the jurisdictional confusion.

The drug and immigration issues intersect when members of the various drug syndicates move across the border into the United States to better control their illicit operations. There is considerable evidence that Mexican drug cartels are now active in most large American cities and that they bring with them the drug-related violent crime that has become endemic on the Mexican side of the border. The numbers of immigrants who are part of criminal immigration are quite small compared to the economic immigrants, but their presence is amplified because of the spikes in violent crime that occur where they are present. This violence is mostly between members of various drug cartels, but inevitably it spills over into broader communities, inflaming anti-immigrant sentiments that are at least partially misdirected. These kinds of problems have already destabilized Mexican national and local politics, and there is a fear that the same thing could happen on the U.S. side of the border.

Responses to the drug and immigration problems are similar. The major response to the drug problem has been interdiction—trying to stop the transit of drugs across the border—but that is largely impossible to do completely. As Andreas suggests, "The amount of cocaine necessary to satisfy US customers for one year can be transported in just nine of the thousands of large tractor-trailers that cross the border every day." The logic of globalization contained in instruments like NAFTA make detailed monitoring of cross-border traffic more difficult, and because such monitoring and inspection takes time, it is clearly counterproductive in globalization terms. It is not at all clear that such "supply-side" approaches to the flow of drugs across the border can be effective.

A more comprehensive view of drugs breaching the border includes an emphasis on reducing the market for drugs in the United States. Just as the availability of jobs has fueled economic immigration, so too has the demand for drugs fueled the growing flow of drugs into the country. If the demand for illegal drugs among Americans were to decrease (analogous to drying up jobs for irregular immigrants), the supply coming across the border would also likely decrease due to a decreased market. During the height of the so-called "war on drugs" during the late 1980s and early 1990s, this approach was known as "demand-side," and although hardly anyone suggested it was a comprehensive solution to the problem, it could help by making the volume of trafficking across the border more manageable.

The difficulty is disentangling the narcotics and illegal immigration aspects of the effects of border leakage. They really are two almost entirely different problems with different sources, dynamics, and largely unrelated consequences. The only thing linking them is the obvious fact that both drugs and unauthorized immigrants come across the border illegally. Even the dynamics of the two enterprises are different, as are the goals and methods of the officials pursuing each priority.

The Terrorism Problem. Although there may be an arguable analogy between the immigration and drug problems, this comparison largely does not extend to the problem posed by the penetration of the United States by terrorists. For one thing, the terrorism threat is not a specifically U.S.–Mexico border problem. Terrorists can enter the United States from Mexico, but also from Canada or at airports or seaports anywhere in the country from different points of origin. Indeed, it is arguable that the greater emphasis placed on the Mexican border may mean a diminution of personnel and effort at other points of entry, making them more likely transit points than they would be in the absence of an immigration emphasis.

The terrorism threat, unlike the other two, is also more of a qualitative than a quantitative problem, and one that is managed in a distinctive way. Irregular economic immigration involves a very large volume of people breaching the border, but where each individual poses little if any specific threat to the United States or its citizens. The problem that people perceive is the result of the overwhelming numbers of irregular immigrants and the collective burdens and problems they create. In contrast, there are relatively few terrorists against whose entry the United States must prepare, but the potential havoc that any one poses means that efforts must be essentially perfect or they can yield disastrous results. Thus, for instance, a boundary system that reduces the flow of economic immigrants across the Mexican border by 90 percent would have an enormous impact on the border issue, but the same effectiveness against terrorist penetration might be entirely unacceptable.

Because the goal of terrorist interception is absolute, the methods employed to prevent the entrance of terrorists into the country is multilayered and more extensive than it is for irregular economic immigrants, as suggested in Chapter 16. The U.S. government operates elaborate intelligence networks to monitor the movement of potential terrorists toward the U.S. border, something it does not undertake for the movement of Mexican peasants. This means, of course, a high level of interaction between government agencies to coordinate antiterrorist activities that are present to some extent in the pursuit of criminal immigrants but not for economic immigrants. Although the problem of terrorist penetration of the border is sometimes linked in discussion to unauthorized people entering the country more generally, it is really *sui generis,* a special problem.

CONCLUSION

The question of irregular immigration across the U.S.–Mexico border has become an explosive, emotional political issue in the United States, where emotions have arguably oversimplified and distorted the nature of the phenomenon. The purpose of this case study has been to place the American situation in its global context and to point out that the U.S. problem is more variegated and complex than simple depictions suggest.

Migration is and has always been a global phenomenon. As noted, 1 in every 35 people alive today is an immigrant in one sense or another and for one reason or another. In many cases, the motivations are economic, and in others they are political. In the most extreme cases, people are pushed out of their native countries: forced to flee their regions or countries and to become refugees. People have been migrating since humankind's forebears left the Great Rift Valley of Africa, and they have done so for a variety of reasons. Escaping a less favorable condition in hopes of finding a better situation has always been the deep underlying motivation.

The U.S.–Mexico border situation mirrors many of the broader global trends. People have been coming across this junction between the developed and developing worlds in large numbers since the early 1990s. Most have been irregulars—the people without official papers ("wops")—of this generation. They have come for the variety of reasons that immigrants always move, but their situation has been complicated because this form of immigration has been augmented and admixed with criminal immigration associated with the flow of illicit narcotics into the United States and the fear of terrorist penetration of the country's borders. Each of these sources of breaches of American national sovereignty as represented by a porous border has different bases and probably different solutions. Although an understanding of immigration as a global problem may not offer the solutions to all these problems, it does at least provide some context within which to consider them.

The American case has its unique attributes, but it is clearly not something that is unique to the United States. Conditions in the most destitute, politically repressive, yet rapidly growing parts of the world continue to push people to emigrate, and more favorable economic, political, and social conditions in the most developed countries continue to pull these immigrants to their boundaries. Much of the EU area is experiencing the same problems as is the United States, with the added factor of sometimes radical Islam complicating their particular situations. The push–pull of migration will not abate until global conditions become much more uniform and remove incentives to migrate. That time is a long ways away.

SUGGESTED ACTIVITIES AND QUESTIONS

1. What is immigration? Into what categories are immigrants normally placed? Especially describe the categories of "irregular immigrants" and refugees.
2. Discuss immigration in terms of why people immigrate, where they immigrate (and why), and why these patterns represent a national and international problem.
3. What are the basic categories of economic immigrants? Why is the distinction important in understanding the current controversy in the United States?
4. Summarize the world situation in terms of immigration. What are the basic trends? Why are they likely to continue? What dilemmas do attempts to restrict immigration present and face?
5. Discuss the general parameters of the physical border security problem facing the United States and the unique problems of the U.S.–Mexico border in that context.
6. What are the three distinct aspects of the U.S.–Mexico border threat? Discuss each, including how each might be solved.
7. Is the United States truly sincere about ending and reversing irregular immigration? What would the consequences of that success be economically and otherwise in the United States? Are Americans really willing to accept these consequences?

SUGGESTED READINGS AND RESOURCES

Alden, Edward. *The Closing of the American Border.* New York: HarperCollins, 2009.

Andreas, Pete R. "Politics on Edge: Managing the U.S.–Mexico Border." *Current History* 105, 695 (February 2006), 64–68.

Campos-Flores, Arian. "Don't Fence Them In: The Arizona of the Future Won't Suffer from Too Many Immigrants—But from Too Few." *Newsweek*, June 7, 2010, 34–35.

Choucri, Nazli and Dinsha Mistree. "Globalization, Migration, and New Challenges to Governance." *Current History* 108, 717 (April 2009), 173–179.

Flynn, Stephen. *America the Vulnerable: How Our Government Is Failing to Protect Us from Terrorism.* New York: Harper Perennials, 2005.

Goldstone, Jack A. "The New Population Bomb: The Four Megatrends That Will Change the World." *Foreign Affairs* 89, 1 (January/February 2010), 31–43.

"International Migration Levels, Trends, and Policies." *International Migration Report 2006: A Global Assessment.* New York: United Nations Department of Economic and Social Affairs/Population Division, 2006.

Jones, Reece. *Border Walls: Security and the War on Terror in the United States, India, and Israel.* New York: Zed Books, 2012.

Kehoe, Timothy J. and Kim J. Ruhl. "The North American Free Trade Agreement After Ten Years." University of Minnesota: Center for Urban and Regional Affairs, 2004. (http://www.econ.umn.edu/~tkehoe)

Koser, Khalid. "Why Immigration Matters." *Current History* 108, 717 (April 2009), 147–153.

Krauze, Enrique. "Furthering Democracy in Mexico." *Foreign Affairs* 85, 1 (January/February 2006), 54–65.

Krikorian, Mark. "Bordering on CAFTA: More Trade, Less Immigration." *National Review Online,* July 28, 2005. (http://www.cis.org/CAFTA)

Maril, Robert Lee. *The Fence: National Security, Public Safety, and Illegal Immigration Along the U.S.-Mexican Border.* Lubbock, TX: Texas Tech University Press, 2012.

Martin, Susan F. "Waiting Games: The Politics of US Immigration Reform." *Current History* 108, 717 (April 2009), 160–165.

O'Neil, Shannon. "The Real War in Mexico." *Foreign Affairs* 88, 4 (July/August 2009), 66–77.

Payan, Terry. *The Three U.S.–Mexico Border Wars: Drugs, Immigration, and Homeland Security.* Westport, CT: Greenwood, 2006.

Rockenbach, Leslie J. *The Mexican–American Border: NAFTA and Global Linkages.* Abingdon, England: Routledge, 2001.

Rozenthal, Andres. "The Other Side of Immigration." *Current History* 106, 697 (February 2007), 89–90.

Shifter, Michael. "Latin America's Drug Problem." *Current History* 106, 697 (February 2007), 58–63.

Snow, Donald M. *Cases in International Relations,* 3rd ed. New York: Pearson Longman, 2008.

2008 Global Trends: Refugees, Asylum-seekers, Returnees, Internally Displaced and Stateless Persons. New York: United Nations High Commission on Refugees, June 16, 2009.

"Unauthorized Immigrant Population, 2000, 2008." Office of Immigration Statistics, U.S. Department of Homeland Security, 2009. Reprinted in *World Almanac and Book of Facts, 2010.* New York: World Almanac Books, 2010.

Van Hear, Nicholas. "The Rise of Refugee Diasporas." *Current History* 108, 717 (April 2009), 180–185.

Secession and Self-Determination: The Case of the Republic of South Sudan

PRÉCIS

Secession, the physical withdrawal of one part of a state from a previous political union, is a traumatic and reasonably infrequent event in international relations, but when it does occur, it generally arises from some perceived threat to the security of the groups that attempt it and also as a threat to the state against which secession is contemplated. The trauma occurs because even the politically divided and fractious states in which secession-ist movements are found are usually integrated in other ways, such as economically, and secessions are often, although not always, violent and bloody. In the contemporary world, secessions are most likely in the highly artificial states of parts of the developing world that have emerged from European colonial rule in the last 60 years. After defining and discussing the dynamics of secession, the chapter moves to an analysis of the conditions most often associated with secessionist sentiments, noting that they are present in many developing-world states, including some very unstable states like Syria.

The case of secession examined is the secession of the Republic of South Sudan from the Islamic Republic of Sudan, the world's most recent successful case of secession. After two long and costly civil wars, the people of the southern part of Sudan finally broke away from Sudan in 2011, ending a bloody confrontation defined along ethnic and religious lines. The two resulting countries are among the poorest in the world, and petroleum exploitation, largely in the new republic, serves as both a hope and a barrier for both.

Redrawing political boundaries has become one of the primary ways by which people have tried to create or reinforce their sense of security in a world where human security is often threatened. One manifestation of this dynamic is found in the migration of populations discussed in the last chapter. When security-seeking populations cannot achieve their goals by moving to other political jurisdictions, they may turn to other, more extreme ways to make themselves safe. One is to break apart an existing state and to carve out a new one from part of it. The act of doing so is secession; the name by which this act is usually justified in the contemporary world is self-determination.

Secession—the formal withdrawal from an organization—is a relatively infrequent phenomenon in international relations, but when it occurs, it is often a very traumatic, bloody event. As applied to members of the international system, secession refers to the physical withdrawal of a territory from an established state. The intent of such an action is normally to create a new sovereign political jurisdiction (a new state), but it also could be to allow the seceding unit to join another existing state with which it perceives a greater affinity.

Secession is thus a quintessentially geopolitical event that may seem at odds with the theme of human security featured in this section of the text. There is, however, a connection. The heart of the idea of human security is the notion of those conditions that make people feel safe and in which they can live well and even prosper. Some of the conditions that threaten human security are natural—violent weather events like tornados and hurricanes, for instance—but many are man-made. All three of the other cases in this section deal with barriers caused directly by other people, such as borders that affect migration, or terrorist activities, or indirectly, as in the actual or potential impacts of global warming.

The principle of self-determination justifying secession is largely a twentieth-century artifact. The major international political theme of the nineteenth century was the consolidation of formerly atomized political jurisdictions in places like Italy and Germany that transformed the core of the contemporary state system. During the twentieth century, that consolidation process has been challenged by the growing assertion of an argued international legal right of all people to seek their common political destiny. The resulting legal right that has emerged associated with this phenomenon is self-determination. With roots in customary international law, this right has been recognized in, among other places, the United Nations Charter of 1945.

The idea and application of self-determination have evolved. The concept first emerged in the early twentieth century as an asserted right among European peoples seeking independence from jurisdictions such as the Ottoman, Austro-Hungarian, and Russian Empires, claims assisted by the outcome of World War I, in place like the Balkans and central Europe. It was one of Woodrow Wilson's principles that underlay the Versailles Peace settlement and the League of Nations and helped justify the emergence of European states like Yugoslavia and Czechoslovakia, both of which experienced further self-determination in the post–Cold War period as Yugoslavia disintegrated and

Czechoslovakia split into the Czech Republic and Slovakia. The principle also helped justify decolonization in the developing world since 1945.

The motivations that give rise to most secessionist movements flow from these dynamics. As a general rule, the desire to withdraw from a particular political union arises when members of some group(s) within a particular state believe that the conditions imposed upon them by the state are intolerable and conclude that the only way their condition can be made more satisfactory is through their independence from the existing union. The ruling social and economic interests of the old American South, for instance, felt their way of life was so threatened by the rapidly growing and increasingly egalitarian North that their "peculiar institution," human chattel slavery, was threatened to the point it might be abolished eventually. The existence of slavery was so fundamental to the structure of the Southern economy and culture that proponents of secession argued, ultimately successfully, that the only justifiable course was to dissolve the union. The result, of course, was the great American tragedy of self-infliction, the Civil War.

Not all withdrawals are so traumatic, although they all have that potential. The prospect of ending the political oppression of Russian-dominated communism caused the various republics of the Soviet Union to withdraw from the Union of Soviet Socialist Republics (USSR) between 1989 and 1991, and the Soviet Union dissolved into history without major bloodshed. More recently (and the subject of the case study in this chapter), the Christian and animist majorities in the southern section of Sudan sought to and succeeded in separating the Republic of South Sudan from what most outside observers viewed as the brutal repression inflicted by the religiously extremist Islamic government of Sudan in Khartoum.

Secession is both an extreme and very controversial act, which may help explain why instances of successful secessionist movements are fairly infrequent. Over time, state jurisdictions develop complex patterns of interactions at all levels that many, often the majority, are reluctant to dismantle. Economies, for instance, become national in terms of production and distribution of goods and services, so that all parts become interdependent to the point that breaking the union apart may present painful dislocations for some or most members of the unit. When these interdependencies advantage some groups or regions at the expense of other groups or areas, the disadvantaged may find the situation intolerable and ultimately conclude that only disunion will produce an equitable outcome. The distribution of oil revenues to different groups and Sunni, Shiite, and Kurdish areas of Iraq presents this kind of dilemma, and the ultimate resiliency of the Iraqi state may depend on whether it is resolved to the satisfaction of all. A similar dynamic that was not satisfactorily resolved contributed to the successful secession of South Sudan.

The resulting divorce is almost always messy and difficult, and often it becomes violent. When all parties can agree that the union should be dissolved, much of the acrimony and trauma can be avoided. When it finally began to dissolve, for instance, one of the more shocking attributes of the secession of states from the Soviet Union was how easily it occurred. There was virtually no violence as even the Russian center whose empire was dissipated in the process acquiesced in ending the union, an outcome which very few apparently regretted very much.

A "RIGHT" TO SECEDE?

Like divorces in families, secessions are rarely as smooth or harmonious as the atomization of the Soviet Union. More typically, there is a strongly held opposition to secession. Those who support the continuation of the existing union deny that there is any right to break apart a sovereign political unit. There may be various rationales for such sentiment. One is there is no inherent right to leave a political union once entered into (this was the position Lincoln took toward the Confederacy, thereby arguing that the Civil War was an illegal attempt to overthrow the government rather than a valid attempt to create a new state). This position may also be based in the calculation of self-interest, effectively based in the perception that union will adversely affect the economic position of those against whom it is carried out, for instance. This perception can be quite strong; there are many Iraqis who might not oppose the secession of Kurdistan, for instance, if such an act did not deprive them of the revenues from Kurdish oil exploitation. For those who support the dissolution of the old union, their battle cry is likely to be the right of self-determination of people, a clarion cry in the contemporary international system. This position is likely to be buttressed by the politico-legal argument that a union that is voluntarily entered into implies the equal right of voluntary withdrawal from the arrangement (essentially the position of the Southern states in the American Civil War).

Who is right in this debate? Does a right to secede exist, or are those who advocate and attempt secession breaking some form of natural or manmade law? The answer is by no means clear. International law, for instance, is ambivalent. Many of the traditional tenets of international law derive from the period, beginning about 400 years ago, when the principle of sovereignty was gaining sway as the basic precept of the evolving international order of sovereign states (Hugo Grotius, often considered the "father" of the subject, published his seminal work, *The Rights of War and Peace: Including the Law of Nations and War,* in 1625). Traditional views tended to be rooted in the absolute authority of the sovereign, normally whoever ruled a country. Because the principle evolved during a period when monarchs were consolidating what became the modern state (see discussion in Chapter 1), views reflected the supremacy of the sovereign over his or her realm, and at least implicitly viewed challenges to that authority as illegitimate. Because the principle of sovereignty reflected the inviolability of sovereign jurisdiction, it also made outside interference in challenges to sovereign control illegitimate as well. Tradition, in other words, is weighted against the notion of the legitimacy of secession.

The assertion of a "right" to secession is effectively a spin-off of the emergence of notions of popular sovereignty. These notions flew in the face and denied the notion of the absolute control of the sovereign over everything that happened within the sovereign realm, including the right of the sovereign to treat those within his or her realm any way the sovereign wanted, including the violation of human rights. How the people were treated was the sovereign's business, and the people had no inherent right to challenge that treatment, particularly by breaking apart the union.

The idea that sovereignty resides with individuals was largely an eighteenth-century construct that gradually grew over time through the publicity of philosophers like John Locke and Jean-Jacques Rousseau and events like the American and French Revolutions (both of which were philosophically rooted in ideas of popular sovereignty). Its basic premise is that the ultimate authority that defines sovereignty resides with all individuals. The sovereign people, in turn, voluntarily cede some of that authority to the state to exist and perform the functions of government. The government has no basis for authority beyond that which is bestowed upon it by the constituent population. Because that grant of authority is voluntary, implicit within it is the right of the people to withhold or withdraw that authority. This line of reasoning creates the basis for the argument that the people have the right to dissolve a political union—in other words, to secede.

The idea that secession is an expression of the self-determination of peoples flows from the right to grant and withdraw support for a political authority and thus to dissolve a particular political union. The philosophical extension suggests that groups of people, regardless of how they define their group affiliation, have the right to withdraw the grant of sovereign authority when the state violates the trust placed in it by those who have effectively "loaned" that authority to them. Because the physical act of disunion is a traumatic and consequential event, this solution has always been thought of as an action *in extremis,* not as a casual action or threat over minor, resolvable dysfunctions. Physical secession is serious business.

The expression of this right of secession flies directly in the face of the traditional sovereignty claim of the absolute authority of the sovereign state (or its ruler). In the process, it denies the claims both of outsider official disinterest in acts of grievance that a ruler may inflict upon his or her citizens and the rights of redress that those aggrieved citizens may have. The impetus for the emergence of popular sovereignty as the overriding principle of contemporary international relations was, of course, the Holocaust, a horror that, according to tenets of traditional international law based in the inviolability of sovereign control, the German government had the right to conduct without outside interference or the sanctioning of internal redress.

Secession has become an increasing phenomenon in modern international politics for at least two reasons. One of these is the greater acceptance of the idea of self-determination. As noted in Chapter 1, some of the basis for acceptance of this principle is a kind of back-handed reaction to the World War II excesses of the Nazis. Given the nature of Nazi atrocities, it is very difficult to gain much support for the argument that governments have a right to treat their citizens in any manner they choose. This does not mean that such excesses have disappeared—the Khmer Rouge extermination of a significant part of the Cambodian population in the early 1970s is dramatic evidence—but it does mean that such actions are no longer acceptable behavior for governments. Self-determination may have some ambivalent impacts on the rights of all peoples in a given state (as discussed later in this case), but the assertion of the right to seek redress under the banner of self-determination is by now a generally accepted proposition.

Second, the rise of secessionist sentiments is also the direct result of conditions that have been created within the international system since World War II. Most of these changes flow from the process of decolonization in the developing world. The result of that process has often been to create imperfectly drawn new political jurisdictions where diverse and often antagonistic groups have been placed under the same national banner. The resulting politics has often devolved into instability where various groups seek to gain control and power at the expense of other groups. When the bases of cleavage are so stark and self-reinforcing that some group(s) or region(s) find the situation intolerable and beyond peaceful resolution, the result can be the emergence of secessionist sentiment.

This discussion lays the groundwork for the rest of the chapter. It begins with a general overview of the sources of modern secessionist sentiments in the contemporary international system, including what dynamics underlay both advocacy and opposition to such actions. It will then move to the kinds of effects that succession can have or has had, both in terms of the establishment of sustainable self-determination or in terms of continuing destabilization and suppression. The complexities and intricacies of possible secessionist solutions is no better illustrated anywhere than in the case of Syria and possible resolutions of the civil war that has torn the country apart since 2011. Cumulatively, these aspects of discussion will form the context for viewing an evaluating the most recent successful secession, that of the Republic of South Sudan from the Islamic Republic of Sudan.

SECESSION IN THE CONTEMPORARY INTERNATIONAL SYSTEM

Two major and contradictory themes dominate the contemporary debate over secession—the principle of justice (usually framed primarily in terms of the right to self-determination in the face of injustice) and the principle of stability (with roots in the assertion of the immutable sovereignty of states). Both sides of this argument typically come into play and have some relevance in any particular case of proposed secession, and generally both have some relevance to determining the outcome in any particular instance.

The topic is increasingly relevant in the contemporary world. As already noted, secessions are relatively infrequent events, although secessionist sentiments can be found almost anywhere. There are, for instance, citizens of the Catalonian region of Spain who still harbor the latent desire for an independent state of Catalonia, even if they do not pursue that goal with particular vigor.

The most serious expressions in contemporary world politics, however, are found in the developing world. In many cases, the outcome of independence movements was to create new states that were largely artificial in structure, either in terms of historical patterns of governance or as reflections of the political sentiments and loyalties of the groups aggregated under particular sovereign jurisdictions. Imperfect political solutions are not uncommon in much of the developing world—especially in Africa but also in the Middle East and other parts of Asia—meaning the potential for the emergence of secessionist movements and sentiment is widespread. Understanding that pattern requires beginning with the sources of secessionism in the contemporary system.

Sources of Secessionist Movements

The roots of modern secession are mostly traceable to the dismantling of the European colonial empires following the end of World War II. The building and maintenance of these empires had been the dominant political experience of much of the Afro-Asian and Latin American areas for over 300 years prior to the second global conflict of the twentieth century (the early colonies date to the sixteenth century, and the last colonies were granted independence in the middle 1970s). The dissolution of these empires was thus a traumatic phenomenon that competed with and overlapped the Cold War. The aftereffects of that dismantling transcended the end of the Cold War and continue to this day as a major source of world patterns of instability and violence. The sometimes successful attempts at secession from states created by the colonial breakup are one of the most extreme expressions of that continuing influence.

The broad underlying cause of secession was imperfection in the pattern of independence granted to the new states by the retreating colonialists. When colonies were established between the sixteenth and the latter nineteenth centuries, they tended to be territorial acquisitions that either ignored or, more frequently, were ignorant about the political realities that preceded them in the new colonies. As argued in Chapter 12, the motivations for colonial acquisition were dominated by profit and prestige. Both motives militated toward claiming the largest hunks of territory they could acquire: profits from economies of scale, and prestige as reflected in the amount of the globe's surface under the control of one European country or another. A major result was to create colonial units that incorporated numerous, diverse peoples whose previous primary loyalties, to the extent such loyalties existed, were to smaller groups or territories than the newly formed political and administrative units. Generally, efforts were not made to integrate the diverse populations with each political unit. Rather, the dictates of maintaining prolonged control suggested that the more parochial and less integrated the populations, the more docile and manageable they were likely to remain.

The effort to enforce and extend colonial bondage inevitably weakened, as such efforts normally do. Subject populations gradually came to resent, reject, and ultimately to resist their subservience. Exhausted by the wartime effort, European countries after 1945 gradually realized (some more quickly than others) they lacked the will and resources to extend their dominion, and they began, with varying degrees of grace and orderliness, to grant independence to the components of their former empires.

The problem was in the circumstances and forms in which independence was granted. In retrospect, there were two major flaws that have contributed to ongoing difficulties: the virtually total lack of preparation of former colonial elites for postindependence rule, and the territorial nature of the units to which the grants were made. The first problem was that many of the new governments lacked people with the political skills to navigate the difficult process of self-determination and especially the delicate compromises to integrate diverse, often feuding populations groups into a harmonious polity, a problem particularly acute in the conditions of poverty that were present in most of these new societies. This shortcoming was critical because independence tended to be granted to the artificial colonial administrative units as a whole or divided more or less arbitrarily. This meant that many of the new countries were diverse polyglots lacking any coherent, unifying political loyalty structure.

Many of these new and diverse states suffered from one (or in some cases both) sources or artificiality and ultimately instability: *multinationalism* or *irredentism*. Multinationalism refers to the situation where more than one national group shares the same political state. An anthropological term, a "nation" is a primary group to which its members feel their most basic allegiance. It can have numerous, often overlapping characteristics that include race, language, culture common history, religion, or a feeling of belonging and identification. Not all national groups possess all or even many of these traits; Americans, for instance, possess only a shared feeling of identification. Despite that, American nationalism is a powerful cohering force among citizens of the United States.

Irredentism, on the other hand, refers to the situation where state boundaries separate members of a nation into separate political jurisdictions and where members of the nation seek to shift state boundaries to allow members of the national group to share a common state. Cases of irredentism are comparatively fewer than those of multinationalism, but where they do exist, the desire of "stateless nations" to carve out their own shared political domain can be particularly intense. The Kurds of Iraq, Iran, Syria, and Turkey are one example of an irredentist movement, as are the Palestinians and the Pashtuns of Afghanistan and Pakistan. It is not coincidental that all three movements are in the greater Middle East.

The problem that both these phenomena present has been manifested in the lack of political loyalties and traditions that plague many developing-world states. A major part of the imperfections of the postcolonial map is the tenuous identification members of multiple national groups have to their new political states. Primary loyalties are not necessarily to being members of the new societies—Nigerians, for instance, may see themselves as Ibos or Hausa-Fulani rather than as Nigerians, and Iraqis may first identify themselves more as Kurds of Arab Sunnis or Shiites rather than as Iraqis. In these kinds of cases, politics can devolve to pitting national groups against one another, often where some groups gain advantage at the expense of others. If this situation becomes sufficiently dire to one national group or another, it may come to believe leaving the union is its only possible salvation.

Imperfectly drawn political maps are, unfortunately, common in much of the developing world, and it should come as no surprise that the most difficult outcomes of multinationalism and irredentist sentiment are also in the places where the most violence and instability exist. The imperfections are most pronounced in Africa and in the Middle East. Almost all states in Africa are multinational, with tribal identifications that predated colonialism as the primary continuing focus of political loyalties. In some cases like Nigeria, literally hundreds of ethnically and linguistically distinct tribes have been aggregated in individual states. These tribes often harbor animosities and hatreds toward other tribes, whom they consider traditional enemies. The animosities between such tribes were never assuaged by the colonialists, and some of the lingering hatreds have been intensified by conversion of different ethnic groups to Islam or Christianity. The latter volatile mix was present in Sudan, and the secession of South Sudan was primarily along reinforcing religious and tribal lines.

Likewise, the modern states of the Middle East, with a few exceptions like Egypt, were all more or less arbitrary outcomes of redrawing boundaries after the collapse of the Ottoman Empire at the end of World War I. The resulting mismatches of nations and states has resulted in multinational states that also sometimes contain irredentist movements as well. Iraq, Pakistan, and more recently Syria are all inflammatory examples of the unstable mix that can result from these dynamics.

Although some elements of multinationalism or irredentism are present in many developing-world countries, overt acts of attempted secession are still the fairly infrequent exception. To repeat, secession is a very fundamental, traumatic, and consequential action, and its seriousness makes it a last resort, both in terms of physical attempts to secede and in international responses to the attempts that do occur. Secessions by no means always succeed; the American Civil War and more recent examples like the attempted secession of Biafra from Nigeria between 1967 and 1970 failed, after all, and irredentist movements among the Kurds and Pashtuns have been dampened by ambivalence or opposition to them internationally.

Dynamics and Effects of Secession

Full-blown secessionist wars are relatively infrequent among the forms that modern political movements take. This is not because there is any shortage of separatist sentiment within the international system and especially in the developing world. Most of the groups advocating separatism never have their sentiment rise to the level of open rebellion. In some cases, the reason may be that the members of the portion of the population that favors separatism are too few in number and too weak to have any hope of seceding, and thus accommodate themselves to a reality they do not prefer but about which they conclude they can do little. Tibetans and the Basques of Spain are examples. In others, the government may reach a formal or informal understanding that grants enough autonomy short of secession to separatists to dampen their ardor or feeling of need for complete secession. Pakistan, for instance, grants considerable de facto autonomy to its Pashtun minority in the tribal areas adjoining the frontier with Afghanistan (a frontier the Pashtuns neither recognize nor respect) partly to dampen sentiment for the formation of a state of Pashtunistan.

When secessions are actually attempted, they have usually failed. One reason already suggested is that those seeking separation are too small or weak to succeed in forcing the existing government to meet their demands. When the Ibo-led Biafran secession movement in Nigeria declared its separation from Africa's most populous country, for instance, the government was able to beat it down over time with superior resources. The American Confederacy, with a population only about one-quarter of the Union (if slaves were not counted) and no real industrial base, was worn down and eventually extinguished by the U.S. government. Many Kashmiris would prefer an independent state either to their continuing inclusion in India or as part of Pakistan, but they simply lack the resources to bring independence about. If the government is ambivalent toward the continuation of the union (a Northern problem during the American Civil War) or faces external pressures to loosen control, secessionist movements may have some enhanced prospects of success, but the government normally enters the competition with considerable advantages.

External assistance or opposition is also a considerable factor in secessionist success or failure. The championing of human rights has been a significant international dynamic which secession is one (if an extreme) way to achieve, but the broader trend has been for the consolidation, not balkanization, of states. The Czech and Yugoslav cases are exceptions to this observation, but they may also prove the harbingers of the future. Yugoslavia in particular was an almost totally artificial state when its consolidation was proclaimed in 1929, with highly different and what proved to be incompatible population segments that included Serbs, Croats, and Bosnians and where cleavages were reinforced by religion and historical tradition. Yugoslavia was a country virtually guaranteed to fail, and it did. Its composition is not dissimilar to that of many contemporary developing world states. Will their fate also be the same?

The creation of new states through secession can, however, create as many problems as it solves. The likelihood of an independent Kurdistan originating in Iraq would certainly please the Kurdish majority in the Kurdish north, but it would create significant internal and external opposition. The oil wealth of northern Iraq would be denied to the rest of the country and particularly to the Sunni minority that happens to sit on virtually no proven oil reserves. Internationally, neighboring states with Kurdish enclaves would also oppose a Kurdish independence that would energize Kurdish irredentism among their own Kurdish populations. Partition is also one of the potential solutions to the Syrian crisis sometimes discussed by outsiders, but both the internal and external consequences of redrawing the Syrian map have generated little enthusiasm among either the internal combatants or neighbors, as discussed later in this case.

Despite its checkered history, the appeal of secession remains high, at least in the abstract. Secession can be a positive expression of self-determination for oppressed groups within multinational states, and those who support secessionist attempts tend to emphasize the act of disunion as an avenue to allow national self-determination. The dynamics of self-determination are not, however, always obviously served by disunion, a point made almost two decades ago by political sociologist Amatai Etzioni.

A major problem identified by Etzioni is that self-determination through secession may create freedom and justice for some peoples but not for others. The process of disassembling and aggregating territories politically may create a liberating sense of freedom and self-determination for some within the new union (presumably those who moved to create it), but may relegate others within the new union to a minority status where they switch roles from being the dominating to becoming the oppressed. This process can be particularly traumatic and bloody. When the Punjab area of the Asian subcontinent was partitioned into Hindu-dominated India and Muslim-dominated Pakistan in 1947, the result was the largest mass migration in human history. Hindus trapped within Pakistan and Muslims on the Indian side of the frontier fled across the new border to join their co-religionists and thus avoid what they feared would be oppression as minorities if they stayed in their homes. The tyranny of a former majority may become the tyranny of a vengeful new majority created by self-determination, in other words, enhancing the status of one group at the expense of others. The current majority can be expected to oppose any proposed secession on those grounds alone.

The causes and consequences of secession are complex and not well understood in general terms, at least partially because of its relative infrequency. Certainly, not enough is known to suggest with any real confidence if secession is the "right" solution to any particular situation, at least partially because different situations are to some extend idiosyncratic and thus beyond confident generalization. There is considerable ambivalence to the idea of secession that has roots in international law, history, and recent experience. The subject has received less attention than other human security concerns at least partially because instances have been less frequent than other causes of international instability and violence and thus as challenges to the security of human groups. The continuing instability in the developed world resulting from imperfectly drawn political maps, however, means that that secession offers at least one conceivable solution to a range of situations that may arise in the future. Nowhere is that set of possibilities more evident than in the volatile Middle East, as a brief examination of the situation in Syria suggests.

Secession as a Syrian Solution?

There is no place on the face of the earth where basic human security is more systematically threatened than in the maelstrom of contemporary Syria today. Civil War broke out in the country of 22 million in 2011 as a kind of adjunct of the Arab Spring phenomenon, and it has raged with an unparalleled viciousness since.

The dimensions of the disaster are staggering, and they continue to mount. United Nations (UN) figures, for instance, estimate that there are over 1.6 million refugees (over 7 percent of the country's population) who have fled across the Syrian border into adjacent countries—principally Turkey and Jordan— which have scant provision to deal with them, and the outflow has no end in sight. The number of displaced persons within the country is probably close to 5 million, although accurate estimates are virtually impossible to collect. The death toll on both sides of the conflict is rising. According to Tabler in the July/August 2013 edition of *Foreign Affairs*, the civil war "has killed 80,000 and displaced nearly one-half of Syria's population." If current casualty rates continue, "Syria will by August hit a milestone: 100,000 killed." There have been reports of war crimes in the form of gas warfare against both sides, but principally by the beleaguered government of Bashar al-Assad, whose removal from power is widely demanded by the international community. By the middle of 2013, there were foreign fighters and resources flowing into the country from both sides that upped the ante and introduced additional sources of instability. According to Tabler, these include terrorists and their supporters: Hezbollah fighters backing the regime; members of Jabhat al-Nusra, an affiliate of Al Qaeda, supporting Sunni resisters; and the Kurdish Workers' Party in the Kurdish north of the country. In June 2013, American President Barack Obama pledged direct American assistance to the insurgents, although to which factions and in what kinds and amounts was largely unspecified.

The country is in shambles, caught in a downward spiraling death hold that no one seems capable of ending. Despite international pressure, the Assad government remains intransigent, and although the tide of war seemed to be turning against it in early 2013, outside fighters had tipped the balance back in its favor by the middle of 2013. As outside support mounted for both sides, it has become increasingly evident that supporters and opponents of the regime are unwilling to let the side they back fail, although they also seem unwilling or unable to ensure the success of their allies. The internal situation in Syria has become so desperate and bitterness between the two sides has become so deep that it is not clear what, if any, form of reconciliation is possible.

The conflict is complicated. The fundamental cleavage that has emerged and around which most outside regional support is based is confessional, based in a widening gulf between the country's Sunni majority and their former partners in governance, the Alawites. Any resolution of the conflict must somehow find a way to either reconcile or separate these two groups. As the war drags on and bitterness becomes more intense, reconciliation seems increasingly unlikely.

The government is effectively controlled by a minority tribal sect, the Shiite Alawites, who have effectively ruled in historic alliance with the Sunnis. The emergence of the Alawites as the dominant force in Syrian politics goes back to the rule of Hafez al-Assad, who consolidated power in 1970 and held it until his death in 2000, at which time power was transferred to his son Bashar. The al-Assad family is Alawite, and while Hafez was in power, he surrounded himself with trusted fellow members of the sect, who dominated the military and civilian government positions, and they historically were supported by the powerful Sunni business community.

As the differences between Sunni and Shiite variations of Islam have become more pronounced, the relationship became strained and was particularly inflamed by Sunni accusations of governmental mismanagement and oppression. Despite very real differences between mainstream Shiism and the Alawite variation (which was only recognized as being part of Shiism in 1974 by a Lebanese cleric, Musa Sadr), Shiite states like Iran (whose population is Persian, unlike the Alawite Arabs) and movements (like Hezbollah) have come to Assad's cause, and the lines have hardened to overlay the ongoing civil war with a significant Sunni–Shiite patina. The heart of this religious division is the political division between the majority Sunnis and the Alawites, who constitute about 12 percent of the Syrian population (there are about 2.6 million of them within Syria). Most of the opposition groups are Sunni and supported by Sunni Muslim regimes (like Turkey, Saudi Arabia, and Qatar) and movements (that allegedly include Al Qaeda). One of the difficulties facing outsiders is that the opposition is splintered among numerous factions sponsored and supported by different outsiders, making it very difficult, and in some cases impossible, to determine who are the "good" and "bad" opponents and thus to whom assistance should be funneled. Not far from the surface of such discussions is the danger that aid could end up supporting something like what became the Taliban and Al Qaeda during resistance to the Soviet occupation of Afghanistan during the 1980s.

It is by no means clear how the Syrian conflict will end, particularly since it has become a confessional confrontation between the Sunni and the Shiites and their outside supporters. Tabler cites the worst long-term prospect: "A prolonged sectarian civil war risks becoming a broader proxy war between Iran and the Sunni powers." Such a war could have very destabilizing impacts on the region as a whole and is one both inhabitants and outsiders would like to avoid. These prospects provide an incentive for the outside world to engineer a settlement. But what is possible?

The key element in any eventual settlement, however, is probably the disposition of the Alawites, a dilemma in which the possibility of partition becomes a potential option. If the majority Sunnis eventually succeed in overthrowing the Assad regime (the overwhelming preference among outsiders), the fate of the minority Alawites remains. As Tabler and others point out, the Alawites have genuine concern that the Sunni majority will engage in retribution against them if Assad falls and is replaced by a Sunni-dominated successor. Most would likely retreat to the Alawite region around Latakia on the Mediterranean, but it is not clear they would be safe if that region remains part of Syria.

One solution that is occasionally raised is a "carved-out ministate" in the Latakia province, the traditional home of the Alawites. There is some precedent for such a state. When the French and British carved up what has become modern Syria from the Ottoman ashes, for instance, they identified three major territories to which they assigned the status of "state": a State of Damascus in the south surrounding the capital, a State of Aleppo in the Sunni north with the country's second largest city at its core, and an Alawite state along the coastline north of Lebanon. Creating an Alawite state would create serious difficulties—it is Syria's only outlet to the sea—for instance, but it might be a way to make more likely postwar peace and even to hasten the end of the war.

Secession may not be the solution in Syria, but it is a possibility worth mention, and similar possibilities exist for other multinational developing world states. The partition of Iraq, for instance, has been suggested as a potential possibility, and there will undoubtedly be more of these in the future. One place where the instinct to break apart has been in the Sudan with the successful secession of the Republic of South Sudan. This action may be the result of idiosyncratic factors in the region that make it difficult to think of Sudan as a precedent, but it is worth examining as part of a potential international trend.

CASE STUDY: THE REPUBLIC OF SOUTH SUDAN

The Republic of South Sudan was officially born on July 9, 2011, when the secession of that state from the Islamic Republic of Sudan was finally consummated in ceremonies in the new capital of Juba. It is an obscure, out of the way place one of whose relatively few points of notoriety is that it is the home of the so-called Lost Boys of Sudan. World leaders from around the globe were present (the United States was represented by then-ambassador to the UN Susan Rice) for the christening of the world's newest country. In short order, the United Nations recognized the new country as its 192nd member. It was the latest successful expression of the principle of self-determination in one of the world's most multinational, blood-stained countries.

The road leading to South Sudanese independence was long and tortured, but it was an outcome that probably represented the only ultimate solution to a violent and conflict-ridden journey for Sudan since the country achieved independence in 1956. That political entity was a tremendously unwieldy, multinational state. The physically largest state in Africa and 10th largest in the world with a land area of almost a million square miles (roughly the size of the United States east of the Mississippi River), it contained, according to Natsios, 597 tribes and sub-tribes who spoke 133 different languages. The population further divided itself imperfectly between Arabs (generally converts to Islam), who constituted about two-fifths of the population, and Africans, who made up a little over half the total, with about 10 percent who considered themselves something else. In terms of religion, about 70 percent of the population, concentrated in the north, was Sunni Muslim, with the other 30 percent, mostly living in the south, divided among adherents to various native, animist beliefs and Christianity. The attempt to force Islam upon the non-Muslims was a recurring source of conflict.

Sudan is itself a largely artificial entity, the product of the colonial geopolitics of the region. Historically, before the Turkish-Egyptian invasion of 1821, the core of what became Sudan was the area around Khartoum, including the tribal entities living in that region. As Teny-Dhurgon puts it, "Sudan in its present boundaries did not exist." What became South Sudan did not have a strong national identity at all and was, for a good bit of time, notable principally as a source of humans for the world slave trade. When the British and Egyptians created an administration of sorts over the Sudan region after World War I, the south was a reluctant adjunct that was also included when Sudan was granted its independence.

The state of Sudan created in 1956 has been more or less constantly at war with itself since its inception. There have been two different and discernible aspects to this internal struggle. The struggle between north and south that eventuated in South Sudanese secession is the oldest: a civil war broke out in the south in 1956 and continued until 1972, when a negotiated settlement created a sense of autonomy from northern Islamic domination for the dissenters concentrated around Juba. Known as the First Civil War, the peace held until 1983, when the central government in Khartoum began a campaign to enforce Islamic values—notably sharia law—nationwide. This caused the south to go into rebellion once again, and the Second Civil War lasted until 2005, when the agreement that ended in secession was negotiated. The second conflict produced the Lost Boys, young men from the Nuer and Dinka tribes of south Sudan who fled the violence in their country and wandered through Africa until the 2005 agreement allowed them to return home. The best estimates are that as many as 2.4 million were killed and another 4 million displaced in the two wars; the majority of the victims were southerners. The other conflict has been within the north and among Sudanese Arabs. Its center of attention has surrounded the province of Darfur. That conflict has been mediated several times but remains unresolved as a problem for the remainder of Sudan after secession of the south.

Based in history and experience, there is little reason for a place called Sudan to exist, at least within the boundaries it occupied before the secession of the south. Williamson summarizes the experience that accumulated in the period since the 1821 invasion forward to the recent past: "No vision unites Sudan, no sense exists that various groups share a stake in the nation, no agreement pertains on what it is to be Sudanese." Rather, he continues, "discrimination—in the economy, politics, public health, and education—has defined Sudan's past 200 years." Instead, the history of the Sudanese region is one of inter-group conflict and division along multiple overlapping lines that made division the only reasonable outcome. The political aspects of conflict and division affect all parts of the country—it is politics, for instance, that divides the government and its supporters in Khartoum from the tribal groups in places like Darfur and in the east and north of the country. The divisions between those in the northern and southern parts of Sudan are more complex and fundamental, which explains why separatism was particularly compelling in what has become South Sudan.

The division between the north and south exists on multiple levels. Much of it is racial and ethnic. Sudanese, for instance, generally think of themselves either as Arab or as Black (or African). It is a distinction that is not precise, as many who consider themselves Arab are, for instance, physically indistinguishable from those who consider themselves African. This intermixture, however, is present in many of the states of the Sahel region, and represents the intermixture of Arabs moving down from the Sahara region into sub-Saharan Africa. It is a distinction that is, for instance, the source of political discord in places like Rwanda and northern Nigeria. In pre-2011 Sudan data from the *CIA World Factbook* (reproduced in *World Almanac and Book of Facts*) found that 52 percent of the population considered itself Black and 39 percent considered itself Arab. The Arab population is concentrated almost exclusively in northern Sudan, whereas Blacks make up the majority in the south. The government in Khartoum is completely dominated by those who consider themselves Arab.

The source of conflict that the Arab–Black distinction creates is mostly religious. The Arabs are Muslims, and like Arab penetrators in other countries, they bring with them a strong sense of Islamic evangelism that is manifested in the forced conversion of non-Muslims to the faith and the imposition of Muslim values and institutions wherever they penetrate. The majority in the south, on the other hand, practices either some form of animism or Christianity, and most of the southern tribes have been particularly resistant to Islamic attempts at conversion. To some extent, this division has its roots in patterns of colonial penetration: the Ottoman Turkish and Egyptian influence on the north and British missionary activity in the south. These influences are further reflected in the fact that the official acceptable language in the north is a local dialect of Arabic, whereas the accepted language in the south is English. This distinction, in turn, probably reinforces some Western sympathy for the southerners.

It is against this backdrop that the secession of the Republic of South Sudan has taken place. The picture that emerges of Sudan is a fractured place where the government in Khartoum, supported by a tribal alliance (known as the Three Tribes) in the area surrounding the capital has attempted to impose its values on parts of the country that reject or resist that imposition. It is not a problem unique to southern Sudan, but it has been most intense in that area. Williamson summarizes the situation: "the people of the south are not the only group on the periphery that has long been marginalized. Peoples of the east, of the central Nuba Mountains, of Darfur in the west, and elsewhere have suffered similar injustices and have rebelled from time to time." Matters came to a head, however, in the south, and because it is the region that has successfully seceded from the center (it is not impossible to imagine other areas like Darfur eventually attempting the same thing), the discussion concentrates on that conflict.

The Bases of Southern Sudanese Secession

North–south animosity preceded the declaration of Sudanese independence and was amplified by the creation of the new state. In pre-colonial times, the south was the source of chattel slaves, either captured by Arabs from the north or transported to "market" through areas of what became northern Sudan, thereby creating a long legacy of southern distrust. The first civil war between north and south broke out within months of the declaration of the Sudanese state and was, according to Natsios, precipitated by events before the new state came into existence: "the prelude to the first civil war began five months before Sudanese independence had even become a formal reality," when the British, whom the south Sudanese considered friends and protectors, announced their withdrawal from the southern region. Upon independence, the new government in Khartoum announced its intention to impose Islamic values country-wide, including in the non-Islamic south. The actions included the mandatory introduction of Arabic in schools and public dealings, the subordination of the region to the central government, and, most infamously, the imposition of sharia law throughout the country.

These impositions were intolerable to southerners, and the first civil war raged between north and south from 1957 to 1972. Casualties from this conflict and the 22-year second civil war between 1983 and 2005 are generally estimated at 2.5 million killed and 4 million displaced, as already noted. The context for this bloodletting is a southern Sudanese population of slightly over 11 million in 2012 and as a contrast with the much more highly publicized casualties in Darfur, where deaths are generally estimated at about 300,000—less than one-eighth of those killed in the wars leading to South Sudanese secession.

The first civil war was ended by the Addis Ababa Agreement of 1972 negotiated in that capital of Ethiopia. The fact of a peace settlement indicated the inability of the much more populous north (whose 2012 population numbered about 34.8 million) to bring the southerners to heel, and under its provisions, as chronicled by Natsios, the north was forced to make significant concessions. These included regional autonomy politically for the south, an independent military structure for military troops from the south (rather than their integration into northern-dominated forces), a secular constitution (that included abrogation of sharia law), and the reinstitution of English as the primary language in the south. After one of its several uprisings in 1977, a new government in Khartoum renounced the central provisions of the Addis Ababa agreement. Most egregious from a southern vantage point was the reinstitution of sharia law in some of its most extreme ways, including the practices of stoning criminals to death and even crucifixion as a means of execution (during the second war, there were occasional reports of southern rebel military captives being crucified, a practice the government denied).

The Process of Secession

The outbreak of the second civil war began the process leading to eventual demands for secession, although these trends were accentuated both by rebellions in other parts of the country and by actions of the Khartoum government that outraged both citizens of Sudan and the outside world. Before the highly publicized rebellion in Darfur, most of this occurred beneath the radar of general international concern, and the discovery of oil in Sudan helped add to the resulting awakening of awareness.

The causes of the second civil war were familiar and centered on the imposition of sharia law countrywide, again in direct violation of the Addis Ababa agreement by an increasingly Islamist regime in Khartoum (Islamists are distinguishable by their adherence to a very fundamentalist—sometimes called salafist—interpretation of Islam). This ascendancy included particularly harsh treatment of non-Muslims in the south and accelerated even more after General Omar Hussein al-Bashir achieved the presidency through a coup in 1989. Bashir's base is in the Islamist portion of the northern population, and his continued possession of power (he is still the president of Sudan) helped flame separatist sentiments in the south. Although the forces available to the government were both more numerous and better equipped than their rebellious southern opponents (they received arms from, among other places, China and Russia), they were unable to subdue the more highly motivated separatists, thus allowing the war to continue for as long as it did.

Several trends developed as the war dragged on that militated toward the separation that eventually occurred. Natsios cites four specific factors that changed the domestic and international landscape of the conflict. First, the "brutality" of the two separate civil wars in the country began to attract unfavorable foreign attention to the Sudan, as well as draining the resources of the regime. Although government suppression of outside observers had managed to obscure most of the worst atrocities in the south, the three rebellions in Darfur (from 1987 to 1989, from 1995 to 1999, and from 2003 to the present) painted an increasingly bleak and negative picture of Sudan and contributed to its progressive isolation in the international system. Second, Africans became increasingly upset by the increasingly aggressive and xenophobic export of Islamism by the regime, cementing regional opposition to Khartoum and, by reflection, support for the two revolutions. Third, one manifestation of the aggressive export of extremism by the regime in Khartoum was its policy in the early and middle 1990s of providing a safe haven for terrorist groups and their leaders. The most famous of these "guests" was Osama bin Laden and his Al Qaeda cohorts. The regime eventually backed away from this policy and, for instance, threw bin Laden out of the country (after allegedly offering to turn him over to the Americans in 1996 before his expulsion to Afghanistan), but the die was cast in terms of an increasingly negative view of the Sudanese regime.

The fourth and, for some purposes, most influential trend was the beginning of oil production from Sudanese oil fields in 1998. Petroleum reserves had first been discovered in Sudan in 1974, but exploitation was inhibited by Sudanese politics and the remote location of the potential oil fields both within Sudan and in relation to facilities for exporting it. The exact size of these reserves is debatable, with estimates from 2–3 billion barrels to as much as 10 billion barrels, and most of these are located in the south, including in areas claimed by both Sudan and South Sudan. Geographic isolation makes the shipment of oil from the fields difficult, and the eventual solution was to build a pipeline to Port Sudan, a Red Sea outlet in the northern region. China, which has had a major stake in Sudanese reserves (see Chapter 2), aided in developing this port. Port Sudan is in the northern region, and there are no obvious alternatives to get Sudanese oil to market.

Oil transformed the situation in Sudan. The country is, and always has been, desperately poor, and oil revenues promised the possibility of increased prosperity. Oil also changed the nature of the civil war. As Natsios explains, "Oil replaced religious expansionism as the reason for war, and since the war was inhibiting oil production, peace became a logical policy." Both sides, the al-Bashir government in Khartoum and the Sudanese People's Liberation Movement/Army (the SPLM/A) representing the South in Juba, need oil revenue, and neither can get that revenue independent of the other: over 75 percent of the reserves are in the south, and there is no alternative to transshipment across the north to Port Sudan. As a result, oil helped push the contending sides toward an accord that both needed and, as it turns out, with which neither has proven especially comfortable.

With the situation on the ground stalemated and heavy outside pressure to end the violence, the north and south agreed to end the fighting in the Comprehensive Peace Agreement (CPA) of 2005. This accord was heavily lobbied for and influenced by the United States and others. In essence, it did several things in addition to creating a cease-fire. First, it created a "'government of national unity' and established an autonomous Government of Southern Sudan (GOSS)." This meant southerners were incorporated into the regime in Khartoum, but most day-to-day decision making affecting southerners was done in Juba. Second, it rescinded the most odious aspects of the Islamist policies of the north, notably the imposition of sharia law on non-Muslims, mandatory Arabic as the official language countrywide (English became the official language of the south), and the attempt to integrate southern military units (mostly SPLA) into Sudanese units controlled by northern Arabs. In particular, it called for the removal of all Sudanese Armed Forces (SAF) northerners from the south and SPLA units from the north. Third, it called for democratic elections throughout the country by 2009 (they were actually not held until 2010). Fourth, it set an interim period that would lead to a referendum in the south in January 2011 regarding continued union. Fifth, it called for a special status for contested areas, notably Abyei.

Events between 2005 and 2011 influenced this process. Prendergast and Thomas-Jensen cite four in particular surrounding 2009. First, the International Criminal Court (ICC) issued an arrest warrant for President Bashir charging him with war crimes in Darfur, a warrant the government refused to honor. Second, the government decided to close down the operation of 16 humanitarian international organizations in the south and north in retaliation for the warrant, an act that further isolated the regime in the international arena. Third, the global economic crisis hit Sudan in the form of sharp drops in the price of oil to about $50 a barrel. Because oil was virtually Sudan's only export, this made a perpetually bad economic situation even worse in both the north and south. Fourth and finally, the election of an Afro-American president of the United States in 2008 raised fears in Khartoum that the new Obama administration might come decisively to the aid of the rebels. Sudan was running out of both friends and options.

In this setting, the CPA-mandated referendum was held under international observation in January 2011. With over 3.5 million southerners registered and voting, an overwhelming 98.6 percent voted for secession, an outcome that was not unexpected (except possibly in its virtually unanimous nature), and the government in Khartoum had no realistic alternative but to accept the results. As noted, the new Republic of South Sudan was born on July 9, 2011, in Juba. What President Obama called on January 8, 2011, an "exercise in self-determination long in the making" had succeeded.

The Prospects of the Sudans

The physical separation of the two parts of Sudan has not been an untrammeled success. Politically, there has not been major conflict or violence between the two sovereign units, but neither have there been the cessation of all differences and the emergence of a spirit of cooperation. Khartoum is still immersed in civil unrest in Darfur, and both sides are still, even increasingly, economically weak and tottering.

There are two major issues that continue to divide the two Sudans. The first and by far most consequential for both states is the question of oil. Neither the CPA nor the separation of the two states resolved the most critical issue, which is how oil revenues are shared between oil-producing South Sudan and oil-transshipping and refining Sudan. Both have limited leverage in achieving their desired outcome, which is as large a share of the revenue as each can get. The leverage of the South Sudanese is obvious: supplies must come from within its borders. So too is Sudanese leverage: those supplies cannot get to market unless they are shipped across the Islamic Republic of Sudan and, in the words of Williamson, "There is no alternative route" either now or in the foreseeable future. This aspect of the evolving differences between the two reached crisis proportions in mid-2012, when the South Sudanese cut off supplies because of the question of revenue sharing, and production remains suspended. Since the governments of both countries rely heavily on oil revenues, the result has been to impoverish each further. Both sides are obdurate and are, in effect, punishing themselves.

The result of cutting off the oil flow has been, of course, reducing to zero the amount of oil revenue that either state receives. Almost all the foreign exchange for both countries—but especially the new and, in Natsios view, "fragile" South Sudanese state—comes from oil revenues. Recent economic data are not particularly reliable, but Prendergast and Thomas-Jensen cite figures for 2008, before secession. "In 2008," they state, "oil sales accounted for 64 percent of revenues received by the government of national unity and a whopping 90 percent of revenue for the GOSS." These figures, of course, predate the global economic downturn. The oil price consequences have been particularly felt in both countries, and the combined result of oil withholding and lower oil prices are reflected in current 2013 per capita income (as cited in the *CIA World Factbook*) for both countries. Pre-secession figures for the whole country in early 2011 stood at about $2,300. Most recent figures show per capita income for the Islamic Republic of Sudan at about $2,400, whereas the equivalent figure for the Republic of South Sudan was virtually the lowest in the world (220th) at $900.

Among the consequences of increasing economic dysfunction is the acceleration of the position of the region on the world's list of failed states. Natsios in 2012 declared that "Sudan is becoming a failed state." The successful secession of South Sudan has added to the position of both resultant entities. The 2013 Failed State Index published in the July 2013 *Foreign Policy* lists Sudan and South Sudan as third and fourth on the list, which is headed by Somalia and the Democratic Republic of Congo. Chad is fifth. The geographical proximity of these "leaders" is probably not a coincidence. A resumption of oil production will ease the situation somewhat, but not relieve it altogether.

The other aspect of continuing disagreement is an area along the border between the two states, the Abyei region. The issue in this region, which is wedged between Sudan and South Sudan and claimed by each, is over sovereignty. It is of particular importance to the South Sudanese because, as Williamson points out, "The Abyei area . . . is home of the Ngok Dinka, the tribe to which many of the most prominent personalities in South Sudan belong." The region has been in contention for some time and is, in Natsios's words, the "powderkeg of Sudan—the Kashmir of the north-south conflict." The current crisis was precipitated before the independence vote when SAF irregular forces swept into the town of Abyei in the manner of Darfur raiders, burning and looting and sending roughly 100,000 residents into the surrounding countryside, from which most of them have not returned. Partially because of this displacement, Abyei was not included in the 2011 referendum, which was one reason for the raid in the first place (the Dinka in Abyei are closely related to the Dinka in South Sudan who make up the largest tribal group in the country). The area remains under contention and is now patrolled by an African Union consisting of 4,200 Ethiopian troops whose presence has not coaxed the displaced Dinka into returning. Natsios argues that Abyei "represents the greatest threat to the peace negotiations" and progress toward normalization in relations between the two states.

On October 31, 2013, a non-binding referendum was conducted in Abyei to allow citizens to express their preferred political future status. The Muslim minority refused to participate in the voting, and over 99 percent of those who did vote said they preferred incorporation into South Sudan. It is unclear what, if any, effect this vote will have, but this clear statement of preference can only add to pressures to incorporate the area into South Sudan. Because of the potential impact on the oil situation, it can only add to the volatility of the situation.

A greater threat to stability erupted in late 2013, when inter-tribal fighting broke out between members of army units from the two largest tribes, the Christian Dinka and the animist Nuer (most South Sudanese army units are tribally defined). The precipitant was the dismissal of Vice President Riek Machar, a Nuer, by the President, Salva Kiir, a Dinka. Nuer units mutinied, sending fearful tribal members into panicked flight to nearby United Nations refugee camps or into the bush. Amid fears of general civil war, peace talks began in the Ethiopian capital of Addis Ababa, where the end of the first Sudanese civil war was negotiated, in late December 2013. These talks continued in early 2014.

CONCLUSION

Secession remains one of the most traumatic potential political actions in international politics. The sentiment that underlies the attempts of areas to separate themselves from existing political entities and to try to form new states is an old one that is only occasionally attempted and that has a very mixed record of success. As an act of proclaimed "self-determination," the idea of secession probably enjoys more legitimacy today than it did in earlier times when it collided with the more prevailing view of the supremacy of state sovereignty as a central value.

The net effect of secession is the partition of existing states, and in an international system of artificial states that are either multinational or irredentist in composition, the underlying appeal of the idea may become broader in the future. The Middle East offers some particularly good examples of where a separatist solution may make some sense in places like Iraq and Syria, but such solutions are always going to be controversial, and their effects uncertain enough to produce both internal and international resistance. The largest partition in recent human history, the secession of the states of the Soviet Union, it must be recalled, was viewed with considerable suspicion and reluctance at the time it was occurring because many were uncertain about what would happen next. On a smaller scale, the same uncertainty surrounds contemporary potential movements.

As the case of South Sudan vividly illustrates, the process and outcomes of secession are often very messy and uncertain. The slaughter in the wars between North and South Sudan was enormous, and more dismemberment of Sudan may lie ahead now that Darfurians and others can see that success is possible. Even when secession is accomplished, however, that does not guarantee a good and positive effect. South Sudan may eventually succeed as a political and economic unit, but for now, it is an extremely poor state, the prospects for which are uncertain. Secession has solved some of the problems its people face, but certainly not all of them.

International reactions to secessionist attempts cannot be taken for granted or counted upon. The South Sudanese example may be an important harbinger for the future. If one assumes that most future secessionist movements will arise in developing-world countries, it follows that successful separations will create some need for assistance if the seceding unit is to succeed. As President Obama put it regarding the independence vote in South Sudan in 2011, "the international community, including the United States, will have an interest in ensuring that the two nations that emerge succeed as stable and economically viable neighbors, because their fortunes are linked. South Sudan, in particular, will need partners in the long-term task of fulfilling the political and economic aspirations of its people." This laudable statement suggests some outpouring of international material support that has not to date been apparent in South Sudan. Given the competing demands for resources within and among states, those contemplating secession should probably not expect much help beyond moral support, and this problem is especially acute in an internationally obscure place like South Sudan. Other than the publicity associated with the 2003 movie "Lost Boys of Sudan," it has remained largely "off the radar" of international concern and awareness.

Will secession become a more important part of the pattern of international relations in the future? The number and variety of unstable political entities in the postcolonial world suggest that there will be no shortage of candidates, but whether they will choose a secessionist path, and especially whether they will succeed, is certainly problematical. Just as the outcomes of individual secessionist attempts is always difficult to predict, so too is the question of whether or not secession is a wave of the future.

SUGGESTED ACTIVITIES AND QUESTIONS

1. What is secession? Why is it relatively infrequent? Why is it described in the text as "traumatic" and often "bloody"? How is it related to the concept of self-determination?
2. Is there a right to secede? Discuss the various sides of the debate. With which side do you agree?
3. Why are contemporary secessionist movements largely associated with the developing world? What are the influences of the pattern of colonization and decolonization? What major flaws in the pattern of decolonization have led to secessionist movements in some cases?
4. How do secessionist movements work? Why do most of them fail? What negative and positive effects do most successful movements share?
5. Apply the arguments about secession to Syria, including multinationalism and irredentism and the key factor of the fate of the Alawites in a possible solution.
6. Why was Sudan a prime candidate for a multinationalist secession? Describe the bases of division among Sudanese, emphasizing sources of cleavage between southerners and northerners.
7. Discuss the chronology and events of the two Sudanese civil wars, including the major issues between south and north and the impact of the discovery of oil. How did events and trends accumulate to make secession inevitable?
8. What are the prospects for the two Sudanese states since secession? What cautions should these provide for the phenomenon and advocacy of secession as a solution in other countries?

SUGGESTED READINGS AND RESOURCES

Arnold, Matthew and Matthew LeRiche. *South Sudan: From Revolution to Independence.* New York: Oxford University Press, 2012.

Brilmayer, Lea. "Secession and Self-Determination: A Territorial Interpretation." Yale University Faculty Scholarship Series 2434. New Haven, CT: Yale University, 1991.

Buchanan, Allen. *The Morality of Political Divorce from Sort Sumter to Lithuania and Quebec.* Boulder, CO: Westview Press, 1991.

Dagne, Ted. *The Republic of South Sudan: Opportunities and Challenges for Africa's Newest Country.* Washington, DC: Congressional Research Service, 2011.

De Waal, Alexander and Julie Flint. *Darfur: A New History of a Long War.* London: Zed Books, 2008.

Etzioni, Amatai. "The Evils of Self-Determination." *Foreign Policy,* Winter 1992/1993, 21–35.

"Failed States: The 2013 Index." *Foreign Policy,* July/August 2013, 68–70.

Feinstein, Lee. *Darfur and Beyond: What Is Needed to Prevent Mass Atrocities.* New York: Council on Foreign Relations Books, 2007.

Finian, William W. Jr. "Darfur and the Politics of Altruism." *Current History* 106, 700 (May 2007), 235–236.

Gordon, David. *Secession, State, and Liberty.* New York: Transaction Books, 1998.

Grotius, Hugo. *The Rights of War and Peace: Including the Law of Nature and Nations.* New York: M. W. Dunne, 1991.

Kohen, Marcela G., ed. *Secession: International Law Perspectives.* Cambridge, UK: Cambridge University Press, 2006.

Lehning, Percy. *Theories of Secession.* New York: Routledge, 1998.

Levy, Patricia and Zawaiah Abdul Latif. *Sudan,* 2nd ed. New York: Marshall Cavendish, 2008.

Natsios, Andrew S. *Sudan, South Sudan, and Darfur: What Everyone Needs to Know.* New York: Oxford University Press, 2012.

Obama, Barack. "In Sudan, an Election and a Beginning." *New York Times* (online), January 8, 2011.

Prendergast, John and Colin Thomas-Jensen. "Sudan: A State on the Brink?" *Current History* 108, 718 (May 2009), 208–213.

Simon, Marlise and Lydia Polgreen. "Sudanese President Accused of Genocide." *New York Times* (online), July 15, 2008.

Straus, Scott. "Darfur and the Genocide Debate." *Foreign Affairs* 84, 1 (January/February 2005), 125–133.

Tabler, Andrew J. "Syria's Collapse: And How Washington Can Stop It." *Foreign Affairs* 92, 4 (July/August 2013), 90–100.

Teny-Dhrghon, Reik Machar. "South Sudan: A History of Political Domination—A Case of Self-Determination." Philadelphia: University of Pennsylvania African Studies Center, 1995 (online).

Wellman, Christopher Heath. *A Theory of Secession.* Cambridge, UK: Cambridge University Press, 2005.

Williamson, Richard S. "Sudan on the Cusp." *Current History* 110, 736 (May 2011), 171–176.

The World Almanac and Book of Facts, 2011 and *2013.* New York: World Almanac Book, 2011 and 2013.

Terrorism: The Changing Global Threat

PRÉCIS

The terrorist attacks of September 11, 2001, are now over a decade in the past, but the problem of terrorism remains a vital international and national concern. Terrorism had been a growing problem for the better part of two decades before 2001 but had not achieved the level of notoriety that the attacks evinced. Largely successful efforts to respond to the actions of Al Qaeda, the group that carried out the 9/11 attacks, have, in turn, caused the nature of the threat to change, and efforts to adapt to and counter new permutations remain a major agenda item for terrorism suppressors.

The purpose of this case is to investigate the nature of the terrorist problem, how it is changing, and what can be done about it. It begins by examining briefly the dynamics of terrorism: What is it; what do terrorists seek to do; who are they; and what causes people to become terrorists? It then moves to how terrorism has evolved structurally as a problem since September 11 and what efforts have been mounted against it. It concludes by examining the current decentralized nature of the threat and social problems posed by so-called lone-wolf terrorists.

The tragic terrorist attack by the Islamic terrorist group Al Qaeda against the World Trade Center towers and the Pentagon 13 years ago on September 11, 2001, was a seminal international and national event. Internationally, it signaled a new and frightening escalation of a problem that had troubled other parts of the world for a long time, and it produced an enormous outpouring of sympathy and support for the United States as the newest victim. Nationally, the attacks traumatized an American population suddenly aware of its vulnerability and spawned a major national priority to deal with this problem under the official sobriquet of the "global war on terrorism" (GWOT).

The GWOT is now over a decade old as well. It has had some successes, capturing or otherwise suppressing elements of the old Al Qaeda network. The crown jewel of this effort was the assassination of Al Qaeda founder and leader Osama bin Laden in 2011. The result has been to change the nature of the threat. The monolithic threat posed by Al Qaeda itself may be less than it was in 2001, but the problem of terrorism remains: New permutations have arisen that are, if anything, more provocative and dangerous. Most share radical Islam as a foundation, but from Chechnya to Indonesia to Somalia, new and different organizations have emerged as new challenges: International terrorism has become a hydra-headed beast.

Some of the ardor and intensity associated with the early post-9/11 period has weakened in recent years. In some ways, this reaction is entirely natural and justifiable. For one thing, the intensity has dissipated as time has passed and no equivalent attacks have followed. Terrorist activities, including some well-publicized attacks and attempts worldwide, continue, but none have risen to a level of violence and atrocity even closely approaching that of 9/11, and there are widespread suspicions that terrorists may simply lack the resources necessary to replicate the attacks on New York and Washington, D.C., by Al Qaeda. The possibility that terrorists might gain access to weapons of mass destruction (WMDs) is the single exception to this train of analysis. The absence of major terrorist follow-on activities against the United States, despite a series of botched attempts, is particularly exemplary in this regard.

None of this means the problem of terrorism has disappeared, of course. Terrorism remains a major and, in some ways, more pervasive force that may or may not pose individual threats of the calamity of 9/11 but that has spread to infect greater parts of the world. Still based mainly in particularly militant, unorthodox interpretations of Islam, the threat has morphed from an apparently concentrated, hierarchical Al Qaeda directed by bin Laden and his close associates to a more diffuse movement directing its mayhem internally in places like the Indian subcontinent and parts of Africa and more broadly to European targets like London.

The changes, examined more systematically later in the chapter, are partially organizational and structural. Al Qaeda is no longer a monolithic, hierarchical entity directing terror; rather, it has become a loosely associated series of "franchises" bound by some ideological affinity. Acts of terror now include highly public acts by independent individuals known as lone wolves. The Internet sometimes serves as a connector between these demented individuals and purveyors of venomous, murderous hatred via so-called virtual networks or leaderless resistance groups.

WHAT IS TERRORISM?

The first step in coming to grips with terrorism is defining the term. It is an important consideration, because so many phenomena in the contemporary international arena are labeled terrorist. This makes a definition particularly important as a means to measure whether a particular movement, or act, is terrorism or not. Without a set of criteria defining what does and does not constitute terrorism, it is hard to tell.

This is not a merely semantic exercise. Take, for instance, the ongoing emphasis on Chechen separatists and their separatist campaign against the Russian government, which that government has called terrorist. Certainly, actions such as enlisting suicide terrorists to blow up two Russian airliners and the brutal siege of the school in Beslan in the Caucasus were hideous, brutal acts that comport with an understanding of terrorism, but is it correct to label the movement that commissioned and carried out the acts terrorist as a result? In context, when the Russian government of the then-president Boris Yeltsin used the Russian army to attack Chechnya in 1995 to wipe out the secessionist movement there (among other things, leveling the capital of Grozny) and president Vladimir Putin renewed the campaign in 1999, there were widespread international accusations that the Russian government was terrorizing the Chechens and engaging in crimes against humanity (acts of state terrorism). So who is the terrorist here?

Having an agreed-on definition of terrorism helps answer defining questions; unfortunately, such a consensus does not exist. Rather, there are virtually as many different definitions as there are people and organizations making the distinctions. There are also some commonalities that recur and will allow the adoption of a definition for present purposes. A few arguably representative examples will aid in drawing distinctions.

The U.S. government offers the official definition in its 2003 *National Strategy for Combating Terrorism:* "premeditated, politically motivated violence perpetrated against noncombatant targets by subnational groups or clandestine agents." In *Attacking Terrorism,* coauthor Audrey Kurth Cronin says terrorism is distinguished by its political nature, its nonstate base, the targeting of innocent noncombatants, and the illegality of its acts. Jessica Stern, in *Terrorism in the Name of God,* defines terrorism as "an act or threat of violence against noncombatants with the objective of exacting revenge, intimidating, or otherwise influencing an audience." Alan Dershowitz (in *Why Terrorism Works*), offers no definition himself, but notes that definitions typically include reference to terrorist targets, perpetrators, and terrorist acts.

These definitions, and similar ones from others in the field, have common cores. All of them share three common points of reference: terrorist acts (illegal, often hideous and atrocious), terrorist targets (often innocent noncombatants), and terrorist purposes (political persuasion or influence). The only difference among them is whether they specify the nature of terrorists and their political base: The State Department, Cronin, and Dershowitz all identify terrorist organizations as nonstate-based actors. Cronin in particular emphasizes that "although states can terrorize, by definition they cannot be terrorists."

For the rest of this case study, terrorism will be defined as "the commission of atrocious acts against a target population normally to gain compliance with some demands the terrorists insist upon." It does not specify that terrorism must be committed by nonstate actors. That may be a characteristic of modern terrorism, but terrorism is terrorism, regardless of who carries it out.

Terrorism thus consists of three related phenomena, each of which must be present in some manner for something to be considered an act of terrorism. The fourth element in other definitions, perpetrators of terrorism, is implicit in the three criteria. Discussing each helps enliven an understanding of what constitutes terrorism.

Terrorist Acts

The first element of the definition encompasses *terrorist acts,* which are the visible manifestation of terrorism and the part of the phenomenon with which most people are most familiar. Several comments can be made about terrorist acts.

One comment is that what distinguishes terrorist acts from other political expressions is that they are uniformly illegal. Terrorist acts upset the normalcy of life through destructive actions aimed at either injuring or killing people or destroying things. Regardless of the professed underlying motives of terrorists, the actions they commit break laws and are subject to criminal prosecution. By raising the rhetoric of terrorist actions to acts of war (currently holy war or *jihad*), terrorists may seek to elevate what they do to a higher plane ("one man's terrorist is another man's freedom fighter"), but the simple fact remains that terrorist acts are criminal in nature.

A second comment is that the general purpose of terrorist acts is to frighten the target audience: The word *terrorism* is derived from the Latin root *terrere,* which means "to frighten." The method of inducing fright is through the commission of normally random, unpredictable acts of violence that induce such fear that those who witness or experience the acts or believe they could be the objects of similar future attacks to conclude that compliance with terrorist demands is preferable to living with the fear of being victims themselves. With the exception of explicitly targeted acts like assassinations, acts of terrorism are not particularly aimed at the actual victims themselves (who are often randomly selected and whose individual fate does not "matter" to the terrorist) but at the audience who views the actions. The dynamic of inducing this fright is the disruption of the predictability and safety of life within society, one of whose principal functions is to make existence predictable and safe. Ultimately, a major purpose of terrorism may be to undermine this vital fiber of society.

Terrorists may, of course, act for a variety of other reasons. Brian Jenkins provides a list of six other, generally less lofty, purposes for terrorist actions. Terrorist actions may be aimed at exacting special concessions, such as ransom, the release of prisoners (generally members of the terrorist group), or publicizing a message. Gaining the release of political prisoners was the stated reason that Hezbollah kidnapped Israeli soldiers in the summer of 2006, triggering widespread violence there. Indonesia's Jemaah Islamiyah carried out its 2004 attack on the Australian embassy and promptly announced that it would perpetrate similar attacks if its leader, Abu Bakar Bashir, was not released from prison.

Terrorists may act to gain publicity for their causes. Before Palestinian terrorists kidnapped a series of airliners and then launched an attack on the

Israeli compound at the Munich Olympics in the 1970s, hardly anyone outside the region had ever heard of the Palestinian cause; the terrorist actions got them that global awareness. The publicity may be intended to remind a world that has shifted its attention away from a particular group and its activities that it is still active and that it is still pursuing its goals.

Another, and more fundamental, purpose of terrorist acts is to cause widespread disorder that demoralizes society and breaks down the social order in a country. This, of course, is a very ambitious purpose, and one that presumably can only be undertaken through a widespread campaign that includes a large number of terrorist acts. The suicide terror campaign by Hamas against Israeli civilians (and the Israeli counterattacks against Palestinians) could be an example of terrorism for this purpose.

A more tactical use of terrorism is to provoke overreaction by a government in the form of repressive action, reprisals, and overly brutal counterterrorism that may lead to the overthrow of the reactive government. This was a favorite tactic of the Viet Cong in the Vietnam War, and evoked the ironic analogy of building schools during the day (as a way to pacify the population) and then bombing those schools at night (because they became the source of Viet Cong actions after nightfall).

Terror may also be used to enforce obedience and cooperation within a target population. Campaigns of terror directed by the governments of states against their own citizens often have this purpose, which is often assigned to a secret police or similar paramilitary organizations. The actions of the KGB in the Soviet Union, the Gestapo and other similar organizations in Nazi Germany, and the infamous death squads in Argentina during the 1960s and 1970s are all examples of the use of government terror to intimidate and frighten their own populations into submission. At a less formal governmental level, many actions of the Ku Klux Klan during the latter nineteenth and early twentieth centuries against Black Americans would qualify as well.

Jenkin's last purpose of terrorist action is punishment. Terrorists often argue that an action they take is aimed at a particular person or place because that person or institution is somehow guilty of a particular transgression and is thus being meted out appropriate punishment for what the terrorists consider a crime. Although the Israeli government would be appalled at the prospects of calling its rescinded counterterrorist campaign to bulldoze the homes of the families of suicide terrorists (or bombing the homes of dissident leaders) as an act of terror, from the vantage point of the Palestinian targets of the attacks, they certainly must seem so.

Stern (in *Terrorism in the Name of God*) adds a seventh motivation that is internal to the terrorist organization: morale. Like any other organization, and especially terrorist groups in which the "operatives" are generally young and not terribly mature, it may be necessary from time to time to carry out a terrorist attack simply to demonstrate to the membership the continuing potency of the group as a way to keep the membership focused and their morale high. As Stern puts it, "Attacks sometimes have more to do with rousing the troops than terrorizing the victims." Improving or maintaining morale may also have useful spin-off effects, such as helping recruit new members to the group or to raise funds to support the organization's activities.

What this discussion seeks to demonstrate is that terrorists commit their actions for a variety of reasons. Some of these are more purposive and "noble" than others, but it is rarely immediately clear what may motivate a particular action. Moreover, different reasons may motivate different groups at different times and under different circumstances. Knowing that a terrorist attack has occurred, in other words, does not necessarily tell one why it has been committed or whether and how to guard against its repetition.

Terrorist Targets

The things terrorists target can be divided into two related categories. The first is people, and the objective is to kill, maim, or otherwise cause some members of the target population to suffer as an example for the rest of that population. The second category is physical targets, attacks against which are designed to disrupt and destroy societal capabilities and to demonstrate the vulnerability of the target society. The two categories are related in that most physical targets contain people who will be killed or injured in the process. Attacking targets in either category demonstrates that the target government cannot protect its members and valued artifices. The desired effect is that the targets question the efficacy or worth of resisting terrorist demands.

There are subtle differences and problems associated with concentrating on one category or the other. Attacks intended to kill or injure people are the most personal and evoke the greatest emotion in the target population, including the will to resist and to seek vengeance. From the vantage point of the terrorist, the reason to attack people is to attack their will to resist the demands that terrorists make. Dennis Drew and I refer to this as *cost-tolerance,* the level of suffering one is willing to endure in the face of some undesirable situation. The terrorist seeks to exceed the target's cost-tolerance by making it conclude that it is physically or mentally less painful to accede to the terrorist's demands than it is to continue to resist those demands. This goal is achieved by maximizing the fear and anxiety that the target experiences because of the often hideous effects of attacks. If the target group becomes so afraid of being the next victim that the target accepts the terrorist demands, cost-tolerance is exceeded and the terrorist wins; if the target remains resolute, the terrorist fails.

Overcoming cost-tolerance is not an easy task, and it often fails. For one thing, terrorist organizations are generally small with limited resources, meaning that they usually lack the wherewithal to attack and kill a large enough portion of the target population to make members of that population become individually fearful enough to tip the scales (blowing up people on airplanes may be a partial exception). One of the great fears associated with terrorist groups obtaining and using weapons of mass destruction is that such a turn of events would change that calculus. For another thing, attacking and killing innocent members of a target group (at least innocent from the vantage point of the group) may (and usually does) infuriate its members and increase, rather than decrease, the will to resist. That has certainly been the case in the reaction to the 9/11 attacks, which both awakened the public to the threat of terrorism and created a steely resolve to resist those who committed them.

When the targets are physical things rather than people per se, the problems and calculations change. When the objective is to terrorize a whole society, the range of potential targets is virtually boundless. In attacking places, the terrorist seeks to deprive the target population of whatever pleasure or life-sustaining or -enhancing value the particular target may provide. The list of what used to be called *countervalue* targets when speaking of nuclear targeting (things people value, such as their lives and what makes those lives enjoyable) covers a very broad range of objects, from hydroelectric plants to athletic stadiums, from nuclear power generators to military facilities, from highways to research facilities, and so on. Compiling a list for any large community and trying to figure out how to protect it all is a very sobering experience.

It is unreasonable to assume that the whole potential list of physical targets for any country can be made uniformly invulnerable. There are simply too many targets, and the means to protect them are sufficiently different that there is little overlap in function (protecting a football stadium from bombers may or may not have much carryover in protecting nuclear power plants from seizure). There will always be a gap between potential threats and the ability to negate all them all. The consequence is a certain level of risk that cannot be removed.

Terrorist Objectives

The final element in the definition of terrorism is the objectives, or reasons, for which terrorists do what they do. For present purposes, the discussion of terrorist objectives will refer to the broader outcomes that terrorists seek (or say they seek) to accomplish. Objectives are the long-range reasons that terrorists wage campaigns of terrorism. In the short run, terrorists may engage in particular actions for a variety of reasons, as already noted (group morale or recruitment, for instance). What they seek ultimately to accomplish is the province of terrorist objectives.

The ultimate goals of most terrorist groups are political. To paraphrase the Clausewitzian dictum that war is politics by other means, so too is terrorism politics by other, extreme, means. Likewise, the objectives that terrorists pursue seem extreme to the target population, if not to the terrorists themselves. Sometimes, terrorist objectives are widely known and clearly articulated, and at other times they are not. Ultimately, however, campaigns of terror gain their meaning in the pursuit of some goal or goals, and their success or failure is measured to the extent that those goals are achieved.

Terrorism is the method of the militarily weak and conceptually unacceptable. The extremely unorthodox nature of terrorist actions arises from the fact that terrorists cannot compete with their targets by the accepted methods of the target society for success. Terrorists lack the military resources to engage in open warfare, at which they would be easily defeated, or in the forum of public discourse and decision, because their objectives are unacceptable, distasteful, or even bizarre to the target population.

The fact that terrorist objectives are politically objectionable to the target sets up the confrontation between the terrorists and the target. Normally, terrorist goals are stated in terms of changing policies (Palestinian statehood or the right to repatriation within Israel, for example) or laws (releasing classes of detained people) that the majority in the target state find unacceptable. Because the terrorists are in a minority, they cannot bring about the changes they demand by normal electoral or legislative means, and they are likely to be viewed as so basically lunatic and unrealistic by the target audience that it will not take those who make them seriously. To the terrorists, of course, the demands make perfect sense, and they are frustrated and angered by the treatment their demands are given. The stage is thus set for confrontation.

Terrorists achieve their objectives by overcoming the cost-tolerance of the target population. The campaign of terrorist threats and acts is intended to convince the target population that acceding to the terrorist demands is preferable to the continuing anxiety and fear of future terrorism.

Determining whether terrorists achieve their goals or fail is complicated by the contrast between the tactical and strategic levels of objectives, making the compilation of a "score card" difficult. Modern terrorists have rarely been successful at the strategic level of attaining long-range objectives. Al Qaeda has not forced the United States from the Arabian Peninsula (although the American presence is declining), Russia has not granted Chechnya independence, and Jemaah Aslamiyah has yet to achieve a sectarian Islamic state in Indonesia. At the same time, the terrorist record at achieving tactical objectives (carrying out terrorist attacks) is, if not perfect, not a total failure either. As long as terrorists continue to exist and to achieve some of their goals, they remain a force against the targets of their activities. Thus, the competition between terrorists and their targets over the accomplishment of terrorist objectives continues to exist within a kind of nether world where neither wins nor loses decisively and thus both can claim some success.

The history of terrorism, moreover, suggests its ability to endure. Different terrorist groups with different objectives come and go, but the use of terrorism as a tool to achieve *some* goals has endured for at least two millennia (most historians of terrorism—see Rapaport, for instance—date the practice to the resistance to Roman rule over Palestine during biblical times). Thus, efforts to suppress terrorism may be more realistic if their goal is to determine a "tolerable" level of terrorist activity and to try to keep instances of terrorism at or below that level rather than adopting the more comprehensive but historically daunting task of eradicating terrorism.

EVOLVING TERRORISM SINCE SEPTEMBER 11

The events of September 11 riveted national and international attention on a specific terrorist threat posed by Al Qaeda. The focus was natural given the audacity and shock value of the actual attacks and by the novelty of an organization such as Al Qaeda. To the extent that Americans had much of any previous understanding of terrorism, it was associated with more "classical" forms, such as highly politicized anticolonialist movements like the Irish Republican Army (IRA); with state terrorism in the form of suppression by totalitarian regimes like Hitler's Germany or Stalin's Soviet Union; or with isolated anarchist assassinations or individual acts like the bombing of the Murrah Federal Building in Oklahoma City.

Understanding the nature of the current threat has been difficult for at least two reasons. First, the contemporary form of terrorism is very different from anything encountered before, certainly by Americans. It is nonstate-based terrorism that does not arise from specific political communities or jurisdictions but instead flows across national boundaries like oil slipping under doors. This makes it conceptually difficult to understand and to counter. It is also religious, showing signs of fanaticism that are present in all religious communities but that are alien to most people's ability to conceptualize. Slaughter in the name of God goes beyond most of our intellectual frameworks. It is also fanatically anti-American and thus in sharp contrast to the general pro-Americanism that Americans at least believed dominated the end of the twentieth century. In addition, it employs methods such as suicide terrorism that, if not historically unique, are deviant enough to go beyond most abilities to conjure.

Second, our understanding is made more difficult by the extremely changeable nature of contemporary terrorist opponents. The Al Qaeda of 2001 was hard enough to understand, but it has evolved greatly since then. Partly this is because international efforts since 2001 have been quite effective in dismantling the old Al Qaeda structure by capturing and killing many of its members. This success, however, has caused the threat to disperse and transform itself into forms that we find even less recognizable and thus more difficult to identify and attack. Thus, a discussion of organizational evolution is necessary to clarify the nature of the current terrorist threat.

The Traditional Threat

Stern, in *Terrorism in the Name of God*, lays out the requirements for a successful terrorist organization. The effectiveness of a terrorist organization is dependent on two qualities: resiliency (the ability to withstand the loss of parts of its membership or workforce) and capacity (the ability to optimize the scale and impact of terrorist attacks). The larger the scale of operations that the terrorist organization can carry out without large losses to its members through capture or death, the more effective the organization is. Conversely, if an organization can only carry out small, relatively insignificant acts while having large portions of its membership captured or killed, it is less effective.

Resiliency and capacity are clearly related to one another. For a terrorist group to carry out large operations like 9/11, it must devise a sophisticated, coordinated plan involving a number of people or cells who must communicate with one another both to plan and to execute the attack. The Achilles' heel in terrorist activity is penetration of the organization by outsiders, and the key element is the interruption of communications that allows penetration into the group and movement through the hierarchy to interfere with and destroy it and its ability to carry out attacks (in other words, to reduce its resiliency). The most effective way for the terrorist groups to avoid penetration is to minimize communications that can be intercepted, but doing this comes at the expense of the sophistication and extent of its actions (reduction in capacity).

The result is a dilemma that is changing the face of contemporary terrorist organizations. Historically, according to Stern and others, most terrorist groups have followed an organizational form known as the *commander-cadre* (or *hierarchical*) model. This form of group is not dissimilar to the way complex enterprises are structured everywhere: Executives (commanders) organize and plan activities (terrorist attacks) and pass instructions downward through the structure for implementation by employees (cadres). In order to maintain levels of secrecy that improve resiliency, terrorist groups compartmentalize themselves so that any one level of the group (cell) knows only of the cell directly above and below it.

Commander-cadre arrangements have advantages associated with any large, complex organization: They can coordinate activities maximizing capacity (the African embassy bombings, for instance); can organize recruitment and absorb, indoctrinate, and train recruits; and can carry out ancillary activities such as fundraising and dealing with cooperative governments. The disadvantage of these organizations is that they may become more permeable by outside agencies because of their need to communicate among units. Modern electronics become a double-edged sword for the terrorist: Things like cell phones facilitate communications in executing attacks, but those communications can be intercepted, leading to resiliency-threatening penetration. In fact, electronic surveillance of terrorist communication has been extremely helpful in the pursuit of Al Qaeda to the point that the old structure of the 1990s, which basically followed the commander-cadre model, has been reduced greatly in size from its zenith.

The result of the campaign against Al Qaeda has been to cause it to adapt, to become what Stern refers to as the "protean enemy" that has "shown a surprising willingness to adapt its mission" and to alter its organizational form to make it more resilient. Al Qaeda is no longer a hierarchically organized entity that plans and carries out terrorist missions. Instead, it has adopted elements of the alternate form of terrorist organization, the *virtual network* or *leaderless resistance* model and has dispersed itself into a series of smaller, loosely affiliated terrorist organizations that draw inspiration from Al Qaeda. If it ever was a monolithic dragon, Al Qaeda has mutated into a hydra-headed monster.

Particularly since the assassination of bin Laden, these mutations, sometimes called "franchises," have increasingly become the public face of terrorism. Terrorist activities are infrequently attributed to the central Al Qaeda organization. Rather, they are carried out by spin-offs like Al Qaeda in the Arabian Peninsula in places like Yemen or by Al Qaeda in the Maghreb in places like Mali. Al Qaeda in Iraq has recently been said to be active in Syria, and al-Shabaab is a major actor in Somalia. What distinguishes the actions of such groups have been the modest size and geographical reach.

The core of this model is to reduce direct communications between the leadership and its members. Rather than planning operations and instructing operatives to carry out plans, leaders instead exhort their followers to act through public pronouncements (for instance, through the use of Web sites). Leaders may issue general calls to action, but they have no direct communications with followers that can be intercepted or used as the basis for suppression or conspiracy indictments. The leader has no direct knowledge or control of individual terrorist acts, which he or she may inspire but not direct. The advantage of this model is that it maximizes the resiliency of the organization and protects its leadership from capture or prosecution; its principal drawback is reduced capacity to order specific "desirable" actions. It has become, however, a major part of the changing environment of the terrorist threat and responses to it.

Increases in electronic forms of surveillance and interdiction by unarmed aerial vehicles (UAVs or drones) are making it increasingly difficult to sustain almost all forms of clandestine activities, and is particularly true of specifically targeted entities like terrorist organizations. Among the few methods available to terrorist groups to evade interruption or destruction are diffusion (organization into small groups), limiting communication that can be monitored, relocating to distant, obscure locations. An effect of these attempts at survival is to limit the size and range of terrorist actions. Another is to change the direction and emphases of those who seek to defeat the terrorists.

DEALING WITH TERRORISM: THE GWOT AND BEYOND

One of the first reactions to the 9/11 attacks in the United States was to declare a "global war on terrorism," or GWOT. The appropriateness of "war" to describe terror or countering it has always been a matter of some debate. The prominence of the terms has gradually faded with time, and American President Barack Obama suggested in May 2013 that the war phase of competition is winding down. "This war, like all wars, must come to an end," he said. The question of how to deal with terrorism thus begins with exploring the nature of the threat.

If the assault on terror is indeed a war, what does that robust rhetoric mean? Is the GWOT really a war at all, or something else (in the immediate wake of September 11, French president Jacques Chirac suggested calling it a "campaign" to remove some of the military emphasis)? Is it really possible to make war, as the term is generally used, against a method or idea, as opposed to some identifiable group of people? How does one attack and defeat a nonstate-based enemy organization that has no territory or identified population base that can be subjected to and subdued by military actions? In addition, what does "victory" mean in this context? Is it the destruction of the opponent, or its containment? What kinds and levels of resources are necessary for the task?

All of these are valid questions about which agreed-upon answers do not exist. Begin with the war analogy. It is frequently argued that it makes no sense to talk about war against an abstraction, and the idea of terrorism is the application of an idea. Can you "kill" an idea in some concrete or abstract manner? If so, how do you know you have accomplished the task? Wars, at any level, are contests between members of different groups to assert control. People and their ideas are not the same things.

The war analogy suffers even if one switches emphasis and says the GWOT is a war on global terrorists. Saying one is making war on terrorists has the advantage of placing the effort on an interpersonal, group-on-group level of violent interaction, which war is. It also, however, has limits given common images of what war is. In normal uses, war refers to armed, organized combat between two (or more) military forces that represent political entities, normally states. Terrorism, however, is a form of asymmetrical warfare (see Chapter 5) where normal descriptions and expectations do not hold. This makes the nature of the competition hard to think about in traditional terms like measuring progress and, ultimately, determining who has won and lost.

The war analogy simply does not "fit" a competition like that against a terrorist organization very well. There is, and has been, for instance, much disagreement within the United States since 2001 about who is "winning" and who is "losing" and by what means one can measure progress. Some of the problem almost certainly derives from the poor fit between conceptions of war and the reality of terrorism and the proper metric for measuring progress against it.

The problem of dealing with terrorists is both physically and intellectually very difficult, and any simple, sweeping approaches to solving the problem of terrorism are likely both to be inadequate and to result in failure. Thinking of the problem as war is an example. That does not mean the task is hopeless or that things cannot be done to manage or mitigate the problem. Certain forms of terrorism suppression are available, and the discussion turns to introducing these. The threat has, as already suggested, changed in recent years, and so some of the clear contemporary forms of terrorist activity will be examined.

Suppressing Terrorists: Antiterrorism and Counterterrorism

In conventional terrorism suppression circles, two methods for dealing with the terrorist problem are most often invoked: antiterrorism and counterterrorism. The two terms are sometimes used interchangeably, although each term refers to a distinct form of action with a specific purpose. Any program of terrorist suppression will necessarily contain elements of each of them, but failing to specify which is which generally or in specific applications only confuses the issue.

Antiterrorism refers to defensive efforts to reduce the vulnerability of targets to terrorist attacks and to lessen the effects of terrorist attacks that do occur. Antiterrorism efforts thus begin from the premise that some terrorist attacks will indeed occur, and that two forms of effort are necessary.

First, antiterrorists seek to make it more difficult to mount terrorist attacks. Airport security to prevent potential terrorists from boarding airliners or the interception and detention of possible terrorists by border guards are examples. Second, antiterrorists try to mitigate the effects of terrorist attacks that might or do occur. Blocking off streets in front of public buildings so that terrorists cannot get close enough to destroy them is one approach, while civil defense measures (i.e., hazmat operations) to mitigate the effects of an attack is another way to deal with the problem.

There are three related difficulties with conducting an effective antiterrorist campaign. One is that antiterrorism is necessarily reactive; terrorists choose where attacks will occur and against what kinds of targets, and antiterrorists must respond to the terrorist initiative. A second problem is the sheer variety and number of targets to be protected. As suggested earlier, the potential list of targets is almost infinite, and one purpose of attacks is randomness so that potential victims are always off guard and antiterrorists will have trouble anticipating where attacks may occur. The third problem is target substitution: If antiterrorist efforts are sufficiently successful that terrorists determine their likelihood of success against any particular target (or class of targets) is significantly diminished, they will simply go on to other, less well-defended targets.

The other form of terrorist suppression is *counterterrorism*, offensive and military measures against terrorists or sponsoring agencies to prevent, deter, or respond to terrorist acts. As the definition suggests, counterterrorism consists of both preventive and retaliatory actions against terrorists. Preventive acts can include such things as penetration of terrorist cells and taking action—including apprehension and physical violence against terrorists—before they carry out their acts. One may not be able to protect all objects in a category of targets (bridges, for instance), but if one can find out which bridge is being targeted, one may be able to intercept and prevent the attack. Retaliation is more often military and paramilitary and includes attacks on terrorist camps or other facilities in response to terrorist attacks. The purposes of retaliation include punishment, reducing terrorist capacity for future acts, and hopefully deterrence of future actions by instilling fear of the consequences.

Counterterrorism is inherently and intuitively attractive. Preventive actions are proactive, taking the battle to the terrorists and punishing them in advance of creating harm. In its purest form, preventive counterterrorist actions reverse the tables in the relationship, effectively "terrorizing the terrorists." Pounding a terrorist facility as punishment after enduring a terrorist attack at least entails the satisfaction of knowing the enemy has suffered as well as the victim.

The problem with counterterrorism, like antiterrorism, is that it is insufficient on its own as a way to quell all terrorism. Preventing terrorist actions requires a level of intelligence about the structures of terrorist's organizations that are quite difficult to obtain, and it has been a central purpose of terrorist reorganization to increase that difficulty. The effect is to make a terrorist network difficult to penetrate, learn of its nefarious intentions, and interrupt those activities. The absence of a state base that can be attacked means it is more difficult to identify terrorist targets whose retaliatory destruction will cripple the organization, punish its members, or frighten it into ceasing future actions.

Ideally, antiterrorism and counterterrorists efforts act in tandem. Counterterrorists reduce the number and quality of possible attacks through preventive actions, making the task of antiterrorist efforts to ameliorate the effects of attacks that do succeed less difficult. counterterrorist retaliation then can hopefully reduce the terrorists' capacity for future mayhem. The result is a more manageable threat confronting the antiterrorists. In practice, however, these efforts sometimes come into operational conflict. The antiterrorist emphasis on lessening the effects of attacks may lead to publicizing the possibility of particular attacks as a way to alert citizens (the color-coded warning system, for instance), whereas counterterrorism prefer to keep operations as secret as possible to facilitate clandestine penetration and interruption.

The Contemporary Threats

Largely due to the success of terrorism suppression efforts since September 11, 2001, the shape of the threat has undergone a protean transformation. Al Qaeda still exists, even if its most villainous figure, bin Laden, is dead, and the monolithic, commander-cadre structure has largely disintegrated under a relentless assault that has killed or captured much of the old network. In its place, the threat has dispersed among a much more diffuse set of loose organizations and individuals. Stern describes this new face of terrorism in a 2010 *Foreign Affairs* article: "The destructive ideology that animates the al Qaeda movement is spreading around the globe, including, in some cases, to small-town America. Homegrown zealots, motivated by al Qaeda's distorted interpretation of Islam, may not yet be capable of carrying out 9/11-style strikes, but they could nonetheless terrorize a nation."

Part of this dispersion has been the result of actions taken by bin Laden and his associates in the 1980s and 1990s. During the period when Al Qaeda operated terrorist training camps openly in Afghanistan, the organization trained thousands of recruits from countries around the globe, and many of these individuals returned to their homes and have organized affiliated movements that now carry out many of the terrorist activities associated with Al Qaeda.

Hoffman argues that the result has been an Al Qaeda–based terrorist threat with four distinct dimensions suggested earlier in the chapter. What he calls Al Qaeda Central contains the remnants of the 9/11 organization. Al Qaeda Affiliates and Associates consist of the spinoff organizations; Al Qaeda in Iraq (Mesopotamia) is a prime example. Al Qaeda Locals are virtual network organizations in different locations; terrorist activity in Mali is exemplary. Finally, there is the Al Qaeda Network, which is composed of "homegrown Islamic radicals"; much of the so-called lone-wolf activity is of this nature.

Two of these permutations are particularly prominent and troublesome in the contemporary scene. One is the problem of the "lone-wolf" terrorist, an individual who commits acts of terror without apparent outside assistance or motivation. The other is the activities associated with virtual networks, a phenomenon greatly accentuated by the exploitation of the Internet to further their activities. The two are connected because Internet appeals may activate both lone wolves and members of virtual networks. Both are troublesome because they are extremely difficult to identify and counter before they act.

Lone-Wolf Terrorists.   The phenomenon of individuals apparently unconnected to any organized terrorist group has been a recurring part of the terrorism problem for a long time. Because their actions are idiosyncratic, isolated, and often erratic, they do not individually receive the level of attention that more systematic, organized movements do. Cumulatively, however, the rise in their prominence parallels the decline in activities by larger, more monolithic organizations.

Interest in lone wolves in the United States peaked in the 1990s with the unrelated cases of Unabomber Theodore Kaczynski (the deranged university professor who killed 3 and wounded over 20 others with letter bombs between 1978 and 1995) and Timothy McVeigh, who killed 159 people in the truck bombing of the Murrah Federal Building in Oklahoma City in 1995. Since these highly publicized cases, there have been episodic instances of domestic lone wolves, such as the pursuit and capture of abortion clinic bomber Eric Robert Rudolph between 1996 and 1998, the May 2009 shooting spree by James von Brunn at the U.S. Holocaust Memorial Museum in Washington, D.C., and even the action of Joseph Andrew Stack III, who crashed a small airplane into the Internal Revenue Service office in Austin, Texas, on February 18, 2010.

Four apparent lone-wolf attacks connected loosely to radical Islamic terrorism galvanized interest again in 2009–2010. The first was the massacre of over 30 fellow soldiers by Major Nidal Hasan at Ft. Hood, Texas, in fall 2009. This heinous act was followed by one during Christmas 2009, when Omar Farouk Abdulmuttalab attempted to detonate a bomb concealed in his underwear aboard a plane en route from Europe to Detroit. Finally, Faisal Shahzad, a naturalized American citizen of Pakistani descent, attempted to explode an amateurishly fashioned bomb on Times Square in New York in April 2010. The 2013 bombing at the Boston Marathon is a more recent example. Each instance pointed to the difficulty of getting a precise handle on terrorism committed by autonomous individuals in advance of their acts; these individuals were, of course, captured, tried, and sentenced for their crimes.

What are the characteristics of the lone-wolf terrorist? The European Union *Instiotuut voor Veilgheids-en Crisismanagement* offers a useful set of interrelated characteristics in a 2007 study. First and foremost, lone wolves act individually rather than as parts of more or less well-organized groups. Second, lone wolves do not belong to any organized terrorist group or network. Third, they act without the direct influence of a leader or hierarchy. Fourth, the tactics and methods they employ are conceived and conducted by the individual without "any direct outside command or direction." Lone-wolf terrorist activities are conceived by individuals who act autonomously in designing and carrying out their acts.

The nature of lone-wolf acts speaks to why they are simultaneously so difficult yet marginal in the greater scheme of terrorism. On one hand, the autonomy of the lone wolf makes him or her extremely difficult to identify in advance, because, by definition, these individuals are usually antisocial loners. Belonging to no terrorist groups, they have no communications that can be intercepted and traced back to them, and they may be able to evade detection for a long time after they commit their acts, unless they make some crucial mistake that leads to their apprehension. The Unabomber, after all, evaded identification and capture for 17 years before his brother recognized his identity through the text of one of his manifestos and turned him in to authorities. On the other hand, acting alone generally limits the sophistication and extent of the destruction the lone wolf can inflict. The Murrah attack by McVeigh or the machine-gunning of a Hebron mosque by Israeli right-wing extremist Baruch Goldstein on February 24, 1994 (which left 29 praying Muslims dead) may well represent the outward limits of mayhem lone wolves can inflict. Blowing up an airplane in flight or car bombings like Times Square may also serve as outer limits.

Lone-wolf attacks are frequent enough, however, to cause concern. The European Union (EU) study, for instance, catalogued instances conforming to its criteria between 1968 and 2007 in the developed world. According to this report, 30 lone-wolf attacks occurred in the United States, followed by 9 in Germany, 7 in France, 6 in Spain, 5 in Italy, 3 in Canada, 2 each in Australia, the Netherlands, Russia, and the United Kingdom, and 1 each in Denmark, Poland, Portugal, and Sweden. From a U.S. view, it is not only the most frequent victim but the vast majority of indigenous attacks within its boundaries are also by lone wolves.

Two other factors make the isolation and categorization of lone-wolf terrorism problematical. One is whether a particular act meets the criteria for terrorism laid out earlier in this chapter, or whether it is an instance of pure depravity. This difficulty is particularly relevant when trying to determine the objective of a lone-wolf attack. McVeigh, in his twisted way, had the apparent objective of avenging the Branch Dravidians who had died at Waco, Texas. What, on the other hand, was the objective of von Brunn in gunning down a security guard at the Holocaust Museum other than an insane expression of anti-Semitism?

The other factor is the degree of autonomy and independence of the apparent lone wolf. Groups with diverse messages of hate increasingly publicize their causes and exhort their followers on the Internet, and it is often unclear whether apparently independent acts have been influenced by such appeals. There is evidence, for instance, that Rudolph was "inspired" by extreme antiabortion appeals on the Internet, and both Hasan and Abdulmuttalab were influenced by the violent preachings of American-born, Yemen-based Muslim cleric Anwar al-Awlaki. These kinds of connections muddy sharp distinctions between lone wolves and virtual networks.

Virtual Networks. The virtual network/leaderless resistance and protean hybrid forms of terrorist organizations are the adaptations that terrorists have had to make in the face of the increased sophistication of terrorist suppressors against traditional commander-cadre groups. They represent ways to deal with the ability of terrorism suppressors to intercept communications and to penetrate terrorist hierarchies. The primary adaptation has been to cease direct communications between terrorist leaders and followers in locations where communications interception is most active and thus where traditional terrorist forms are most vulnerable.

The genesis of this adaptation was apparently the reaction of Louis Beam and his Aryan Nation followers to government discovery and harassment of their activities based on wire taps. The response was to cease direct communications among group members. One advantage of severing communications was to deprive the government of advanced knowledge of Aryan Nation plans; another was to shield Beam from direct responsibility for illegal actions. As adapted by others, it has also made penetration of terrorist organizations more difficult.

The heart of this model is to eliminate a direct link between leaders and followers. Direct contact is replaced by indirect communication, often in the form of Internet postings that seek to attract new members, spread the group's message, and even exhort members to actions. The posting of sermons by al-Awlaki from Yemen, for instance, effectively served to help radicalize lone-wolf terrorists like Hasan and Abdulmuttalab. Given the vastness and portability of Internet access, it is an effective tool to protect the identity and location of leaders and thus to reinforce resiliency in the organization. For example, despite concerted efforts to capture and eliminate al-Awlaki, he remained at large in the mountainous desert of Yemen until he was killed in a drone attack in 2011.

Operating virtual networks has both advantages and disadvantaged. The advantages are primarily in increasing resiliency, particularly in places where the government's electronic surveillance capabilities are greatest. It should, for instance, come as no great surprise that the model was spawned in the United States where, over the years, American authorities (notably the Federal Bureau of Investigation) have developed very sophisticated means of penetrating subversive organizations of all kinds, including terrorists. Eliminating virtual organizations, however, is much more difficult, especially for identifying terrorist followers and their plans in advance. Because leaders exhort or suggest attacks rather than organizing and ordering them, the timing and nature of any specific act is largely left to the individual follower, who is effectively acting as a lone wolf, albeit one with outside inspiration. Regardless of who inspired the Times Square bombing attack by Shahzad, for instance, the act itself was largely his own.

Increased resiliency, however, comes at a price in terms of capacity, a trait shared by lone wolves. Individuals generally cannot plan and execute operations on the same scale as larger groups. As University of Michigan analyst Juan Cole put it in a *Foreign Policy* article, "they cannot hope to accomplish much. At most, they can carry bombs on trains (a reference to the 2004 Madrid train bombings)." This limit on capacity has in turn helped inspire a hybrid form by combining elements of both traditional and virtual network models.

The hybrid model seeks to combine the "best" of both models. In an October 2005 speech, President George W. Bush summarized this new form: "Many militants are part of global borderless terrorist organizations like Al Qaida, which spreads propaganda and provides financing and technical support to local extremists and conducts dramatic and brutal operations. They are found in regional groups associated with Al Qaida. . . . Still others spring up in local cells inspired by Islamic radicalism but not centrally directed." Where conditions permit (some of the tribal areas of Pakistan, for instance), these hybrids may function as near-traditional organizations; where they cannot, they necessarily become more like virtual networks.

The point is not so much the forms that are most prevalent as the process they represent. Terrorists and their organizations practice a form of asymmetrical warfare, and, as discussed in Chapter 5, a major characteristic is the adaptability of such movements. Asymmetrical warfare is a methodology, not a method, and so is terrorism. Stern's protean analogy is apt. The Greek god Proteus, after all, was noteworthy for his ability to take on various forms or appearances, and so do terrorists. The protean analogy thus suggests that the terrorist challenge is dynamic, not static. Like Proteus, terrorists adapt to challenges to their existence and abandon forms and practices that prove dysfunctional or self-destructive. The implication is clear: Today's terrorist threat is different than the threat that existed in 2001, and the challenge of the future will not be the same as it is today.

CONCLUSION: WHENCE THE THREAT

The problem of international religious terrorism has changed and gained dubious celebrity since 9/11. Before the attacks, acts of terror were considered a horrible aberration, not an integral part of international existence. The single most deadly terrorist act in history changed that perception. The threat of terrorism is now considered ubiquitous and efforts to suppress it a pervasive part of everyday life. The war on terrorism—whether the war analogy is apt or not—is now an accepted, institutionalized part of the political environment nationally and internationally.

The terrorism environment is clearly changing. Although Al Qaeda remains the central threat with which many people identify, the problem has become less centralized and more diffuse as the efforts of terrorism suppressors have forced terrorists to adopt different forms and approaches to attaining their lethal goals. At the same time, the absence of follow-on attacks on the order of magnitude of 9/11 has also eroded some of the urgency that surrounds the terrorism issue.

In this atmosphere, whence the war on terror? Will the emphasis continue to erode in the popular minds if there is not another major attack in the United States? Has the terrorism suppression effort become adequately proficient that a major terrorist attack is decisively less likely than it was in 2001? If the current threat continues to appear increasingly impotent, will support (or the need) for high-priority, expensive terrorism efforts decline? Will there be a slow retreat in the threat and efforts to contain it to pre-9/11 levels, as international religious terrorism recedes and before another wave of terror takes its place?

The terrorism future is hard to predict. If history is a faithful guide, the current spate of international religious terrorism will indeed fade away eventually, although it is not clear how long that will take. History also suggests that a new cycle of terrorists will emerge with different, and as-yet unknown, reasons for being. Terrorists come and go, but terrorism persists. The effort and desire to eradicate both terrorists and their methods is both laudatory and understandable, but it may be hopelessly utopian and unrealistic. Terrorism has been so enduring because its practitioners have indeed emulated Proteus; today the emphasis is on lone wolves and virtual networks. But who knows about tomorrow?

SUGGESTED ACTIVITIES AND QUESTIONS

1. Define terrorism. What are its common elements? How does the elaboration of the elements help us understand the nature of terrorism?
2. What do terrorist acts seek to accomplish? In what circumstances do they succeed or fail?
3. What kinds of targets do terrorists attack? What is cost-tolerance? How does it factor into resistance to terrorism and terrorist success?
4. Why do terrorists engage in terrorist activities? What do they seek to accomplish? Why do terrorists adopt asymmetrical means to achieve their objectives?
5. How has international terrorism changed since 9/11, notably in terms of terrorist organization? What are the implications of these changes for dealing with terrorists?
6. What are the three ways of dealing with terrorism discussed in the text? Describe each as an element in lessening or eliminating the problem of terrorism.
7. What are the future prospects for terrorism? Specifically, what threats are posed by lone-wolf terrorists and virtual terrorist networks? What does it mean to describe the terrorism threat as protean?

SUGGESTED READINGS AND RESOURCES

Art, Robert J. and Kenneth N. Waltz. *The Use of Force: Military Power and International Politics*, 7th ed. London: Rowman and Littlefield, 2008.

Atran, Scott. "Mishandling Suicide Terrorism." *Washington Quarterly* 27, 3 (Summer 2004), 67–90.

———. "The Moral Logic and Growth of Suicide Terrorism." *Washington Quarterly* 29, 2 (Spring 2006), 127–147.

Benard, Cheryl. "Toy Soldiers: The Youth Factor in the War on Terror." *Current History* 106, 696 (January 2007), 27–30.

Bergen, Peter and Swati Pandrey. "The Madrassas Scapegoat." *Washington Quarterly* 29, 2 (Spring 2006), 117–125.

Burke, Jason. "Think Again, Al Qaeda." *Foreign Policy*, May/June 2004, 18–26.

Bush, George W. "Transcript: Bush Discusses War on Terrorism." *Washington Post* (online), October 6, 2005.

Clarke, Richard A., ed. "Terrorism: What the Next President Will Face." *Annals of the American Academy of Political and Social Science*, 618 (July 2008), 4–6.

Cole, Juan. "Think Again: 9/11." *Foreign Policy*, September/October 2006, 26–32.

Cronin, Audrey Kurth. "Sources of Contemporary Terrorism." In Audrey Kurth Cronin and James M. Ludes, eds., *Attacking Terrorism: Elements of a Grand Strategy*. Washington, DC: Georgetown University Press, 2004.

Dershowitz, Alan M. *Why Terrorism Works: Understanding the Threat, Responding to the Challenge*. New Haven, CT: Yale University Press, 2002.

Fleishman, Charlotte. *The Business of Terror: Conceptualizing Terrorist Organizations as Cellular Businesses*. Washington, DC: Center for Defense Information, May 23, 2005.

Gunaratna, Rohan. "The Post-Madrid Face of Al Qaeda." *Washington Quarterly* 27, 3 (Summer 2004), 91–100.

Hoffman, Bruce. "From the War on Terror to Global Insurgency." *Current History* 105, 695 (December 2006), 423–429.

———. *Inside Terrorism*, 2nd ed. New York: Columbia University Press, 2006.

Jenkins, Brian. "International Terrorism." In Robert J. Art and Kenneth N. Waltz, eds., *The Use of Force: Military Power and International Politics*. New York: Rowman and Littlefield Publishers, 2004, 77–84.

"Lone Wolf Terrorism." *Instituut voot Veilgheids-en Crisismanagement* (online), June 2007. (http://www.transnationalterrorism.eu/tekst/publications/Lone-Wolf.%20Terrorism.pdf)

Laqueur, Walter. "The Changing Face of Terror." In Art and Waltz, eds., *The Use of Force*. New York: Rowman and Littlefield Publishers, 2004, 451–464.

Nacos, Brigette. *Terrorism and Counterterrorism: Understanding Threats and Responses in the Post-9/11 World*. New York: Penguin Academics, 2006.

National Strategy for Combating Terrorism. Washington, DC: The White House, 2003.

The 9/11 Commission Report: Final Report of the National Commission on Terrorist Attacks upon the United States (authorized ed.). New York: W. W. Norton, 2004.

Pillar, Paul D. "Counterterrorism After Al Qaeda." *Washington Quarterly* 27, 3 (Summer 2004), 101–113.

———. "Dealing with Terrorism." In Art and Waltz, eds., *The Use of Force*. New York: Rowman and Littlefield Publishers, 2004, 469–476.

Rapaport, David C. "The Four Waves of Terrorism." In Cronin and Ludes, eds., *Attacking Terrorism*. New York: Rowman and Littlefield Publishers, 2004, 46–73.

Sloan, Stephen. *Beating International Terrorism: An Action Strategy for Preemption and Punishment*. Montgomery, AL: Air University Press, 2000.

Snow, Donald M. *National Security for a New Era: Globalization and Geopolitics After Iraq*, 3rd ed. New York: Pearson Longman, 2008.

———. *September 11, 2001: The New Face of War?* New York: Longman, 2002.

——— and Dennis M. Drew. *From Lexington to Baghdad and Beyond: War and Politics in the American Experience*, 3rd ed. Armonk, NY: M. E. Sharpe, 2009.

Stern, Jessica. "Mind over Martyr: How to Deradicalize Islamic Extremists." *Foreign Affairs* 89, 1 (January/February 2010), 95–108.

———. *Terrorism in the Name of God: Why Religious Militants Kill*. New York: ECCO, 2003.

———. "The Protean Enemy." *Foreign Affairs* 82, 4 (July/August 2003), 27–40.

Yew, Lee Kwan. "The United States, Iraq, and the War on Terror." *Foreign Affairs* 86, 1 (January/February 2007), 2–7.

WEB SITES

Official U.S. government Web sites dealing with terrorism:

The Department of Homeland Security: http://www.Whitehouse.gov/homeland

The State Department: http://www.state.gov

Reports on Future Trends from Federal Research Division: http://www.loc.gov/rr/frd/terrorism.html

UN action against terrorism: http://www.un.org/Docs/sc/committees/1373/

RAND Corporation on terrorism and homeland security: http://www.rand.org/research_areas/terrorism/

Terrorism Research Center: http://www.terrorism.com/

CREDITS

INDEX